Translocal China

In recent decades, China has experienced an explosion of new types of mobility. *Translocal China* details how this mobility affects diverse localities and identities across China. Much previous scholarship has focused on the rapid increase in migration within China, particularly that of rural laborers moving to the booming coastal cities. This volume, however, assembles a broader array of mobilities, including finance capital, print and visual media, disease, tourists, brides, and entrepreneurs, as well as migrant workers. The contributors suggest that identities and other ties in contemporary China have not been simply uprooted from their localized cultural foundations to float free in the rapidly urbanizing reform era. Rather, people and institutions have come to be *translocal*, that is, to belong to more than one locality simultaneously. The volume breaks new theoretical ground by bringing the concepts of place, space, and scale to bear on China's current transformations.

With contributions from well-respected China specialists, *Translocal China* offers a multidisciplinary approach to understanding China's new networks through raising issues such as how meanings and germs travel with tourists, how the Internet generates new exchanges between formerly isolated localities, and how business location strategies are defying conventional spatial hierarchies. *Translocal China* presents a comprehensive study of the connections between location and culture, politics, economics, gender, and technology, and as such will have huge appeal to both students and scholars of China studies as well as those interested in the burgeoning mobilities of our globalizing world.

Tim Oakes is Associate Professor of Geography at the University of Colorado at Boulder, USA.

Louisa Schein is Associate Professor in the Departments of Anthropology and Women's and Gender Studies at Rutgers University, New Brunswick, USA.

Routledge Studies on China in Transition
Series Editor: David S. G. Goodman

Translocal China

Linkages, identities, and the
reimagining of space

Edited by
Tim Oakes and Louisa Schein

Routledge
Taylor & Francis Group

LONDON AND NEW YORK

First published 2006
by Routledge
2 Park Square, Milton Park, Abingdon, Oxon OX14 4RN

Simultaneously published in the USA and Canada
by Routledge
270 Madison Ave, New York, NY 10016

Routledge is an imprint of the Taylor & Francis Group

© 2006 Tim Oakes and Louisa Schein, selection and editorial matter;
the contributors, their own chapters

Typeset in Times New Roman by
Newgen Imaging Systems (P) Ltd, Chennai, India
Printed and bound in Great Britain by
MPG Books Ltd, Bodmin

British Library Cataloguing in Publication Data
A catalogue record for this book is available from the British Library

Library of Congress Cataloging in Publication Data
A catalog record for this book has been requested

ISBN 0–415–36920–7

Contents

Illustrations

Figures

Tables

Notes on contributors

Carolyn Cartier is Associate Professor of Geography at the University of Southern China. She is the author of *Globalizing South China* (2001) and co-editor of *The Chinese Diaspora: Space, Place, Mobility, and Identity* (2003).

David Faure is University Lecturer in Modern Chinese History and Fellow, St Anthony's College, University of Oxford. He works on Chinese social history from the Ming Dynasty to the Second World War.

David S. G. Goodman is Professor of International Studies at the University of Technology, Sydney. His most recent publication is *China's Campaign to "Open Up the West": National, Provincial and Local Perspectives* (2004).

Feng Chongyi is Associate Professor in China Studies at the University of Technology, Sydney and adjunct Professor of History, Nankai University, Tianjin. His research focuses on intellectual development in modern and contemporary China. He is the author of several books such as *Peasant Consciousness and China*, *Bertrand Russell and China*, and *From Sinification to Globalisation*. He is also the editor of several books, including *The Political Economy of China's Provinces* and *Constitutional Government and China*.

Hans Hendrischke is Associate Professor and Head of Chinese Studies at the University of New South Wales, Sydney. His recent research focuses on the emergence of private entrepreneurship and local business systems in China.

Helen F. Siu is Professor of Anthropology at Yale University. She conducts fieldwork in South China, exploring the nature of the socialist state and the refashioning of identities through rituals, festivals, commerce, and consumption. She is the author of *Agents and Victims in South China: Accomplices in Rural Revolution* (1989) and co-editor of *Down to Earth: The Territorial Bond in South China* (1995) and *Empire at the Margins: Culture, Ethnicity and Frontier in Early Modern China* (2006).

Lisa Hoffman is Assistant Professor (Cultural Anthropology) in the Urban Studies Program at the University of Washington, Tacoma. Her interests include new forms of governing, subjectivity, and urban transformation in contemporary China. She is currently completing a book manuscript on the emergence of young professionals in Dalian City.

Louisa Schein is Associate Professor in the Departments of Anthropology and Women's and Gender Studies at Rutgers University. She has conducted long term research on gender and ethnic politics among the Hmong/Miao in China and in diaspora and is the author of *Minority Rules: The Miao and the Feminine in China's Cultural Politics* (2000).

Tim Oakes is Associate Professor of Geography at the University of Colorado at Boulder and Visiting Professor at Guizhou Nationalities Institute, Guiyang. He is the author of *Tourism and Modernity in China* (1998) and co-editor of *Travels in Paradox: Remapping Tourism* (2005).

Wang Gan received her PhD in anthropology at Yale University. Her dissertation is on conspicuous consumption activities and business networking in Shenzhen, China. She is a researcher in the Social Anthropology Department, Sociology Institute, Chinese Academy of Social Sciences. Her current academic interests include parenting, the Internet, and volunteering organizations.

Wanning Sun is a Senior Lecturer in media and communication at Curtin University of Technology in Western Australia. She is a Visiting Professor at State University of New York (Binghamton) from 2005 to 2006. She is the author of *Leaving China: Media, Migration and Transnational Imagination* (Rowman & Littlefield, 2002). She is the Chief Investigator for an Australian Research Council project "Maid in China: Gendered Mobilities, Internal Migration, and Transnational Imagination" (2004–2006), and is working on a book-length manuscript on this topic.

Weng Naiqun received his PhD in Anthropology from the University of Rochester in 1993, and now is a senior research fellow in the Chinese Academy of Social Sciences. Most of his research has been carried out in southwest China.

Zhan Changzhi is Professor of Sociology at Hainan University and deputy editor-in-chief of *The Journal of Market and Population*. His publications include *The Chinese Population: Volume on Hainan* and *Progress and Setbacks: A Study on Modernization in Hainan Special Economic Zone*.

Preface

This volume draws together a diverse set of perspectives on the question of translocality in China. These perspectives were initially the basis of a rich and rewarding set of discussions in Haikou, Hainan, at a conference titled "Translocal China: place-identity and mobile subjectivity," sponsored by the UNSW-UTS Centre for Research on Provincial China, in June 2002. All of the chapters in the present volume were presented in Haikou, with the exception of Hoffman's, which was solicited in preparation for a special issue of the journal *Provincial China*, titled "Reimagining Chinese mobilities and spaces" (Schein and Oakes 2003). That issue also featured earlier versions of the present volume's chapters by Hendrischke, Faure and Siu, Cartier, and Wang.

Participants in the Haikou conference were asked to consider the ways new kinds of mobility affected the localities with which they were most familiar in their research. The term "translocal" was suggested as an organizing concept for these considerations for a number of specific reasons. First, while mobility in the form of internal migration was garnering more and more scholarly attention in China, there seemed to be less attention paid to the *relationship* between mobility and place in China. With "translocal" we sought to focus our attention simultaneously on mobility and locality. Second, work on mobility in China was dominated by an emphasis on migrants and, specifically, China's "floating population." In raising the question of translocality, we sought to broaden the inquiry to examine a broader network of social, cultural, and financial linkages that mobility forges between, for example, city and country, interior and coast. Third, while the concept of "translocality" was being developed in the context of studies of transnationalism, we sought to explore the applicability of the concept within the more limited sphere of mainland China. We sought to develop an appreciation of China itself as a space of mobility, rather than just a sending or receiving zone of transnational linkages.

Fourth, we wanted to deploy "translocal" not just as a descriptor of different kinds of mobility and their relationship to place, but as a vehicle for thinking about subjectivity in China in new ways. As we considered a new kind of mobile subjectivity in China, we did not want to lose sight of grounded localities and the importance of place. For this reason, we wanted to emphasize how space in China is being wrenched from the particular structures of self-sufficiency and hierarchy that dominated the Mao era (and, in some cases, earlier times as well) to be reorganized in ways that create new spaces of difference. For instance, the rural–urban divide is increasingly undercut by the networks that bring urban images, goods, and aesthetics to the countryside while at the same time injecting the city with the often harsh realities of the rural political economy. Non-state flows of financial capital are also affecting patterns of regional development, and the spatial gap between wealth and poverty, in ways that remap the spatial legacies of state socialist development. Yet while the development of translocal networks is explained partly in terms of the economic unevenness that has induced the uprooting of vast numbers of laboring migrants, we wanted to suggest that the unevenness of social and cultural capital, along with ideas of prestige and legitimacy, is also an important factor in creating such networks.

Finally, we wanted to ask how historical patterns of mobility have conditioned contemporary patterns, and consider the extent to which translocality represents a new phenomenon in China.

In addition to the above themes, much of the discussion in Haikou focused on issues of identity and identification. Much of the workshop discussion centered on the definition of the term "translocal." Apropos of this discussion, David Goodman proposed a definition of translocality which became the main working definition used throughout the conference: *translocality means being identified with more than one location.* What this definition captured was the double meaning of identity or identification, and this helped link our interest in subjectivity with broader sociopolitical issues. Identity does not have to be subjective, but can refer to one's household registration identity or one's official nationality identity or an undocumented migrant identity imposed by the state. This definition helped focus attention on the relationship between identities, subjectivity, and the networks that link places together. By the end of the conference, presenters were asked to consider the following specific question in addition to those posed earlier: In what ways does peoples' sense of belonging relate to their social/political/economic connections across China?

The thirteen contributors to this volume have all taken up these issues, with different emphases according to the nature of their research and their disciplinary perspectives. We would like to acknowledge their enthusiasm for the project and their efforts to push their own research interests in some new directions. We would also like to thank the UNSW-UTS Centre for Research on Provincial China for making the Haikou conference possible. In addition to the volume's contributors, the following individuals contributed to the success of the project in various ways: Kate Barclay, Beatriz Carrillo, Cindy Fan, Guo Yingjie, Caroline Hoy, Jo Illingsworth, Elaine Jeffreys, Jian Zhang, Koh Sunhui, Diana Lewis, Li Tianguo, Liao Xun, Ma Jianzhong, Chip Rolley, Tang Zhenle, Wan Wangming, Wei Hongyun, Xie Liuzhang, and Ye Bin.

Reference

Schein, L. and Oakes, T. (2003) "Introduction: reimagining Chinese mobilities and spaces." *Provincial China*, 8(1): 1–4.

1 Translocal China

An introduction

Tim Oakes and Louisa Schein

The most obvious and most commented upon element of spatial change in today's China has been the unprecedented geographic mobility of millions of labor migrants, tourists, brides, entrepreneurs, and many others. What we seek by deploying the term "translocal," is to complicate this literal notion of mobility with many other forms and functions of connectedness, both past and present, and to ask how they have transformed localities and relations among localities within China. The term "translocal" has been appearing in recent work by cultural theorists (Clifford 1997: 7), geographers (Massey 1999; Cartier 2001: 26; Katz 2001; Castree 2004), anthropologists (Escobar 2001: 147; Eriksen 2003; Peleikis 2003), and historians (Rafael 1995; Dirlik 1999; Wigen 1999), and while it has sometimes been used simply as a substitute for more common terms like "transnational" or "global," we use it here to highlight a simultaneous analytical focus on mobilities *and* localities.[1] Translocality, then, draws our attention to the multiplying forms of mobility in China without losing sight of the importance of localities in people's lives. To elaborate, we note four complications to any simplistic notions of what constitutes translocality.

First, translocality does not only mean people. It is crucially constituted as well by the circulation of capital, ideas and images, goods and styles, services, diseases, etc. It involves myriad technologies over and above those such as busses, trains, and airplanes that transport people. Translocality is also fashioned out of the rise of instantaneous modes of communication—especially the telephone, the Internet—and out of the profusion of media forms—television, video, VCD/DVDs—that transmit images of other places. Because of these multiple modalities, we emphasize the interdependence of the subjective dimension of translocality—vicarious mobilities and translocal imaginaries—with the physical movements we document here.

Second, the notion of the translocal draws us to images of connectedness, flows, networks, rhizomes, decenteredness, and deterritorialization. But we must emphasize that China's translocality is not a phenomenon of simply crosscutting and undifferentiated lateral connections. We might go so far as to say that it is precisely China's reform era differentiation, its unevenness, that constitutes and spawns current translocalities. Concomitantly, inequalities are produced and exacerbated by translocal flows. The dependence of much of the Chinese economy on migrant remittances is but one example. Just how it is that uneven development spawns a boom in translocal linkages should be high on the agenda of any investigation of the flows we call translocal.

Third, the transgression of spatial boundaries and the movement between scales characteristic of translocality by no means implies the effacement of place, region, province, or their accompanying identities. Instead, we observe, in tandem with the explosion of translocality in the current era, a revitalization of place-making and place differentiation, only some of which is market-driven. If, as geographer Doreen Massey has put it, "The identity of a place does not derive from some internalized history. It derives, in large part, precisely from the specificity of its interactions with the 'outside' " (1994: 169), then we might expect an increase in interactions to generate more identity production around places. Our chapters reveal this process happening on multiple scales—from the body to the native place to the city, the county, the province, the region, the nation, and even the cosmopolitan. Moreover, we see these scales coming into question, potentially being renegotiated through the proliferation of productive activity around belonging and place identity.

Fourth, we stress the dilemma of how to talk about what's new in China's reform period without eliding the existence of older translocalities. How might earlier forms and practices of translocality have conditioned what we see in the present? Conversely, how might they contrast with current phenomena? Relatedly, through an examination of the late imperial and Maoist eras, we ask what the role of the state might be in the emergence and fostering of translocal ties. While the current translocal boom might appear to be an artifact of the marketization and liberalization of Chinese society, a straightforward causal relation between the two is belied by the occurrences of translocality earlier in Chinese history. In order to pursue this line of inquiry, we begin by unpacking forms of power in relation to mobilities during earlier moments of Chinese history. We proceed with discussions of scale and place, followed by interrogations of issues around symbolic translocality, subjectivity, and the body.

Power and the state: genealogies of translocality

If the contemporary concept of translocality is to be understood in a context of social differentiation and spatial unevenness, then there are significant histories of state practice which have also played key roles in laying the framework within which translocal practices now emerge. Here we trace some of these historical trajectories to identify the genealogies of translocality that preceded current patterns. Our purpose is to consider how the state itself has maintained an interest in approaches to territorial administration and empire- or nation-building that might be called prototypes of translocality. More to the point, tensions in central-local relations in Chinese history have consistently been resolved by appealing to a translocal imaginary. Although today the state is by no means the only entity powerful enough to condition social relations in China, it offers a key entry-point into understanding how translocal practices have emerged in contemporary

China. Drawing attention to the historical link between the Chinese state and a translocal imaginary suggests that the state has sought to dominate representations of place not simply by drawing and controlling boundaries around localities, but by defining the very geographical imaginations by which people understand their place in relation to the greater civilization.

By beginning our discussion with an examination of the state's interest in translocality, we also seek to delink translocality with any necessary spatial politics of resistance to power. Because advocates of a progressive place politics have invoked the idea of a translocal imagination to convey a locally-rooted resistance to broader spatial relations of dominance (Massey 1994; Katz 2001), it is all the more necessary to acknowledge the state's interest in controlling such a potentially subversive arena of representation. While the idea of translocality has been used, particularly by geographers, to capture the relational quality of place identity—and thus to describe place as unenclosed and unbounded—we hope to further develop the term in such a way that it be not limited to one specific context for interpreting place identity. Thus, we note here the interests of the state and, later, of capital in producing and maintaining translocal imaginations. We further note, in a later section on scale, that translocality offers an innovative approach to interpreting scale politics. With these interventions, we hope to use this introduction to both solidify the meaning of translocality and convey some of its potential for theoretical innovation not only within the China studies field, but also within the broader disciplines of geography, anthropology, cultural studies, and other relevant fields.

The late-imperial state

Why did the imperial state seek to define a translocal imaginary? In order to address this question, we might want to first ask about the state's interest in the local. Citing work by Kishimoto Mio on seventeenth-century scholars Gu Yanwu and Wang Fuzhi, Duara (2000: 15) argues that the local was represented in orthodox Confucianism as a site of reform and an object of cultivation. The state maintained an official position of paternal guidance through moral leadership to revitalize the local (always assumed to equate with the rural village) in the face of commercial development, urbanization, and social class formation. Such a position would therefore entail a larger formation toward which the reform and cultivation of the local should aspire, and this of course was the high civilization of the empire with its pantheon of orthodox rituals, celestial beings, and cosmologies. The object of reform would be for the local to be fashioned as a microcosm of the empire, just as the empire was a microcosm of the cosmos. Such mimetic referencing has been observed throughout late-imperial China's cultural landscapes from housing compounds (Knapp 1999) and city walls (Dutton 1998; Knapp 2000), to gardens (Foret 2000) and sacred mountains (Hahn 1988; Kleeman 1994). Ultimately, or ideally, the local would be the irreducible "essence" of civilization, but this would be the product of the state's cultivation, rather than a natural quality of the local itself.

The local was thus a kind of project for the late-imperial state, one that required an ideology capable of linking the local firmly with the larger formation of the empire without sacrificing its symbolic value as the very foundation of Chinese civilization. This would presumably be difficult to maintain given the apparently isolated and self-sufficient nature of "the village." Indeed, orthodoxy held such self-sufficiency as a virtue, for how else could the local withstand the ever-growing impurities of commerce, class differentiation, and urbanization? In fact, the power of the local as the ultimate "seed" of Confucianism's enduring habits and values (as Fei Xiaotong would have it) necessitated a paradoxical ideology that both insisted on its isolated and irreducible nature *and* universalized it as an equivalent to the empire, civilization, and the entire cosmos. Faure and Siu's chapter sets out by noting this paradox and resolves it by demonstrating the power of the state's translocal imaginary to make the local appear as a vital part of the whole even though in practice most localities were indeed the isolated and "cellular" communities orthodoxy held them to be. "The belief that the local community was part of a wider whole was present in all of China's earth-bound villages," they argue. "It was part of Ming and Qing state ideology, expressed as much through the learned works of the literati as in village religion." They continue, "The Chinese state, one might say, encouraged the translocal imagination; the ideology which drew the local community into the state assumed, not that state power could be extended into the village from the outside, but that state rituals would be drawn into the village from the inside." In his study of territorial cults, Stephen Feuchtwang (2001) identified this project as the "imperial metaphor." Thus, imperial cults of kinship and lineage extending beyond the official network of cities and towns provided a metaphorical reference with which local territorial cults negotiated their relations with the center.

We could summarize this by arguing that the late-imperial state's interest in translocality was to cultivate subjects who identified themselves in exactly the same ways, whether in relation to the family, the village, or the empire. A translocal imagination enabled subjectivities to be tied not *just* to the locality but also to *any and all* localities simultaneously (and thus the empire as a whole), even if these were never seen, visited, or even really understood. As Faure and Siu put it, the goal would be for everyone to carry the same mental map, weaving together the rituals of daily (village) life with the larger formation of imperial administration. If they are correct, it suggests an interesting connection with the new localisms seen in the post-Mao era. Goodman and Feng and Zhan observe comparable translocal projects in Shanxi and Hainan, respectively. In their chapters, the post-Mao state seems to share a similar interest in translocality with its late-imperial predecessor. Goodman, for instance, describes the state's efforts to build and promote "Shanxi culture" as resulting in a new translocal identity that is neither local nor provincial but which represents a network of multiple local identities. Like its late-imperial predecessor the post-Mao state remains interested in harnessing the power of the local for the purposes of regional development and nation-building.

Yet, Goodman also shows that a much broader set of processes is at work. The translocalism in Shanxi, he argues, cannot be attributed solely to the state's development project. And so we might also ask whether late-imperial versions of translocality also went beyond the state ideological project described by Faure and Siu. It is tempting to assume so, but it is also necessary to remember that there is almost no comparison between the volume of today's mobilities, networks and flows (of people, electronic communication, and other media, investment capital and remittances, commercial goods and services) and that which existed a century or two ago. Indeed, Faure and Siu caution against the assumption that late-imperial "translocality" was much more than an ideology. However, ideologies, if effective, do tend to take on lives of their own when received, resisted, or negotiated by those at whom they are directed. Thus, late-imperial attempts to produce a translocal imagination also provided a space for place-making within localities, as has been argued by both Feuchtwang (2001) and Wang Mingming (1995) with reference to local territorial cults which were able to produce meaningful local spaces within the constraints of the imperial system. Their work should remind us that while the state may maintain an interest in translocality, we should not assume that the state was in fact able to monopolize the production of spatial representations in China.

The Maoist state

As Faure and Siu remind us, whatever volume of non-state commercial trade, networking, and sojourning did exist among localities in late-imperial China was severely truncated under three decades of Maoist spatial restructuring. The ideology of "earth-bound" China ironically achieved its greatest success under the modernization and development of Mao's socialist state, which oversaw unprecedented restrictions on personal mobility and a severe reduction in the commercial trade which accompanied such mobility. With the implementation of the system of household registration (*hukou zhidu*) China came to be spatially and occupationally classified into four categories (rural, urban, agricultural, and non-agricultural).[2] As a number of scholars have argued (Cheng and Seldon 1994; Chan and Zhang 1999), the *hukou* system was not implemented to limit population movement, much less keep people out of China's cities, as is typically construed today. What it did was tie one's identity and fortunes to a specific place of residence. As it was very difficult to change one's registration status, it became a kind of caste-like system (Potter 1983), but one with specific *spatial* qualities. *Hukou* institutionalized one's particular slot in the state's organization of space, meaning that one's relation with and access to the state was defined, at least in part, spatially. Any change in that relation or access, then, would be initiated by one's ability to relocate within the state's spatial organization. What this system established, in short, was a situation (still very much present in the contemporary era) where geographical mobility was tantamount to social mobility. While this dramatically reduced the possibility for translocal relations to develop outside of the state purview, the Maoist state nevertheless maintained an interest in fostering a kind of "universal localism" similar to that explored by Faure and Siu for late-imperial China. Accordingly, Mao recognized the need to appropriate the local by engendering the organic growth of "local" culture which was synonymous with the nation and with socialism (Levenson 1967; Holm 1991). Like its predecessors, the Maoist state regarded the local as a project for cultivation, but the success of this project was thought to lie in the state's ability to reform the local from inside out, to cultivate what we might now see as translocal subjectivities which identified with the local and the nation simultaneously.

At the same time, the Maoist state was engaged in another sort of translocal project. In its efforts to redress the material imbalance between industrial coast and agricultural interior, as well as address perceived external threats to the nation's security, thousands of skilled workers were sent inland from cities such as Beijing, Tianjin, Shanghai, and Nanjing, and thousands of urban youth were sent to the countryside to labor alongside peasants. A translocality of sorts resulted from such movements, for these migrants tended to maintain a dual sense of identity between their home cities and their new villages or work-unit (*danwei*) compounds in the interior. Many dreamed of return and eventually did return home, maintaining their long-distance ties at the subjective level even when actual travel was impossible.

These non-local identifications had material manifestations as well. As discussed in Sun's chapter, many Anhui intellectuals, like those in the research and design institutions of Bengbu, lived "both separate from and above local economic life." While shopping locally and sending their children to local schools, these migrants nevertheless lived in clearly delineated compounds, and maintained Beijing dialects. It is even possible to suggest that such translocal identities be seen as a continuation of the longer-term state project of translocal ideology identified by Faure and Siu, for Sun comments that, "Very often the *danwei* (workplace) is not separate from the nation-state. Instead it may be the material embodiment of the nation-state per se." Dutton (1998: 194) has in fact made similar observations of the *danwei*, arguing that it be regarded as part of the socialist state's apparatus of spatial technologies aimed at producing "a very definite kind of subjectivity and intersubjectivity" in which one's position within a much broader macro-scale hierarchy was manifest in the micro-spatiality of the work unit compound itself. A similar kind of translocality could also be identified in relation to the Mao state's practice of sending youth to the countryside, a practice that has led to a fascinating legacy of multilocal nostalgia, marriage, collective memory, and urban consumption today.

The post-Mao state

Since the early 1980s, Mao-era restrictions on mobility have been gradually relaxed as the state has encouraged the development of township and village enterprises, responded to the rural demand for access to urban markets, incomes, and standards of living, and orchestrated the transfer of surplus rural labor from agricultural to industrial occupations, and from interior to coast. More broadly, the state has gradually recognized the need for mobile labor markets to meet the demands of regional specialization and China's integration into the global manufacturing assembly line. The result has been an explosion of new translocal practices, only a few of which have been encouraged or anticipated by the state, but all of which have been conditioned by the state's policies of macroeconomic restructuring and liberalization. As indicated above, these translocal practices have emerged within a context of increasing spatial unevenness such that it is difficult to speak of translocality in China without recognizing that it almost always occurs in relation to the spatial inequalities that pervade contemporary Chinese society. Spatial mobility, in other words, continues to be equated in most people's minds with social mobility.

In this context, the state remains interested in translocality in a number of ways. As mentioned above, both Goodman and Feng and Zhan find the state interested in cultivating a new provincial identity, such that a new translocal imaginary—in which the province becomes a meaningful mediating scale between the locality and the nation—may emerge. Such provincial identity formations entail translocal imaginaries—we could also call them ideologies of translocalism—in that they do not seek to displace the locality or the nation, but cultivate subjects who identify with the province just as they do with the locality and the nation. Such identification would presumably lead to looking out for the interests of the province and supporting the province's economic development, just as one would look out for and support one's locality or China more generally. A similar attention to translocality is seen on the part of the state in Hoffman's analysis of Dalian. The municipality's interest in cultivating "enterprising subjects" also entails an ideology of translocalism, for such subjects must clearly identify with the interests of Dalian just as they would those of China. At the same time, such subjects must maintain a global outlook, be "at home" any place along the circuits of global capital, and possess a sense of identity with the global economy enabling them to lead Dalian through the tumultuous waters of market capitalism.

Hoffman's case also reminds us of a related interest in translocality on the part of the state. Having unleashed unruly market forces capable of undercutting the state's ability to maintain macroeconomic (and thus social and political) stability, there is a clear interest in territorial regulation, planning, and governance to manage the uneven accumulation of capital. Indeed, state territorial regulation remains, for the most part, a facilitating, rather than inhibiting (as is often assumed to be the case) factor in the rapid globalization of capital (Swyngedouw 1992; Cox 1997; Storper 1997). Furthermore, "competitive advantage" in the global economy often depends on place-specific factors that are created or encouraged by state practice (Dicken 1998: 271–273). This can be most clearly seen in cultural industries such as tourism (see Weng, this volume; Oakes 1999; Wang 2001) and regional product manufacturing. But, as Hendrischke shows in this volume, for "first generation" privatized enterprises, locally specific *institutional* relations—particularly those that entailed the involvement of local authorities with capital accumulation—also accounted for much business success. For localities, benefiting from globalization may thus entail cultivating place-specific development advantages while at the same time conforming to global standards of (de)regulation in local labor and financial markets. As potential sites of capital accumulation, localities like Dalian (or even Shanxi or Hainan) remain important spaces for the state to cultivate as distinctive (i.e. *vis-à-vis* the nation). But at the same time, localities must be standardized if they are to attract investment capital. Indeed, they must be "commodified" in the sense that they become exchangeable for capital in the national interest. As such, the locality becomes translocal in the sense that it is identified as part of a broader network of market exchange and capital flows. Also, as Hendrischke chronicles, the move toward translocal openness has ended up being precisely one of the shifts that has proven beneficial to the "second generation" of private enterprise.

Translocality also plays a role in the state's cultivation of investment linkages between communities of overseas Chinese and their native places on the mainland. While this would equally qualify as an aspect of transnationalism, referring to it in terms of translocality focuses our attention on the fact that the flows creating translocal identities need not be restricted to people themselves, as is typically assumed to be the case in the literature on transnationalism. In relying on a "Greater China" network of finance capital, the Chinese state has encouraged sending regions to cultivate a translocal approach in tapping into overseas capital markets (Olds and Yeung 1999). Not only are overseas Chinese communities encouraged to see themselves as extensions of the mainland native place but those native places are also encouraged to see themselves as translocal endpoints of a global network of capital flows.

The state also manifests an interest in translocality by sanctioning the conditions of spatial unevenness which have prevailed in the post-Mao era. Just as it is now having an impact on the development of China's western regions through the *Xibu Dakaifa* (Opening the West) program, state policy is also the major factor explaining the early rapid growth of the coastal region beginning in the mid-1980s. The timing of that growth—the early boom of the Zhujiang Delta region, followed by Jiangsu, Zhejiang, Shanghai in the early 1990s—is very much tied to specific state decisions regarding the granting of special policies for these regions at specific times. The resulting "southern boom" and the patterns of labor migration associated with it can thus be seen as products of state planning.

In other words, the spatial unevenness of post-Mao development in China has been deliberate, and, from the state's perspective, translocality might be regarded as a factor in the mitigation of that unevenness. The central government has, for instance, encouraged localities which have benefited from favorable policies and "gotten rich quick" to link up with poorer regions, facilitating the establishment of "window enterprises," making charitable contributions for basic health and education projects in impoverished areas, and making it lucrative for firms from rich areas to set up operations in poor regions. And this transfer has been formalized and spatialized in the form of the *Xibu Dakaifa* program (Goodman 2004). The state, in other words, would like localities to assume a more independent translocal perspective as they navigate and negotiate the inequalities of the market transition.

On the level of individual subjects, the state has also encouraged the translocality of labor migrants by encouraging a rural exodus through the "Labor Export for

Development" policy, while maintaining a system of household registration which denies all but the most elite migrants permanent residence in the places to which they move for work. The state treats the majority of its internal labor migrants as "guest workers" or "temporary migrants" and thus stimulates their translocal identification with home place and work place. Their location can only be formulated as shifting or circular. From the state's perspective, such translocality is a mitigating factor in the extreme hardship endured by many labor migrants, with impermanence being framed as more of a comfort than an injustice for laborers enduring abusive working conditions. Translocality can also be seen as a kind of strategy of keeping internal migration from becoming excessive while not attenuating the labor market required by capitalist development. The state has long been committed, for instance, to a policy of limiting migration to large cities while encouraging surplus agricultural workers to join the industrial labor force while staying in the countryside (*litu bulixiang*) or moving to local towns or regional cities.

The success of this must ultimately depend on the state's ability to bring a satisfactory standard of living to poorer regions. But it also depends, at least in the short term, on the creation of a translocal imagination, in which those who don't leave can imagine themselves to be *part of* a broader network of (wealthier) places, rather than *segregated or excluded from* such places. Such an imaginary is, of course, not solely a state creation, nor can it really be controlled or manipulated by the state. It is, rather, part of what Sun identifies as a new spatial subjectivity that is less mobile than translocal.

In addition to material mobilities and exchanges, the state has also been instrumental in promoting translocal flows of messages and ideologies through media. An explicit policy throughout the 1990s and into the 2000s has been to improve the *suzhi* (quality) of rural people through promulgating market *sixiang* (mentalities) (Yan 2003). To this end, the state has made considerable investments in the establishment of satellite television hookups in remote areas. This is understood as a strategy of development and poverty alleviation, since the hope is to "modernize" the minds of television viewers, marketizing them through inciting in them both consumption desires and a consequent willingness to pursue entrepreneurial endeavors. The flow of media messages represents a chief form of translocality that does not entail human movement. Because of the pedagogical function that is scripted for television, we might think of the increasing ubiquity of standard programming as akin to what Appadurai referred to as an ideoscape. Appadurai contrasted his notion of mediascapes, which provide "repertoires of images, narratives, and ethnoscapes to viewers throughout the world, in which the world of commodities and the world of news and politics are profoundly mixed" (1996: 35), with ideoscapes, which were more "directly political and frequently have to do with the ideologies of states and the counterideologies of movements explicitly oriented to capturing state power" (1996: 36). What this bifurcation—of media- and ideoscapes—did not allow for, however, was an ideological climate in which the display of commodities and lifestyles is itself a political message, especially on the heels of the Cultural Revolution. The market message conveyed is one that can be thought of as persuasively political—aggressively promulgating market thinking in a society that spent decades being allergic to it. We might also think in terms of ideoscapes for the circulation of the notion of authenticity described herein by Oakes, since it is aligned with a normative formulation of modernization.

Scale

As the earlier discussion of the Mao and post-Mao era restructuring of space begins to suggest, scale is a crucial component in understanding translocal China. By arguing for a translocal perspective on contemporary China, we are in fact implying an argument about scale. Cartier (2001: 26) has already made this argument explicit by pointing out that "dialectical scale relations may be thought of as a set of 'translocal' processes for the ways in which the translocal are those multiple places of attachment experienced by highly mobile people." In other words, translocality draws our focus to local scales of activity while not losing sight of the broader scales of interaction that link the local to the regional and national scales. The term also seeks to recognize that because of increasing time-space compression, the spatial scales of identity have in many ways expanded greatly. But despite this, "the urge to identify with localities seems to have become stronger" (Thrift 1994: 225). It is not so much that people *insist* on staying local *despite* all the changes going on around them, but that time-space compression has made it possible to translate identity into various scales *simultaneously*, by identifying with multiple localities in both practical and imaginary ways.

Here, we want to suggest that translocality offers an important contribution to theories concerning the social production of scale. In the discussion that follows, we hope to point out that it is important to interpret multiple scales of identity not only in the vertical terms of a scale-hierarchy (i.e. local-regional-national-global), but also in the horizontal terms of multiple locales or multiple regions of identity. Translocality therefore does not necessarily impose a hierarchical rendering of scale-relations, making it possible to articulate conceptions of scale alternative to those imposed by, for example, the state, capital, or other powerful interests. To develop this argument, we trace some of the theoretical approaches to scale as a dynamic social construction before moving more directly to scaled processes in China and their implications for translocality.

Shifts in international political economy since the late 1970s—including the breakdown of the Bretton Woods agreement, the fall of the USSR, and the growing power of regional, political, and economic formations at subnational and supranational scales—have led to an increasing willingness in the social sciences to question the assumption that scale is a given, neutral attribute of spatial phenomena (Gregory and Urry 1985; Soja 1989; Agnew 1994). On one level, the idea that the scales at which social phenomena express themselves are always changing seems too obvious to warrant mention. As Neil Smith puts it (2003: 228), all one has to do is compare medieval London's walled city to contemporary

Sao Paulo or Los Angeles to see that the "urban scale" has shifted in size considerably. As society changes, the scales at which we live our lives and interact with others change too. But the rise of theoretical work on the "social production of scale"—much of it inspired by Lefebvre's *La Production de L'espace* (1974)—managed to push these banal observations toward more radical conclusions. Perhaps the most influential of these is the idea that the nation-state as the basic or even most effective scale of economic and political force should not be taken for granted, for it is in fact only a contingent manifestation of political and economic forces as they emerged in Europe after the seventeenth-century Treaty of Westphalia. This sense of contingency is affirmed in Benedict Anderson's (1983) treatment of the rise of nationalism which argued that it was in large part a common imaginary of print-reading publics—as collectivities defined by their vernacular languages—that allowed for the emergence of translocal national sentiments.

This is not to imply that contemporary globalization might herald the end of the nation-state. Rather, it is merely to note that the nation-state is subject to a complex array of contemporary struggles which contest the exercise of state power on a national scale (Dirlik 1999). These include struggles over the control of transnational capital flows, subnational, indigenous and regionalist struggles for autonomy or independence (there being both political and economic versions of these), and supranational political or economic alliances which seek to displace various aspects of state power at the national scale. Such struggles are in fact not unique to the contemporary era (Arrighi 2003), and the persistence with which the scales of political and economic power are contested, shifted, and transformed only makes clear that such scales are never fixed but subject to change as well as active and ongoing maintenance by the states or other forms of power that benefit from them. It follows, of course, that assumptions about the ordering of the world into fixed scales of global, national, regional, and local not only err in viewing such an order as natural, given, and unchanging, but also miss the fact that new scales are always emerging to displace the old. For instance, supranational institutions like the North American Free Trade Agreement (NAFTA) and the European Union (EU) have created new "regional" scales somewhere between the global and the national. Transnational business networks have done the same thing (e.g. "Greater China"—see Ong 1999; Sum 2003). Other regional scales of political or economic force are asserting themselves at the subnational level, but not according to regional boundaries to which we're accustomed.

These observations emerge from a body of work that has conceptualized scale as a spatial arena where social power relations are contested and temporarily resolved (Swyngedouw 1997: 140). Neil Smith (2003: 228) calls scale a "*spatial resolution of contradictory social forces.*" Such social forces, for example, might include capitalist enterprises that find the scale of the nation-state too constraining on accumulation. However, they would also include political institutions that represent labor on a national scale and these institutions tend to insist on the nation as the optimal scale of labor's negotiated relations with capital. There are also regional movements which seek to establish or fix new scales for their political claims. Existing scales that reinforce the power of some groups might be constraining to others. One example of this situation comes from Europe, where Smith finds capitalist firms seek to operate at a scale greater than that of the nation-state, with the growing institutions of the EU facilitating this move. Smith refers to such efforts to expand the scale at which an organization (in this case, a firm) operates as "jumping scale," or "the reorganization of specific kinds of social interaction at a higher scale and therefore over a wider terrain, breaking the fixity of 'given' scales" (2003: 229). For certain European firms, jumping the nation-state scale can be a means to higher profits; in more abstract terms, jumping scale is an effort to gain power. "This applies whether we are considering national claims to empire, a city's efforts to annex surrounding suburbs, or feminist efforts to dissolve the boundaries between home and community" (ibid.). One could also see this as a closing of gaps between uneven scales of development and thus power, and marginal groups may seek to close the development gap by jumping to a scale that is more empowering.

While much of the geography literature sees scale jumping as a practice of translocality, we seek to explore the possible distinction between "jumping up" scale hierarchies and "jumping across" scale gaps via the cultivation of multi-locale networks. This distinction seems particularly important in China, where mobility up the scale hierarchy remains difficult whereas mobility across development gaps is much easier. But the implications for conceptualizing non-hierarchical scale relations hopefully go well beyond the specific context of China.

In order to explore the distinction between "jumping up" and "jumping across." It is important however to first consider whether such agentive and often contentious scale-jumping practices are necessarily extra-state or counter-state phenomena. To the contrary, Jing Wang (2005: 3) has suggested that there is no necessity for the common formulation, typical of scholars accustomed to analyzing neoliberal economies, that scalar production is "always" a contested and heterogeneous process entailing negotiation between state and non-state agents. By contrast, a state such as China's, especially given its command legacy, might be seen, according to Wang, to be quite capable of unilaterally producing scales and enforcing their rankings at certain moments. With this caution in mind, it is worth watching carefully, with China's specificity in mind, for historical and political conjunctures that might mitigate toward more contested against more authoritarian productions of scale.

At present, China offers fertile ground for exploring the implications of jumping across the uneven scales of socio-economic development. Reforms have created broad patterns of unevenness between north and south, east and west, coast and interior, and rural and urban. These broad geographies of inequality have in turn informed strategies of mobility and indeed the nature of flows between regions throughout China. No longer is Chinese space organized in terms of the pyramidical spatial hierarchy imposed during imperial and Maoist times in which Beijing (or another capital) constituted the unequivocal apex. Instead, Cartier's chapter documents the growing symbolic appeal of southern cities, and details the gendered representations of such "symbolic city regions" which convey the manufacturing of desire that accompanies inequality. Similarly, Sun's chapter explores the lure of "the south" among the professional elite of Anhui, and that by Feng and Zhan shows how swiftly Special Economic Zone (SEZ) status created unprecedented desirability for Hainan. Hoffman's chapter also notes the trafficking in symbolic north–south differences through examining Dalian's attempts to transplant some of southern China's "miracle" success back to the north. The crossing of rural–urban and interior–coast gaps likewise forms the basis of Schein's chapter on Miao women migrants from Guizhou, while Oakes's and Weng's deal with the reverse flow of tourists from wealthier eastern urban places to China's exotic but impoverished interior. In short, nearly all the chapters deal with the crossing of gaps of some sort.

Meanwhile, though none of the chapters in this volume explicitly touch on it, the current campaign to "open up the west" offers perhaps the most sensational recognition by the state that gaps it expressly intended are now creating pressures with potential consequences for the long-term viability of the regime (see Goodman 2004). The preponderance of so many development gaps appears to be a product of the state's particular approach to ordering space in China. Chinese state space has been intensely hierarchical for centuries and certainly was under Mao. While there has always been movement across the hierarchical scales that have ordered the empire and the nation, the contemporary era is perhaps unique in the degree to which that hierarchy expresses one of the world's highest rates of income inequality, something which creates enormous pressure for movement across space and consequently tremendous pressure on the scales that fix state power spatially. Such pressures elicit the state's renewed tinkering with and refashioning of scalar relationships, including the promotion of what Wang (2005: 16–18) calls a transboundary planning vision that is more "relational" and "networked."

China has one of the world's oldest and most enduring systems of territorial scale hierarchy, defined primarily in terms of counties (at the most local level), districts or prefectures, provinces, and nation-empire. Of these, the county has remained the most "fixed" over time, with current boundaries showing remarkable continuity over the past two millennia. Introduced during the Yuan Dynasty in the thirteenth century, provinces have been the next most enduring scale of administration and offer a telling lesson in the construction of scale. Most provinces were initially established to facilitate state military control over the empire's vast regions. But as John Fitzgerald (2002) notes, the province's function as an instrument of military power evolved into one of mediator between the interests of the empire with those of counties (see also Guy forthcoming). It thus emerged as a scale of negotiated interests between center and locality. In fact, the center would have preferred to maintain a direct and unmediated link with the locality (i.e. county or "village"). Fitzgerald (2002: 33) argues:

> The art of government appeared to lie in linking the national capital with the counties and villages to educate and mobilize the common people, extract resources, develop the country, and defend the realm. Little allowance

was made either for cities or provinces as relatively autonomous units of government. From the panoptic perspective of the metropole, all intermediate echelons of territorial administration, including provinces, prefectures, special zones and cities, appeared either as obstacles in the way of consummating the special relationship between the capital and the counties, or as expedient intermediaries arising from the temporary postponement of the romance of county and metropole, people and state.

Such a view of governance is consistent with the "earth-bound ideology" discussed in Faure and Siu's chapter, and gives us additional perspective on why a translocal imaginary capable of transcending this vast divide between center and locality was necessary to construct and maintain. As it turned out, however, the center always found it necessary to turn to an intermediate scale as direct administration was never feasible. If Smith (2003) sees scale as expressing compromise, or "resolution," between contending forces, then the province seems to provide a textbook illustration, being the best compromise between the center's need for absolute power and the locality's need for effective decisions and policies that reflected local concerns and conditions.

If the province is the geographical resolution of contending forces, then the balance of forces has shifted somewhat in the reform era, with fiscal and macro-economic decentralization policies allowing provinces greater political and economic autonomy. This move makes sense in the context of Fitzgerald's (2002) argument that provinces not only mediate between center and locality, but also help build the state in a more fundamental sense. Periods of state crisis in China have typically been resolved by devolving more authority and autonomy to local and regional scales (Lary 1974), and this is what the center seems to have done following the death of Mao and the convulsions of the Cultural Revolution, when the re-establishment of state legitimacy was crucial. The chapters by Goodman and Feng and Zhan illustrate some of the outcomes of this decentralization, as the state has recently shown interest in shoring up the scale of the province not simply as a scale of negotiation between center and locality, but as a cultural and economic entity in its own right. This reminds us that despite their "constructed-ness," scales always accrue meanings and identities which tend to indeed convey a "fixed" or "natural" quality. But in the case of China's provinces the picture gets somewhat more complicated. Not only have provinces mediated central-local relations, but they have at key moments been called upon to either maintain the legitimacy of the center (Fitzgerald 2002: 35) or to even articulate an alternative vision of what the center *should* be (Duara 1993). In this respect, the meanings associated with the province imply a translocal imaginary, in which the scales of empire-nation and region symbolically collapse into one. Goodman and Feng and Zhan both examine the province as a constructed scale and translocal imaginary, and they find that the state's project of constructing a provincial identity in fact involves the marshalling of resources from several scales and collapsing them together. Hainan identity, Feng and Zhan argue, consists of ideas attributed to a more broadly regional scale of "southern" China, while Goodman finds Shanxi identity to be partly an amalgamation of cultural practices and customs with much more localized connections. Translocality, then, helps us see the multiple scales of identification that are often drawn together for the state's specific spatial projects.

While provinces remain an important scale project for the state, the most significant issue to arise in relation to scale and hierarchy in China today has been the expansion and scope of the urban (Guldin 1992; Chen *et al.* 2001). Fitzgerald argues that cities are posing a significant challenge to the scale of the province, and could even displace the province as the key mediating scale between center and locality. With the policies of *shixiaxian* (cities leading counties) and *chexian gaishi* (abolishing counties and establishing cities), cities have been "jumping scale" all over China as the state seeks to rescale its territorial administration and capture—for the purpose of revenue accumulation—the rapid economic growth in suburban regions, or what Guldin describes as "a dense web of transactions [that] ties large urban cores to their surrounding regions" (1997:62). But that the increasingly superior rank of cities remains a historically and economically contingent phenomenon, arising at this recent moment in the reform transition, is nonetheless underscored by two developments that temporarily put the prestige and desirability of cities under threat: first, the period in the 1980s when peasants in certain regions of China suddenly stood to gain unprecedented wealth through agriculture and village enterprises while urbanites struggled along with relatively sluggish wage increases, and second, the severe acute respiratory syndrome (SARS) scare when dense urban aggregations became sites of avoidance for fear of epidemic contagion (Wang 2005: 4). Clearly, the rank of the city in China's scalar hierarchy is subject to a myriad of economic and political variables over time.

In these terms, cities "jumping" to district, province, or even national scales of activity has clearly been an avenue to maintaining state power over these potentially chaotic realms of socio-economic change (Cartier 2001: 25; Fitzgerald 2002: 30). Cartier's chapter in this volume captures an additional dimension of this process by examining the popular spatial imaginations associated with the rising cities of southern China. Her chapter reminds us that scale jumping as a means to power is not only appropriated by the state, but can also be read as a signifying practice in which identities are "scaled up" as people set their sights on those high-flying cities as the locus of actual or potential migration, or simply of desire. The rural Miao migrants in Schein's chapter reflect such a subjectivity, struggling to find ways to move to or stay in cities not always simply for wage opportunities but also because cities bear the mark of modernity.

At the same time, the increasing relative wealth and power of Chinese cities is driving a widening rural-urban income gap which is probably the single most significant social issue facing China today. Given the pressures, as mentioned above, to close that gap and jump scale from the rural to the urban, translocality offers an important tool for understanding scaled strategies of mobility and their relationship to identity formation and subjectivity. Chapters by Cartier, Sun, and Schein each focus on this issue in distinct ways. More explicitly than the others in this volume, Schein's chapter explores the implications of scale jumping as a way of negotiating the spatially uneven social relations that are obtained in China today. She points out something that is also clear in the above discussion: that much of the focus of the literature on scale has been on the fragile nature of the nation-state and the struggles to displace the nation-state with other scales of power, as well as on relatively large economic and political institutions instead of smaller or less powerful groups or individuals. As do all the chapters in this volume, Schein explores the implications of changing social relations for scales *within* a nation-state framework, but she aims her analysis more explicitly at the question of hierarchy in scale productions by focusing on Miao women who migrate "across scale."

As noted briefly earlier, this represents a significant shift in the conceptual potential of translocality to intervene in theories of scale. Schein raises the question of whether the translocality of Miao women who shuttle across the rural-urban and interior-coast gaps entails not only the jumping up in scale which Smith (2003) identifies as an avenue to power, but also a horizontal jumping across scale. By pointing out that some movement "across the gap" itself does not necessarily mean an improvement in status or living standard, Schein asks whether such moves are reproductive of established scale hierarchies, or whether they entail a renegotiation of scale in new terms. Translocality indeed seems to imply more of a horizontal than vertical orientation, and thus perhaps offers an alternative approach to conceiving the social production of scale. Schein puts it this way:

> If scale is always in process, "under construction," as it were, then what does this mean for the shift from envisioning one-time unidirectional moves "up" the social–spatial ladder from villages to cities to envisioning the production of translocal connectedness across China? One possibility is that migrants may be renegotiating the ranking of scales, potentially (though not necessarily) remaking the relation between urban and rural into something more horizontal.

Horizontality, then, becomes another way of expressing an unbounded local scale. It is also suggestive of a non-hierarchical rendering of scale, as seen in Schein's finding that Miao peasants supplement their use of terms such as "*shangmian*" (above) or "*xiamian*" (below) to designate state-ordered administrative scales with the more colloquial "*da*" (big) or "*xiao difang*" (small place) to describe more urban or more rural places respectively. This usage would be suggestive of what Herod and Wright (2002: 7) offer as an alternate scale metaphor to that of ladder-like hierarchy:

> concentric circles, with "smaller" scales such as the local being represented by circles which are closer to the central point (representing the location of the observer) and "larger" scales represented by bigger circles located further from the central point. Moving between scales, then, would be a process of traversing from a central point outwards to ever larger scales in which the global scale, being the most distant circle, is seen to enclose all other scales.

We might go so far as to read these instances as struggles that seek to "equalize" social relations across scale, to replace the ladder with more traversable concentric circles. The vast numbers of rural migrants in China's cities have, for example, been viewed by Kate Zhou (1996) not exclusively as evidence of continuing dis- crimination against the rural, but also of the ability of farmers to "ruralize" the cities, effectively claiming them as their own space (see Solinger 1999; Zhang 2002). Schein too notes the potential consequences for seemingly rigid scale hier- archies of "an aggregate of quotidian practices" undertaken by millions of rural migrants. This conceivable erosion of existing scale structures not only marks a "loosening" of the *hukou* system, as Cartier observes, but perhaps even a ques- tioning of the much older and more stable system of administrative hierarchy that *hukou* has been used to reinforce.

Hendrischke's chapter offers another version of this horizontal theme. Examining the growth strategies of Zhejiang enterprises, he finds that while the privatization of enterprise leads to increased mobility, the state still plays the key role in defining the spatial scale structure in which that mobility occurs. Because of this, the advantages of access to state power are still very much defined by the localities within which businesses operate. In other words, and perhaps unlike the European firms discussed in Smith's (2003) scale jumping example discussed earlier, the benefits of remaining tied to localities make it attractive to become translocal rather than, say, "regional" or "national" in scale. The difference between these strategies is subtle but important. The latter strategy of scale jump- ing assumes a clear move *up* in an established hierarchy of scales, while the former—or translocal—approach indicates less a struggle to join or create a new scale of operation than to cultivate multiple local scales of operation in a kind of network (Castells 1996) or rhizomic strategy.

Indeed, it is tempting to push further with the notion of the rhizome, developed by Deleuze and Guattari (1987), as an image for the multiplicity of translocal connections that have come to crosscut China. Unlike "centered (even polycentric) systems with hierarchical modes of communication and pre-established paths," the "rhizome connects any point to any other point" (1987: 21). One needs only to think of the chaotic patterns of road building in China's reform era—departing from the Mao era tracing of administrative hierarchy and instead crisscrossing the landscape to mirror all manner of diverse flows—to see the rhizomic strategy in action. Deleuze and Guattari describe this profusion of flows as an intrinsic func- tion of capitalism, which supercedes the despotic state and "decodes" and "deter- ritorializes" precisely that coding by which that state had ordered and governed the *socius*. The hallmark of capitalism, for them, is this move toward an undiffer- entiated *socius* constituted by promiscuous flows based on the abstractions of money-capital and "free" labor (1972: 33), where power, as Foucault would put it, is more regional, more "capillary" (1972: 96). Yet, at the same time, "capitalism institutes or restores all sorts of residual and artificial, imaginary, or symbolic territorialities, thereby attempting, as best it can, to recode, to rechannel persons who have been defined in terms of abstract quantities" (1972: 34). We can see this move toward recoding in the proliferation of symbolic markings by which places come to be individuated through market processes, producing the jockeying for place distinction recounted, for instance, in Hoffman's treatment of Dalian, or in Oakes's treatment of tourist villages. We might also note the proposals recounted by Wang (2005: 15) to rescale China's vertical hierarchy into "administratively independent trans-boundary networks of urban zones," and the contemporary ascendancy of certain Chinese cities as autonomous centers of accumulation each with particular characteristics. Decoding then, should not be taken as any annihilation of difference, but rather, as Harvey might have put it, as a "postmodern" feature of burgeoning capitalism accompanied by an aesthetic that "celebrates difference, ephemerality, spectacle, fashion, and the commodification of cultural forms" (1989: 156) at the expense of any abiding state-enforced codifications.

Place

In addition to the possibility of a more rhizomic approach to the production of scale, translocality can also be developed to convey a more subjective interpretation of social space. Much of the existing scale literature, while inspired by the pioneering work of Lefebvre, has not really explored the micro-scale of the body, nor ventured into the realm of spatial subject formation, despite Lefebvre offering some brilliant observations regarding these areas of inquiry. As a later section will explore in greater depth, the concept of translocality maintains a focus on the body as a scale of spatial struggle and meaning by considering what mobility does to the body on the move and in place. Here, we begin exploring these more subjective dimensions of translocality by first exploring its relationship to place. With its focus on connections among multiple localities, one might assume that translocality is another way of indicating a "multi-placed" person or phenomenon. But the concept of place is not simply another word for locality, which typically assumes a site of relatively limited scale. Instead, place is not defined by scale at all, but rather by the meanings, histories, and practices associated with being in a given space. As such, place can be conceived as a scale-transcending idea and thus speaks more to how a translocal perspective implicates questions of subjectivity and identity in relation to scaled processes. Here we examine both the Chinese concept of "native place" in relation to translocality as well as the theorizations of place in academia to illuminate these implications.

The concept of translocality both extends from and works in tension with the idea of native place in China studies. The native place (*guxiang*) has been one of the most fundamental markers of identification throughout the late imperial and modern eras. While the importance of native place seems to reinforce Fei Xiaotong's idea of an "earth-bound" China, it is ironically an idea that derives at least as much from mobility as from the rootedness with which it is typically associated. Literary renderings of *guxiang* have always evoked the traveler's or exile's melancholy longing for home (Strassberg 1994; Tang 2000: 74–75; Wang 2004). In more modern articulations, the literary *guxiang* took on the symbols of refuge as urban writers confronted China's revolutionary changes in the context of treaty-port colonialism (Duara 2000). Native place was also institutionalized in the form of sojourning merchant associations (*huiguan*) (Ho 1966; Skinner 1976; Rowe 1984: 213–251). Bryna Goodman (1995: 12–13) has argued that the native place sentiments conveyed by these associations were not necessarily "localistic and parochial" but, in being derived from one's mobility *beyond* the native place, were grounded in a larger political ideology of nationalism. "Love for the native place," she comments, "was virtuous because it helped to constitute and strengthen the larger political polity of China." Thus, in Goodman's modern Shanghai, we see a kind of scale-transcendence which again reminds us of the translocal imaginary identified by Faure and Siu for late-imperial times.

Contemporary manifestations of translocality in part emerge from this history of native place as a fluid process of identification. Yet translocality also suggests a tension with this history in that it implies a shift from an assumed local site of identification (the native *place*, however fluid and linked to broader networks of exchange, travel, or administration) to *multiple* sites of identification. Rather than simply assuming the on-going construction of home in relation to mobility, translocality suggests that home itself becomes complicated, its roots to a single locality multiplied to a network of localities. Late-imperial and early modern place identities were typically associated with the trade skills of their sojourning merchants, the scholarly abilities of their scholar-officials, or even the conditions of poverty which might have forced migrants to take to the road and go begging (as in the case of northern Anhui, see Sun 2002). In contemporary China, however, many "places" are self-consciously constructed as consumable spaces of attraction, investment, and development (Oakes 2000). Identity is now a complex discourse *within* places, rather than simply among those who have traveled away from them. This has, in turn, helped spur the proliferation of what Cartier identifies as "trait geographies" within China, in which place images multiply and circulate as part of the process of constructing consumable places through entertainment and other commercial media, state development policies, marketing strategies, and other processes related to increasing integration of China with regional and global capital markets. The result, as Cartier points out, is a saturation of place identities and a complication of one's sense of home and belonging. In short, we are suggesting that native place identity in contemporary China might be fruitfully reconfigured as translocal identity to accommodate the recent shifts in opportunities for spatial identity construction.

To better understand these shifts, some further exploration of academic conceptions of place might be helpful. There is of course a vast literature dealing with place, and only a very small portion of it comes out of academic geography. Place has been a subject of study in literary criticism, philosophy, anthropology, sociology, and history, and its meaning has varied accordingly. But in general there has been a trend over the past couple of decades toward a relational understanding of place as socially constructed (Castree 2004), and this relational approach has had two general areas of focus: materialist approaches to place as produced by the broader political and economic processes of capital accumulation, and cultural approaches to place as produced in association with the construction of identity, subject formation, and processes of social differentiation. There is considerable overlap between these two broad approaches, of course, but while the former has emphasized the unbounded and networked quality of place, the latter has been more concerned to articulate a sense of local knowledge and experience as an alternative to the universal pretensions of abstract scientific discourse. Materialist approaches to place have tended to dominate in recent human geography (e.g. Pred 1984; Jackson 1989; Massey 1992 and 1994) while cultural approaches have been emphasized in anthropology (Basso 1996; Feld and Basso 1996; Gupta and Ferguson 1997; Escobar 2001) and in philosophy (Casey 1997; Malpas 1999).

Translocality can be seen as drawing on both of these trends in the following ways. First, the idea that place is unbounded, dynamic and expressive of multiple scales of material processes means that place constitutes an intersection of local and translocal processes and thus offers a concept that can link different scales together in a meaningful way. The translocal imaginary is thus a kind of place per-ception (or "sense of place") in that it agentively links one locality to another, or links a locality to a broader set or scale of processes. Translocality deliberately confuses the boundaries of the local in an effort to capture the increasingly com-plicated nature of spatial processes and identities, yet it insists on viewing such processes and identities as place-based rather than exclusively mobile, uprooted, or "traveling." Second, by insisting on this place-based perspective on mobility, translocality also seeks to view subject formation as a place-making process imbricated with the experience (real or imaginary) of mobility and connection across space and scale. Drawing on the work of Merleau-Ponty, Casey argues that while place is the most fundamental component of subjectivity, it is from *mobil-ity* of the body that place-making occurs. Place anchors the body to a site of lived experience and is produced by the body as it moves through space. "The lived body is itself a place. Its very movement, instead of effecting a mere change of position, *constitutes place*, brings it into being" (1997: 233). In this sense, place itself is mobile, traveling with the body as it is constantly being made and remade as part of the ongoing process of subject formation.

The association of place with the body and with mobility, then, suggests the potentially disruptive nature of place as what Lefebvre (1991) would call a "differ-ential space." In producing its own space, Lefebvre argues, the body produces space that may subvert dominant spatial practices and spatial representations. Deleuze and Guattari (1972), mobilizing an isomorphism between body and society, might call this disruptive entity the "body without organs" for it is not codified according to dominant categories. Another way of saying this is to argue that what Casey calls the body/place nexus is disruptive of fixed scales produced by dominant political and economic systems of administration and production. The implications of this go far beyond the practice of "jumping scale" discussed in the previous section. If local knowledge itself emerges from such place-making, then there are further epistemo-logical implications to consider. Place-making, in other words, potentially disrupts other categories of knowledge than just scale. Casey puts it this way:

> Whatever place is, it is not the kind of thing that can be subsumed under already given universal notions—for example, of space and time, substance or causality. A given place may not permit, indeed it often defies, subsumption

under given categories. Instead, a place is something for which we continually have to discover or invent new forms of understanding, new concepts in the literal sense of ways of "grasping together."

(1996: 26)

In the concept of translocality, we hope to convey the potential for such transgressive place-based subjectivities while insisting that such potential is entwined with the mobile dimension of place-making. With contemporary China experiencing unprecedented degrees of mobility, new kinds of subject formation may reflect the kinds of disruptions that Casey's place-based philosophy identifies.

It is important to also recognize that, just as the above-identified trends represent material and symbolic components of place-making, translocality can also be seen as constituting material and symbolic forms of mobility among places. Material forms of translocality, then, would include people who themselves travel and migrate; capital in the form of investments, loans, remittances, and currencies exchanged; electronic communications and other virtual media which bring images and text to television and computer screens, or carry voices through telephones; popular print media such as newspapers and magazines; viruses or other microorganisms which carry diseases such as HIV or SARS; drugs and related commodities; and of course all the other commercial goods which make up the networks of trade that have always tied localities together. These material flows clearly overlap with the symbolic aspects of translocality as discussed later, especially when we are talking about media and electronic communication. The point is not to insist on two separate categories of translocality (material and symbolic) but rather to convey the complex processes currently at work in translocal China. Material flows carry symbolic baggage. The intensification of these material flows has not led to a diminishment of place as a resource for identity or a process of subject formation. Rather, with translocality we suggest a perspective that sees an intensification of place-making since the material and symbolic resources for that place-making are multiplied with the flows that increasingly link places together.

Symbolic aspects: imaginaries and subjectivities

We return here to the premise that one of the ways in which China has become translocal is through the relational or contrastive partitioning of the country into what Cartier has called "symbolic cities and regions." As Sharon Zukin has argued, "The cultural power to create an image, to frame a vision, of the city has become more important as publics have become more mobile and diverse, and traditional institutions—both social classes and political parties—have become less relevant mechanisms of expressing identity" (1995: 2–3). Another way of talking about the process of attribution of certain features to certain places is "trait geographies," and in China we see them as artifacts of both state and non-state discourses. Honig's (1992) classic study of the characterization of Subei (northern Jiangsu) people by Shanghai urbanites as coarse and uncivilized is a prime example of this fusing of imputed traits with places. One of the phenomena emerging with the progressive differentiation of regions within China is an ever more vibrant sphere of symbolic production that depicts these differences, often in agonistic terms that produce contrast precisely to argue the superiority of one place over another. We might, following Zukin (1995: 7) and Molotch (1976), call the manufacturers of these symbologies "place entrepreneurs." Ironically, this type of social agent has, perhaps, become particularly relevant in this era in which the increasing mobility of persons across China has untethered place from pure identities creating more heteroglot places with mixed populations and with subcommunities coalescing within larger localities.

As we have noted, the two largest symbolic partitions of space are those of north-south and east-west. In Cartier's, Feng and Zhan's, and Sun's papers we see a certain romance of the south associated with openness, dynamism and being "hot." In Cartier's case these more socio-economic traits are supplemented by gendered notions and fantasies about different types of bodies. It is with these images that a place like Dalian must compete in articulating the advantages of the north, and it is not surprising that the notion of the unified coastal region is deployed to ameliorate this competition. This leads to the east-west partition which has had several incarnations (for instance, the key interior projects of the First Five Year Plan, and the military-industrial relocations of the Third Front project), but appears in these works (especially in Weng's, Schein's and Oakes's papers) in terms of the west as signifying a remote locus of natural, cultural, and labor resources which are increasingly put in the service of the coastal regions.

A full sense of translocality entails the fundamental insight that people do not need to move in order to have their subjectivities transformed by translocal processes. We ask: what sort of occurrences precipitates peoples' thinking in terms of elsewhere, or experiencing belonging at scales greater than their local place? What do people think, imagine, fantasize prior to moving or deciding not to? This latter type of query has often been addressed using Appadurai's emphasis on media:

> In the past two decades.... More persons throughout the world see their lives through the prisms of the possible lives offered by mass media in all their forms. That is, fantasy is now a social practice; it enters, in a host of ways, into the fabrication of social lives for many people in many societies.
>
> (1996: 53–54)

To be sure, the proliferation of forms of mass media, especially television, but also VCDs, audio cassettes, promotional media such as billboard advertising, and print media such as magazines and posters, has been transformative in reform China. Messages about other places are being transmitted through all these media at a remarkable pace and density. And desires to tour or live in these places seem to have burgeoned concomitantly. But we wish to push beyond the formulation of media providing the material for imagining elsewhere(s) in two ways.

First, we emphasize alternate types of imagining, distinct from the imagining of "other places" per se. The most salient, perhaps, is the process of subjectification to belonging at greater scales, be it the province, the region, the nation, or the transnation. As Schein shows, for Miao women, operating beyond the villages of the Miao mountains meant preconceiving of oneself as occupying negotiable scales of city, province, and country. Goodman offers a case in which a notion of provincial cultural identity comes to be inculcated in the minds of Shanxi locals. For Wang's "net-moms", translocal connectedness is spatially unbounded, hence it potentially puts scale under erasure, and yet, as she argues forcefully, such virtual translocality is, far from being epiphenomenal, one of the most meaningful sources of connection in the consciousness of these mothers.

Feng and Zhan's paper provides an especially intriguing example in which mainland migrants to Hainan, far from identifying with Hainan as their new place, formulated a translocal understanding of themselves as contributing to the national project of substituting a maritime for a landlocked China. Here, instead of being a province, Hainan came to be recast (along with Dalian, as discussed by Hoffman in Chapter 6) as part of a massive and symbolically freighted "coast," a springboard for China's transnational participation. Additionally, with Hainan set up as a Special Economic Zone to model the socialist market economy, the fostering of "SEZ consciousness" (*tequ yishi*) was a specific place-transcending goal of Hainan development. As Feng and Zhan point out, to possess SEZ consciousness was tantamount to being modern or cosmopolitan.

Here we come to the more placeless imaginaries—of, say, cosmopolitanism and modernity—that also circulate so promiscuously under Chinese translocalism. In Oakes's paper we learn that contemporary Chinese notions of authenticity, particularly the crafting and marketing of a certain kind of authenticity, can be indices of the modern, and that this authenticity travels as a genre that brings diverse tourist destinations into translocal dialogue with one another. Because of this tacit dialogue, "authentic replication [in tourism practice] becomes a claim of national authority and representation." What both Feng and Zhan's and Oakes's papers emphasize is that translocality exceeds the meaning of connections between localities, connoting as well the plugging in to a circuit (Deleuze 1995: 8) that is sometimes signified as the nation, sometimes as the cosmopolitan, but is in any event, supralocal. In Hoffman's paper, what is valorized is not only "enterprise culture" but also a quality of "openness" or "outward lookingness." It is a quality that any good citizen of Dalian should possess, and connotes reconfiguring one's outlook so as to imagine Dalian as a node, even a hub, in a network of global capital circulation.

The rhizomic network is, of course, epitomized by the "net-moms" described by Wang. They have created a community for which place is increasingly irrelevant. Locations such as Beijing or the United States may be terms in their discussion of different parenting approaches, but these are despatialized terms, sites of certain orientations rather than physical locations. One of the liabilities of thinking cosmopolitanism is that there is a tendency to smuggle in various versions of universalism that elide the discrepancies between places. What we learn from Wang's account is that participating in the net discussions may be, in one sense, entering into an undifferentiated virtual space, but at the same time, it is shot through with newfangled forms of place-making, as participants debate the merits of western and Chinese mothering styles.

Moreover, we believe that the media are only one of the vehicles creating the translocal imaginary, and should not be overprivileged. Concrete practices and material exchanges are crucially important to the formation of symbolic translocality. For instance, types of consumption and style become highly marked signifiers of places and mobilities. They contribute to the constitution of what Cartier calls "trait geographies." As we see in Feng and Zhan, Goodman, Cartier, Sun, and Schein, people associate places with certain types of food, clothing, and other commodities and they signal their translocal motion by adopting the consumption emblems of another place. Relatedly, as we will see later, bodies and body practices are also implicated in the translocal imaginary. Cartier's example of gendered bodies being imagined differently by place, particularly in the characterization of Shanghai men and women, illustrates this elegantly.

Another type of non-media agent creating the translocal imaginary are translocal businesses and industries themselves. For many Chinese, of course, their lives have been transformed by the arrival of translocal and transnational investments and enterprises at the doorstep of the places they call home. This creates the shift, best seen in Hoffman, toward a self-perception that is more connected, that sees nodes in networks rather than the bounded localities fostered by decades of *hukou* immobility and command economy. One of the industries that explicitly traffics in place differences is that of tourism. In Oakes's article we see the effect of an industry which must, by definition, trade in the juxtaposing of what are crafted to be authentic distinctions between sending and receiving sites. But even as it manufactures difference, the business of tourism brings about a dissemination of an approach to marketing certain forms and values, particularly authenticity, as a way of participating in a translocal modernity. The point, here, is that it is the practices of the industry, not only mediated representations, that produce this supralocal modern toward which to strive.

With Weng's article we have the notion of multiple flows whose trajectories are determined by specific institutions, and by recent improvements in China's infrastructure, especially in terms of transportation. Here the interplay of symbolic and material aspects of tourism come into play more concretely, for, with tourists flow money and HIV. Weng's is perhaps the most intensely embodied inquiry into translocality in that he deals with the transmission of infectious disease through the bodily intimacies of sex and intravenous drug use. The role of the symbolic takes on a special freight in discussions of HIV spread, for it is often specific imaginaries about types of places and peoples that allows individuals to deny or efface their exposure to risk. In an extraordinary example, we see how place imaginaries become the basis for transmission: in a Lijiang township, tourists fantasize about the indigenous custom of *tisese* or visiting marriage (*zouhun*) as promoting a sexual promiscuity that is marked as traditional. Since it is kept conceptually distinct from any kind of sex trade, tourists are able to partake in it without confronting its potential dangers of infection. Abstracting from Weng's example, we see how generalized imaginaries about the Chinese remote could produce elisions of urgent realities—the endemic drug addiction near the border with the Golden Triangle being one especially poignant illustration.

A final example of symbolic processes other than media is that of language, for with the mobility of people comes a greater admixture of dialects, as well as the possibility of mutual incomprehension. As demonstrated in both Schein's and Feng and Zhan's articles, language politics constitute significant social dynamics which are intensified with the movements of people. Importantly, again, those who don't move also stand to be impacted by transformations in their linguistic environments. For Miao women living away from home, the capability to communicate in their own Miao language or in a southwest dialect of Chinese meant the ability to form tiny subcommunities insulated from the Han who were dominant in the areas to which they migrated. For a previously homogeneous Jiangsu Han peasant linguistic environment, the presence of these other languages created a dramatic rupture in their insularity and their daily realities. By contrast, in Feng and Zhan's, and to some extent Sun's examples, what migrants brought with them was the elite dialect of Mandarin. In (formerly) backwater Hainan, the possession of Mandarin could operate as a form of social capital, making it possible for newcomers to set new terms for status and create desires on the part of locals to transform their linguistic usages.

The transnational and the global

One of the challenges for a developed discussion of translocality is to identify the paradigms that have become salient in the much more elaborated field of transnational studies, and to weigh their usefulness within national contexts. Certainly we see strong parallelisms with notions such as "transnational subjects ... live in, or connect with, several communities simultaneously.... They construct and utilize flexible personal and national identities" (Yeoh *et al.* 2003: 3), or with definitions of transnationalism as "the processes by which immigrants forge and sustain multi-stranded social relations that link together their societies of origin and settlement" (Basch *et al.* 1994: 8). While linkages across space offer a commonality of themes, we can see more divergence in terms of notions of nationalism and citizenship. Speaking of transnationalism Michael Peter Smith has averred: "The once taken for granted correspondence between citizenship, nation, and state has been questioned as new forms of grassroots citizenship have taken on an increasingly trans-territorial character" (2003: 15). Transnational migrants begin from the vantage point of marginal citizenship in their destinations, and we speak of the anomaly of long-distance (Anderson 1998) or deterritorialized (Appadurai 1993) nationalisms practiced from overseas. The situation shifts, however, when we are speaking of internal migrants who at one level should be able to claim citizenship rights wherever they find themselves within the nation space, but at another level may find they still have to struggle for legitimacy once they are on the move. This is most dramatically illustrated in China by the legacy of the *hukou* and the tensions over urban citizenship for rural migrants, the "floating population" (Solinger 1999; Zhang 2004).

Recently, much has been made of the notion of flexibility in relation to shifts in the global economy. Perhaps most notable is David Harvey's (1989) notion of "flexible accumulation" to denote, in part, the strategies of transnational corporations to render production mobile and malleable, inaugurating an era of offshore processing in which the globe is relentlessly scoured for the most inexpensive labor. What is significant about this type of strategy for our purposes here is that the mobility of capital and processing is prompted by differentials in wealth within, not beyond, the level of the nation-state. Comparable differentials within China may, as we have suggested, be considered to generate much of the mobility we see here as well, but there is a difference: no national borders prevent the flow of labor to existing sites of processing, nor do great geographical distances. So instead of corporations needing to chase cheap labor, they are able to draw it across China, and the accumulation of capital that takes place in those sites creates a draw for service labor as well. So much attention has been paid to China as an offshore receiving site within the transnational frame that the internal dynamics of wealth differentials have gone overlooked. Only by China being differentiated both in terms of distribution of labor opportunities and in terms of the local economics of such things as wage standards can we expect to see such tremendous human mobility.

Neoliberal formations seem consonant with the development of flexibility, or seem to canalize those developments, producing both structures and subjects that are characterized by their ability to shift and adapt. Anthropologist Emily Martin (1994) has identified the recent era as one in which subjects and their bodies need to cultivate a range of flexibilities in order to keep pace with ever-changing demands on them. No one skill, asset or talent, nor any particular cluster of them, can be relied upon; rather, those who thrive are those who are continually developing new skills and refashioning themselves. Likewise, those who are spatially mobile, must readily recast their notions of home and belonging. Sun compares the elite migrants out of Anhui to these masters of flexibility, calling them postmodern nomads who feel at home everywhere because of their highly portable professional skills.

Anthropologist Aihwa Ong has developed this notion in relation to another form of transnational accumulation—that of the traveling businessperson, the "flexible citizen." Her focus is particularly Hong Kong Chinese who maintain more than one national base—that is, Hong Kong and a city in the West—for their enterprises, and they shuttle across the Pacific to manage business. This kind of flexibility is also being cultivated inside China; indeed, in contrast to the instances discussed earlier, it appears to be more a program of the state rather than an effect of the globalization of capital. In withdrawing many of the regulations and social provisions that scripted people's lives in the Maoist era—*danwei*s, grain coupons, assigned jobs, price controls, etc.—the state has effectively created a social and economic environment in which the flexibility to rise to the demands of a fluctuating economy becomes paramount, even for peasants.

The flexibility that reform era China requires, then, is not only seen in the willingness to move, to cross China in search of opportunities (see Chapters 4, 11, and 12), but also in terms of other translocal ventures, from setting up sideline enterprises which require traveling to market one's wares, to investing in distant provinces (as in the current campaign to open up the west, see Chapter 5), to crafting versatile selves for employment (as in Chapter 6). As Hoffman points out, these "rationalities and discourses of enterprise" in turn reveal themselves to be "new modes of regulation." As Foucaultian and other scholars of advanced liberalism (Burchell *et al.* 1991; Heelas and Morris 1992; Barry *et al.* 1996; Rose 1999) have argued, fashioning neoliberal subjects entails a form of governance that promotes (rather than dictates) "autonomization." Under conditions of privatization in China, we see this playing out in the valorization of enterprising individuals who take charge of their own welfare and, even better, that of their communities, in what sociologist Nikolas Rose has called the "double move of autonomization and responsibilization" (Rose 1999: 174).

Even as we see the national and transnational scales blurred with the hegemonic circulation of neoliberal ideologies of flexibility and enterprise under globalization, we would like to retain a distinction of scales for another reason. We would like to unpack the articulation of translocal with transnational processes. Translocality in China and elsewhere is in part shaped by the international border. Put another way, certain places, their economies and social lives, are imbricated with the transnational; others are not. And this differential accounts for much of the unevenness that characterizes Chinese reform. This is most evident in the instances offered by Weng and by Feng and Zhan in which development is, at least in part, a direct consequence of border proximity. We might think of certain locales as switching points for the transnational: some of these are deliberately crafted by the state, as in the designation of Hainan as a Special Economic Zone, but some are the product of illicit exchanges, as in the drug trade on the Yunnan–Burma border. In both we can identify specific nodes that serve as the connection between the domestic and the transnational. What is striking, however, is that the presence of the unofficial nodes is yet another decoding of China's administrative hierarchy. In other words, hot spots for economic activity and human transit will not necessarily be centers designated by the state, but may have more to do with their geographic positioning or their ethnic make-up. We might return here to the notion (in Deleuze and Guattari 1972, 1987) of capitalist reterritorializing of space, privileging a new set of places based on their articulation with the transnational.

Body

Speaking to the mutual imbrication of body and place, Casey writes:

> the lived body—which is perhaps what human beings take to be the most self-enclosed and intimate thing they experience—shows itself to be continually conjoined with place, however impersonal and public in status it may be in given instances. The conjunction itself is made possible precisely because the body is already social and public in its formation and destiny—as Foucault would insist—while places for their part are idiosyncratic in their constitution and appearance.
>
> (1997: 241)

David Goodman's discussion of Shanxi noodles provides an intriguing starting point for a consideration of the social/material character of bodies. On the one hand, Shanxi could be identified by noodles simply because of the hard material fact of the lack of rice agriculture in most of the province, giving rise in turn to a distinctive grain culture. But Goodman is quick to point out that no sooner is grain particularity practiced in subsistence than it becomes an element of identity production, now taken up by the efforts to create a more arbitrary provincial identity.

The way in which cultural production overwrites basic material production allows us to talk about yet another form of symbolic place making. Bodies are not simply *in* places; bodies *are* places. Probably the best-known incarnation of this in China is the north-south grain divide. Southern bodies are made of rice, whereas northern bodies are made of wheat and other dry grains, and these are understood as qualitatively different bodies. These differences map relatively smoothly onto the topographical features of the Chinese landscape; what Goodman's study adds is a concrete case of grain identity being mobilized in the service of the much more arbitrary administrative boundary of the province.

If bodies index placement, and places shape bodies, then what happens when these once-emplaced bodies are on the move, are out of place? Sun makes an important point about the way in which bodily styles and conventions become transmuted into aspects of identity under displacement. She describes, for overseas Chinese, the melancholic memory of a time when "food was associated with bodily satisfaction, rather than a signifier of ethnic desire" (2002: 145). Within China, of course, we might think in terms of regional as well as ethnic desires. Another popularly cited regional distinction that territorializes Chinese places is that of the chillies of the southwest. Schein's example of the Miao women from Guizhou transporting chillies to their marital homes in Jiangsu allows some insight into mobile body cultures. At the outset, what we might observe about migrants is that their places travel with their bodies, creating the condition of "*bu xiguan*" or feeling unaccustomed and hence displaced. In Steven Feld's and Keith Basso's words, "places naturalize different worlds of sense" (1996: 8), making it seem like the inert body will never shed its particular constellation of *xiguan*—in this case, the taste for chillies. But the process does not stop at collisions of body cultures, for the movement of migrants eventually creates bodily minglings, and refashionings of bodies. In the most literal sense, what this meant in Schein's instance, was that Miao women brought chillies to Jiangsu, and not only ate them themselves, but also introduced them into their cooking for their families, creating a hybridized cuisine.

We might think of the flows of bodily culture created by translocality, then, as producing palimpsests, in which local practices are overwritten by imported ones, creating new layerings and a more complex bodily experience for all. We must be cautious, however, about implying that hybridities and palimpsests—the heterogenization of places consequent upon recent mobilities—are entirely new phenomena. As can be amply gleaned from Siu and Faure's chapter, that traveling merchants and goods created a lively circulation across Chinese space is a much older phenomenon. Body cultures would, of course, not have been pristine and discrete before reform, nor before Mao, no matter how much discourses protested to the contrary. Rather, they would have to have been hybridized much earlier with the vigorous dissemination of, for instance, culinary ingredients and customs.

Writing of postcolonial dispersals of populations, May Joseph emphasizes tactile and sensory memories that are activated at moments as basic as eating alloyed cuisines: "For people whose social knowledge comprises composites of multiple space/time continuums fractured by the experience of decolonization and migration, the striated spaces of modernity's folds are dense with texture" (2000: 44). Not only between nation-spaces, but also within them we might expect to see dense texturings of body experiences as populations undergo dramatic displacements. It is perhaps the phenomenal *volume* of population shifts in the Cultural Revolution and in the *dagong* migrant era that distinguishes the last few decades from late imperial China. The movement there and back of urban youth sent down to the countryside in the Cultural Revolution, has, for instance, spawned an extensive bodily memory transported back to the cities and commodified for twice-displaced customers in the form of the Cultural Revolution nostalgia restaurants. Here consumers pay for sensory awakenings of youthful memories through eating and smelling foods, and seeing and listening to spectacles, evocative of their erstwhile rural sojourns. It is not insignificant that the longings of translocals scattered across China have, as in this instance, increasingly come to be addressed by the market, and we can expect to see a proliferation of translocal enterprises and trade goods tailored precisely to the memories and longings of persons out of place.

In addition to the ways that places constitute bodies, we also need to explore the imbrication of representations with bodies. The virtual mothering world described herein by Wang presents an intriguing example, for it takes that eminently corporeal world of maternal care and transposes it to the scale of the globe. As members of the Yaolan network, mothers mobilize the translocal insights of women across China and beyond to deliver better care to their child in terms of health, education, and well-being. Moreover, their children live in part on the screens of the website, as pictures are mounted and exchanged. Indeed, the babies and their mothers enjoy practices of materializing the virtual space, through idioms such as the "small sofa in the home," by which they refer to babies' links for friends. Although these babies might not have ever met in person, their mothers are actively engaged in making their virtual meetings reality.

Whereas, in Wang's account, virtual communication in a sense brings life to remote persons, Weng's case might be thought of as a counter-example in which the harsh facts of disease transmission, that is threats to life, are obfuscated by representations of particular places. Weng begins from the premise that people on the move experience a "change in socio-cultural environments [that] might induce them to have risky behaviors, including becoming drug users or practicing unsafe sex or working as sex workers." Given this substrate of erotic contact occurring in practice, Weng unpacks the accompanying imageries that contribute to a denial of risk. In one village, peasants maintain that only transnational border crossers can be infected by HIV, that transmission within Chinese borders is unlikely. In another, locals and tourist promoters alike contribute to the discursive project of "eroticizing culture," making the traditional culture of Na people a vehicle for sexual exchanges which, because of their appearance of moral correctness, masquerade as cleaner than straightforward sex work.

Conclusion

With this introductory chapter we have attempted to diversify and nuance the meanings of translocality for China. Rather than present an overly unitary para-digm, we have emphasized differences at several levels. Most fundamental to our argument is that the contemporary translocality we see documented in most of the chapters is an artifact of China's economic and social *unevenness*. Despite connotations of grassroots connectedness and lateral ties, we insist that Chinese translocal processes arise out of and reproduce the constitutive inequalities of China's market reform era.

That said, no study of translocality in China can ignore the practices of the state, and we look back at the late imperial and Maoist eras to reveal the antecedents of contemporary translocality embedded in state ideology and prac-tice. Moving forward in time, we, on the one hand, see a decoding of Chinese territory produced by frenetic, crisscrossing movements across the terrain, but we also see powerful efforts of recoding, of reorganizing space, on the part of the state and capital. Added to this tension is the increasing articulation with the transnational which yields a configuration of space revolving around hot spots or switching points for transnational engagement, which in turn generate particularly patterned flows.

Throughout, we stress the doubleness of translocality, as both material and symbolic, as involving both horizontal and vertical dimensions and, most impor-tant, as relevant not only to mobilities but also to fixities, to localities, and to people that do not move. Translocality heightens China's internal differentiation, and much of this process is accomplished through the production of imaginaries, whether in media or in popular practices. The subjective dimension of translocal-ity is so crucial precisely because it is the awareness of China's internal differ-ences that spawns so much of translocal practice. And this awareness may be bodily as well as cognitive/emotional, prompting us to interrogate myriad intimacies of ingestion, sexuality, maternity, and disease transmission.

The doubleness of translocality is thus seen in the simultaneous micro-scale experiences of the body and macro-scale production of spatial imaginaries. We stress, however, that such a scale-transcending concept not only captures mobili-ties through vertical scale hierarchies, but also horizontal movements across scales. We thus find an untapped rhizomic approach to the production of scale embedded within translocality, compelling us to interpret multiple scales of iden-tity not only in the vertical terms of a scale-hierarchy, but also in the horizontal terms of multiple locales or multiple regions of identity. Translocality therefore does not necessarily imply a hierarchical rendering of scale-relations, making it possible to articulate alternative conceptions of scale to those imposed by, for example, the state, capital, or other powerful interests. In this regard, translocality can convey a more subjective interpretation of social space, one which brings the work on scale back to the realm of spatial subject formation. Ultimately, then, translocality encompasses the experience of those people living in China who find their lives increasingly lived at several scales, or in numerous places, simultaneously.

Notes

1 This body of work on translocality is further based on a broader set of scholarship which, while not necessarily using the specific term, has helped to build the idea of translocality by questioning the boundaries of the local. Some of this broader work includes, among others, Pred (1984), Watts (1991), Appadurai (1996), and Gupta and Ferguson (1997).
2 *Hukou* has a dual classification system. One is the place of registration (*hukou suozaidi*)—this is simply the locality, but it can then be grouped as rural or urban; it is the basis for determining one's rights according to place of residence—that is the distribution of collective grain, and so forth. The other is *hukou* "status" (*hukou leibie*) which is either agricultural or non-agricultural; *hukou leibie* determines eligibility for state entitlements such as grain coupons. According to Chan (1994: 29), roughly 77 percent of the population was rural and agricultural, 14 percent was urban and non-agricultural, and the remaining 9 percent were divided between urban agricultural and rural non-agricultural, based on 1981 data. See also Chan and Zhang (1999: 821–822).

References

Agnew, J. (1994) "The territorial trap: the geographical assumptions of international relations theory," *Review of International Political Economy* 1: 53–80.
Anderson, B. (1983) *Imagined Communities: Reflections on the Origin and Spread of Nationalism*, London: Verso.
—— (1998) *The Spectre of Comparisons: Nationalism, Southeast Asia and the World*, London: Verso.
Appadurai, A. (1993) "Patriotism and its futures," *Public Culture* 5(3): 411–429.
—— (1996) *Modernity at Large: Cultural Dimensions of Globalization*, Minneapolis, MN: University of Minnesota Press.
Arrighi, G. (2003). "The rise of East Asia and the withering away of the interstate system," in N. Brenner, B. Jessop, M. Jones, and G. Macleod (eds), *State/Space: A Reader*, Oxford: Blackwell, 131–146.
Barry, A., Osborne, T., and Rose, N. (eds) (1996) *Foucault and Political Reason: Liberalism, Neo-Liberalism and Rationalities of Government*, Chicago, IL: University of Chicago Press.
Basch, L., Glick Schiller, N., and Szanton Blanc, C. (1994) *Nations Unbound: Transnational Projects, Postcolonial Predicaments and Deterritorialized Nation-States*, Basle: Gordon and Breach.
Basso, K. (1996) *Wisdom Sits in Places*, Albuquerque, NM: University of New Mexico Press.
Burchell, G., Gordon, C., and Miller, P. (eds) (1991) *The Foucault Effect: Studies in Governmentality*, Chicago, IL: University of Chicago Press.
Cartier, C. (2001) *Globalizing South China*, Oxford: Blackwell.

32   *Tim Oakes and Louisa Schein*

Casey, E. (1996) "How to get from space to place in a fairly short stretch of time: a philosopical prolegomena," in S. Feld and K. Basso (eds), *Senses of Place*, Santa Fe, NM: School of American Research, 13–52.
—— (1997) *The Fate of Place: A Philosophical History*, Berkeley, CA: University of California Press.
Castells, M. (1996) *The Rise of the Network Society*, Malden, MA: Blackwell.
Castree, N. (2004) "Differential geographies: place, indigenous rights and 'local' resources," *Political Geography* 23: 133–167.
Chan, K. W. (1994) *Cities With Invisible Walls: Reinterpreting Urbanization in Post-1949 China*, Hong Kong: Oxford University Press.
Chan, K. W. and Zhang, L. (1999) "The *hukou* system and rural-urban migration in China: processes and changes," *The China Quarterly* 160: 818–855.
Chen, N., Clark, C., Gottschang, S., and Jeffery, L. (eds) (2001) *China Urban: Ethnographies of Contemporary Culture*, Durham, NC: Duke University Press.
Cheng, T. and Selden, M. (1994) "The origins and social consequences of China's *hukou* system," *The China Quarterly* 139: 644–668.
Clifford, J. (1997) *Routes: Travel and Translation in the Late Twentieth Century*, Cambridge, MA: Harvard University Press.
Cox, K. (ed.) (1997) *Spaces of Globalization: Reasserting the Power of the Local*, New York: Guilford.
Deleuze, G. (1995) *Negotiations, 1972–1990* (trans. M. Joughin), New York: Columbia University Press.
Deleuze, G. and Guattari, F. (1972) *Anti-Oedipus: Capitalism and Schizophrenia* (trans. R. Hurley, M. Seem, and H. Lane), New York: Viking Press.
—— (1987) *A Thousand Plateaus: Capitalism and Schizophrenia* (trans. B. Massumi), Minneapolis, MN: University of Minnesota Press.
Dicken, P. (1998) *Global Shift*, Third edn, London: Guilford.
Dirlik, A. (1999) "Place-based imagination: globalism and the politics of place," *Review, A Journal of the Fernand Braudel Center for the Study of Economics, Historical Systems and Civilizations* 22(2): 151–187.
Duara, P. (1993) "Provincial narratives of the nation: centralism and federalism in Republican China," in H. Befu (ed.), *Cultural Nationalism in East Asia*, Berkeley, CA: University of California Institute for East Asian Studies, 9–35.
—— (2000) "Local worlds: the poetics and politics of the native place in modern China," *South Atlantic Quarterly* 99(1): 13–45.
Dutton, M. (1998) *Streetlife China*, Cambridge: Cambridge University Press.
Eriksen, T. H. (2003) "Introduction," in T. H. Eriksen (ed.), *Globalisation: Studies in Anthropology*, London: Pluto.
Escobar, A. (2001) "Culture sits in places: reflections on globalism and subaltern strategies of localization," *Political Geography* 20: 139–174.
Feld, S. and Basso, K. (eds) (1996) *Senses of Place*, Santa Fe, MN: School of American Research Press.
Feuchtwang, S. (2001) *Popular Religion in China: The Imperial Metaphor*, Richmond, Surrey: Curzon.
Fitzgerald, J. (2002) "The province in history," in J. Fitzgerald (ed.), *Rethinking China's Provinces*, London and New York: Routledge, 11–39.
Foret, P. (2000) *Mapping Chengde*, Honolulu, HI: University of Hawaii Press.
Foucault, M. (1972/1980) *Power/Knowledge: Selected Interviews and Other Writings 1972–1977* (ed. C. Gordon), New York: Pantheon Books.

Goodman, B. (1995) *Native Place, City, and Nation*, Berkeley, CA: University of California Press.

Goodman, D. S. G. (2004) "China's campaign to 'open up the west': national, provincial-level, and local perspectives," *The China Quarterly* 178: 317–334.

Gregory, D. and Urry, J. (eds) (1985) *Social Relations and Spatial Structures*, Basingstoke: Macmillan.

Guldin, G. (1992) *Urbanizing China*, New York: Greenwood.

—— (1997) *Farewell to Peasant China: Rural Urbanization and Social Change in the Late Twentieth Century*, Armonk, NY: M.E. Sharpe.

Gupta, A. and Ferguson, J. (eds) (1997) *Culture, Power, Place: Explorations in Critical Anthropology*, Durham, NC: Duke University Press.

Guy, R. Kent (forthcoming) *Inspired Tinkering*, Seattle: University of Washington Press.

Hahn, T. (1988) "The standard Taoist mountain and related features of religious geography," *Cahiers d'Extreme-Asie* 4: 145–156.

Harvey, D. (1989) *The Condition of Postmodernity*, Oxford: Blackwell.

Heelas, P. and Morris, P. (1992) *The Values of the Enterprise Culture: The Moral Debate*, London: Routledge.

Herod, A. and Wright, M. (2002) "Placing Scale: An Introduction," in A. Herod and M. Wright (eds), *Geographies of Power: Placing Scale*, Malden, MA: Blackwell.

Ho, P.-T. (1966) "The geographical distribution of hui-kuan (landsmannschaften) in central and upper Yangtze provinces," *Tsing Hua Journal of Chinese Studies* 5(2): 120–152.

Holm, D. (1991) *Art and Ideology in Revolutionary China*, Oxford: Clarendon.

Honig, E. (1992) *Creating Chinese Ethnicity: Subei People in Shanghai, 1850–1980*, New Haven, CT: Yale University Press.

Jackson, P. (1989) *Maps of Meaning: An Introduction to Cultural Geography*, London: Unwin Hyman.

Joseph, M. (2000) "Old Routes, Mnemonic Traces," *The UTS Review* 6(2): 44–56.

Katz, C. (2001) "Vagabond capitalism and the necessity of social reproduction," *Antipode* 33(4): 709–728.

Kleeman, T. (1994) "Mountain deities in China: the domestication of the mountain god and the subjugation of the margins," *Journal of the American Oriental Society* 114(2): 226–238.

Knapp, R. G. (1999) *China's Living Houses: Folk Beliefs, Symbols, and Household Ornamentation*, Honolulu, HI: University of Hawaii Press.

—— (2000) *China's Walled Cities*, Oxford: Oxford University Press.

Lary, D. (1974) *Region and Nation: The Kwangsi Clique in Chinese Politics, 1925–1937*, Cambridge: Cambridge University Press.

Lefebvre, H. (1974) *La Production De L'espace*, Paris: Anthropos.

—— (1991) *The Production of Space* (trans. D. Nicholson-Smith), Oxford: Blackwell.

Levenson, J. (1967) "The province, the nation, and the world: the problem of Chinese identity," in A. Feuerwerker, R. Murphey and M. Wright (eds), *Approaches to Modern Chinese History*, Berkeley, CA: University of California Press, 268–288.

Malpas, J. (1999) *Place and Experience: A Philosophical Topography*, Cambridge: Cambridge University Press.

Martin, E. (1994) *Flexible Bodies: The Role of Immunity in American Culture from the Days of Polio to the Age of AIDS*, Boston, MA: Beacon Press.

Massey, D. (1992) "A place called home?" *New Formations* 17: 3–17.

—— (1994) *Space, Place, and Gender*, Minneapolis, MN: University of Minnesota Press.

—— (1999) *Power-Geometries and the Politics of Space Time*, Heidelberg: University of Heidelberg Press.

34   *Tim Oakes and Louisa Schein*

Molotch, H. (1976) "The City as a Growth Machine," *American Journal of Sociology* 82: 309–331.

Oakes, T. (1999) "Selling Guizhou: cultural development in an era of marketization," in H. Hendrischke and C. Feng (eds), *The Political Economy of China's Provinces*, London and New York: Routledge, 27–67.

——(2000) "China's provincial identities: reviving regionalism and reinventing 'Chineseness' ," *The Journal of Asian Studies* 59(3): 667–692.

Olds, K. and Yeung, H. W. (1999) "(Re)shaping 'Chinese' business networks in a globalising era," *Environment and Planning D: Society and Space* 17(5): 535–555.

Ong, A. (1999) *Flexible Citizenship: The Cultural Logics of Transnationality*, Durham, NC: Duke University Press.

Peleikis, A. (2003) *Lebanese in Motion: Gender and the Making of a Translocal Village*, Bielefeld: transcript-Verlag.

Potter, S. H. (1983) "The position of peasants in modern China's social order," *Modern China* 9(4): 465–499.

Pred, A. (1984) "Place as an historically contingent process: structuration and the time-geography of becoming places," *Annals of the Association of American Geographers* 74(2): 279–297.

Rafael, V. (ed.) (1995) *Discrepant Histories: Tanslocal Essays on Filipino Cultures*, Philadelphia, PA: Temple University Press.

Rose, N. (1999) *Powers of Freedom: Reframing Political Thought*, Cambridge: Cambridge University Press.

Rowe, W. (1984) *Hankow: Commerce and Society in a Chinese City, 1796–1889*, Stanford, CA: Stanford University Press.

Skinner, G. W. (1976), "Mobility strategies in late-imperial China: a regional systems analysis," in C. Smith (ed.), *Regional Analysis, Vol. I: Economic Systems*, New York: Academic Press, 327–364.

Smith, M. P. (2003) "Transnationalism and Citizenship," in B. S. A. Yeoh, M. W. Charney, and C. K. Tong (eds), *Approaching Transnationalisms: Studies on Transnational Societies, Multicultural Contacts, and Imaginings of Home*, Boston, MA: Kluwer Academic Publishers, 15–38.

Smith, N. (2003) "Remaking scale: competition and cooperation in pre-national and post-national Europe," in N. Brenner, B. Jessop, M. Jones, and G. Macleod (eds), *State/Space: A Reader*, Oxford: Blackwell, 227–238.

Soja, E. (1989) *Postmodern Geographies: The Reassertion of Space in Critical Social Theory*, London and New York: Verso.

Solinger, D. (1999) *Contesting Citizenship in Urban China: Peasant Migrants, The State, and the Logic of the Market*, Berkeley, CA: University of California Press.

Storper, M. (1997) *The Regional World: Territorial Development in a Global Economy*, London: Guilford.

Strassberg, R. (1994) *Inscribed Landscapes: Travel Writing from Imperial China*, Berkeley, CA: University of California Press.

Sum, N.-L. (2003) "Rethinking globalization: re-articulating the spatial scale and temporal horizons of trans-border spaces," in N. Brenner, B. Jessop, M. Jones, and G. Macleod (eds), *State/Space: A Reader*, Oxford: Blackwell, 208–224.

Sun, W. (2002) "Discourses of poverty: weakness, potential and provincial identity in Anhui," in J. Fitzgerald (ed.), *Rethinking China's Provinces*, London and New York: Routledge, 153–177.

Swyngedouw, E. (1992) "Territorial organization and the space/technology nexus," *Transactions of the Institute of British Geographers* NS 17: 417–433.

—— (1997) "Excluding the other: the production of scale and scaled politics," in R. Lee and J. Wills (eds), *Geographies of Economies*, London: Arnold, 167–176.

Tang, X. (2000) *Chinese Modern: The Heroic and the Quotidian*, Durham, NC: Duke University Press.

Thrift, N. (1994) "Taking aim at the heart of the region," in D. Gregory, R. Martin, and G. Smith (eds), *Human Geography: Society, Space, and Social Science*, Minneapolis, MN: University of Minnesota Press, 200–231.

Wang, J. (2001) "Culture as leisure and culture as capital," *Positions* 9(1): 69–104.

—— (2005) "Introduction: the politics and production of scales in China: how does geography matter to studies of local popular culture?," in J. Wang (ed.), *Locating China: Space, Place and Popular Culture*, London and New York: Routledge, 1–30.

Wang, M. (1995) "Place, administration, and territorial cults in late imperial China: a case study from south Fujian," *Late Imperial China* 16(1): 33–78.

Wang, Y. (2004) "Literary nativism, the native place and modern Chinese fiction," Paper delivered at the workshop "Place Imaginaries, Mobilities, and the Limits of Representation," June 7–9, New South Wales, Australia.

Watts, M. (1991) "Mapping meaning, denoting difference, imagining identity," *Geografiska Annaler* 73B(1): 7–16.

Wigen, K. (1999) "Culture, power, and place: the new landscapes of East Asian regionalism," *The American Historical Review* 104(4): 1183–1201.

Yan, H. (2003) "Neoliberal governmentality and neohumanism: organizing suzhi/value flow through labor recruitment networks," *Cultural Anthropology* 18(4): 493–523.

Yeoh, B. S. A., Lai, K. P. Y., Charney, M. W., and C. K. Tong (2003) "Approaching transnationalisms," in B. S. A. Yeoh, K. P. Y. Lai, M. W. Charney, and C. K. Tong (eds), *Approaching Transnationalisms: Studies on Transnational Societies, Multicultural Contacts, and Imaginings of Home*, Boston, MA: Kluwer Academic Publishers, 1–12.

Zhang, L. (2002) "Spatiality and urban citizenship in late socialist China," *Public Culture* 14(2): 311–334.

—— (2004) *Strangers in the City: Reconfigurations of Space, Power and Social Networks within China's Floating Population*, Stanford, CA: Stanford University Press.

Zhou, K. (1996) *How the Farmers Changed China*, Boulder, CO: Westview.

Zukin, S. (1995) *The Cultures of Cities*, Cambridge, MA: Blackwell.

2   The original translocal society and its modern fate

Historical and post-reform south China

David Faure and Helen F. Siu

Fei Xiaotong, the doyen of Chinese anthropologists, summarizing Chinese society in the 1930s, described it as essentially "earth-bound". In rendering his Chinese term *xiangtu* as earth-bound, rather than rural or rustic, he emphasized land and its essential part in Chinese society. He said so without ambiguity: rural people carry the smell of the earth; they do because they depend on it for their livelihood. His whole book of essays builds upon this concept. The land-based community rests upon interpersonal relationships, governed by custom rather than law, dependent upon an oral rather than a written tradition. It consists of clusters of families, may best be described as a mini-clan, and is essentially closed to outsiders (Fei 1948: 1–7). This cellular society, to borrow from a term created in the 1970s, was crisscrossed by the common culture of the scholarly class, often denoted as the gentry, and, foreshadowing G. William Skinner (1971), who argued that rural markets in China opened and closed to the outside world as their relationship to the city changed over time. For Skinner, opening and closing had to do with political stability; for Fei, they stemmed from the exploitation of the countryside by the city (Fei 1949: 16–23).

Rural China, as Fei Xiaotong described it, was an ideal. It filled the social science literature of the Republican period, and it continued from there, through the work of Hsiao Kung-chuan (1960), Chang Chung-li (1955) and others, mostly at the University of Washington in Seattle, into the North American sinology of the 1950s and 60s. It had continued, as Fei himself acknowledges profusely, from the Confucian tradition. Of course, the word is a misnomer, for it was less the teaching of Confucius than the borrowing of the classics as a source of legitimacy for imperial rule. We know of it now as more of a cycle of events dating from no earlier than the early Ming (*c*.1364) when with the revival of the examination, the imperial government began a continuous process in the manufacturing of elites. So successful was it that titles which granted the right to government jobs were, by the end of the Qing, purchased for no other purpose than social status, the employment of degree holders in official capacities notwithstanding. The examinations, therefore, created a national elite living at home, or an amalgam of local leadership aspiring to or putting on the pretense of a national elite, but either way, men who had roots at home but who thought of themselves as acting within the state (Dardess 1983; Elman 2000).

As Fei Xiaotong himself makes clear, the view of earth-bound China linked by an elite produced by examination was at odds with the expansion of population, the splintering of communities and migration beyond home. He sees the process of scattering as being akin to seeds falling from a tree. Where they become bound to the earth, they grow into new communities, maintaining a connection—often nominal—with the parent from which it was issued. He cites his own example of the "native place of origin" familiar now not only to scholars of Chinese society but to anyone having had any experience in China, of his family being described as having come from Wujiang and the Wujiang Fei surname as claiming that they have come from Jiangxia. The translocal element, according to this view, is secondary to the local. Earth-bound China is, according to Fei, fundamental, and translocal community arises out of it (Fei 1948: 76–83). Nevertheless, it does not always follow that migrants succeed to set up their own communities: many hang on as "outsiders" in some village, sometimes for generations, or, failing even that, disappear from view.

Translocal communities in late imperial Chinese history

In this chapter, we argue that the three elements of Chinese society as summed up in Fei Xiaotong's essays, that is to say, the view that Chinese society was earth-bound, the unity given this society by the gentry class, and migration, gave rise to ideas of translocalism. But we want to add that most of that is imagined. People who see themselves as translocal are not necessarily tied to more than one place, and those who do not are not necessarily tied to the earth. The truly earth-bound community does not see itself as being isolated from the rest of the world: there simply is no rest of the world to be separated from and so it must itself be the be all and end all of the universe. Translocalism, we shall argue, is an element of the earth-bound ideology, conveniently appealed to in the incidence of early migration where home and work are separately located, and made to look real by the despatch of information and resources (money, women, and recognition). In this, Chinese society was not different from any other society, the overseas Chinese notwithstanding.

Massive migrations taken place in historic times are well documented in the historical records. They took place at the end of war to reclaim devastated cultivated land and during famine because, until the railway and the steamer changed the economics of transport, it was more cost-efficient to move people to food than food to people.[1] More to the point, migration follows economic development: on each occasion the Chinese economy expanded, people moved. Dwight Perkins's calculations of how China had succeeded in feeding its rising millions in the five centuries from the sixteenth century to the twentieth century show that increase in yield accounted for perhaps half of the grain needed by population increase, and the other half had had to come from the reclamation of land which had previously not been put under cultivation (Perkins 1969). In effect, that meant doubling the Chinese cultivated acreage between the fifteenth century and the nineteenth century, a feat brought about only by migration into previously unpopulated areas: the hills of Hunan and Hubei, the swamps at the mouth of the Yangzi and the Pearl, more hills on the uplands of Jiangxi, pushing into the edges of Lake Tai, and by the Qing, the expanses of the Northeastern provinces. None of this was new to Chinese history by the sixteenth century. The centre of population itself, no less, shifted from the Yellow River to the Yangzi between the Tang and the Song (Chi 1936: 96–112; Elvin 1973: 204–215).

Migrations and land reclamation brought about the splintering communities which Fei Xiaotong had in mind, but as he knew well, movement came about also from trade. In fact, the land reclamation would not have come about but for the fact that food grain was among the most important items of trade since 1500. Trade opens an entire vista for the construction of translocal communities: the boatmen's chapels on the Grand Canal coming under the cult of Luozu, the Heaven and Earth Society and its various affiliated brotherhoods, ranging from the Triad groups in the tin mines of the Straits Settlement to the pseudo-surname brotherhoods documented on Taiwan, and from there to the pseudo-networks along the salt-and-opium smugglers' trails across Fujian, Guangdong and Jiangxi; the trade guilds, including common-origin associations as busy setting standards for settlement of accounts as shipping home the corpses of sojourning merchants, to the owners of the markets and the temple alliances which ensured continuation of control and which were the sources of many inter-village feuds (Skinner 1964; Weng 1975; Kelley 1982; Zhuo 1990; Owmby 1996; Wang 1996). Communities founded on trade might be imbued with the earth-bound ideology no less than the farming community, but they would have included people, temporarily or permanently, making a living away from "home."

It is evident that movements of people transporting goods around China seeking a market constitute "trade," but in what sense is land reclamation on the hills or the swamps not equally a "trading" activity? Fei Xiaotong was not naive to the situation: population expanded and so the excess was driven out of the village to become laborers somewhere else, hence the need to seek settlement rights from incumbents. He does not, however, consider where the incumbents might have come from, and the answer does not have to be, as assumed by the image of earth-bound China, that forced out of their own villages, they begged entry from incumbents. In the Pearl River Delta, laborers on reclaimed land were known as the *dan*, just as elsewhere, notably in Jiangxi and Hunan, they were known as the *pengmin*, or shed people, terms indicating the lack of settlement status where they lived (Siu 1995b; Zheng 1997). This view neglects the heavy investments required for land reclamation. In the Pearl River Delta, where we know about the process in greater—although never enough—detail, investment groups come together through share partnerships to provide the funds and the political clout, and cultivators were kept as outsiders for as long as possible. Historians who write about the uprooting of the poor without pointing out the need for an infrastructure that allowed them to be uprooted are as guilty of the simple-minded view of migration subscribed to by physiocratic Ming and Qing officials. Trade, as Fei Xiaotong knew well, was part of earth-bound China, and if trade creates translocal communities, it must do so not in its periphery, but right in its heart.

Yet, even at the periphery, the establishment of land rights came together with the growth of business. On top of a hill above the Qingshui river in remote Jinping county in Guizhou province, is situated the village of Wendou.[2] This village inhabited by the Miao people has in recent years yielded land deeds in the thousands, dating from the eighteenth century when the timber trade opened up the region (Guizhou sheng bianzhi ju 1988; Daniels *et al.* 2001; Zhang 2003). The land deeds tell of outsiders coming in from Hunan to rent Wendou's land and to purchase its trees. They came because the timber trade turned the trees into a commodity. Centuries of deforestation had cleared the forests of the middle Yangzi, and by the eighteenth century, timber merchants from Huizhou and Jiangxi were advancing into relatively unopened Guizhou. The villages on the river became centres of the timber trade, and the villages on the hillside lorded over the hill land on which trees were planted. Land rights were created as trade boomed, and, as in any situation of economic development, the market created for labor drew in the outsiders. Once again, Karl Polanyi (1957) is vindicated, for it was long-distance trade that led to the population expansion, not the other way round. The extension of trade turned the resources of the periphery into a commodity, and in response, incumbents established their rights, hence the proliferation of land deeds and the exclusion of newcomers from incumbent status.

The establishment of land rights and the growth of business called for different communal ideologies. To assert land rights in the situation where common resources were intensely competed for, dominant groups sought to exclude outsiders. To attract business, nevertheless, outsiders not only had to be tolerated, they must also be made welcome. This is the difference between the village and the town in late-imperial China, and if historians have not made this vital element of Chinese social history more explicit, it is because they have been asking the wrong question about land. The rights of settlement are asserted not by restrictions over the ownership of farmland, but by restrictions imposed on building houses, and with those, the right to claim hitherto unallocated resources, such as, grass cutting on the hillsides, access to burial sites, foraging in the rivers, and, most importantly, the reclamation of "wasteland." Villages assert settlement rights, while towns, such as Foshan, are lax in their enforcement. Settlement rights, where obtained, are not abandoned lightly. For many, the ability to build a house represented the ability to found a family. Given the male dominance among migrants in towns and cities, houses in the home village meant the settlement of the family in the home village even as the man worked away from home (Faure 1986, 1990).

The late imperial Chinese state was cautious about men who gathered outside their village environments. It was also concerned with raising tax and recruiting for its bureaucracy, for which the tax measures and official examinations were implemented. In the early Ming dynasty, that is, in the second half of the fourteenth century, these various strands came together in the form of *lijia* household registration. This very important institution has often been misunderstood. It was not, as China historians have always argued, imposed from above. It was not even implemented over very much of China in the fourteenth century. Moreover, it did not go into decline in the fifteenth century, a time, in fact, when it was popularised over much of Ming China. Instead, by *lijia* registration, the Ming government recognized the power structures inherent in the village and expressed through rotas that had been established for sacrifice at local earth god shrines. While in the early Ming, *lijia* registration was implemented only in those areas in which the Ming government established its rule and demanded corvee service, from the second half of the fifteenth century and into the sixteenth century, increasing efforts at land registration and the payment of tax in silver transformed the registered household into a tax account under which property rights to land were maintained. Finally, when successive examinations added accumulatively to the reservoir of degree holders, degree holding families, invariably making some claim that they had settled down in some part of the realm—for the simple reason that the examination quotas were tied to administrative units such as the county—built their family history upon *lijia* records. As *lijia* was superceded by collection of tax through land-holding, a process which was not completed until the early eighteenth century, the *lijia* registration record itself gave way to the concept of collective responsibility in the *baojia* registration, designed for the maintenance of law and order rather than tax collection. By then, the idea had been accepted that the household (*hu*), was rooted not where it resided, but where it registered (Liu 1997).

To this very brief description of early Ming registration must be added the ritual transformation of the Chinese state, and for that it is necessary to begin with the southern Song. The Song government extended its rule over south China not only by implementing an administrative structure, but also by recognizing local deities. Deities made famous in the process, such as the Tianhou, were then installed in local communities far away from their origin, for example in Putian in Fujian province, and it might be argued that a translocal element was built into the communal ideology even in the spread of the religious cult (Hansen 1990; Dean 1993). Had we known more about pilgrimages at major temples in late imperial times, we might even be in some position to describe the extent of the translocal communities formed in those places (Schipper 1977; Naquin 1992). The sixteenth-century transformation in rituals, however, gives this development a complicated twist. Unlike the Song, the Ming state did not depend on the recognition of deities for the absorption of local society into itself. Instead, following the Great Rituals controversy (Fisher 1990), it advocated filial piety, in the interest of which territorial groups were encouraged to build ancestral halls for the repose of their ancestors, and the practice of sacrificing at ancestral halls came to be universally adopted as a mark of the scholarly gentry household. The same practice went hand in hand with the compilation of written genealogies, which carefully record not only the first ancestor to settle in the village (known as the "founding ancestor" *shizu*), but which also made every effort to relate him to an origin outside the village. The belief in ancestry, coupled with the recording of it in writing, and its celebration in rituals, together made up a powerful tool for the construction of an imagined community known as the lineage. One need not have seen a written genealogy or sacrificed in an ancestral hall to believe that some such must exist in the home village, wherever that might be (Faure 1999).

Without minimizing the importance of translocal contact, we think, therefore, that much of translocalism existed only in the imagination. This is not to say that the imagined community was unimportant, because it was precisely because community might be imagined that the institutions for business were created whereby land might be reclaimed and guilds might be established. On this point, Maurice Freedman's contribution to studies of the lineage must come to the fore, for Freedman argued that we must not be taken in by the genealogy-keeping of territorial groups to forget that in this process incorporation was built into social structure (Freedman 1958, 1966). The groups that claimed common descent were not strictly brought about by descent (thus going against the oft-held view among Chinese scholars that the blood-connection *xueyuan* might be equated with the territorial connection *diyuan*). Instead, these were territorial groups that were built upon an understanding of common descent, real or imagined. Property was held in the names of ancestors, and by extension, in the names of voluntary associations formed to celebrate the birthdays of deities and to take charge of affairs at their temples, and it was precisely in this manner that Ming law provided the loophole whereby property might be held in trust beyond the lifetime of any single individual party to the contract. Where the law had not provided explicit recognition for incorporation, therefore, ritual took over, the rules of inheritance standing in for the rules of equity. The partnership structures on remote Wendou village, like the ones observed in the Pearl River Delta, therefore, were brought about by the same application of written deeds, the same backing in the law of the Ming and the Qing and the same assumptions on inheritance and share-holding as in the heartland of China. The building blocks of the translocal community were much more varied than the sacrifice at common deities, and shared meals at common-origin associations. They were none other than the tools by which investment and banking were facilitated. To call all this networking borders on insulting these long-established and well-tried institutions. They were the cogs that made the China machine work.

The sixteenth century, it must be remembered, saw no less than a commercial revolution that extended through much of Ming China. The ritual reforms that arose in the process were as much its results as the tools of business which went into its land reclamation and banking ventures. The merchants' guild (*huiguan*) was as much a variation of the same theme as the Heaven and Earth Society, but it is useful now to see how the two differ in order to provide a perspective, if not between fiction and reality, at least between different sorts of realities. Trade, by its very nature, required merchants to live within multiple local communities. Merchants residing as outsiders, establishing themselves in a guild hall built in the style of an official residence, propagating the view that the building served not only trade but also candidates on their way to the examination, appealed to their translocal roots as well as to the literati's status connections. Just as the Southeast Asian Chinese common-origin association is formed not to carry its weight in China but in the country in which it is formed, the appeal to an official connection suggests a quest for status not at home but in the city in which the association is located (Wang 2000). Behind the translocal skin, therefore, the merchants' guild is an instrument for indigenization. However, if even the merchant guild's translocal character is open to doubt, the Heaven and Earth Society's translocal connections are a matter of myth. Where Chinese males had settled overseas they had adopted rituals that placed them within pseudo-families. There is nothing in that which has to be translocal: these pseudo-families might claim to be part of a greater whole but for the most part, the claims were no more than that. It was widely believed by the early years of the nineteenth century that pockets of the Heaven and Earth Society worked like branches within a wide network extending through the whole of south China. Not a shred of evidence supports that view. Quite to the contrary, ample reasons may be cited to demonstrate that despite the belief in the greater whole, individual cells of the Heaven and Earth Society had no dealings whatsoever with one another.

The belief that the local community was part of a wider whole, taken to the extreme by the Heaven and Earth Society, was present in all of China's earthbound villages. It was part of Ming and Qing state ideology, expressed as much through the learned works of the literati as in village religion. The toiler at his or her soil, living in imagined communities of lineages and village alliances, centered on temples, governed by degree holders or pretenders to be the same, many holding properties in the village but the more senior being quite closely attached to city, made up part of a long continuum which saw the emperor at the apex of society and the lowly village at its bottom. The Chinese state, one might say, encouraged the translocal imagination; the ideology which drew the local community into the state assumed, not that state power could be extended into the village from the outside, but that state rituals would be drawn into the village from the inside. The ambiguity of state influence, expressed through administration and ritual, placed the village, that is, the territorial community, as much at the center of the state as it did imperial power. State ideology, ritual and the place of the individual within society produced three sorts of maps: administrative, ritual and mental. The administrative map divides the realm into counties, prefectures and provinces; the ritual map ties the territorial community to the greater whole by tracing the movements of gods and ancestors, but it was the mental map, taking in the locations of buildings, temples, markets, relatives and friends which wove together the administrative and ritual maps in daily life.

A very curious result of this state ideology was the peripheralization, not of the translocal, but of towns and cities. It was only natural that the majority of the urban population was rooted in the villages from which they had come. Political ideology did not recognize that towns or cities had any place within the individual or the household identity, for it was the household that was absorbed into the Ming and Qing state. The corollary of that, however, must be that the household had to be part of a wider whole. The household was only a household if it could be recognized as such within the state, and that was why, by extension, membership to a lineage was an essential mark of status.

There were translocal communities in the Ming and the Qing, to be sure. There must be as long as people and capital moved around. But the translocal communities founded on movement were supplemented by imagined translocalism. The two could appear so similar that it is not always easy to tell them apart.

The twentieth century and the Maoist imprint

The ideology enforced between *lijia* and the official examination came to its demise when by 1905, the imperial examination was abolished, and by 1911, the monarchy itself gave way to a republic. Instead of an ideology which said that household and emperor were one and recognition was to be had by members of the household for achievement of success in the examination, the new ideology, enforced through a constitution, required elections to be held by towns, counties and provinces, and gentry status, divorced now from degree holding, to be acquired through service in voluntary associations. The brave new world of the 1900s saw the centre of the Chinese state shift from the village to the cities.[3] Where the lineage with its roots in the village had been central, the rural population of the Republican state was viewed as the backward portion of Chinese society that held back economic progress. All this went on as means of movement and communication were advanced by technology: the railway, the steamship, the printing press, the newspaper, the post office and Western banks made it possible for people, news and capital to move about with hitherto unknown ease, while industry and the possibility for moving food into the cities added to the urban populations.

For emerging regional cities in the Pearl River Delta (such as Foshan and Guangzhou) in the Ming and Qing period, "outside elements" were economic and human assets and eventually absorbed. The urban populations remained differentiated. This was largely due to the highlighting of cultural, ethnic and differences in geographic origin for the organization of business, livelihood, and social order.[4] In areas of population fluidity, it was precisely when physical differences were blurred and economic stakes highly competitive that culturally constructed boundaries were imposed by the powerful. The lines between "us" and "other" were drawn with the intention to distinguish, at times to marginalize, but not necessarily to exclude. The work of Siu and Liu (2006) on the relationship of established lineages and the dan fishermen in the Pearl River Delta, and that of Emily Honig on the Subei in Republican Shanghai (1992), are historical examples.

When Siu started fieldwork in the Pearl River Delta in the late 1970s, the villages appeared curiously "cellular" (Donnithorne 1972; Shue 1984; Siu 1989a). Compared to the prosperous, vibrant, and pluralistic images she was able to glean from historical sources, life in the Maoist era seemed bare, one-dimensional, colorless, and earth-bound. Town or village made little difference. The locals would have said to the anthropologist, "We are but peasants, what is it that interests you?" Their self-perception—poor, immobile, weighed down by an overpowering bureaucracy determined to include them in a revolutionary language—came to be the starting point of her exploration in rural Guangdong. By the 1990s, a few hours into the ten-hour drive from Xiamen (Fujian) to Chaozhou (Guangdong), town after town, village after village, the material environment looked almost identical—the physical layout of the shops and houses, the architecture, the size and color of the bricks, the activities and the look of the inhabitants. No doubt there were more commodities to be consumed (Beck's beer produced in Fujian was abundant), and one found an occasional hair saloon or karaoke bar, all with the name "Hong Kong." Local details might have escaped us. Historians and economists might argue that we were observing the homogenizing march to modernity and development. But it was ironic that nearly fifteen years after turning their backs on Mao, and after the state machinery appeared willing to give its subjects some space, the local inhabitants seemed to have little imagination left. Communities continued to appear earth-bound, and everyday life lacked diverse details. What had happened to the historically rich, multi-tiered translocality and its imageries?

During the Qing period, in Xinhui county on the Pearl River Delta, a highly capitalized land reclamation and extensive grain production in the sands were interwoven with the mature, cash-crop growing core of the delta through a complex system of collective and private land ownership, multi-layered tenancy and finance, and cultural politics (Siu 1989a). Higher-level lineage halls, regional temple and charity associations, county academies, and merchant guilds were public arenas where local leaders and officials negotiated, colluded and contested to create fluid cleavages and alliances among their kinsmen, tenants and clients. By the Republican period, overseas Chinese merchants and military bosses, with varied resource bases and new claims to legitimacy, added to the plurality and contingency. There might not have been modern motor road, but the dense network of rivers linking villages to towns, county capitals and regional cities bustled with traffic, goods and people. Eighty-year-old farmers in the 1970s identified the 1930s under the Guangdong warlord Chen Jitang as the "golden age." "From then on," they said, "it was downhill all the way." Their mental horizons seemed broad and they were able to recall detailed price fluctuations of the cocoons their families sold in the specialized markets in the neighboring county of Shunde when a big fire in Japan diminished the supply.[5] Women were also visible contributors to the regional culture and economy. Historical studies on the various phases of the silk industry in Shunde and Zhongshan counties of the delta provide ample evidence that women were not confined to home or village (Topley 1975; So 1986; Stockard 1988; Siu 1990a).

After 1949, the layers of vertical and horizontal social institutions (and their leaders) were destroyed, along with the operations and associated cultural meanings of which were integral to village life in pre-revolution Guangdong. The land reform in 1950 physically and symbolically removed the cultural nexus of power shared by former land-owning merchants, ancestral estate managers, and militaristic local bosses. Collectivization and the corresponding replacement of rural marketing by state channels of distribution grounded the farmers and reduced alternative sources of livelihood and information. When periodic markets were abolished in 1957, the policy shrank the farmer's social world by at least two thirds.[6] The imposition of the household registration system soon afterwards further barred the farmers from movement to towns and cities. The anti-commercial policies of the Party reduced thriving market towns to petty administrative sites dependent on crumbs from state factories. The once elegant ancestral halls in the township centers were torn down to provide for much needed building materials.

The ones that remained were put to use as village schools, nurseries, storage houses, and occasionally as tractor stations and primitive factories. The Great Leap Forward and subsequent political campaigns highlighted the mobilization power of the party, with its language of class and revolution, and with increasing quiescence and complicity from local cadres and commune members. There were ebbs and flows in ideological and organizational intensity. At the local community levels, there were foot dragging and resistance. But informants said with resignation, "We dug the canals, demolished the temples and ancestral halls, and cut down the fruit trees, did we not?"

By the 1970s, the once mobile *dan* fishermen in the delta were mostly moved onto land, their boats collectivized. They functioned as fishing brigades. For centuries, the floating populations, their identities ambiguous in historical records, had eluded the reach of the state and the town-based landlords. They were finally grounded under the Maoist state. The shrinking of cultural imaginings was most evident among a younger generation of villages. In Chaolian xiang during the 1980s, an ancestral hall still stood tall in the physical center of the community, adjacent to the focal ancestral hall of the major Lu lineage. What remained of the grand stone pillars and elaborated carved hard wood beams that had withstood the red guards' attempts to destroy it suggested that the hall had been a rather significant ritual site for the lineage. When asked about that building, after much prodding, the villager could only answer by asking the curious question, "Do you mean the shoe factory?"

The general transformation of village life in the delta during the decades following 1949 has been described as "cellularization," in physical and cultural terms. The traditional channels for social mobility, and the once open arenas for circulation of cultural meanings, became fragmented and truncated if not outright destroyed. The stripped-down "villages" in the 1970s were products of a Maoist era. Without appreciating the historical cultural nexus of power that bonded villages and their inhabitants to layers of non-local influences and imaginings, it is easy to regard these cellularized units as the original "village China" and to analytically diminish the impact of the Maoist state (Siu 1989a).

By 1986, market towns in the delta were being revived on the development of small-scale enterprises, private or collective (*xiangzhen qiye*). Xiaolan *zhen* of Zhongshan county was one of them. Perched on the edge of one of the delta's most extensive sands, the town was known historically for its thriving grain trade, its rich and varied ancestral estates, temples, neighborhood shrines, and most important of all, its Chrysanthemum Festivals.[7] Like many commercial centers that were home to traditional cultural elites, the Maoist revolution reduced it to a petty administrative site, with the local government (then an urban commune) managing small-scale collectives for producing farm tools, handicrafts, and processed agricultural goods.

The rural economy was liberalizing in 1986, triggered by the dismantling of the communes and the reintroduction of the household responsibility system. However, contrary to expectation, amidst desperate maneuvers to put the Maoist politics behind them and to get ahead, town residents consciously avoided what they believed to be official power and interests, and channeled their entrepreneurial energies into less competitive or profitable businesses. The options they pursued were few—hair saloons, small food and clothing stalls. In "Socialist peddlers and princes in a Chinese market town," Siu cautions against the analytical idea that the retreat of the state leads to market advances or societal gain. Local cadres, with lingering monopoly power over supply channels and distribution information, were able to capture the market initiatives. Between the town government and private residents, there was no level playing field for creating new opportunities in economic or social mobility. More importantly, it seemed that even if the town cadres had intended to liberalize in earnest, individual entrepreneurs, having internalized the institutional power of the party-state in the Maoist era, were reproducing that power in their everyday choices and practices. Siu terms the process "state involution" (Siu 1989b: 195–212).

Likewise, "state involution" might characterize the cultural politics of the post-Mao decades. Funeral and wedding rituals, dowry and brideprice, and community festivals were not "rural traditions," repressed and frozen for decades under Mao, now being revived with a vengeance. Instead, they were fragments of local practices that were decimated, partially destroyed and removed from everyday consciousness for decades, being reconstituted by a new generation of practitioners. The new ritual energies target the uncertainties of livelihoods, social networks, and statuses at a time of profound ideological redefinition.[8] The lack of resourcefulness and diversity of imagination contrasts sharply with the energies exhibited in entrepreneurial pursuits. The feverish energies (*re*) are localized and one-dimensional. Cultural "paralysis" was being institutionalized. If there were translocal elements left in local imaginations and everyday practices, the language of the state continues to provide an ordering framework.

Moreover the late 1980s, saw the newly converted municipality government of Zhongshan pushing for the merging of Xiaolan *zhen* (an urban commune) with the rural communes surrounding it.[9] The power play between the two sets of local officials aside, the town leadership was most reluctant to merge with their rural counterparts. The town's expanding industrial enterprises were already hiring tens of thousands of migrant workers from the surrounding countryside and from provinces such as Guangxi, Hunan, and Jiangxi, the number reaching that of its original "town registered" residents. The town's regional rural markets had been growing with a larger variety of goods and traders coming from neighboring counties (e.g. Jiangmen, Panyu, Shunde) linked by waterways. Building sites for factories, offices, and new residences were scarce. The town's roads were clogged with noisy and polluting tractors. The town offices were inundated with demands for registering, rationing, and controlling the complicated categories of residents, temporary residents, and non-residents. Violent crimes became an issue, and in most cases, the migrant laborers were blamed.

Merging the two communes would allow for tighter management of resources and more long-term, infrastructural planning, but the town cadres dragged their feet. They were worried that the merge politically justified once more, a relocation of urban resources to the poorer parts of the rural hinterland. Their predecessors had seen it before, when ancestral halls and other public buildings were torn down, ancestral graves dug up, and the previous materials transported to the surrounding villages for dikes and bridges. They also remembered the "Four Cleanup Campaigns" just before the Cultural Revolution, when work teams consisting mostly of "peasant activists" humbled the town cadres. Their adversaries were from the sands, traditionally discriminated as *dan* fishermen, and quite eager to settle accounts. Political strategy aside, "rurality" is a stigma highlighting poverty, immobility, isolation and backwardness, and to be avoided at all costs.

Town residents shared such feelings with their leaders. However meager their "town" resources were, they continued to believe that they were far better off than the peasants "out there." Most held onto their poorly paid jobs in the town factories, unwilling to move to the surrounding rural brigades where manufacturing enterprises were beginning to mushroom and where industrial skills were highly valued. They dug their heels anxiously, unwilling to make a drastic move. The only time town families wished that they had lived across the narrow waterways separating the town from the rural brigades was in the wake of the Cultural Revolution. Their children, who had "*zhen*" household registrations and thus considered "urban," were sent off to Hainan Island as educated youths, while their rural neighbors escaped such a fate because they were already "in the countryside." The line drawn on the ground was tenuous, but it had meant a world of difference for many families in the area (Siu 1991: 61–82). Like their rural neighbors, the town residents found themselves locked into caste-like statuses defined by the language of an organized state machinery (Cohen 1994: 151–170). The entrenched divide, material and mental, was shaping their mobility strategies in the post-Mao liberalizations.

The initial policies to introduce the market in the region produced visible results by the mid 1990s. The Pearl River Delta is connected by Hong Kong financed super highways serving indigenous and foreign operated high-tech industrial parks, shopping malls, and private housing estates. The roads are filled with foreign luxury sedans, many driven by young professionals commuting between the regional cities on business and for leisure. The long lines of trucks waiting at crude river crossings were things of the past. Shabby long-distance public buses continue to shuttle migrant laborers, but locals travel in air-conditioned mini buses and taxis. A trip from Shenzhen to Guangzhou takes less than two hours. From Guangzhou to Jiangmen at the western edge of the delta (a distance of about 110 kilometers), the drive has been reduced from four hours to just over an hour. On the ring roads, one speeds past major municipalities like Dongguan, Foshan, and Shunde without even realizing it. The movement of goods, people, capital, and information between the delta and Hong Kong has long blurred the political border.[10] Among coastal China where similar market-driven developments and the consumer revolution have taken shape, the Pearl River Delta is probably one of the most thoroughly transformed, the speed and fluidity of the changes most dramatic.[11]

Since Xiaolan *zhen* and the neighboring rural commune merged, infrastructural changes have been remarkable. An entire new town area is created from farmland on the outskirts of the old town. One finds grand government and public security buildings with Hong Kong style office towers clustering around. Its industrial park proudly displays numerous town enterprises whose individual annual production value has long exceeded 100 million yuan.[12] The southern super-highway between Guangzhou, Zhuhai and Jiangmen cuts through the district. By the mid 1990s, Xiaolan had more than 70,000 migrant workers in its factories, adding another 50 percent to its original 130,000 population. A dozen or so luxury guest houses/hotels have been in operation, the most exclusive in partnership with a Hong Kong business. Nearly every household has private telephone connections. The enlarged town, having claimed the most prosperous northern part of the former Zhongshan county, maintains a competitive relationship with the municipal government in Zhongshan *shi* 27 kilometers south, on the way to the Special Economic Zone of Zhuhai, and Macau.[13] In this era of high growth, market changes and mobility, what is Xiaolan's self perception as a locality? In a recent article, Siu uses the once-in-sixty-year Chrysanthemum Festival celebrated by the town in 1994 to explore the issues (Siu 2002: 233–249).

In the past, the festivals were part of the town elites' self-fashioning. Since early nineteenth century, an alliance of emerging lineages and merchants with vast estates in the sands, flaunting their self-claimed literati statuses, staged the festivals for two purposes. The occasion drew local and regional boundaries by showing off their wealth and resources at the *dan* tenants in the sands who were excluded, and maintaining alliance networks with competitors in neighboring rural counties. Their literati imaginings were pursued to claim respective places in the imperial order. Every sixty years, a new elite with different power bases staged the festivals, improvising on the themes and symbolisms, and negotiating with officials at the county and provincial capitals. In 1934, when the town's traditional lineages were in disarray, militaristic bosses with new merchant allies took over the festivities. They too were improvising on the emerging translocal languages of power to carve territorial spheres of influence in the local political economy (Siu 1997: 139–185).

The town government in the post-1949 decades continued to use the chrysanthemum as a symbol of the town's identity. The flower had been associated with the settlement history of the town's earliest inhabitants, although the ownership claims of town based lineages to the valuable farmland in the region were long replaced by the revolutionary agenda. Some festivities associated with chrysanthemum continued, although they were used to highlight particular political landmarks—the tenth anniversary of the People's Republic, for example. During the radical days of the Cultural Revolution, particular floral displays were debated. "Feudal designs" such as "fairy maidens in a shower of flowers" were balanced by a figure of the revolutionary soldier "Lei Feng." The activities involved local identities, but the underlying themes were intimately engaged with national campaigns and ideological debates.

The town cadres turned entrepreneurial when signals from Guangzhou and Beijing indicated that political winds had changed. In the early 1980s, the town commissioned a team of local historians to reconstruct the identity Xiaolan as "the chrysanthemum town." The Overseas Native Place Associations of Xiaolan and Dalan (a rural brigade adjacent to the town, known also as a site of the original settlement) organized small-scale festivities with the theme of the flower. Natives who had been successful merchants in Hong Kong and Macau were invited to the town as potential investors. Cadres believed that if the town government embarked on activities formerly denounced as "feudal," it would at least show that it was liberalizing in earnest. Investments did follow. To an extent, the politics of native roots worked.

In 1994, the town government staged the once-in-sixty-year festival, with the grandest of schemes and visions. It was to show off the new town with over a 100 major items of infrastructural development. With highways, a brand new stadium, modern school buildings, hospitals, and factories boasting hundreds of millions of production value, and clusters of Hong Kong style luxury villas for sale, the town promoted its aspirations to be part of China's march toward market modernity. But the language of the market and liberalization is intertwined with initiatives coming directly from the government bureaucracies. The town invited several thousand guests from overseas, and including high-ranking retired officials from Beijing and Guangdong. Both Hong Kong and Guangdong media gave the festivities wide coverage. Every work unit, rural or town, were to mobilize natives and friends to visit. The organizers expected at least half a million spectators. At the center of the floral displays, art shows, operas and song, parades and banqueting, stood the grand industrial exhibition hall. Potential investors were eagerly invited to initiate businesses on the spot.

The 1994 Chrysanthemum Festival of Xiaolan *zhen* was undoubtedly a government staged, top-down event. Work units and residential neighborhood were mobilized to contribute funds, labor and content. Despite the hype to forge a modern Xiaolan identity, a majority of local residents seemed to be involved only as spectators. Older residents complained that there was no tradition left. The skilled cultivators and connoisseur of the art had long disappeared due to previous political persecutions. So were temple operas. They could not understand the Canto Pop that replaced the opera singers. They stuck to the floral displays in the park at the center of the old town, and watched the parades via television at home. Few were invited to the town's banquets. Except for Dalan, a rural district with its own economic resourcefulness and historical claims to the area, few rural residents from the outlying districts were visible in the crowd. Still, hundreds of thousands of visitors from Hong Kong, Guangzhou, Macau, and other municipalities jammed the streets in the new part of town. The migrant laborers put on their holiday clothes and enjoyed their days off from miserable factory work. Even after the stage on the parade ground collapsed in the middle of the ceremonies, local residents acted distant and cynical. It was the message from the gods, some said, because the town cadres, mostly recruited to the Party with poor peasant backgrounds over the decades, had no knowledge of history or local tradition. They chose an inauspicious site (on the outskirt of town where the dead and the sick were abandoned during famine and war), did not perform the necessary religious rituals, and were too arrogant to consider local sentiments.

The 1994 Chrysanthemum Festival of Xiaolan is illuminating. The monopolizing political presence of the town government is clearly visible. The officials have shrewdly captured market initiatives to boost their administrative control over local economy and society. They use cultural means to forge a territorial identity in which they have privileged positions as "urbanites," aspiring to becoming China's new consuming middle class. To an extent, they are not unlike the organizers in the previous festivals who self-fashioned as literati. The difference, however, is that while previous elites sank social roots in local society through a variety of culturally defined and competing institutional channels (such as lineages, trade and temple networks, charities and regional associations), the cadre's legitimate claims are largely administrative and political, and not necessarily urbane. Constructing and marketing the locality under their control continue to dominate the town officials' visions of engaging liberalization. The question is whether such organizational intensity to forge a local identity allows them and the town residents to imagine alternative means of social mobility.

The rural migrants working in the town are also locked into a similar mind-set. The lack of horizontal channels of association means that if social capital is mobilized, it is along the lines of administratively defined territorial localities. This form of social networking is prevalent among migrant labor groups in many other parts of China, as reflected in Ching-kwan Lee's portrayal of *dagongmei* in Lee (1998) and of the residents of Beijing's "Zhejiang cun" by Jeong-ho Jong (2000) and Zhang Li (2001). Rather than taking native place identities as cultural given, we like to historicize their construction, reconstitution, and application in the Maoist and late socialist periods. Coupled with the Maoist legacy in which rural and urban statuses are sharply defined and enforced with a powerful party machine, these localized identities continue to have salience in shaping contemporary livelihoods and perceptions, even among those whose physical movements have long crossed territorial boundaries. In the present consumption-driven, "state development" mode of thinking, populations with a "rural" labeling are often viewed as commodities to be consumed—as cheap labor in the field and factories, as cheap services in karaoke bars and homes, as gendered bodies to reflect the patrons' good life on the fast track.[14]

Feeling local, feeling translocal: the ideology of the bounded universe

In this chapter we have argued that the localized peasant community was but an image for the convenience of imperial rule. It was a means to make spaces and their occupants legible for officials.[15] The various incarnations of *xiangtu* Zhongguo in the twentieth century served similar functions for the Republican and Communist regimes. The peasant, portrayed as poor, backward, tied to his land, lineage and community, was a subject for modern reform and revolution, led by urban elites or socialist vanguards.

Posed against historical experiences, the cultural construction of peasant community was anything but local. Lineage charters and settlements narratives started with histories of migration. The hierarchy of marketing systems, higher order lineages, temple networks, academic and official mobility provided maximum circulation of translocal resources and cultural imageries. War and natural disasters triggered other waves of circulation, be they demographic, economic, social or cultural. Resources reaching far beyond the local were used to make and legitimize locality. Multiple state and local agencies are involved in constructing this vibrant complex. It took the massive organizational and ideological powers of the Maoist revolution to "ground" the Chinese peasants to administrative cells, after significant layers of social life beyond these cells were truncated, marginalized, destroyed.

With such Maoist baggage, rural populations now embark on their new movements with an ironic twist. We explore several nodes of translocal fluidity in south China today—township enterprises, migrant enclaves, community festivals and the consumption craze. They highlight processes by which rural populations and urbanites, locked into lingering parameters of the rural/urban divide, guide their global reach with the most localized assumptions.

At every age, therefore, we rediscover translocal China. We have to rediscover it because we believe that China must be earth-bound. But Chinese society could not be earth-bound unless it was also translocal. This had to be because the agrarian economy on which earth-bound China rested was serviced through trade, in goods, in labour and in capital, and because the ideology evolved from the mid-Ming dynasty, say the sixteenth century, that relegated every household to a unique location within the realm. Even for communities at the margins of the empire that could be extremely localized in material terms, their imaginings were not. These translocal meanings were at the heart of community identity.

Notes

1 Fei (1949) 36–38 noted the same; also Mallory (1926) argues that better transportation, including the railway, could allow food to be moved to victims, and Buck (1931) has some vivid descriptions of famine victims traveling on the railway to the lower Yangzi.

2 On Faure's visit in 2002, reaching Wendou required an hour's journey by motor upriver from the county city, and then a solid two-hours' walk up the steep hillside. The nearest village, Jiaci, was another two-hours' walk from Wendou.

3 See Siu (2001) on the intertwining of state ideology, merchant identities, and the construction of native community in late imperial China in Guangdong, and the disintegration of that unity in the Republican period.

4 See David Faure "What made Foshan a town?" and David Faure and Helen Siu (eds) *Down to Earth: The Territorial Bond in South China*; see also William T. Rowe, *Hankow: Conflict and Community in a Chinese City, 1796–1895*.

5 These were two elderly farmers from Chaolian *xiang* near Jiangmen Municipality. Interviewed in the late 1980s.

6 In 1957, rural markets were held only on the first and sixth day of the ten-day cycle. The lack of modern transport did not allow itinerary traders to travel to more than one market in the same day, thus reducing circulation that had been possible with staggered periodic marketing days.

7 For a town with 12,000 residents before 1949, it had 393 ancestral halls and 139 temples and shrines. The rich ritual complex was reinforced by a legendary Chrysanthemum

Festival, conducted once every sixty years since the early nineteenth century. See Siu (1990b) "Recycling tradition", and Siu (2002) "Redefining the market town."

8 See Siu (1989c) "Recycling rituals: politics and popular culture in contemporary rural China; Siu (1993) "The reconstitution of brideprice and dowry in south China," Siu (1995a) "Community festivals in south China: economic transformations and cultural improvisations."

9 This was the general policy to have urban nodes taking over the administration and reorganization of rural units—shi dai xian, zheng dai xiang, for more coordinated development in the post-Mao period.

10 On the intense cross-border traffic between Hong Kong and Guangdong, see Siu (2005), "The changing cultural landscape and luxury housing in south China: a regional history." Carolyn Cartier (2001) also stresses the importance of a regional construct in assessing such traffic and fluidity.

11 See Davis *et al.* (1995) and Davis (ed.) (2000) for comparative cases.

12 A metal-lock factory and Jinri Group, one that produces milk health drinks (recently bought by Danone) are the well-known ones.

13 There is historical rivalry between local leaders in Xiaolan zhen and those in the county capital (Shiqi zhen). Zhongshan municipality, together with Nanhai, Panyu, Shunde, Dongguan, has been one of the five "small dragons" of high growth in south China.

14 For the consumption of migrant rural women's bodies by city men, see Tiantian Zheng (2003). For a parallel situation with "minorities," Louisa Schein analyses how urbanites consume the image of Miao women in ethnic tourism. See Schein (2000).

15 On a general point of legitimate state spaces, see James Scott (1998).

References

Buck, P. (1931) *The Good Earth*, New York: John Day.

Cartier, C. (2001) *Globalizing South China*, Oxford: Blackwell.

Chang, C.-l. (1955) *The Chinese Gentry: Studies on Their Role in Nineteenth-Century Chinese Society*, Seattle, WA: University of Washington Press.

Chi, C.-t. (1936) *Key Economic Areas in Chinese History*, London: George Allen & Unwin.

Cohen, M. (1994) "Being Chinese: the peripheralization of traditional identity," in Tu Wei-ming (ed.), *The Living Tree: The Changing Meaning of Being Chinese Today*, Cambridge, MA: Harvard University Press.

Daniels, C., Yang, Y., and Fusaji, T. (eds) (2001) *Kishu byozoku ringyo keiyaku bunsho kaihen (1736–1950 nen)*, Tokyo: Tokyo gaikoku daigaku ajia afurika gengo bunka kenkyujo.

Dardess, J. W. (1983) *Confucianism and Autocracy: Professional Elites in the Founding of the Ming Dynasty*, Berkeley, CA: University of California Press.

Davis, D. (ed.) (2000) *The Consumer Revolution in Urban China*, Berkeley, CA: University of California Press.

Davis, D., Kraus, R., Naughton, B., and Perry, E. (eds) (1995) *Urban Spaces in Contemporary China*, Cambridge: Cambridge University Press.

Dean, K. (1993) *Taoist Ritual and Popular Cults of Southeast China*, Princeton, NJ: Princeton University Press.

Donnithorne, A. (1972) "China's cellular economy: some economic trends since the Cultural Revolution," *China Quarterly*, 52: 605–619.

Elman, B. A. (2000) *A Cultural History of Civil Examinations in Late Imperial China*, Berkeley, CA: University of California Press.

Elvin, M. (1973) *The Pattern of the Chinese Past*, Stanford, CA: Stanford University Press.

Faure, D. (1986) *The Structure of Chinese Rural Society, Lineage and Village in the Eastern New Territories, Hong Kong*, Hong Kong: Oxford University Press.

—— (1990) "What made Foshan a town? The evolution of rural-urban identities in Ming–Qing China," *Late Imperial China*, 11(2): 1–31.

—— (1999) "The Chinese emperor's informal empire: religion and the incorporation of local society in the Ming," in S.-m. Huang and C.-k. Hsu (eds), *Imagining China: Regional Division and National Unity*, Taipei: Institute of Ethnology, Academia Sinica, 21–41.

Faure, D. and Siu, H. (eds) (1995) *Down to Earth: The Territorial Bond in South China*, Stanford, CA: Stanford University Press.

Fei, X. (1948) *Xiangtu Zhongguo*, Shanghai: Guancha she.

—— (1949) *Xiangtu Chongjian*, Shanghai: Guancha she.

Fisher, C. T. (1990) *The Chosen One: Succession and Adoption in the Court of Ming Shizong*, Sydney: Allen & Unwin.

Freedman, M. (1958) *Lineage Organization in Southeastern China*, London: Athlone Press.

—— (1966) *Chinese Lineage and Society: Fukien and Kwangtung*, London: Athlone Press.

Guizhou sheng bianji zu (ed.) (1988) *Dongzu shehui lishi diaocha*, Guiyang: Guizhou minzu.

Hansen, V. (1990) *Changing Gods in Medieval China, 1127–1276*, Princeton, NJ: Princeton University Press.

Honig, E. (1992) *Creating Chinese Ethnicity: Subei People in Shanghai*, 1850–1980, New Haven, CT: Yale University Press.

Hsiao, K.-c. (1990) *Rural China: Imperial Control in the Nineteenth Century*, Seattle, WA: University of Washington Press.

Jong, J.-h. (2000) "Renegotiating with the state: the challenge of floating population and the emergence of new urban space in contemporary China," PhD thesis, Department of Anthropology, Yale University.

Kelley, D. (1982) "Temples and tribute fleets: the Luo sect and boatmen's associations in the eighteenth century," *Modern China*, 8(3): 361–391.

Lee, C. K. (1998) *Gender and the South China Miracle*, Berkeley, CA: University of California Press.

Liu, Z. (1997) *Zai guojia yu shehui zhi jian: Ming Qing Guangdong lijia fuyi zhidu yan-jiu* (Between state and society: a study of lijia tax and corvee in the Ming and Qing), Guangzhou: Zhongshan daxue chubanshe.

Mallory, W. H. (1926) *China: Land of Famine*, New York: American Geographical Society.

Naquin, N. (1992) "The Peking pilgrimage to Miao-feng Shan: religious organizations and sacred site," in S. Naquin and C.-f. Yu (eds), *Pilgrims and Sacred Sites in China*, Berkeley, CA: University of California Press, 333–377.

Ownby, D. (1996) *Brotherhoods and Secret Societies in Early and Mid-Qing China*, Stanford, CA: Stanford University Press.

Perkins, D. H. (1969) *Agricultural Development in China 1368–1968*, Edinburgh: Edinburgh University Press.

Polanyi, K. (1957) *The Great Transformation*, Boston, MA: Beacon Press.

Rowe, W. T. (1989) *Hankow: Conflict and Community in a Chinese City, 1796–1895*, Stanford, CA: Stanford University Press.

Schein, L. (2000) *Minority Rules: The Miao and the Feminine in China's Cultural Politics*, Durham, NC: Duke University Press.

54   *David Faure and Helen F. Siu*

Schipper, K. M. (1977) "Neighbourhood cult associations in traditional Tainan," in G. W. Skinner (ed.), *The City in Late Imperial China*, Stanford, CA: Stanford University Press, 650–676.

Scott, J. (1998) *Seeing Like a State*, New Haven, CT: Yale University Press.

Shue, V. (1984) *The Reach of the State*, Stanford, CA: Stanford University Press.

Siu, H. (1989a) *Agents and Victims in South China: Accomplices in Rural Revolution*, New Haven, CT: Yale University Press.

—— (1989b) "Socialist peddlers and princes in a Chinese market town," *American Ethnologist* 16(2): 195–212.

—— (1989c) "Recycling rituals: politics and popular culture in contemporary rural China," in R. Madsen, P. Link, and P. Pickowicz (eds), *Unofficial China: Essays in Popular Culture and Thought in the People's Republic*, Boulder, CO: Westview Press, 121–137.

—— (1990a) "Where were the women? Rethinking marriage resistance and regional culture in south China," *Late Imperial China* 11(2): 32–62.

—— (1990b) "Recycling tradition: culture, history and political economy in the Chrysanthemum Festivals of south China," *Comparative Studies in Society and History*, 32(4): 765–794.

—— (1991) "The politics of migration in a market town," in D. Davis and E. Vogel (eds), *China on the Eve of Tiananmen*, Boston, MA: Harvard University Press, 61–82.

—— (1993) "The reconstitution of brideprice and dowry in south China," in D. Davis and S. Harrell (eds), *Chinese Families in the Post-Mao Era*, Berkeley, CA: University of California Press, 165–188.

—— (1995a) "Community festivals in south China: economic transformations and cultural improvisations," in C.-k. Lo, S. Pepper, and K.-y. Tsui (eds), *China Review*, Hong Kong: Chinese University Press, 1–17.

—— (1995b) "Lineage, market, pirate and *dan*: ethnicity in the sands of the Pearl River delta," paper presented at the Annual Meetings of the Association for Asian Studies.

—— (1997) "Afterword" and "Recycling Tradition," in S. Humphreys (ed.), *Cultures of Scholarship*, Ann Arbor, MI: University of Michigan Press, 139–185.

—— (2001) "The grounding of cosmopolitans: merchants and local cultures in south China," in W.-h. Yeh (ed), *Becoming Chinese*, Berkeley, CA: California University Press, 191–227.

—— (2002) "Redefining the market town through festivals in south China," in D. Faure and T. T. Liu (eds), *Town and Country: Identities and Perception*, St. Antonys-Palgrave, England, 233–249.

—— (2005) "The Cultural landscape of luxury housing in South China: A regional history," in Jing Wang (ed.), *Locating China: Space, Place, and Popular Culture*, London and New York: Routledge, 72–93.

Siu, H. and Liu, Z. (2006) "Lineage, market, pirate and *dan*: ethnicity in the sands of south China," in P. Crossley, H. Siu, and D. Sutton (eds), *Empire at the Margins: Culture, Ethnicity, and Frontier in Early Modern China*, Berkeley, CA: University of California Press.

Skinner, G. W. (1964/1965) "Marketing and social structure in rural China," *Journal of Asian Studies* 24(1–3): 2–43, 195–228, and 363–399.

—— (1971) "Chinese peasants and the closed community: an open and shut case," *Comparative Studies in Society and History* 13(3): 279–281.

So, A. Y. (1986) *The South China Silk District: Local Historical Transformation and World-System Theory*, Albany, NY: SUNY Press.

Stockard, J. (1988) *Daughters of the Canton Delta, Marriage Patterns and Economic Strategies in South China, 1860–1930*, Stanford, CA: Stanford University Press.

Topley, M. (1975) "Marriage resistance in rural Kwangtung," in M. Wolf and R. Witke (eds), *Women in Chinese Society*, Stanford, CA: Stanford University Press, 67–88.

Wang, G. (2000) *The Chinese Overseas: From Earthbound China to the Quest for Autonomy*, Cambridge, MA: Harvard University Press.

Wang, R., Xiangtu zhi lian (1996) *Ming–Qing huiguan yu shehui bianqian*, Tianjian: Tianjian renmin.

Weng, T. (1975) *Kangxi chuye "yi Wan wei xing" jituan yudang jianli Tiandi hui*, occasional papers series, no. 3, Singapore: Institute of Humanities and Social Sciences, Nanyang University.

Zhang, L. (2001) *Strangers in the City*, Stanford, CA: Stanford University Press.

Zhang Yingqiang (2003) "Mucai liudong: Qing dai Qingshui jiang xia you diqu di shichang, quanli yu shehui" (The movement of timber: market, power and society in the lower reaches of the Qingshuijiang River) PhD thesis, Zhongshan University.

Zheng, R. (1997) "Yimin, huji yu zongzu: Qingdai zhi Minguo qijian Jiangxi Yuanzhou fu diqu yanjiu," unpublished M. Phil. thesis, Hong Kong University of Science and Technology.

Zheng, T. (2003) *From Rural Migrants to Bar Hostesses: Gender and the Politics of "Becoming" in a Post-Mao City*, unpublished PhD thesis, Department of Anthropology, Yale University.

Zhuo, K. (1990) *Qingdai Taiwan de shangzhan jituan*, Taipei: Taiyuan.

3 Shanxi as translocal imaginary
Reforming the local

David S. G. Goodman

During the 1990s in Taiyuan, the capital of Shanxi Province, one of the great economic success stories was the emergence of restaurants and eateries named after the province—its noodles, pancakes, and pasta. These new enterprises came in all shapes and sizes: *Shanxi Noodle King*, *Shanxi Pasta World*, *Shanxi Noodles*, to name a few. This phenomenon was all the more remarkable because while the territory of Shanxi had long been famous for its noodles, pancakes, and flour-based food, they had not previously been marketed with specific reference to the name of the province. On the contrary, such foods were more likely to have place descriptors, where these existed at all, to more limited territories, such as towns and counties. For example, the Linfen *shuaibing* (a very large and thin, flat pancake, cooked folded in layers) or Wenshui *jubing* (a deep fried doughy ball with a sweet filling) and then only because they had become known (largely through sales) outside their area of origin.

The emergence of Shanxi noodles (and indeed a provincial cuisine of any kind) in the 1990s was part of the deliberate construction of a provincial identity by the party-state, designed primarily to assist the cause of economic development. Shanxi was being identified as a new local imaginary that would help mobilize the enthusiasm, productivity and even the resources of its inhabitants. Indeed, both because the province is clearly a higher order of the "local" than the towns and counties that might be thought the more usual level of local identification, and because the social construction of a specifically Shanxi identity emphasizes the networks that bind its inhabitants, this result is perhaps better described as the emergence of a translocal imaginary. In this process of identity formation, the idea of the local was effectively reformed by the party-state in two further regards: localism was being openly articulated and becoming politically respectable; and the province was being highlighted as the prime scale of identification.

The "local" as a focus of socio-political interaction had an undoubtedly ambiguous existence from the establishment of the People's Republic of China (PRC) in 1949 to the start of the reform era in the 1980s. From the point of view of the party-state created by the Chinese Communist Party (CCP) a strong center required the identification of the local, but necessarily only in subordinate positions. At least partly in consequence, the descriptor "local" was applied to everything from village, to county, district, and province. While the activism and voluntarism of local government at all these levels was encouraged, "localism" was a significant political crime that invariably resulted in loss of office (Teiwes 1979: 366ff.).

This started to change in the 1990s as the party-state built on the ambiguities resulting from the definition of local as both province and village and everything in between as part of its deliberate strategy to encourage development. Although the term "localism" has not been depoliticized, the negative approach toward it has started to change with reform and the introduction of an effective state-sponsored discourse of localism. There has been an emphasis on the importance of local feelings of identification by entrepreneurs and managers as motivators of economic behavior. To rephrase a well-known description of capitalism in the USA, the implicit operating principle for economic development became "what's good for Haizhou is good for China." There has also been, in contrast to past practice, the crafting of explicitly provincial discourses of development by the party-state itself (Goodman 1997; Hendrischke and Feng 1999; Oakes 2000: 667).

Concerns about localism escaping the state are entirely understandable from a number of perspectives influencing the current leadership of the PRC, including China's history of warlordism in the twentieth century and the implosion of the state in post-communist Russia and Eastern Europe. However, a series of interviews in Shanxi during 1999–2002, in particular the responses to questions about migration and perception of place, suggest that networks of translocalism may be more important and stronger than any more divisive identifications. During the 1990s economic development was almost inherently localist, not least in response to the party-state's new discourse of development. Almost all those interviewed had lived in the province all their lives; very few others had lived and worked there for almost all their adult lives; and there had clearly been very few social interactions with the rest of China. All the same an apparently intense social localism would seem to have been offset to some considerable extent by the emergence of a provincial translocal imaginary that aids an even wider political cohesion.

Migration and mobility within Shanxi

Shanxi is a north China province that in 2000 had 32.97 million people, a GDP of 164.4 million yuan RMB, and a GDP per capita of 5,137 yuan RMB.[1] Although it is, and has been for about eighty years one of China's major heavy industrial bases, with exceptionally large and high quality resources of coal, its reputation within the PRC is one of poverty and peasant radicalism. It was the site of the major front-line base areas against Japanese invasion during the War of Resistance of 1937–1945; and the once Mao-era model production brigade of Dazhai is located in the east of the province. Since the 1920s Shanxi has been an established major center for heavy industry, and it currently produces large proportions of China's coal, coke, aluminum, electricity, and specialist steels. In the past, the lack of understanding of Shanxi's local conditions more generally was not too surprising given its mountainous topography and lack of transport links with the rest of China. Other Chinese were effectively hindered from visiting Shanxi, let alone doing business there, until a massive road-building program made the province more accessible during the mid-1990s (Gillin 1967; Breslin 1989: 135; Goodman 1999: 323).

Before 1992, provincial economic development had depended heavily on central government investment, growing fastest with that investment during the mid-1950s and mid-1980s. It was only during the mid-1990s that sustained, though still only extremely modest, above-national-average rates of growth were achieved without that support. During the last decade Shanxi's economic structure has ceased to revolve solely around the central state sector, though it still plays a sizeable role in provincial development, not the least through its control of energy prices. There has remained relatively little foreign interaction with the province though there has been considerable domestic investment from and trade with other parts of China, particularly in the development of the private sectors of the economy. By 2000, 10.9 percent of the province's GDP was produced by the primary sector of the economy, compared to the national average of 15.9 percent. A provincial GDP of 50.3 percent came from the secondary sector of the economy, compared to the national average of 50.9 percent; and 38.7 percent was derived from the tertiary sector, compared to the national average of 33.2 percent. Heavy industry, centering on coal, coke, and steel production is the backbone of the provincial economy, with rapid growth in the new technologies, foodstuffs, and textiles (*Touzi daokan* 1996). In 2000, about 10 percent of GDP was derived from the foreign-funded sector of the economy, compared to a national average of about twice that figure.

In the context of another project it has been necessary to try and collect social and demographic data, as well as perceptions of place and culture from a more general sample of the Shanxi population.[2] As a group those interviewed have been selected to reflect regional diversity across the province (drawing on people living in each of the province's eleven administrative districts) age and gender differences, as well as residence between rural and urban areas. In the process of creating a control group for comparison, information about migration, mobility and perceptions of place are readily available. The information discussed here is taken from those interviews, a group who predominantly might be described as the middle classes. The extent to which the sample of 210 interviewees is drawn from those social categories is apparent from a brief consideration of their current occupations and educational backgrounds. Of those interviewed 10 percent were businesspeople, 25 percent teachers, 22 percent worked in administrative positions of various kinds, 5 percent described themselves more generally as workers, and 18 percent were different kinds of professionals—doctors, nurses, accountants, engineers. Of the sample, 49 percent were university educated, 23 percent had and completed a three-year college program, and 15 percent were graduates of a two-year technical college program.

An understanding of "home" is clearly central to any consideration of migration as well as the local in this context. However, "home" may well be a series of operations for those interviewed, with a complex set of interrelations. "Home" might be where someone was born (birthplace); the location of the interviewee's parent's long-term family home, certainly regarded as having been the major cultural identification of place in the past (native place); the place where the interviewee's parent's lived when they were growing up (parental home); and the place where the interviewees settled to live when they married and started their own family (family home).

Those interviewed during 1999–2002 were predominantly from Shanxi, in the sense that they were either born there (89 percent), their parents' native place was in the province (86 percent), or they had grown up there (89 percent). Even where people were not province-born they had spent almost all the years since the late 1940s in Shanxi.

Perhaps more remarkable is the extent to which birthplace, native place, and parental home location of those interviewed were identical and in Shanxi, as well as where birthplace, native place, and parental home though not identical, are located within the same district. District in this sense being the fundamental cultural sub-areas of the province: central Shanxi, centerd on the Taiyuan Basin; southeast Shanxi, centered on Changzhi and Jincheng; southern Shanxi, centered on Linfen and Yuncheng; north Shanxi centered on Datong; the Liuliang Mountains; and the area in the northeast of the province centered on Yuanping, Xinzhou and the Wutai Mountains.

Over half of those interviewed were born and brought up in their parents' native place. In addition, more than a quarter of all those interviewed had their birthplace, native place and parental home location all within Shanxi Province. Moreover about two-thirds of all those interviewed had their birthplace, native place, and parental home place all located within the same district of Shanxi.

Education is a significant determinant of migration and social mobility, particularly when attending university presents one of the first opportunities for the individual to move away from the parental home. Attendance at college is usually more local. Those interviewed were relatively highly educated. Though there are clear gender and age differences, 72 percent had graduated from either a four- or three-year higher education award program. The middle-aged and the males were more likely to have attended university; the females, were more likely to have graduated from three-year college programs.

Although the interviews revealed that native place remains an important cultural association for those interviewed, it would seem that it is less a determinant of economic behaviour than the location of the parental home. While almost half of those interviewed might have left the parental home to study for degrees and professional qualifications, just over half of them ended up working in the location of their parental home. Of those interviewed, 53 percent were found to be working in the location of their parental home; while only 33 percent were working in their parents's native place.

The provincial boundaries of migration would also seem to be strongly indicated by the information available on the relationships between birthplace, native place, parental home and family home location. While not (quite) all those interviewed might have regarded Shanxi as "home" all were long-term residents of the province. The overwhelming majority had been born in the province, had their native place there, and had grown up there too. Though the dominant pattern is an identity of birthplace, native place, and parental home, there is additionally a secondary pattern of mobility within the province with individuals moving for education and work.

As might be expected, given both the provincial socio-economic trends of the last decade and the results of other surveys also focussing on the Shanxi middle classes (Goodman 2001: 132) those interviewed appear to have been generally upwardly mobile in socio-economic terms. Other surveys in Shanxi have highlighted a number of different routes to socio-economic advance during the 1990s with urbanization; the development of light industry, particularly in suburban villages and townships; and the growth of service industries. While people (and their children) from social categories previously excluded from social and political advance have played a significant role in the creation of new businesses, parental levels of education and participation in the leadership of the party-state (especially at the local level) have also played important roles in the creation of the new middle classes of the reform era in Shanxi (Goodman 1998: 39, 2003: 187). A survey of leading cadres suggested a three-generation pattern of peasant to cadre to business person: while the cadres themselves had been recruited overwhelmingly from the ranks of the poor and less privileged, their children went on to become the backbone of the business middle class (Goodman 2000: 180).

A higher percentage of the fathers of those interviewed were either peasants or workers (42 percent) compared to the interviewees themselves (9 percent). Although a third of the fathers of those interviewed had been white collar workers, well over three-quarters of the interviewees were. Significantly, a large number of those interviewed had fathers who had been cadres, though not necessarily leading cadres.

A migration pattern that is almost completely within the province, with a closer relationship to the place of growing up, rather than native place as such, is further indicated by the location of the family home established once those interviewed had married and settled down. Only just under half of those interviewed had established their own family home in the place where they had grown up, and where their parental home was located. On the other hand, less than a quarter of them had settled in their family's native place.

Constructing the provincial

These trends are part of the essential context for examining the emergence of a translocal imaginary. Another is the development of a provincial discourse of development by the leadership of the Shanxi party-state during the mid-1990s, which explicitly attempted to construct a provincial identity that would create wider feelings of solidarity and mobilize local economic activism (Goodman 2002: 837). The new distinctive Shanxi identity of the 1990s was constructed from local cultures and practices in an often very confused and *ad hoc* way. In one or two cases, it was possible to highlight a near common characteristic for much of the province, as with the identification of noodles or vinegar as provincial cultural icons. Sometimes a specific cultural element of one locality was transformed into a provincial trope, as with the transformation of Fenyang County's *Fenjiu*—a sorghum-based liqueur—into the provincial drink; or with the recognition of local opera and theatre traditions. There was even the creation of a completely new "tradition" as a provincial characteristic through the elaboration of a previously highly localized cultural practice, as with the development of Drum and Gong Troupes.

The provincial discourse of development was promoted in and after 1992 under the slogan of "A Prosperous Shanxi and a Wealthy People." The legitimacy for this approach was grounded in the length of the history of the area of today's province. The sense of history was often quite exaggerated: the media and provincial leaders were quite capable of describing anything since the Tang Dynasty as "recent" or "modern" (*Linfen ribao* 1996: 2; *Shanxi ribao* 1996: 8). Linguistically, Shanxi was often referred to as *San Jin* (Three or Tripartite Shanxi) or *Jin* (the classical Chinese character for the province) rather than the modern Shanxi, thereby reinforcing the notion of a long heritage. The description of the province as *San Jin* refers to the Warring States period that started around 453 BCE. At that time today's Shanxi south of the Beiyue Mountains (i.e. everything except the region centered on Datong in the north) was divided into three principalities, corresponding to the areas around today's Yuncheng, Changzhi, and Taiyuan.

In practical terms, a sense of Shanxi identity was cultivated through the media as part of the reform agenda. The propaganda system of the provincial government produced a whole series of publications dedicated to the promotion of local culture. These included magazines such as the bi-monthly *Materials on Shanxi's Literature and History*; culturally broad magazines such as *Vicissitudes* and more literary journals such as *Yellow River*, *Spark*, *The Wind on the Beiyue Mountains*, and *Metropolis*; as well as a series of compendia, such as the fifty-two volume *Shanxi Encyclopedia*.

A determined encouragement of the reconstructed Shanxi identity was to be found in the regular media—the radio, television, and newspapers—which carried stories and items of local content. Where the more establishment newspapers and programs carried stories of strategic interest in terms of economic development, the more popular media concentrated on items of more cultural or general interest. Thus not surprisingly the CCP's *Shanxi Daily* featured development of the Shanxi coal industry (Zhao Shurong 1996: 4), as well as the development of other industries. Papers such as the *Taiyuan Evening News* and *Morning Life* concentrated on issues such as local foods, vinegar consumption, and local history, both ancient and modern (Qu Shaosheng 1996: 8; Zheng Sheng 1996: 6; Kang Yuqin 1998: 7; Liu Fang 1998: 3).

To support this construction of the new translocal identity, the provincial leadership ensured the development of a whole network of institutes, study groups, and associations dedicated to popularizing the idea of Shanxi. These included a Shanxi Culture Research Association, and a Shanxi Overseas Exchange Committee. The provincial leadership also established a Shanxi

Research Institute under its Provincial CCP Committee, with an initial staff of just under 100 people. Perhaps even more remarkably, it also appointed 165 local historians in different locations around the province. In absolute terms this figure is clearly not large in a population of some 30 million, but given the other challenges that were facing the provincial leadership at the time, and that required funding, these appointments reflect the importance attached to the development of provincial (and inherently translocal) knowledge. A major feature of the work of these historians was to supply news stories of various kinds to the official media.

The new idea of Shanxi being created in these ways was not intended to represent a radical break with either the recent past, or the idea of China as a whole. The distinctiveness of Shanxi people was described very much in terms of social characteristics and cultural practices, with little if any attempt to identify core values as the basis of solidarity. In particular, considerable attention was paid to food, especially noodles and vinegar, as well as music and folk traditions.

The centrality of food in general and noodles in particular to an identification of Shanxi is not hard to understand since this is an aspect of life in the province that (though varied) is different to much of the rest of China, especially to the south and east (Li Defu 1998: 3). Agriculture is largely dry-land farming, with almost no rice cultivation and considerable grazing land. Except in the far southwest, where there is rice, the major staples are millet, sorghum, wheat, and oats, as well as potatoes. All grains, including potatoes, are often ground and their flour used to make noodles, as well as dumplings, griddlecakes, and breads. Stews and casseroles are commonplace, and lamb is the meat of choice.

The transformation of noodles and pancakes, and indeed all flour products, from everyday, highly localized, and commonplace to iconic status in public culture has been a major feature of the 1990s. The media have been full of stories and articles that have raised the profile of "noodle culture" not only generally, but more specifically as part of Shanxi distinctiveness (Yi Fan 1998: 2). Numerous books about noodles of different kinds have been published (Dou *et al.* 1992; Wang and Ya 1994) and as already noted the province has seen the emergence of specialist noodle restaurants in quite some numbers. In the process, types of noodle once thought of as specific to a town or county—such as Yuanping's potato flour noodles; or Shangdang's fried, red sorghum flour noodles, eaten cold with a spicy sauce—have now become "provincialized."

The consumption of noodles is one explanation often advanced for Shanxi's high vinegar consumption, which has also come to be regarded as a mark of provincial distinctiveness. Vinegar consumption in Shanxi is officially regarded as such an essential part of the diet that its price remains state-controlled, if through devolution to the Qingxu County authorities, a major center for vinegar production. Vinegar is said to aid the digestion of noodles.

The promotion of Shanxi distinctiveness in these ways was very much part of a process of province building. There had not, for example, previously been a specifically designated "Shanxi cuisine" before the provincial leadership encouraged its promotion. Nor had there been restaurants named specifically for the province before the 1990s though these now started to proliferate. On the contrary within Shanxi it was (and remains) often explicitly recognized that the province is characterized by its intense localism (Fan Changjiang 1937: 21). It is, for example, commonly accepted that people from adjacent counties are almost certain to speak distinctly different languages and to have difficulties in communication. Though they are usually somewhat too heavy to be used as guidebooks, many county gazetteers in Shanxi provide a fairly lengthy section on the local language used in each county, and particularly its distinct characteristics.

Far from a single provincial cuisine, there had been (and remain, even if perceptions are changing) different food traditions, tastes and special foods and dishes characteristic of various parts of the province. To the end of developing a provincial identity, these were all brought together and described as "Shanxi" dishes (Li Binhu 1998: 3). Vinegar too remains locally differentiated with many counties having their own traditions, of production, even though *Laochencu* vinegar from Qingxu remains privileged as the provincial brand. Around the province the grains used to make vinegar vary, as does the process of production (Li Jianyong 1998: 86).

Beyond noodles and vinegar, the idea of Shanxi was also extended to theatre, music, folk traditions, and literature, though more through the celebration of the local within the province. As in other provinces during the 1980s and 1990s, the plethora of new literary and cultural magazines produced in the province stressed their provincial focus, and provided a site where a specifically Shanxi culture and local identity could be explored. For theatre and music this was not difficult. Shanxi has a rich history of local opera and theatre forms. However, these are all highly localized and mostly not general across the province (Shi and Zhi 1996: 62). In the 1990s search for a Shanxi identity, all were encouraged and resurrected after their suppression during the Cultural Revolution, with some such as *Puju* (an opera form from Shanxi's southwest corner) and Shangdang Theatre (the local theatre tradition of Changzhi and the province's southeast) being recognized and often described as provincial opera and theatre, respectively (Zheng Xiaoyu 1996: 2).

The search for a distinctive Shanxi folk tradition that could be promoted as part of the new provincial identity led straight to a process not unknown in other localities seeking to identify and market their own unique cultural representation. A highly localized and disparate folk tradition was made more formal and structured (Vickers 1997) in this case with the emergence of Drum and Gong Troupes. Folk music in southwest and southeast Shanxi had long centered around the playing of drums, though each locality has its own traditions of drum, drumming and accompanying percussion. A more structured and marketable approach to this kind of folk drumming, albeit related to north Shanxi, had been demonstrated in the film *Yellow Earth* during the 1980s. Where in Beijing the organization of *Yangge* folk-dance teams was promoted during the 1990s as a popular, community-building form of participatory culture, Shaanxi saw the emergence of Drum and Gong Troupes. They rapidly proved themselves to be a very popular and fairly lucrative activity, with their public performances, especially at weekends outside stores and restaurants, and for special occasions. For example, a dozen Drum and Gong Troupes each in action separately participated in the opening ceremony for the newly built Yingze Road Bridge over the Fen River in the center of Taiyuan on October 1, 1998.

Apart from food, drama, and music, the newly emergent provincial identity also drew on "traditions" authenticated by the CCP, and appeals to popular history. Shanxi's role as a heavy industry center for China was reemphasized with the expansion of the electricity generation industry and aluminium production (Zhao Shurong 1996: 4; Zheng *et al.* 1997: 1). Similarly, Shanxi's role in the formation of CCP authority continued to be publicized, especially during the period of the War of Resistance to Japan. This was also part of a process, typical in the construction of collective identity, to establish an uninterrupted history from an earliest, often mythic age to the present day (Tian Qizhi 1993). The essence of the message was clearly to emphasize Shanxi's long-term centrality to the project of China, as well as to appeal to provincial pride.

The origin of Chinese civilization was found in the large number of pre-historic settlements—a quarter of all those known in the PRC—located in Shanxi's south-west, in particular around Linfen. From these origins, Shanxi's place at the heart of the later development of Chineseness was repeatedly emphasized in a number of ways. For example, a "Three Kingdoms City" was built in Qingxu (to the south of Taiyuan) as a theme park to commemorate the Chinese classic *Romance of the Three Kingdoms* written by Qingxu native Luo Guanzhong about the period in Chinese history from 220 to 265. Inside, a temple was built and dedicated to one of the heroes of the *Romance of the Three Kingdoms*, Guan Yu (later immortal-ized and widely worshipped as Guan Di) who was also a native of the current provincial area, from Haizhou in present-day Yuncheng. Elsewhere, Hongtong County, in the Linfen District of southern Shanxi was promoted as the mythical site of origin of Han Chinese, building on its role as a source of migration to the rest of China[3] (Zhao Fulong 1999: 4). More generally, Shanxi's architecture, espe-cially in its smaller towns and villages, was publicized as "traditionally Chinese," (Li Yuxiang 1994) and its villages and rural landscapes used in television programs and films for that reason. Most notably, the award-winning *Raise the Red Lantern* was filmed at the Qiao family mansion in Qixian.

Shanxi's role as a "living museum" of Chinese culture was repeatedly stressed, partly in line with the provincial leadership's goal of developing tourism in the province but also partly to emphasize Shanxi's role in the development of a wider Chinese culture. The more obvious sites of historical and cultural interest include Wutaishan, the entry point of Buddhism into China; the UNESCO-listed World Heritage sites of Pingyao's walled city and the Yungang Grottoes outside Datong; the Daoist frescoes of the Yongle Gong; and the life-size funerary figures at Jinci. The claim was often made that Shanxi had more temples, frescoes, and pagodas than other provinces (Tian Lei 1996: 1).

Identifying the translocal

Somewhat paradoxically, the claim that Shanxi Province lies at the heart of China's development was matched by a recognition within the province that it was not well connected, other than politically, with the rest of the country. Indeed its poor physical integration both internally and with the rest of the country led to a massive road-building campaign during the 1990s (Gong Guoqiang 1998: 1). There has clearly been only a very limited migration into Shanxi from the rest of China, and only a muted migration around the province even for the middle classes. Nonetheless, the evidence from interviews during 1999–2002 is that a new, translocal imaginary has begun to emerge since the mid-1990s.

In order to attempt to assess the understandings of local characteristics, and generally their perception of and identification with place—the immediately local, the provincial and China—those interviewed were asked a series of questions about different aspects of popular culture, in particular about food, music, and dance. Interviewees were asked, amongst other questions, to nominate three foods they saw as typical of separately Shanxi, China as a whole, the world outside China, and their home location; as well as to identify typical musical forms and dances similarly for Shanxi, China, the rest of the world, and their home location.

The interview sample was divided into four categories of respondents, reflecting degrees of migration, possible perceived social mobility and distance from their origins. The first "Local" category refers to those whose movement was most restricted in these terms. This category includes people who still live and work in their native place, which was also the place where they had been born and brought up. The second "District" category identifies those whose movement in terms of birthplace, native place, parental home, and family home is within the boundaries of one of Shanxi's administrative districts, but excludes those already classified in the Local categorization. The third "Provincial" category includes those whose movement in terms of birthplace, native place, parental home, and family home has taken place within the province, but who have moved either in their youth or through their career away from their provincial administrative district of origin. The fourth and final "External" category refers to anyone who was born, has a native place, or had grown up outside the province. Of those interviewed, 37 percent were in the Local category, 20 percent in the District category, 25 percent in the Provincial category, and 18 percent were External.[4]

Those interviewed were asked to nominate up to three items of food they identified as most typical of Shanxi Province. Almost everyone nominated noodles at least once, some rather enthusiastically even additionally nominated specific kinds of noodles. Well over 80 percent of those interviewed recognized the existence of the "Shanxi noodle culture" much promoted during the 1990s. Perhaps more surprisingly, only 40 percent of respondents also nominated vinegar as typically from Shanxi. Given that almost every county has its own vinegar plant and tradition of vinegar making, this relatively low rating may well be because some interviewees did not regard vinegar as a "food." Equally as remarkable, no other single item was nominated by even a quarter of respondents, though potatoes were so recognized by more than one in five.

The interviewees were also asked to nominate up to three items of food most typical of food elsewhere in China. Unsurprisingly seafood (72 percent) and rice

(69 percent) head the list. Shanxi is not only well inland, but until the recent advent of airfreight rarely had fish, let alone other fresh seafood. In the past it was customary for wealthy families to place a highly decorated wooden fish on a banquet table—not least to encourage good fortune (*youyu* homophonically can be read as to have either "fish" or "a surplus" which has become by extension "good fortune")—in the absence of more edible varieties. With economic development and increased communications (including airfreight for fresh sea food from Australia) since the mid-1990s a large number of seafood restaurants have emerged, not least to cater for the expanding tastes of the provincial new rich. Similarly, as already noted, Shanxi's agriculture is dry-land farming and rice is not a provincial staple and fairly uncommon outside the far southwest. In addition, those interviewed also nominated (Beijing) Roast Duck (30 percent) and Sichuan (or Chongqing) Hot Pot (28 percent) in relatively large numbers.

When interviewees were asked to nominate food types that typified (for them) the world outside China, "the world" was clearly equated in their mind's eye with the USA. The hamburger was nominated by over two-thirds of interviewees as a typical food outside China. Almost a quarter indicated that salad was also typical, followed in lesser quantities by sandwiches, chocolate, and coffee. A feature of the responses to this question was not only the predominance of fast food associated with the USA as the marker for the "Rest of the World" but also the emergence of known brands originating in the USA. While this was not at all surprising, it was interesting to see confirmation that McDonalds (32 percent), KFC (11 percent), and Coca Cola (25 percent) were lodged in the collective consciousness, though it may be that these results are exaggerated by middle class bias of the interview sample, and their greater real disposable income.

In order to test whether interviewees had different perceptions of the provincial and the more local (in this context, county or town) they were also asked to nominate typical food (and later music and dance) for their home locations. These nominations were then subsequently compared to those made as typical of the province to examine the degree of identification.

When asked to specify the three most typical foods from their home locations the interviewees responded overwhelmingly in terms of noodles. Unsurprisingly, given the culinary environment in Shanxi, the most nominated items were noodles (76 percent), dishes made with noodles (47 percent), and steamed bread (37 percent). In addition, other flour-based dishes, as with noodles and breads, made from a variety of grains, but including maize, wheat, potatoes, oats, buckwheat, sorghum, and millet, were also mentioned in large numbers.

Table 3.1 provides an index derived from comparing the responses of interviewees asked to nominate three typical provincial types of food and three typical local types of food, to see whether there was overlap in the perception of the provincial and the more local. Where all three items were the same in the answers to both questions a score of three was recorded; where two were identical, a two; and so on. The data presented in Table 3.1 suggest a distribution centered on an overlap factor of one item. Given the predominance of noodles as a factor in any consideration of Shanxi cuisine this is probably not a high degree of overlap at all.

Table 3.1 Index of identification of home county/town food with provincial description (number (percent))

Migration status	Degrees of identity				
	Three	*Two*	*One*	*None*	*Total*
Local		12	58	9	77
District	3	16	17	6	42
Provincial	3	16	31	3	53
External		3	19	16	38
Total	6 (2.9)	45 (21.4)	125 (59.5)	34 (16.2)	210

Source: Shanxi interviews, 1999–2002: local and provincial food.

Indeed, though several highly localized food items—for example, and most famously, Pingyao Beef, Taigu Cakes, Qingxu grapes—were mentioned by respondents when asked to nominate food typical of Shanxi, they were never suggested by individuals who had connections of birthplace, native place, parental or family home with those specific locations. At the same time, the responses when asked to nominate foods typical of the interviewee's home location suggest a more clearly expressed sense of local cuisine than at the provincial level, with greater variety, and complexity.

Similar patterns in the perception of the world outside China, Shanxi, and the local county or town attend the interviewees' responses to questions about music and dance, though the clarity of understanding about the world beyond the borders of the PRC is often a little suspect. Almost half of those interviewed identified Shanxi Theatre (as already noted, a local popular opera, originating in the southeast of the province, and sometimes also known as Wuxiang Theatre after its county base in the Changzhi District) as typical of the province. Just under half (40 percent) of those interviewed also identified *Jinju* (an opera form often associated with the southwest of the province). It is more than likely that the existence of the provincial name (Shanxi or *Jin*) as descriptor reinforces identification of these musical forms with the province as a whole in the minds of those interviewed. *Puju* (as previously noted, an older high culture opera form also associated with the southwest of the province) was also nominated by a substantial number of respondents. When asked to nominate musical forms most typical of China outside Shanxi, respondents mentioned Peking Opera most frequently (60 percent) and somewhat surprisingly TV variety shows (52 percent). Somewhat vague references to "Western classical music" and "Western popular music" often filled out with specialist knowledge of individual composers and performers were provided in response to requests for nomination of music typical of the world outside China.

Table 3.2 presents an attempt to indicate the extent to which nominations of typical music types of county and town, on the one hand, and the province, on the other, overlap. Once again this evidence, crude as it must inevitably be, suggests that interviewees were able to distinguish between the musical forms of their

Table 3.2 Identification of local with provincial musical form
            (number (percent))

Migration status	Yes	No	Incomplete
Local	29	43	5
District	15	24	3
Provincial	10	41	2
External	3	34	1
Total	57 (27.1)	142 (67.6)	11 (5.2)

Source: Shanxi interviews, 1999–2002: local and provincial musical performance.

home location and of the province more generally. Only a little over a quarter of respondents identified the music type of their home location with that of the province. Given that the party-state's construction of a provincial identity has indeed built on local musical forms and turned them into provincialized concepts, these comparative figures would seem to suggest that those interviewed might even have some consciousness of the process of identity formation.

When asked to nominate dance forms typical of the province, those interviewed overwhelmingly specified the *Yangge* (77 percent). No other dance form was chosen by more than one in ten of respondents, though a fairly large variety of nominations were made for various different kinds of lion dances, dragon dances, and waist-drumming. The *Yangge* also featured highly in the number of nominations from respondents as a dance form typical of China though not to quite the same extent as at the provincial level of identification (38 percent). On the other hand almost half of those interviewed nominated the lion dance as typical of China as a whole (48 percent). Ballroom dancing was the most frequently nominated as a dance form typical of the world outside China, by a long way, chosen by over two-thirds of all respondents.

Table 3.3 extends the attempt to assess the extent to which interviewees equate their local experience with the provincial identity, by comparing the overlap in perceptions of typical local and provincial dance forms. On the whole, it indicates that those interviewed were well able to distinguish between the local and the provincial. However, it also suggests that slightly more respondents than was the case with perceptions of music forms saw the dance form nominated as typical of their home location as also typical of the province. The explanation of this difference, muted though it may be, is undoubtedly a function of the sense of either identification with (or ownership of) the *Yangge*.

The nomination of the *Yangge* stands in interesting contrast to the perception of Drum and Gong Troupes. As already noted, the emergence and activities of Drum and Gong Troupes have been encouraged by the provincial party-state since the mid-1990s, very much as part of its construction of a new provincial identity. It is even clear that Drum and Gong Troupes have become a popular participant activity for some urban residents in the bigger cities, as well as a popular event to

Table 3.3 Identification of local with provincial dance form
(number (percent))

Migration status	Yes	No	Incomplete
Local	34	40	3
District	14	26	2
Provincial	17	33	3
External	7	30	1
Total	72 (34.3)	129 (61.4)	9 (4.3)

Source: Shanxi interviews, 1999–2002: local and provincial dance.

be observed by others. Nonetheless, very few of those interviewed during 1999–2002 saw them as most typical of Shanxi, either as music or as dance.

Reforming the local

Caution would clearly be prudent in drawing conclusions from a survey based on a fairly limited sample, largely drawn from the middle classes, in one north China province. Nonetheless, the evidence from this examination of Shanxi during 1999–2002 would seem to indicate fairly certainly that the idea of the "local" has been or is in the process of being reformed quite radically compared to the Mao-dominated era of China's politics, by both the party-state and by those who live in the province. From the party-state's perspective one startling indicator of change is the extent to which discourses of localism are now acceptable; another is the extent to which the provincial has become emphasized as the prime translocal level of identification. However, a third and potentially more important way in which the local has been reformed is with the emergence of a new translocal imaginary. To be sure the party-state's actions in attempting to create a new provincial identity have played a central role in that process, but they do not provide a complete explanation of these new networks of understanding.

Shanxi's development since 1992 has most definitely been driven by a strong and state sponsored discourse of localism which has attempted to create a new provincial identity and in the process remind society of its past entrepreneurial practices, emphasize the importance of investing in one's place of residence, and provide opportunities for local networking. There is a creative tension in this new provincial discourse of development. Local identity is clearly being provincialized, but in that process the local is being privileged almost as much as the provincial. Sometimes the provincial party-state has attempted to develop new provincial tropes (either *ab initio* or by selection of existing specific local manifestations) but equally, sometimes simply emphasizing the local in general has been seen as adequate provincialization. The result is a neither a new local identity nor a new provincial identity alone, but rather a new translocal scale of identity, based on an emergent spatial network of ideas.

These complex relationships highlight the emergence of a translocal imaginary, not least because of the party-state's acceptance and encouragement of multiple and scale-transcending groundings. Clearly though explaining the development of a translocal imaginary solely in terms of the party-state's interventions and its creation of a new provincial identity does not tell the whole story. It almost certainly fails to engage with the long-term importance of a new translocal imaginary, not linked to any short-term regime configuration, and hence likely to be more a permanent feature of social politics in Shanxi. Increased communications and interactions within Shanxi have provided the necessary contrasts that lead to more, greater, and wider (not to say overlapping) understandings of place, and have highlighted the role of networks in identity formation.

Analysis of the interviews undertaken in the province during 1999–2002 suggests three more specific sets of conclusions about the emergence of the new translocal imaginary in Shanxi. The first, and most obvious, is that those interviewed have a fairly well articulated sense of place, that differentiates while associating the PRC, Shanxi, and their home county or town. While knowledge of the world outside China is clearly more limited, there are definite perceptual differences maintained between the idea of China and that of the rest of the world. There are also strong distinctions made between Shanxi and the rest of China, though these are often more sharply etched about the identification of the rest of China than of the province itself. As might be expected, given both the intensity of the party-state sponsored discourse of localism and increased communications within the province, the result is a commitment to a translocal Shanxi identity that is built upon a network of multiple local identities.

A second set of conclusions relates to the impact of the party-state's intervention in identity formation. Most importantly it is clear that the emerging Shanxi provincial identity is not simply a product of the party-state's publicity machine during the 1990s. Some of the directions about provincial identity the party-state and the media have produced during the last decade certainly seem to have entered the public consciousness. The identification of "Shanxi noodle culture" and its attendant emphasis on vinegar production are clear examples. Though not discussed in this chapter, another is a long-term provincial tradition of commercialism, associated with the "Exchange Shops" of central Shanxi (Pingyao, Taigu, and Qixian in particular) and a native banking tradition, which were a significant part of social and political life in Shanxi during the nineteenth century. The party-state has publicized this "tradition" during the second half of the 1990s to emphasize, not least to local citizens, that Shanxi has not always been characterized in terms of either the less economically outgoing and adventurous era of Yan Xishan's corporatist warlord state during the 1920s and 1930s, or the state socialism of the PRC after 1949 (Goodman 2004).

At the same time it is also clear that there are levels of popular culture and consciousness that are not so easily manipulated by the party-state, while remaining inherently translocal. The most obvious example from the information generated in the interviews is the identification of the *Yangge* folk dance as the most frequently cited typical Shanxi dance. During the 1990s little publicity has been given to the *Yangge* in Shanxi. To the contrary, as already indicated, there has been an attempt through the construction of a new Shanxi identity to emphasize the role of "Drum and Gong" Troupes as a popular form of performance, which has indeed been very successful. Nonetheless, the identification of the *Yangge* as distinctively provincial remains a clearly articulated aspect of public consciousness. It is possible that the strength of provincial identification with the *Yangge* results from its popularization in Shanxi through the more "revolutionary" reminiscent phases of the PRC when the CCP was emphasizing the legacy of the War against Japan. At that earlier time the CCP was not only, as already noted, particularly active in Shanxi, but had also adopted the *Yangge* as a popular art form for propaganda and mobilization purposes (Holm 1984: 3, 1991: 115 ff.). Another explanation may be that even before the CCP came to Shanxi in large numbers, Yan Xishan had similarly popularized the *Yangge* as a mobilisatory device, building on the dance forms of the southern Taihang Mountains (Gillin 1967: 169; *Zhongguo xiqujuzhong dacidian* 1995: 268 ff.).

A third set of conclusions relates to the relationship between migration and translocality, and is perhaps the most important in terms of understanding the dynamics of translocalism. It indicates that migration is of itself not a necessary ingredient for the emergence of a translocal imaginary, even though spatial networks and some forms of mobility (especially of ideas) may be. The interviews suggest that there is little difference in translocal imaginary for the various categories of those interviewed. Those who have moved around the province share an almost identical translocal imaginary with those who still live where they initially grew up. Perception of place is always determined by contrast with elsewhere, and clearly in many ways can be considered a translocal process. However, in the case of the interviews considered here such contrasts result very little from the movement of people, which has been both clearly relatively limited and not very important in shaping alternative local identities in Shanxi. Rather, strong local identities are being shaped by networks linked to other places. A clear demonstration of this network determination of the translocal imaginary is found in the observation that Shanxi foods were rarely identified as typically provincial by those who themselves come from the places of origin of those food types. The idea of the "local" has always been ambiguous under the PRC. The experience of Shanxi since the mid-1990s would suggest that its has shifted yet again, not this time in terms of the relations between the center and the local so much as in the emergence of a multiple place based "translocal" for the province.

Notes

1 Data for Shanxi and comparative national data, unless otherwise indicated, are taken from *Zhongguo tongji nianjian 2001*.
2 The project is concerned with an investigation of Christianity in Shanxi, and has been supported by a research grant from the Australian Research Council. Professor Tian Youru of the Modern Shanxi Research Institute, and Li Xueqian of Shanxi University provided help and assistance without which this project would not have taken place. Neither they nor indeed anyone else in Shanxi who has contributed to this project,

72   *David S. G. Goodman*

including those interviewed for this study, is in any way responsible for the interpretation or views expressed here.
3 After the Anlushan Rebellion and during the Ming Dynasty the repopulation of parts of China was officially organized in Hongtong. The names of those who migrated are recorded on its Scholar Trees that are now a place of pilgrimage for many Chinese.
4 For those interviewees who were not married, family home and parental home were assumed to be identical.

References

6Breslin, S. (1989) "Shanxi: China's powerhouse," in David S. G. Goodman (ed.) *China's Regional Development*, London: Routledge, 135.
Dou, N., Jia, B., and Li, J. (1992) *Shanxi miantiao* (Shanxi noodles), Taiyuan: Shanxi renmin chubanshe.
Fan, C. (1937) "Shanxi jixing" ("Record of a journey through Shanxi"), *Guowen zhoubao* (National Weekly) March 29: 21.
Gillin, D. G. (1967) *Warlord Yen Hsi-shan in Shansi Province 1911–1949*, Princeton, NJ: Princeton University Press.
Gong, G. (1998) "Wosheng gonglu jianshe xingaochao zaiqi" ("Another high tide for highway construction in Shanxi"), *Shanxi jingji ribao* (Shanxi Economic Daily) June 25: 1.
Goodman, D. S. G. (ed.) (1997) *China's Provinces in Reform: Class, Community and Political Culture*, London: Routledge.
—— (1998) "In search of China's new middle classes: the creation of wealth and diversity in Shanxi during the 1990s," *Asian Studies Review* 22(1): 39–62.
—— (1999) "King Coal and Secretary Hu: Shanxi's third modernization," in C. Feng and H. Hendrischke (eds) *The Political Economy of China's Provinces: Competitive and Comparative Advantage*, London: Routledge, 323–356.
—— (2000) "The localism of local leadership: cadres in reform Shanxi," *Journal of Contemporary China* 9(24): 159–183.
—— (2001) "The interdependence of state and society: the political sociology of local leadership," in C.-m. Chao and B. Dickson (eds) *Remaking the Chinese State: Strategies, Society and Security*, London: Routledge, 132–156.
—— (2002) "Structuring local identity: nation, province and county in Shanxi during the 1990s," *The China Quarterly* 172: 837–862.
—— (2003) "New entrepreneurs in Reform China: economic growth and social change in Taiyuan, Shanxi," in H. Dahles and O. van den Muijzenberg (eds) *Capital and Knowledge in Asia: Changing Power Relations*, London: Routledge, 187–197.
—— (2004) "Localism and entrepreneurship: history, identity and solidarity as factors of production," in B. Krug (ed.) *The Rational Chinese Entrepreneur*, London: Routledge.
Hendrischke, H. and Feng, C. (eds) (1999) *The Political Economy of China's Provinces: Comparative and Competitive Advantage*, London: Routledge.
Holm, D. (1984) "Folk art as propaganda: the Yangge movement in Yan'an," in B. McDougall (ed.) *Chinese Popular Literature and Performing Arts in the People's Republic of China, 1949–1979*, Berkeley, CA: University of California Press, 3–35.
—— (1991) *Art and Ideology in Revolutionary China*, Oxford: Oxford University Press.
Kang, Y. (1998) "Shanxi de gudu" ("Ancient capitals of Shanxi"), *Taiyuan wanbao* (Taiyuan Evening News) December 24: 7.
Li, B. (1998) "Jincaide xingcheng yu fazhan" ("The formation and development of Shanxi cuisine"), *Shanxi jinri* (Shanxi Today) November 19: 3.

Li, D. (1998) "Shanxi yinshi wenhua shuoyuan" ("The origins of Shanxi's food culture"), *Shanxi jinri* (Shanxi Today) November 19: 3.

Li, J. (1998) "Cujingshen" ("Vinegar spirit"), *Huohua* (Spark) 6: 86.

Li, Y. (ed.) (1994) *Laofangzi: Shanxi minju* (Old Houses: Shanxi Folk Architecture), Nanjing: Jiangsu meishu chubanshe.

Linfen ribao (1996) "Yiyannanjin Shanxiren" ("Some comments on Shanxi people"), *Linfen ribao* (Linfen Daily) January 19: 2.

Liu, F. (1998) "Techan mingchi" ("Local specialities and famous food"), *Shenghuo chenbao* (Morning Life) April 7: 3.

National Bureau of Statistics of China (ed.) (2001) *Zhongguo tongji nianjian 2001* (China Statistical Yearbook 2001), Beijing: China Statistics Press.

Oakes, T. (2000) "China's provincial identities: reviving regionalism and reinventing 'Chineseness'," *The Journal of Asian Studies* 59(3): 667–692.

Qu, S. (1996) "Yan Xishan tuixingde tuhuo yundong" ("Yan Xishan's native goods campaign"), *Taiyuan wanbao* (Taiyuan Evening News) August 14: 8.

Shanxi ribao (1996) "Shuo chi" ("Speaking and eating"), *Shanxi ribao* (Shanxi Daily), January 22: 8.

Shi, X. and Zhi, M. (1996) "Zhijiang Guangzhi de Shanxi minsu diaoyian" ("Zhijiang Guangzhi's Shanxi Folkways"), *Cang Sang* (Viccissitudes) 3: 62.

Teiwes, F. C. (1979) *Politics and Purges in China*, New York: M. E. Sharpe.

Tian, L. (1996) "Rang Shanxi wenwu fang yicai" ("Let Shanxi's historical relics develop greatly"), *Shanxi zhengbao* (Shanxi Gazette) September 13: 1.

Tian, Q. (1993) *Dangdai Shanxi shehui kexue* (The Social Sciences in Modern Shanxi), Beijing: Shehui kexue wenxian chubanshe.

Touzi daokan (1996) "Shanxi Jianhang xindai zhanlue he zhizhu chanye xuanze" ("The Shanxi Construction Bank's credit strategy and selection of industries for support"), *Touzi daokan* (Investment Guide) 1(February 1): 9.

Vickers, A. (1997) *Bali: A Paradise Created*, Hong Kong: Periplus Editions.

Wang, C. and Ya, F. (1994) *Shanxi mianshi* (Shanxi pasta) Taiyuan: Shanxi kexue jishu chubanshe.

Yi, F. (1998) "Zhongguo mianshi shu Shanxi" ("Shanxi noodles are tops in China"), *Shenghuo chenbao* (Morning Life) June 2: 2.

Zhao, F. (1999) "Shanxi yiminshi" ("Shanxi emigration history"), *Shanxi fazhan dabao* (Shanxi Development News) November 11: 4.

Zhao, S. (1996) "Shanghai gongye huoju shi Shanxi meitan gongye dianrande" ("The torch of Shanghai's industry is lit by Shanxi's coal"), *Shanxi ribao* (Shanxi Daily) November 15: 4.

Zheng, F., Gao, X., and Chang, J. (1997) "1996: wosheng caisheng shouru chao'e wancheng fengdou mubiao" ("1996: Shanxi's public revenue surpassed the desired target"), *Shanxi ribao* (Shanxi Daily) January 19: 1.

Zheng, S. (1996) "Guanchang" ("Guanchang (A traditional Shanxi snack)"), *Shenghuo chenbao* (Morning Life) August 2: 6.

Zheng, X. (1996) "Qiantan Shanxi 'Sida bangzi' " ("A brief talk about Shanxi's 'Four theatres' "), *Datong wanbao* (Datong Evening News) December 28: 7.

Zhongguo xiqujuzhong dacidian (1995) "Shandang luozi," in *Zhongguo xiqujuzhong dacidian* (Encyclopedia of China's Theatre, Opera and Music), Shanghai: Cishu chubanhse.

4 Openness, change, and translocality

New migrants' identification with Hainan

Feng Chongyi and Zhan Changzhi

The massive spontaneous population movement, from villages to towns, from towns to cities, from one county to another county, and from one province to another province, is part of the fundamental social change in China since the 1980s. It is not the case that there were no population flows in Mao's era, but the command economy and totalitarian control during that period meant that the population movement was largely organized and controlled by the party-state. It is a stark irony that the Chinese communist regime with a self-appointed mission to eliminate feudalism and localism would greatly enhance the native-place identity throughout China by introducing the *hukou* system, the *danwei* system and other controlling mechanisms (Cheng and Selden 1994; Yan and Yu 1996; Lu and Perry 1997; Li and Li 2000). The transition to a market economy coupled with the ease of social control, the decline of the *hukou* system and the *danwei* system in particular, has generated opportunities for not a small part of the population in China to move around and renegotiate their place-based identities.

Hainan has always been a destination for internal population flows in Chinese history, including the period of the People's Republic of China. The emerging social openness and the new economic development in Hainan have resulted in new waves of migrations to the island since the mid-1980s, particularly after its establishment as China's new province and largest Special Economic Zone (SEZ) in 1988. The trend of migrations has changed with economic cyclical fluctuations as the primary purpose of migration is economic. Since the mid-1990s some migrants have returned to the mainland due to the economic fluctuation, but others have chosen to stay and settle there. A process of identification with the host society has taken place for those new migrants choosing to stay. They have become a crucial force for the development of Hainan and interacted positively with the local population. Largely based on a survey of 100 new migrants to Hainan, this paper is an attempt to assess the psychological impacts on the migrants, the degree of their identification with the host society, and the extent to which they have transgressed the geographic and cultural borders between their place of origin and the new home.

The analysis on the phenomenon of translocality in Hainan aims to shed new light on the identity issues resulted from internal migration in China. The usual image is that migrants tend to adapt to whatever existing local culture and to be eventually absorbed into the host community. Furthermore, Faure and Siu in Chapter 2 in this volume argue that the post-Mao efforts to reconstruct local culture along the lines of market development does not offer much for locals to identify with. A different dynamism seems to be at work in Hainan. Our findings in the case study of Hainan indicate that, rather than identifying with existing Hainanese culture, New Mainlanders on the island are determined to change the local culture and construct a new place identity that is distinctly translocal. In the meantime, local communities are also adapting to the new environment and joining in the efforts to create a kind of newly constructed Hainan provincial identity or a new Hainanese culture. The result is nothing less than a new translocal identity combining the mainland links carried by the migrants, the existing local culture, and the new constructs generated by both migrants and locals in their march to modernity.

Hainan's market reforms and opening-up

Using language and history as two major indicators, three major communities are most obvious on the island: the Li, Hainanese, and the Mainlanders (Feng and Goodman 1997: 53–88). The Mainlanders can be easily further divided into two major groups of the Old Mainlanders, who came to Hainan during the Mao Era, and the New Mainlanders, who have come to the island during the reform era since the 1980s. Unbalanced economic development is inevitable for a country as large and diverse as China. At the early stage of a market economy extending from the south east coast to other parts of China, it is understandable that the massive population flow by and large follow the same direction as the capital flow. Hainan has stood out as a major destination for both massive capital flows and populations from other parts of China and beyond, simply because it has been privileged in the reform process to become a pioneer of economic openness and development in China.

The shape of the economy in Hainan has changed beyond recognition since the early 1980s, due largely to external investment and involvement. By the end of 1996, a total of 7,898 foreign-funded enterprises had registered to engage in direct foreign investment in Hainan, with contracted direct investment of US$15.86 billion, of which US$6.3 billion had been utilized. During the same period, 17,296 enterprises had been set up by investment from elsewhere of China, with net investment of RMB¥40 billion (Xing 1997: 7). As shown by Table 4.1, given the small size of the Hainan economy, the involvement of foreign investment and trade in Hainan has been remarkable indeed. By mid-1999, the foreign-funded sector accounted for one-third of GDP in Hainan (Lin 1999). In the meantime, the construction of freeways around and across the island and the reconstruction of all cities and towns throughout the island have completely changed the landscape of Hainan. The improvement of transportation, communication, energy supply and other infrastructure is a world of difference compared to that of the 1970s. GDP per capita increased seven times from RMB¥354 in 1980 to RMB¥6022 in 1998, with the proportion of urban population increased from 8.93 to 26.64 percent during the same period (Statistical Bureau of Hainan Province 1999).

Table 4.1 Foreign investment and trade in Hainan, 1987–1998

Year	GDP (in million US$)	FDI		Foreign loans		Foreign trade	
		Total (in million US$)	AS % of GDP	Total (in million US$)	AS % of GDP	Total turnover (in million US$)	AS % of GDP
1987	716.25	13.61	1.90	N/A	N/A	292.41	40.83
1988	964.13	381.89	39.61	5.26	0.55	664.62	68.93
1989	1,142.50	280.60	24.56	51.53	4.51	1,096.20	95.96
1990	1,281.13	128.82	10.06	33.22	2.59	936.97	73.14
1991	1,506.38	396.67	26.33	139.72	9.28	1,348.76	89.53
1992	2,271.38	2,261.14	99.55	332.23	14.63	1,694.50	74.60
1993	3,226.00	4,194.44	130.02	300.42	9.31	2,568.66	79.62
1994	4,136.88	1,224.72	29.60	340.58	8.23	2,697.19	65.20
1995	4,552.13	2,780.77	61.09	288.91	6.35	2,267.44	49.81
1996	4,869.13	273.94	5.63	851.64	17.49	2,286.67	46.96
1997	5,123.25	281.86	5.50	392.35	7.66	1,949.01	38.04
1998	5,486.50	143.21	2.61	590.22	10.76	1,909.13	34.80

Source: Calculated from Statistical Bureau of Hainan Province (ed.), *'99 Hainan tongji nianjian* (Hainan Statistical Yearbook of 1999), China Statistical Publishing House (1999: 23, 331, 341).

External participation in Hainan's economy has been facilitated by and has given great stimuli to marketization reforms in Hainan. Right after its establishment as a province, Hainan took the lead in China in publishing a *Collection of International Regulations and Practices* to educate and guide the government and public in bringing down tariff barriers and offering low tax and long tax holidays, despite the failed attempt to establish a free port and free trade zone on the island; in computerizing tax collection to reduce red tape and close loopholes; in opening sensitive areas such as mining, natural resource exploitation, financial markets, infrastructure, and agriculture to foreign investment; in establishing long-term leases on large areas of land to foreign as well as domestic companies; in liberalizing the price of grain and the means of agricultural production; in creating the new pattern known as "company plus peasant households" to develop "highly profitable agriculture"; in introducing share-holding arrangements in the construction of public facilities such as freeways and airports; in replacing the previously complicated procedure for approval of the establishment of a new firm with a simple system of registration as practiced in the advanced societies; in granting national treatment to all enterprises regardless of their nature of ownership; and in setting up a comprehensive social security net for the entire urban workforce across the state, collective, private, and foreign sectors (Feng and Goodman 1998: 342–371).

It is not an exaggeration to proclaim that a world-oriented market economy has firmly taken root in Hainan, although the plan did not come true to separate Hainan from the national customs system and establish it as a Special Customs Zone and a free port fully integrated into the international economy along the lines of another Hong Kong. After two decades of economic globalization, marketization and partial privatization, a "mixed economy" consisting of a diversified ownership such as the state sector, domestic private sector, and foreign sector has emerged on the island, with a market framework to guarantee a basically free flow of goods, capital, technology and personnel. *The Tenth Five-Year-Plan for Economic and Social Development* passed by the Fourth Plenary of the Second Hainan Provincial People's Congress in February 2001 made it clear that during the next five years "enterprises solely owned by the state or dominated by the state shares will on the whole withdraw from ordinary industries and areas open to commercial competition." It also elaborated the detailed plans to "actively clear away institutional obstacles for the vigorous development of private and non-public economy" and "attract foreign companies to participate in the restructuring of the state-owned enterprises (SOEs) through share-holding arrangement or annexation" (Hainan Provincial Government 2001).

Aided by China's entry into WTO, the pace of globalization and marketization in Hainan will be definitely accelerated. As shown by Table 4.2, compared to other sources, the state finance has even become an insignificant player in the area of investment in fixed asset of the state units, although the items of "internal loans," "self-raised funds," and "bonds" are actually still drawn from the state sector. More importantly, Table 4.3 shows that the state sector, which used to overwhelmingly dominate the industrial production, has now been balanced by the foreign and private sectors. It is also worth mentioning the fact that foreign capital has deeply involved itself in agricultural production in Hainan. Originally, this foreign capital mainly came from Taiwan, and these Taiwan-funded enterprises made huge profits by introducing new technologies and new varieties of cash crops. This highly profitable business was soon joined by business people from elsewhere. By the end of 1995, a total of more than 400 foreign-funded agriculture enterprises from Taiwan, Hong Kong, Malaysia, Thailand, Singapore, the United States, Japan, and other countries had been set up in Hainan, with an investment

Table 4.2 Sources of investment in fixed assets in Hainan's state units, 1990–1998

Year	Total (in million yuan)	State	Foreign	Internal loans	Bonds	Self-raised funds	Other
1990	3,049.69	328.23	420.85	602.63	N/A	1,279.03	418.95
1991	4,056.93	347.16	263.85	1,356.23	N/A	1,431.64	658.05
1992	7,889.16	474.36	1,004.91	2,315.53	N/A	3,476.72	717.64
1993	17,529.26	470.09	1,961.12	4,026.08	675.55	6,570.59	3,825.83
1994	20,313.06	465.34	2,687.14	5,163.03	56.48	9,357.58	2,583.49
1995	17,789.95	355.35	5,537.54	3,289.25	937.65	5,031.77	2,638.39
1996	16,802.48	445.37	4,735.35	2,774.41	310.00	6,774.81	1,762.54
1997	14,480.67	419.40	3,237.91	2,487.93	229.53	6,837.69	1,268.21
1998	15,460.78	1,138.28	3,233.03	2,719.20	146.15	7,102.74	1,121.38

Source: Statistical Bureau of Hainan Province (ed.), '99 *Hainan tongji nianjian* (Hainan Statistical Yearbook of 1999), China Statistical Publishing House (1999: 84).

Table 4.3 Gross industrial output value by sectors in Hainan, 1987–1998

Year	GIOV in total (in) million yuan	State		Collective		Other (private and foreign)	
		Sum	% of total	Sum	% of total	Sum	% of total
1987	2,154.63	1,635.66	75.91	158.91	7.38	360.07	16.71
1988	3,124.61	2,335.59	74.75	196.91	6.30	592.11	18.95
1989	3,894.42	2,888.62	74.14	225.53	5.79	782.27	20.08
1990	4,431.89	3,355.85	75.72	219.88	4.96	856.16	19.32
1991	5,668.76	4,028.64	71.07	297.14	5.24	1,342.98	23.69
1992	7,625.29	5,419.31	71.07	389.82	5.11	1,816.16	23.82
1993	12,827.09	7,420.92	57.85	642.00	5.01	4,764.14	37.14
1994	16,475.25	8,243.01	50.03	1,220.43	6.19	7,211.81	43.77
1995	17,680.92	7,052.11	39.89	780.46	4.41	9,848.35	55.70
1996	21,599.08	7,125.17	32.99	1,034.98	4.79	13,438.93	62.22
1997	23,104.49	8,147.68	35.26	1,150.79	4.98	13,806.02	59.75
1998	24,858.01	6,128.44	24.65	1,311.02	5.27	17,418.55	70.07

Source: Calculated from Statistical Bureau of Hainan Province, (ed.), *'99 Hainan tongji nianjian* (Hainan Statistical Yearbook of 1999), China Statistical Publishing House (1999: 225).

Notes
The sharp decline of the state sector and rise of the private and foreign sector after 1995 in the table partly resulted from the change of calculation. Since 1995 many "share-holding companies" with various proportion of the state shares have been eventually counted as private or foreign companies if foreign or private investment is involved.

of about US$375 million, involving in growing cash crops and flowers, livestock farming, aquatic farming, and agricultural produce processing (Xing 1997: 25).

However, Hainan's economy has been in trouble since the mid-1990s, due partly to the bad luck of property speculation and partly to the partial reform. There are those who argue that "market communism" and "bureaucratic entrepreneurs" have been the key factors contributing to the steady growth of China's economy during the last two decades (Gore 1998). However, the syndrome of low SOE efficiency has become one of the most persistent ailments of China's economy. Viewing from the provincial perspective, the provinces with a stronger private sector, such as Zhejiang, Jiangsu, and Guangdong, have been faring much better than those provinces with a stronger state sector, such as Heilongjiang, Shaanxi and Shanxi. Hainan shares the characteristics with several special provincial units, such as Beijing and Shanghai, where the state and foreign sectors are both strong. Whereas due to their strategic positions and close connections with the central government Beijing and Shanghai have been able to guarantee state investment to weather the bad times, Hainan experienced a sharp economic downturn in 1994, when the policy of tightening money supply by the central government resulted in a burst property bubble, followed by the negative impacts of Asian financial crisis (Liao and Zhang 1996: 54). In 1992, the growth rate of Hainan's GDP reached 40.2 percent, the highest in the country. It was still at a high level of 20.9 percent in 1993, next only to Guangdong and Shandong.

Hainan's economy took a sharp downturn in 1994, when the GDP growth rate dived to 11.9 percent, ranking sixteenth on the national scale. The rate fell further to humiliating figures of 4.3, 4.8 and 6.7 percent in 1995, 1996, and 1997, respectively, lowest among all provincial units, most of them maintaining double-digit annual growth rate during the same period. Hainan's economy has slowly recovered since 1998 and managed to achieve a growth rate slightly higher than the national average, but it is still facing a grim situation characterized by the slack market demand, the decline of foreign investment, and underdevelopment of the domestic private sector. In his recent report the provincial governor admitted that these "difficulties and problems have to be sufficiently understood and solved" for Hainan to move ahead (Wang 2001).

New migrants in Hainan: origins and types

It is the favorable social and economic conditions described above that have drawn thousands of migrants from the mainland to the island during the 1980s and early 1990s. These migrants can be categorized in terms of motivation, social background, time span, and place of origin. Except for a handful of democratic activists taking refuge on the island after the June Fourth Movement in 1989, all new mainland migrants to Hainan are economic migrants motivated by economic considerations, responding primarily to the push and pull of market forces. However, they are by no means homogeneous.

Little research has been done on the new mainland migrants in Hainan and no sufficient empirical information is available for in-depth analysis. The 100 subjects of this research are not selected strictly through random sampling. Rather, they are selected among the candidates recommended to us by friends, with an eye on representativeness in terms of age, level of education, length of stay, profession, and place of origin, as shown by Tables 4.4–4.8 respectively. It is

Table 4.4 Age groups

Age	20–30	30–40	40–50	50 and above
Number	20	50	20	10

Table 4.5 Level of education

Level	Primary	Junior High	Senior High	University
Number	15	35	12	38

Table 4.6 Length of stay

Years	Less than 3	3–5	5–10	More than 10
Number	6	23	22	49

Table 4.7 Occupation

Occupation	Number
Civil servant	5
Manager	12
Journalist	4
Self-employer (*getihu*)	18
Lawyer	4
Teacher	7
Retiree	8
Servicemen	4
Clerk	8
Engineer	6
Laborer	24

Table 4.8 Place of origin

Province	Number
Sichuan	20
Hubei	11
Henan	11
Jiangxi	10
Hunan	8
Anhui	8
Guizhou	5
Guangxi	4
Yunnan	4
Shanxi	3
Shaanxi	2
Fujian	2
Shandong	1
Zhejiang	1
Jiangsu	1
Dongbei (Liaoning, Jilin, and Heilongjiang)	6
Other	3

regrettable that we failed completely in maintaining the balance of gender due to the reluctance of women to participate in our research. The 100 subjects of our research not only answered our survey questionnaires, but also accepted our brief interviews on a wide range of topics.

In terms of social background, to use McNeill's model pointing not only to different social composition but also to the different capacities of migration groups, they can be neatly divided into two categories, elite migrations and mass migrations (McNeill 1978). The elite group constitutes highly trained, highly skilled, and well-connected officials and professionals organized or recognized by the party-state. After September 1987 when the central government issued a circular announcing the plan to establish the SEZ province of Hainan, thousands of applications were sent all over China to the Preparatory Committee for Establishing Hainan Province, which decided to set up a special "Provincial Centre for Qualified Personnel Exchange" to deal with the applications. By July 1988, three months after the establishment of the Province, the Center had received more than 170,000 applications from the mainland. Most of them did not wait for approval but landed on the island by themselves. A sensational news headline of the year was, "100,000 qualified personnel flood into Hainan." Many of those who were not lucky enough get immediate appointments ended up selling food, newspapers, and other small commodities on the street in Haikou and Sanya (Lu and Xu 1998: 52–54). However, many of them did succeed in getting good jobs and staying in Hainan. For a number of years after the establishment of Hainan Province and the SEZ about 40,000 people migrated officially to the island from the mainland every year, more than half of them taking up positions in Hainan, particularly Haikou, the capital of the province, as entrepreneurs, technicians, managers, or administrators (Zhan 1993: 42–43).

The mass migrants, on the other hand, fall into the official category of the "blindly floating population" (*mangliu*), who usually held a rural *hukou* and just crossed the Qiongzhou Straits with no government approval or any guarantee of work. In the first quarter of 1989, 200,000 such migrants landed in Hainan alone. After taking resolute measures to deter this category of migrants, the number still remained at the level of 120,000–140,000 each year during the period from 1990 to 1992. If lucky, these migrants would become blue-collar workers, but they were predominantly young, and even well educated according to the Chinese standard. A survey in 1992 showed that only 1 percent of them were under 18 and 1.2 percent above 35, with the age group of 18–24 accounting for 81.6 percent. Most of them have received high school or vocational education, with less than 2 percent illiterate (Zhan 1993: 43–44).

As to the place of origin, the establishment of the SEZ province of Hainan attracted migrants from every province in China, as shown by Table 4.9. The provincial distribution of these migrants is uneven. Originally, the majority of these migrants were from the neighboring provinces of Guangdong and Guangxi. The proportion of Guangdong migrants was surprisingly high, accounting for almost 40 percent of the total. However, Guangdong migrants seem to be overwhelmingly sojourners rather than settlers. After the mid-1990s less and less migrants have come from Guangdong and those who had already crossed the Qiongzhou Strait went back home one after another, due to the setback of the Hainan economy and new development opportunities emerging in Guangdong. It is the migrants from those less developed provinces, such as Sichuan, Henan, Anhui, Hubei, and Hunan, that have settled and become permanent residents of Hainan.

Table 4.9 Spatial distribution of migrants in
Hainan by province, 1985–1990

Province	Proportion (%)
Guangdong	39.56
Guangxi	23.05
Sichuan	12.57
Hunan	5.31
Fujian	4.23
Zhejiang	2.50
Hubei	2.11
Henan	1.87
Shandong	1.87
Jiangsu	1.29
Jiangxi	1.29
Anhui	1.16
Guizhou	0.64
Hebei	0.43
Yunnan	0.40
Beijing	0.39
Jilin	0.35
Heilongjiang	0.34
Shaanxi	0.34
Gansu	0.31
Liaoning	0.31
Xinjiang	0.30
Shanghai	0.21
Hong Kong, Macao, and other countries	0.18
Tianjin	0.12
Xizang	0.11
Inner Mongolia	0.08
Qinghai	0.08
Shanxi	0.06
Ningxia	0.01

Source: Calculated from the 10% sample of the fourth
national population census in 1992. Quoted
in Zhan Changzhi, chief editor, *Zhongguo
renkou—Hainan fence* (Population of China—
Hainan Volume), Beijing: Zhongguo caizheng
jingji chubanshe (1993: 91).

Chineseness, Hainaneseness, and translocalism

In dealing with the issues of translocality in Hainan, it might be useful to compare
the concepts of translocalism and transnationalism. Transnationalism is usually
defined as a social process whereby migrants operate in social fields that
transgress geographic, political and cultural borders (Glick Schiller *et al.* 1992).
The core of this concept refers to communities spreading across national borders,
creating networks beyond national borders, and taking part in exchange between

or among spatially separated component groups. These communities are characterized by the multiple affinities, and troubled by ambivalent or divided loyalties toward "home" in the country of residence or "home" in the country of origin (Van Hear 1998: 241–250). Translocalism is similar in that it also connotes multiple place attachments identities. However, translocalism does not usually involve a conflict of political and national loyalties. Translocalism in China points to the idea and practice of turning place identities into ambiguity and complexity. It does not necessarily apply to just migrants, but a broader set of networks link-ing people's identities to more than one place. In the case of Hainan, since the 1980s both Hainaneseness and Chineseness have been negotiated anew, fashioning a translocal mode of identification.

Translocal networks are very important for the new migrants, as well as for locals. In answering the question "Who is the first person you seek help from when you run into difficulty?," 71 percent of our respondents nominated "friends." As a matter of fact, for those who have settled in Hainan, most of them have done it through the assistance of social networks. Few, if any, mainlanders who are appointed to a senior position in a company or the government in Hainan have not brought over some acquaintance, usually *laoxiang* (fellow-townsman or fellow-villager). In the meantime, locals see the new migrants as a new source of skills and social capital. Among the 170,000 applicants mentioned earlier and other applicants handing in their applications to the Hainan Provincial Centre for Qualified Personnel Exchange, only less than 10,000 of them have succeeded in getting a position through the official channel of the Centre from 1987–2000 (Zhan 2001: 266). Others have found their way through their own networks, either the existing old one or the new one created after landing on the island. Many of the new migrants and locals join together to establish commercial networks for the sales of local specialities, such as tropical fruits, on the mainland.

After being settled, many of the new migrants have continued to maintain the networks of *laoxiang* as well as the linkage with their relatives and friends left behind at their native place. The governing style of the party-state has prevented them from organizing "common native place associations," common among the migrants during the period of the Republican China and among overseas Chinese all over the world. Instead, restaurants specialized in provincial cuisines have become the most important meeting points for *laoxiang*, many of them joining together regularly to speak their native dialects, enjoy their native dishes of food, exchange information, and provide mutual moral support. The elite groups usu-ally meet at the private rooms of these restaurants to enjoy native delicacies and discuss job opportunities and business opportunities, whereas the mass groups usually meet at the hall for consumption at a lower price. Locals and migrants from other parts of China for their part also come to these specialized restaurants, enjoying different provincial cuisines and customs, which would otherwise not be available but for the mass migration.

Remittance to relatives back home at the place of origin is a common practice among blue-collar *mingong* (peasant-workers) from less developed provinces, but not among the elite groups of migrants, who usually do not have poor families or

Table 4.10 Monthly remittances to native place by migrants in Hainan

Amount (RMB¥)	Less than 50	50–100	100–200	More than 200
% of total Interviewees	17	46	27	10

relatives back on the mainland to support. Since the majority of these *mingong* earn a monthly income of RMB¥300–1,200, the amount of remittances to support their relatives back home is quite significant, as shown by Table 4.10. Given the fact that most of them come from rural areas where monthly household income is less than RMB¥300, their remittances amount to 25–50 percent of the household income. For those migrants who have left their families behind, their remittances form the major sources of their household income back home. For those who have established their own families, their remittances are also very important for their parents, brothers, and sisters.

Close ties with the place of origin notwithstanding, a slow process of integration is also underway in Hainan. Integration of migrants with the host society is a complicated issue. People move with their cultures, and the presence of immigrant communities inevitably generates a point of comparison and contrast with indigenous cultures. The interaction between immigrant and host communities is bound to create and transform patterns of social relationships and cultural power. The Hainan experience is quite special in China. As usual, the mainland migrants to Hainan before 1949 tended to localize themselves and adopt local culture, including local dialects and customs. In other words, they had been assimilated into the host society. Their followers after 1949, however, have been too proud to learn from local culture. In the Mao era, "internal colonialism" was the best term to describe the relationship between the mainland and Hainan. After the "liberation" of Hainan in 1950, particularly after the crackdown on "Hainanese localism" and the purge of Feng Baiju and his followers in 1957, Hainan's politics became dominated by cadres from the mainland who supplanted the relatively numerous and well-organized local Hainanese communists who had fought against the Nationalist regime and the Japanese for three decades (Wu and He 1996). From 1950 to 1980 industrialization and urbanization of the "treasure island," which could supply strategic materials such as rubber and iron ore for China, were sacrificed for development elsewhere in China. Hainan has always had abundant natural resources, but there was little attempt from either central or Guangdong governments to provide the additional processing industries for their development. Locals were required to almost exclusively cultivate grain, particularly rice, to feed themselves and the mainland immigrants, rather than the other profitable tropical crops suited to the environment. Many of the New Mainlanders regard themselves as explorers, pioneers, and pathbreakers to develop the "backward" island. (Jiang 1991). They have exploited the hierarchical ordering of languages and dialects to reverse the positions of the host and the guest on the island. While a thick local accent is common everywhere in China, mainlanders in Hainan have succeeded in establishing proficiency in standard Mandarin as one of the most important factors for appointment in government and other professions.[1] This has contributed to the tension between the mainland and native communities on the island and the contestation for different versions of the Hainanese identity or Hainanese culture (Feng and Goodman 1997: 53–88; Feng 1999).

It is precisely the dominant position that provides a key incentive for the elite group of New Mainlanders to identify with Hainan. Given Hainan's policy of importing "qualified personnel" many of the new mainlanders have been able to secure desirable positions before leaving the mainland. Because few Hainanese can speak anything like unaccented Mandarin, the restructuring of Hainan government, the reopening of Hainan University, the restructuring and expanding of Hainan Teacher's College, Hainan Provincial Party School, and art and mass media institutions, and the establishment of new research institutes, new research centres and new firms have created golden opportunities for the mainlanders to seek dominant positions. Except for several token appointments, the native Hainanese communities have been very poorly represented in the top provincial leadership consisting of provincial Party secretaries, governors and vice-governors since the establishment of Hainan province. Among current officials at the provincial level, three quarters of them are not from Hainan. Among the total of seven members of the university leadership and nine deans at Hainan University, only one is from Hainan for each group. Those from the community of New Mainlanders have even accounted for two-thirds of the "Outstanding Entrepreneurs of Hainan" and "Model Entrepreneurs of Hainan" selected through the ballot organized twice by the Hainan Provincial Entrepreneurs Association. The normal case of the "immigrant other" being dominated the host society has been reversed on the island.

When first crossing the Qiongzhou Strait to accept those promising appointments, many new migrants even left their families behind or kept their official residence registration back on the mainland. They have contributed to and benefited from the development of the new province. Of those interviewed, 49 percent have stayed for more than ten years and 70 percent range from 30 to 50 years of age. This means that most of them were between 20 and 30 years of age when they came to Hainan in the late 1980s or early 1990s. These mainland professionals have laid down a solid foundation for their career and established stable families and social networks on the island, which has become their only home or at least the second home (*di er guxiang*). Most of them (70 percent) regard themselves as a Hainanese.

Professor Cheng, 56, from Yunnan, was a manager of a firm back in Yunnan. He came to the island in 1987 when Hainan Province was about to be formally established. He has changed his occupation and serves as an academic now. He told us that he enjoyed very much the free atmosphere in Hainan. His annual income is more than RMB¥50,000 and he already owns a private car, although he has not achieved his original goal in terms of his career development. He regards close relationships with native Hainanese very important for the mainland migrants. He has a Hainan *hukou* and many Hainanese friends, and believes the *hukou* system should be abolished. Mr Hu, 40, divorced, from Anhui, has a BA degree and is editor-in-chief of an Internet website. He came to Hainan in 1988 when it became a province. He has now got Hainan *hukou* and proudly regards himself as Hainanese. He has many friends of Hainanese origin and is very satisfied with his life in Hainan. Mr Huang, 47, from Jiangxi, is a university graduate. He came to Hainan with his wife in 1996, leaving behind their only child who had graduated from university, and got a job. He works in Haikou as a private medical practitioner and has made many native Hainanese friends. He likes Hainan very much and is in the process of getting a Hainan *hukou*. Mr Wang, 23, from Shandong, is a university dropout and trained as a computer technician. He has been in Hainan for only four years but has done a lot and become much better off. He once owned a small shop, ran an Internet cafe, worked as an Internet administrator and created many Web sites. He is collaborating with several friends from Hainan and other parts of China to set up a company specialized in tourism and the Internet. They have rented a house of more than 100 square meters for that purpose. Mr Wang is very confident of his future and has a plan to settle in Hainan. He has found a girlfriend of Hainanese origin and they will get married soon.

The group of the mass migration are not as lucky in settling in Hainan, nor are they as strong in identifying with Hainan. The topic of *hukou* commands serious attention during the interviews with the elite group, but it is not hard for them to acquire a Hainan *hukou* for permanent residency. The outmoded *hukou* system remains the single most important obstacle for migrant peasant-workers to be integrated into the host society of Hainan. Among 100 interviewees 67 percent are originally from the countryside before their migration, leaving 17 percent from towns and 16 percent from cities. However, 94 percent of them give a positive answer to the question "Are you satisfied with your overall situation of work and life in Hainan?" The result of this survey has clearly shown that the group of peasant-workers are also willing to stay longer or permanently if possible in Hainan. The most important reason emerging during the interviews is that it is relatively relaxing and easier to make money in Hainan as a SEZ. However, they are fully aware of their vulnerability of not having a status of the government employee and a permanent residency *hukou* in Hainan. Hainan is the first province in China to set up a comprehensive social security net covering "all sectors" by ownership, but actually covers only the urban workforce with a permanent Hainan *hukou*. Unlike the migrants of the elite group, peasant-workers do not have access to the state benefits, including housing, health care, pensions, unemployment insurance, kindergartens, and schools. During the interviews they repeatedly explained that they did not expect any benefits or assistance from the government, and what they did expect from the government was to trouble them less and leave them alone. They rely entirely on their social networks newly created on the island for survival and development. Even for those who have successfully established their promising small business on the island, they are still facing great uncertainty for their future. Mr Zhang, 21, is an owner operator of an audio/video shop. He enjoys the favourable climate, environment and economic opportunities. He expressed a strong desire to settle down in Hainan, and even find a local bride. But the lack of a local *hukou* may prevent his dream from coming true.

Apart from these two groups of professionals and peasant-workers, Hainan in recent years has also become a destination for the migration of retirees from the mainland. According to one newspaper report, there are no less than 50,000 retirees from the mainland buying property and living in Hainan permanently (Wang 2002). They are no doubted attracted by the relaxing lifestyle, as well as the favorable climate and environment on the island. Mr Wang, over 50, is a retiree from Shanxi. He came to Hainan in 1998 for the purpose of enjoying his life of retirement. He clearly enjoys the fresh air, the friendly environment, and the relaxing social atmosphere on the island. He is trying his best to adapt to the host society. Mr Wang admits that his life has changed in some ways since he came to Hainan. He used to prefer meat and wheaten food for meals, but now he likes seafood and rice too. Wang also goes to local teahouses frequently, the "old dad teahouse" in particular, to meet his friends.

Current mainland migrants in Hainan regard native Hainanese as warm, easy to get along with, and trustworthy, contrary to the overwhelming perception of Cantonese xenophobia (*paiwai*) among the migrants from other provinces in Guangdong (Wang 1992). In answering the question "Do you have many friends of Hainanese origin?," the replies of "many" and "not a few" accounted for 96 percent, leaving only 4 percent of our respondents with a reply of "few." Yu Qiuyu, a famous cultural critic from Shanghai praises Hainanese culture as a "maternal civilization (*muxing wenming*)" with the virtues of a "soft, peaceful and natural beauty" and a "homeland civilisation (*jiayuan wenming*)" attaching more importance to daily family life than anything else. According to him, "it is lucky that the strait shelters Hainan from the dryness, bitter cold and restlessness, enabling the island to develop and keep a natural and hence normal maternal civilisation and homeland civilisation. However, such a civilisation is bound to become challenging and subversive when encountering the mainland," which for thousands of years has followed an abnormal track, indulging in manoeuvre, erection of monuments, endless struggle, persecution and rehabilitation (Yu 1994). This seems to reflect the perception of Hainan by those mainland migrants who feel at home among locals, although Yu's assertion reveals more of his own disappointment with the politics on the mainland rather than providing a faithful account of the reality on the island.

At the level of popular culture there are also signs of joint efforts by migrants and locals to create a new Hainanese culture. As many as 65 percent of our respondents replied that they would not learn to speak Hainanese even if they were provided with opportunities to learn it, with the reason that they do not feel it's difficult to communicate with native Hainanese. This statement does contain a strong element of mainlander superiority, but it is partly true that most locals, including those villagers over middle age who never spoke Mandarin before, have managed to speak Mandarin and are ready to accept the mainland communities. The vocabulary of daily language on the island has grown rapidly during last two decades due to massive imports from other parts of China. New traditions catering to the needs of both locals and migrants have been invented on the island.[2] One striking example of these new traditions is the annual International Coconut Festival. The idea of the festival came from three mainlanders who felt homesick and wanted to celebrate the brotherhood of mainlanders on the island. The first Coconut Festival was organized in 1992 with corporate sponsorship. It was taken over by the provincial government in the second year, but after several years it was handed back again to the corporate sector due to financial difficulties of the provincial government. The coconut is believed to be the symbol of Hainan among the Chinese. And the time is set in early April to coincide with the Qingming Festival highly valued by the locals and the Third March Festival (lunar calendar) which is the most important festival of the Li.[3] Major features of the festival include various programs of entertainment for visitors from the mainland and abroad, exhibitions of local products, and bids for investment projects and other commercial activities.

Another example is the emergence of Mrs Xian (*Xian Furen* 522–602) as the most important deity on the island. Mrs Xian was born into a prominent family of a tribe active in Gaoliang Prefecture (now Yangjiang in west Guangdong) and became the most powerful tribe leader herself. This period is known in Chinese history as Northern and Southern Dynasties (420–581), characterized by chaos of wars, successive turmoil, and frequent change of dynasties. Mrs Xian succeeded in conquering various tribes and maintaining stability in the vast area of today's west Guangdong, east Guangxi, and Hainan. More importantly to the Chinese, she kept the tribe leaders of this area loyal to the central government in spite of frequent change of dynasties and accelerated the process of assimilating various tribes to the Han. According to Chinese history, Hainan was first brought into the Chinese territory by the Han Dynasty, but the rule of the central government from north China over this island was at best nominal. It was Mrs Xian who put down tribe rebellions and finally convinced the tribe leaders in Hainan to submit to the central government. As a matter of fact, the Li in Hainan remained rebellious throughout Chinese history until modern times. This explains why Mrs Xian has been turned into a deity in Hainan but not at her hometown in Guangdong. No later than during the Ming Dynasty (1368–1644) temples were built and the *Junpo* (military slope) Festival was created in the northeast part of Hainan for the worship of Mrs Xian. The peculiar part of this festival is that the date varies from one place to another starting from February 9 until June 21 in the lunar year. It features a large-scale parade, entertainment performance and fair trade, and is celebrated by the entire population at a given locality regardless of geographical or ethnic origins. The origin of this tradition and translocal deity can be attributed to the desire of mainland migrants for celebration of "harmony" between migrants and locals, and between the Han and other ethnic groups. After establishment of Hainan Province, Mrs Xian has been upgraded to the most powerful deity in Hainan, due to promotion by the local state media and the involvement of the provincial government in the celebration of the *Junpo* Festival at the outskirts of the provincial capital Haikou on February 9 in the lunar year, attracting thousands of visitors to offer joss sticks at the Mrs Xian Temple for their better future, such as promotion for officials, wealth for business people, and safety for taxi drivers.

This leads us again to the theme of translocalism. The mainland migrants' identification with Hainan definitely means to identify with the place of their residence to various extents, but not necessarily identify with cultures or the existing set of practices on the island. Instead, there seems to be an emerging consensus among the mainlanders and native communities on the island to join their efforts in creating a New Hainan characterized by a new-found modernity. Substitution of a maritime China for a landlocked China is a national project, as exemplified by the national policy of and public discourse on *kaifang* (opening to the outside world). Due to its strong overseas links particularly with overseas Hainanese in south-east Asia and beyond, the outward-looking Hainanese culture is constructed as a contrast with the allegedly inward-looking and conservative culture of traditional China. The single most important objective for reformers to establish a provincial-level SEZ on Hainan was to precisely carry out "ahead-of-time experiments (*chaoqian shiyan*)" for economic and political reforms in China. The new province was expected to build a new and distinct political and economic system based on new principles such as the "socialist market economy" and "small government, large society." The special image of the New Hainan is linked by local officials and academic alike with the "SEZ consciousness (*tequ yishi*)," which is interpreted as a sense of mission for Hainan to take the lead in China in transforming the old style party-state and establishing a market economy articulated with the international practice (Bao 1998). For all communities in Hainan, cosmopolitan Hong Kong is the best model, as indicated by their zeal to "create another Hong Kong (*zaizao xianggang*)" (Zhong 1995). This is a clear indication that a new place identity is informed by translocal imaginary. In response to the campaign launched by the provincial government in 1999 to "make concerted efforts in creating Hainan image (*qixin suzao Hainan xingxiang*)," they argue that "openness is the most important image of Hainan." It is because of the "image of openness" that Hainan has been able to attract investment from other parts of China and the world, to attract qualified people of various talents, and to achieve high speed reforms and development. According to them, Hainan should adopt even more liberal policies in China to attract investment and talents, and experimenting bolder reforms to shape up its economy and administrative systems (Shi 1999; Zhou 2002).

Conclusion

The reform and erosion of many of the traditional party-state control mechanisms, the *danwei* system and *hukou* system in particular, have contributed to the emergence of a relatively open labor market on Hainan, which in turn has attracted massive migrations from the mainland. They have managed to keep their old identities of their place of origin while acquiring a new identity linked to their place of residence; and they have maintained the social networks while seeking integration with the host society. In this way, they have become a translocal community characterized by varying commitments, varying allegiance, and multiple affinities and loyalties toward their place of origin and their place of residence.

Internal colonialism of mainlanders is still evident in Hainan and tensions between communities are not far from the surface. However, it has been argued elsewhere that cultural contest on the island may also lead to a synthesis (Feng 1999). In the long run, it is not beyond imagination that the Li, Hainanese and the mainlanders will reach the same destination in creating a new Hainanese culture centered on the concepts of opening and internationalization, which is not only pursued by all communities on Hainan with great enthusiasm but also entailed and facilitated by the position of Hainan in the forefront of China's reform and opening. This goal can be achieved through mutual assimilation and enrichment between different communities on the island as well as increasing exposure to intense foreign influence. The Li are exposed to unprecedented external influence and more ready to make changes and meet challenges than at any time in the past. Despite resentment Hainanese are learning from the mainlanders and improving their skills in every aspect, including Mandarin. The mainlanders, arrogance notwithstanding, may not be able to maintain the purity of the Mandarin culture and resist localization over time, as the experience of their predecessors would seem to indicate. At least a minority of mainlanders have made great efforts to learn the Hainanese dialect. As early as in 1993, a mainlander took the lead in editing and publishing a Hainanese–Mandarin–English dictionary to assist the endeavor (Wang and Li 1998). In spite of tensions and conflicts, a new Hainan is emerging where localization of the mainlanders, sinicization of Hainanese and the Li, and everyone's internationalization are all well under way.

In the history of modern China, Shanghai once played a dominant role in defining Chinese modernity or modern Chineseness (Wang 1999: 118–134). During the reform era, the SEZs, Shenzhen and Hainan in particular, have been thrusting to repeat the role played by Shanghai in modern China. At least this has been one of the objectives pursued by the reformers. After China being virtually sealed off from the Western world for three decades, the establishment of the SEZs did send a shockwave throughout China and the world. The SEZs, as Shanghai in modern China, have attracted a galaxy of innovative or venturous talents drawn by the approved openness allowing far more leeway to challenge the Confucian and Maoist convention, to adopt international practices, and to experiment new approaches. In this sense negotiation of a Hainanese identity is but a continuation of the unfinished modern transformation of Chineseness started in Shanghai and elsewhere more than a century ago.

Notes

1 According to Pierre Bourdieu's theory on symbolic power, by legitimating the official language, the policy of linguistic unification would subordinate those who knew only a local dialect to those who already possessed the official language as part of their linguistic competence. Pierre Bourdieu, *Language and Symbolic Power* (English

translation by Gino Raymond and Mathew Adamson, Cambridge: Polity Press, 1991),
chapter 1. For a brilliant elaboration of correspondence between a hierarchical ordering
of languages and political power in Europe, see Ralph D. Grillo, *Dominant Languages:
Language and Hierarchy in Britain and France* (Cambridge: Cambridge University
Press, 1989), chapter 1 in particular. For an interesting discussion on Gramscian theory
of hegemony, see Paul Ransome, *Antonio Gramsci: A New Introduction* (London:
Harvester Wheatsheaf, 1992).

2 For the difference between "traditions" and "invented traditions," see Eric Hobsbawm,
"Introduction," in Eric Hobsbawm and Terence Ranger (eds), *The Invention of Tradition*
(Cambridge: Cambridge University Press, 1983), 1–14.

3 According to the Li myth the Li and even the entire humankind are descendants of the
Li couple who met on March 3, lunar year. For the Li, March 3 is a festival for both love
affairs and commemoration of the ancestry.

References

Bao, Y. (1998) "Jian sheng shi nian de tequ yishi" ("Special zone consciousness in the last
ten years since the establishment of Hainan Province"), *Hainan Ribao*, March 7.

Cheng, T. and Selden, M. (1994) "The origin and social consequence of China's Hukou
System," *The China Quarterly* 139 (September 1994): 644–668.

Feng, C. (1999) "Seeking lost codes in the wildness: the search for a Hainanese culture,"
The China Quarterly 160 (December 1999): 1037–1056.

Feng, C. and Goodman, D. S. G. (1997) "Hainan: communal politics and the struggle for
identity," in D. S. G. Goodman (ed.) *China's Provinces in Reform: Class, Community
and Political Culture*, London and New York: Routledge: 48–88.

——(1998) "Hainan in reform: political dependence and economic interdependence,"
in P. Cheung, J. H. Chung, and Z. Lin (eds) *Provincial Strategies of Economic
Reform in Post-Mao China: Leadership, Politics and Implementation*, Armonk, NY:
M. E. Sharpe.

Glick Schiller, N., Bash, L., and Blanc-Szanton, C. (eds) (1992) *Towards a Transnational
Perspective on Migration: Race, Class, Ethnicity, and Nationalism Reconsidered*,
New York: New York Academy of Sciences.

Gore, L. L. P. (1998) *Market Communism: The Institutional Foundation of China's
Post-Mao Hyper-Growth*, Hong Kong: Oxford University Press.

Hainan Provincial Government (2001) "Hainan sheng guomin jingji he shehui fazhan di
shi ge wu nian jihua gangyao" ("Outline of the Tenth Five-Year-Plan for Economic and
Social Development in Hainan Province"), *Hainan Ribao* (Hainan Daily), March 2.

Jiang, W. (ed.) (1991) *Tequ sheng de guanlizhe men* (Administrators in the Provincial
SEZ), Beijing: Zhongguo Jingji Chubanshe.

Li, L. and Li, H. (2000) *Zhongguo de danwei zuzhi: ziyuan, quanli yu jiaohuan* (China's
Danwei: Resources, Power and Exchange), Hangzhou: Zhejiang renmin chubanshe.

Liao, X. and Zhang, J. (1996) *Zouchu "paomo": Hainan jingji fazhan zhanlue zhuanzhe*
(Getting Over the "Bubble": An Abrupt Turn in Hainanese Economic Development
Strategy), Hakou: Nanhai Chuban Gongsi.

Lin, D. (1999) "Situation and Strategies of Attracting Foreign Capital to Hainan," *Hainan
Ribao* (Hainan Daily), June 14.

Lu, B. and Xu, B. (1998) *Zhongguo da tequ de shinian biange* (Changes in the Big SEZ
of China during the Last Ten Years), Beijing: Zhongyang dangxiao chubanshe.

Lu, X. and Perry, E. (eds) (1997) *Danwei: The Changing Chinese Workplace in Historical
and Comparative Perspective*, Armonk, NY: M.E. Sharpe.

McNeill, W. H. (1978) "Human migration: an historical overview," in W. H. McNeill and R. S. Adams (eds) *Human Migration: Pattern and Politics*, Bloomington, IN: Indiana University Press.

Shi, F. (1999) "Nuli shuli Hainan de kaifang xingxiang (Make efforts to create an openness image of Hainan)," *Hainan Ribao* (Hainan Daily), February 8.

Statistical Bureau of Hainan Province (ed.) (1999) *'99 Hainan tongji nianjian,* (Hainan Statistical Yearbook of 1999), Beijing: China Statistical Publishing House.

Van Hear, N. (1998) *New Diaspora: The Mass Exodus, Dispersal and Regrouping of Migrant Communities*, Seattle, WA: University Washington Press.

Wang, G. (1999) "Chineseness: the dilemmas of place and practice," in G. Hamilton (ed.) *Cosmopolitan Capitalists: Hong Kong and the Chinese Diaspora at the End of the Twentieth Century*, Seattle, WA and London: University of Washington Press.

Wang, S. and Li, Q. (eds) (1998) *Hainan hua putong hua yingyu changyong kouyu duizhao 888 ju* (888 Sentences of Spoken Language in Hainanese, Mandarin and English), Haikou: Hainan chuban gongci, 1993; reprinted 1998.

Wang, X. (2001) "Guanyu Hainan sheng guomin jingji he shehui fazhan di shi ge wu nian jihua gangyao de baogao" ("Report on the outline of the Tenth Five-Year-Plan for Economic and Social Development in Hainan Province"), *Hainan Ribao* (Hainan Daily), March 3.

Wang, Z. (1992) *Nan zhongguo jishi* (True Stories from South China), Chengdu: Sichuan renbin chubanshe.

Wang, Z. (2002) "Hainan de yimin" ("Migrants in Hainan"), *Hainan Ribao* (Hainan Daily), January 18.

Wu, Z. and He, L. (1996) *Feng Baiju Zhuan* (A Biography of Feng Baiju), Beijing: Dangdai zhongguo chubanshe.

Xing, Y. (ed.) (1997) *Hainan gaige chao* (Reform Tides in Hainan), Haikou: Hainan chubanshe.

Yan, Z. and Yu, Q. (1996) *Zhongguo huji zhidu gaige* (The Reform of China's Household Registration System), Beijing: Zhongguo zhengfa daxue chubanshe.

Yu, Q. (1994) "Tianya gushi" ("Stories from the end of the earth"), *Shouhua* (Harvest) 2.

Zhan, C. (ed.) (1993) *Zhongguo renkou—Hainan fence* (Population of China—Hainan Volume), Beijing: Zhongguo caizheng jingji chubanshe.

—— (2001) "Jiasu renli ziben jilei shi shixian ke shixu fazhan de biyou zhilu" ("Accelerating accumulation of human capital is the only way for sustainable development in Hainan"), in *2001 nian Hainan lilun yantaohui lunwenji* (A Collection of Articles from the Hainan Theoretical Conference in 2001), Haikou: Hainan chubanshe.

Zhong, Y.(1995) "Hainan zai zao xianggang de neihan jiqi yunzuo" ("The way to create another Hong Kong on Hainan"), in Zhong Yechang (ed.) *Hainan tequ gaige kaifang yu fazhan* (Reform, opening and development in the Hainan SEZ), Beijing: Zhongguo shehui kexue chubanshe.

Zhou W. (2002) "Laoji jingji tequ de diwei he renwu" ("Keep firm in mind the position and mission of SEZ"), *Hainan Ribao* (Hainan Daily), March 13.

5 Corporate locality and translocality of private enterprises in China

Hans Hendrischke

Introduction

New found economic mobility has been one of the hallmarks of Reform China. Mobility of people, capital, goods and services is changing the country more thoroughly than any time in the past when long distance trade moved goods and people across boundaries and created new settlements and local cultures (see the chapter by David Faure and Helen Siu's in this volume). Private entrepreneurs in particular have benefited from the new found mobility as they engage in national and international trade. Economic mobility primarily and most obviously relates to the operational reach of enterprises into national and international markets. From a current globalized market perspective, operational mobility is easily taken for granted, even though China's domestic markets are the product of institutional reforms that lasted through most of the 1980s and 1990s (Findlay 1992). The operational mobility in business transactions, however, does not find its correspondence in the structural corporate mobility of private enterprises, that is, their ability to move their corporate structure from one territorial jurisdiction to another. There is a general consensus in research literature that private enterprises in China are thoroughly embedded in their localities. "Local" enterprises are subject to formal and informal institutional restrictions that tie them to the locality from where they have emerged. In spite of their wide-spread and expanding business transactions, these enterprises are characterized by strong local ties and resulting corporate immobility. Putting aside the issue of operational translocality, this chapter will focus on structural or corporate locality and translocality of private enterprises in China.

The translocal research agenda presented by Oakes and Schein in their introduction to this volume provides useful concepts for analyzing the locality of Chinese enterprises. For Oakes and Schein, China's translocal vision of the past tied "subjectivities not just to the locality but to any and all localities simultaneously" and was an ideology as much as a material reality. This equally applies to the present. Ideological aspects of corporate translocality have been addressed in Hoffman's chapter on Dalian in this volume. Arguably, even official Chinese statements proclaiming that translocality exists across national, regional or even provincial unified markets and institutions can be normative or ideological.

Material aspects of translocality are not only manifest in the movement of goods and people, but also in the formation and operation of economic institutions. In a transition economy like China it is not at all clear how governments and enterprises at different local levels create formal and informal institutions for enterprises to be established and to operate. This involves the agenda of the state, because institutions do not necessarily have the same boundaries as the territorial subdivisions of the state and can be contested. Taking up Lefebvre's (1974) suggestion that the state can be opposed to the local, the following analysis of how institutions are formed at different local levels will specifically explore the interlinkage between the state and the local; in brief, how localities fill the institutional void that is left by the Chinese state with its weak formal economic institutions.

Private enterprises come with a variety of local ties. A large proportion of the small and medium sized enterprises which have emerged from two decades of privatization are local because they were either owned by local state organizations as county-level state-owned enterprises (SOEs) or collectives, or under the control of township and village institutions as township and village enterprises (TVEs). Other types of enterprises were set up by private entrepreneurs or by networks linking different forms of shareholders (Krug and Hendrischke 2003). These enterprises have undergone various stages of transition to privatization which depended on support or patronage from local authorities and institutions. "Local enterprise" is therefore often used synonymously with private or small enterprise. The various institutional set-ups for corporatization and privatization of these enterprises, whether they are characterized as state entrepreneurialism, local state corporatism or public–private network structures, share one point in common: they tie enterprises firmly to local authorities and specific local institutional set-ups.

Recent interviews with private enterprises in Zhejiang and Jiangsu indicate that this situation is gradually changing as a result of the current full-scale privatization at local level and concomitant tax reform. For local governments at township (*zhen*) or city district (*qu*) level, the focus of economic policy is shifting from internal control of enterprises (Walder 1995) to external control and maximization of tax revenue. Where local authorities before profited from their control over individual enterprises, they now benefit from creating a better and more open institutional environment that attracts more enterprises and investment into their jurisdiction. However, this does not create a unified institutional environment across different localities. After full privatization, the most efficient way for local authorities to maximize their revenue is to offer incentives to enterprises. This has resulted in horizontal and, to a lesser degree, vertical competition between local state authorities. Private enterprises, intent on exploiting different local incentives, have responded with new localization strategies and by developing translocal enterprise structures. This trend signals the beginning of a new phase in public and corporate governance in China and brings to the fore the continued relevance of locality and translocality for China's private enterprise sector.

This chapter explores the institutional aspects of locality and translocality for private firms. Their locality and translocality are seen as constructed through specific institutional mechanisms. Locality for a firm is defined less by the administrative territorial unit in which it resides, than by where the firm is embedded in an institutional set-up. Structural translocality is not achieved by expanding business reach nor is it a matter of perception. Instead, translocality has to be constructed in the form of institutional linkages that enable enterprises to cross jurisdictional boundaries. Analysis of public–private interaction between local authorities and enterprises has to shift its focus from one locality to multiple localities. Translocality in the process of China's privatization and economic transition is unfolding in varying ways and speeds in different localities. Eventually, this process might lead to an open institutional environment which provides for full enterprise mobility and where local differences become irrelevant. At this stage, however, locality of private enterprises remains strong and the conditions for corporate translocality have to be constructed locally by enterprises and governments, leading to specific local and potentially specific Chinese forms of corporate mobility.

The following sections will first provide an explanation for the institutional diversity at local level, in particular in terms of property rights and business environments; second, argue that recent large-scale privatization and improved local tax administration created the conditions for competition between local authorities and delocalization of enterprises; third, detail forms of corporate translocality by analyzing institutional responses of enterprises; and fourth, draw some conclusions.

The study is part of a larger project which so far has produced over 100 extensive interviews with private entrepreneurs conducted between 2000 and 2004 in Hangzhou and Suzhou and surrounding areas in Zhejiang and Jiangsu, plus additional interviews with local tax officials and local government and Party cadres.[1] Each enterprise interview had an open-ended part which focused on the types of links between enterprises and local state authorities and their impact on privatization. The interviews with entrepreneurs are the primary sources for this report and are given more weight than public policies or official studies which confirm local variations, but provide little institutional detail (Huang 2003). One caveat that applies to every study based on local information is that the findings do not claim to be representative for the whole of the country, even though the experience of the early movers presented here may spread to other provinces, as will be shown.

Localization of enterprises

The local embeddedness of China's small private enterprise sector has drawn attention from different academic disciplines. Sociologists have looked at the political alliances of private enterprises (Wank 1995) and explored their links with the local socio-political environment (Unger and Chan 1995; Unger and Chan 1999; Goodman 2000). Political scientists and institutional economists have developed the concepts of local state corporatism (Oi 1999), state entrepreneurialism (Duckett 1998) and entrepreneurial culture (Krug 2002). Detailed studies exist on the role of the local environment in transforming SOEs (Guthrie 1999; Wank 1999) and TVEs (Vermeer 1996; Sun *et al.* 1999; Sun 2000). These studies, including some detailed provincial studies published in China (Hu and Cao 2001; Wan 2001; Huang and Fu 2002), note the wide local variance that exists at every level of local administration, in particular with regard to economic reform policies. In most detailed studies, local variance is seen as a positive aspect of China's transition process and less as an inability of the central state to provide a unified legal environment with strong formal institutions. While there is ample descriptive evidence on informal institutions, little systematic work has been done on how these informal institutions do make up for the lack of formal institutions (but see Xin and Pearce 1996; Nee 2000). One important aspect of how informal institutions differ from formal institutions is their localized nature. Localized ties between authorities and individual enterprises create the informal institutional basis for the local private economy to function. Enterprises depend on local authorities to provide a degree of institutional security. Local authorities in turn rely on their links with enterprises for local economic and social welfare, mainly for revenue and employment. In the absence of a general institutional consensus between state and local enterprises, mutual benefit in the transition process is achieved by intertwining local authorities and enterprises through various forms of shareholding, stake holding or networks. The diversification in local institutional environments finds an exemplary explanation in the process of enterprise reform and privatization in the two provinces of Zhejiang and Jiangsu which are ahead of most other provinces in establishing private property rights.

From the enterprise interviews in Zhejiang and Jiangsu emerges a tiered process of implementation of national privatization policies that allows local governments at different levels in the hierarchy to adapt central policies to the economic and political preferences within their administrative reach. National policies can be adapted to "local circumstances." As a consequence, property rights for private enterprises issued at central level in the form of new laws or government regulations are not automatically enforced at local level. Central laws and regulations may be phrased as binding regulations and presented as such in official publications, but at local level they are perceived more as policy recommendations and implemented in a trickle down process through the various layers of local governments. It is important to note that the layers of local governments down from provinces to townships (provinces, prefectures, counties, townships as well as cities at the various levels) function as nested hierarchies where one level only reaches down to the next level. At each level, local authorities have a degree of discretion to adapt these policies to their local circumstances and to differentiate themselves from neighboring communities. This applies even to village level authorities which do not possess formal government status. As each subsequent level of administration is not obliged to fully enforce the implementation of policies that are passed down the hierarchy, no two localities are necessarily the same. This produces a wide variety of informal local institutions. In analogy to Kornai's (1986) hard and soft budget constraints, this situation could be described in terms of "soft institutional constraints." Soft institutional constraints allow localities to delay (or anticipate) the implementation of central policies. At the same time, hardening of institutional constraints occurs as more localities gradually implement central policies and a local consensus emerges. This consensus puts political pressure on lower-level local authorities to avoid lagging too far behind other localities. The remarkable feature is that the actual institutions are built up from below.

One set of "soft institutional constraints" can be observed in the implementation of national policies at provincial and local levels. These are documented in the research literature on government negotiations and bargaining (Lieberthal and Lampton 1992) and on the effects of "nested hierarchies" in local taxation (Wong 2002). Another set of "soft institutional constraints" operates in the relationship between local authorities and enterprises undergoing privatization. Local authorities are able to claim "local circumstances" if they want to modify provincial or national policies for their locality. As a consequence, local enterprises are forced to make arrangements and solve conflicts with their local authorities and without legal recourse to national (or provincial) legislation. This point is crucial in order to understand the functioning of the so-called "fuzzy" or hybrid property rights. Under China's decentralized reforms, hybrid property rights occur in localized form as a mixture of formal property rights that are not fully implemented and informal property rights agreed upon between local authorities and local enterprises.

From an enterprise perspective, the fuzziness of property rights reflects on an agreement with local authorities to solve economic conflicts through negotiation and bargaining at local level, that is, to localize conflicts. Private enterprise have little choice in this, as the relative independence of local political authorities makes it impossible for entrepreneurs who are in conflict with them over property rights to appeal to higher authorities. As there is no strict hierarchical implementation of policies, the position of higher level authorities is unpredictable from an entrepreneur's perspective and the outcome of an appeal would be more unpredictable and potentially carry more risk than informal negotiations with local authorities. In their own locality, entrepreneurs can still bring their economic and social power to bear. Fuzziness of property rights also means that higher level government echelons are excluded from interfering in local property rights disputes. Even if local authorities seem to be in conflict with the letter of the law or official regulations, enterprises under their jurisdiction have no means to enforce those laws and regulations as long as the local government's position is in line with "local circumstances." The right to vary policy implementation according to local circumstances at each level of the government hierarchy means that there is no hierarchical line of appeal. One could argue that if institutional regulations and customary economic exchange were completely separated and unmediated, this could lead to institutional breakdown. This does not happen because both local authorities and entrepreneurs are accustomed to negotiate their local *modus vivendi* and do not primarily rely on external authorities. The institutional mechanism that is used to routinize these negotiations consists of public-private networks which create an alternative informal forum of exchange between enterprises and local governments and whose function has been described elsewhere (Hendrischke 2004). The point to stress here is that local embeddedness of property rights ties enterprises to one specific locality (Nee 1992).

This seems to be in contradiction with the official Chinese view on privatization as a national policy. From an official perspective, there are broad similarities in local policies at least on a provincial if not on a larger regional scale. For example, the two provinces of Zhejiang and Jiangsu are generally seen as very similar in privatization to the degree that sometimes a Zhejiang/Jiangsu model of privatization and corporatization is postulated. Yet, from the interviews we find that there are considerable differences in the way provincial governments as well as local authorities in Zhejiang and Jiangsu reacted to national laws, regulations and policies and implemented privatization at various levels. This in turn has significant repercussions for the way privatization and property right reforms proceed—to the degree that it is possible to differentiate provincial and subprovincial trajectories of privatization. For example, respondents in the two provinces defined different national policies and dates as the main events in their local process of privatization.

In Zhejiang, the conversion to shareholding cooperatives under the Standard Regulations for Shareholding (*gufenzhi guifan tiaoli*) in 1988 (So 2000), the promulgation of the Company Law in 1994 and, less frequently mentioned, the constitutional amendments on private enterprises in 1997 and 1999 were defined as the major events in corporate histories. Conversely, respondents in Jiangsu reported that although the establishment of private enterprises was propagated (but not enforced) as a policy as early as 1993, the initial step of conversion to shareholding cooperative occurred from 1995 or later. Whereas enterprises in Zhejiang anticipated the Company Law or started to incorporate from 1994, the majority of enterprises in Jiangsu only started to incorporate in the late 1990s or was considering incorporation and change of ownership only after 2000.

Zhejiang Province has played a leading role in the privatization of enterprises since the early 1980s when the "Wenzhou Model" was first propagated (Nolan and Dong 1990; Forster and Yao 1999; Shi *et al.* 2004). For Zhejiang respondents, the initial phase of institutionalization of property rights came as early as the 1988 promulgation of the Standard Regulations for Shareholding. The Regulations enabled enterprises to define property rights and to separate collective and private enterprise shares. While they were issued nationally in 1988, the times for their local implementation varied by locality. The earliest instances of implementation was among respondents in Zhejiang, where the Regulations were immediately implemented, although their initial impact was mitigated by the economic recession during the years 1989–1991, when many small enterprises suffered economic decline or were forced to close down. The Standard Regulations were followed by the Company Law which came in force in 1994, but in some places in Zhejiang was implemented locally on a trial basis as early as 1992. Beginning from 1992, enterprises in these locations were offered the chance to change to a limited liability structure in anticipation of the Company Law, which at that time was still under consideration by the National People's Congress in Beijing. The interviews indicate that propagation of the Company Law by provincial and local authorities all over China did not mean that it was also implemented once it had come into force in 1994. Local authorities set their own timelines. For example, in Zhejiang, the separation of collective or state-owned and private shares under the new law happened faster than in Jiangsu, Shanghai or Beijing (Duckett 1998; Guthrie 1999; So 2000). Respondents reported that some local authorities in Zhejiang requested enterprises under their jurisdiction to convert to limited liability companies as early as 1992 or 1993, without, however, enforcing specific levels of private ownership shares or local state shares. These ratios were left to local discretion.

In Jiangsu we find that policies promoted at provincial level propagated institutional structures that were already obsolete in Zhejiang. For example, enterprises were still transformed into shareholding cooperatives in Jiangsu at a time when in Zhejiang incorporation under the 1994 Company Law was already the dominant form of property rights transformation. Respondents in Jiangsu changed to shareholding cooperatives in 1997 and even as late as 1999. Incorporation under the Company Law as a result of provincial policies began for most Jiangsu respondents only in 2000. They mentioned that incorporation on a broad scale was meant to be completed by 2002, but by mid-2001 many of them had still not made any preparations for determining future shareholding and governance structures and were not expecting to be under pressure to do so in the near future. At a stage when full privatization had already become a provincially enforced policy priority in Zhejiang, enterprises in Jiangsu still maintained large public shares that had become obsolete in Zhejiang years earlier.

An apparent hardening of institutional constraints to privatize and for provincial policies to converge occurred from the year 2000, when provincial authorities in Zhejiang as well as in Jiangsu propagated a "deepened reform of the system" (*shenhua gaizhi*) for the years 2000 and 2001. This reform aimed at reducing all public shares in enterprises of mixed ownership to less than 50 percent. In other words, provincial government policy required private entrepreneurs to become the majority shareholders in local enterprises. At the time of interviews in September 2001, localities in Zhejiang seemed to be ahead in these reforms to reduce state or collective shares, while respondents in Jiangsu expressed confidence that their local authorities were also committed to these plans, in spite of their slower pace of implementation. In September 2003, the situation had changed radically, as localities in Zhejiang as well as in Jiangsu had not only concluded the reduction of state and collective shares, but were now in the process of large-scale full privatization and complete withdrawal of government shares from local enterprises.

The basic reason for the local nature of small enterprise is that local authorities exercise insider control, either through direct administrative interference or through network structures. This insider control characterizes the first phase of privatization up to around the year 2001. Insider control by local authorities amounts to a joint exploitation of resources controlled by the entrepreneurs on the one hand and local authorities on the other. Local authorities had to attract managerial expertise in order to benefit from local enterprises, while the new firms obtained institutional protection and access to non-tradable input in return for their financial and social contributions to their communities. For enterprises, this cooperation made up for the lack of markets. For local authorities it was a way to ensure revenue flows from enterprises, which were largely tax exempt, and to restrict enterprise mobility so as to secure local employment. Economically, this was an inefficient solution, as the localization of control and operation prevented mobilization and wider allocation of resources. This is what characterizes the first generation of privatized enterprises. Large-scale privatization changed this situation, as it led to a stronger formalization of institutions and a second generation of private enterprises.

Delocalization of enterprises

The main feature of this new stage is the transition from internal control of enterprises to external, more formalized administration. With full privatization of all local enterprises and the withdrawal of all state or collective shares from the enterprise sector, local administrations lose their direct control over enterprise assets, cash flow and operational decisions. Administrations at township or district level can no longer control enterprises internally, as they are not able to cope with the (transaction) costs for administering the large number of enterprises. Some townships in the south of Suzhou have thousands of enterprises and only small local administrations. As a result, the initial direct links between local authorities and local enterprises are weakened and enterprises become "delocalized." This process is driven by a strong economic rationale. Internal control means interference with and reduced efficiency in local markets and a concomitant drop in business-based potential tax revenue. In other words, if reduced administrative interference leads to more efficiency, the loss of internal control for local authorities will be counterbalanced by increased tax revenue. Improvements in local tax administration and the allocation of tax shares to local authorities have created the formal institutional conditions for this to happen. Once local tax revenue is tied to the economic performance of enterprises in a specific jurisdiction, the stage is set for competition between local authorities trying to attract enterprise settlement. Under soft institutional constraints this will take the form of horizontal competition between different localities as well as vertical competition between different scales of administration, depending on the registration policies for enterprises.

From the perspective of interviewees, the decisive administrative layer for large-scale privatization is the city (*shi*) or county level, from where the relevant documents for township-level governments were issued. Respondents emphasized that these documents are internal and are not made public. However, the available information indicated that these documents are not the same for all localities. Local differences exist in specific timelines for transition to overall privatization as well as in prescribed forms of privatization. Timelines can vary according to local circumstances. Concrete examples of such "local circumstances" were, for example, funding requirements for the closure of SOEs. In one instance in Jiangsu, a locality had to wait for budget allocations to pay out former state employees before privatization could be concluded. In neighboring localities where no SOEs were left, these restrictions did not apply. Other examples of deferred privatization concerned enterprises which had complex ownership structures or enterprise groups that had to be disassembled before privatization.

Apart from the time horizon, local regulations also stipulate the specific procedures for complete privatization. While it was not possible to ascertain these in exact detail, a sequence in procedures that gradually reduced the local influence could be verified in locations in Jiangsu as well as in Zhejiang. There were two sets of procedures. For an initial period, local authorities at township level had the right to conduct "internal negotiations" (*neibu xieshang*) for the transfer of ownership. These internal negotiations gave them flexibility to find local investors to take over the assets to be privatized. "Internal negotiations" also entailed some leeway in setting prices and arranging finance, for example, allowing managers to borrow against assets they were buying. There was a time limit for conducting "internal negotiations." In one city district local authorities were entitled to choose between public auction and internal negotiation for a transition period in 2002. Depending on the asset they could opt for whichever procedure they preferred in what was called a dual-track system. This entitlement ended by the end of March 2003, and from April 2003 all privatization had to proceed by public auction. In preparation for public auctions, local authorities had to go through an asset evaluation in order to obtain a reserve price for the asset. The asset then had to be advertised publicly and a date set by which interested parties from anywhere in China could express their interest and submit their bids. If the reserve price was met by any of the bids, the sale would be concluded. If offers did not reach the reserve price, the asset was to be readvertised and could then be sold for a price below the reserve price. At this stage the local authorities were no longer able to express preferences for specific bidders, although respondents reported of cases where local authorities managed to get extensions for conducting internal negotiations for assets that were of special interest to them. Respondents, however, agreed that in the second stage it had become much harder, if not impossible, for local authorities to enforce protectionist measures that would exclude outsiders from acquiring assets.

Once privatization is concluded, township governments oversee thousands of enterprises. Their main administrative hold over these enterprises is through the ability to allocate land and, more generally, to offer material or physical, procedural, or commercial incentives. Indirect links also exist through the local tax offices (*dishui ju*). After the severing of ownership ties with local administrations enterprises have the option to exit their original locality, while local authorities can actively attract enterprises from outside their jurisdiction. In the relatively rich and booming region around Suzhou, local township administrators present functioning local tax offices as one of their competitive advantages. They explain this in terms of the benefits for their own administration accruing from orderly procedures, which in turn gives enterprises a predictable basis for calculation and reasonable compliance costs. There was a discernable trend among interviewees and administrators to emphasize regular taxation, although respondents confirmed that they still were called upon to contribute to specific local projects, such as school and community buildings, in addition to their extra-budgetary contributions. However, it was obvious that taxation as well as local fees are seen by local administrators in the larger context of incentives and public goods provided to enterprises. Taxes and fees constitute an important element in intergovernmental competition for investment and enterprises.

In horizontal government competition, the most important incentive is still the allocation of land. While in the earlier stages of privatization the administration of land had become a target for greater transparency, there are now clear signs that land has become a scarce commodity that local authorities use at their discretion to influence industrial settlement in their jurisdiction. The physical availability of land is one aspect; another is the price of land. Even for land in industrial zones where land prices are fixed, local authorities can lower land prices and forgo profit from land sales in order to attract investors. In one case, a local township Party secretary pursued a policy of targeted settlement of specific industries by offering highly competitive land prices. Other material incentives to attract investors include provision of infrastructure such as transport routes, water, energy supply, and communication.

While these are standard incentives that had existed throughout the reform period, local authorities also offered new forms of procedural incentives as a competitive device in targeting enterprises from other jurisdictions. Examples are simplified approval procedures for setting up enterprises and for registration of investments or easy access to the local Party secretary. Respondents confirmed that local administrators or Party secretaries use their power to simplify procedures to attract investors. In addition, local administrators use their influence to secure financial guarantees required for bank loans. These guarantees are issued by local credit guarantors at different levels.

One surprising element of competition is the provision of what could be called "administrative non-interference." Local administrators commit themselves to let enterprises look after their affairs without requiring constant and specific information. This forms part of transition know-how that local administrations have accumulated. The acquisition of this transition know-how, that is, the ability of local administrators to deal with private enterprise, is pursued systematically and as a learning experience. One respondent reported that local administrators from southern Jiangsu had organized tours to successful industrial locations in Zhejiang to study their administrative procedures and learn about the requirements of investors. They then tried to systematize what they had learned with the specific purpose of enticing investors from neighboring Zhejiang with better conditions.

Respondents also reported commercial incentives, where local administrations had opened up previously closed local industries to outside investors or tried to find usage for under-utilized local resources. Not all of these attempts were successful, especially if they failed to meet market demand. One city in Zhejiang had advertised itself a partner city of Shanghai and coined the slogan "Merge with Shanghai" (*yu Shanghai jiegui*). The city offered special discounts to any Shanghai business willing to invest, with the disappointing result that neither business people from Shanghai nor those from other localities, which were excluded from the discounts, responded to what seemed to be an empty slogan. Local enterprise respondents expressed dissatisfaction with this kind of local government policy and regarded this as undue market interference that discouraged potential investors.

Apart from these forms of horizontal competition between local authorities, there are forms of vertical competition. These are less easy to tie down, as vertical competition happens in a more fluid environment of frequently changing regulations. One of the best examples, though, is tax competition. Hangzhou City, for example, has created special tax incentives designed to attract settlement of high-tech industries in one urban area. Enterprises in this area designated as a high-tech zone are granted three years of tax exemption and two years of a 50 percent tax reduction as long as they can make a claim to high-tech status. The high-tech status is only loosely defined and has attracted respondents from surrounding townships to move into the city. Above township levels, higher levels of administration can bring into play their access to preferential funding for enterprises and obtain either higher volume of credit guarantees for enterprises registered with them. In the case of one respondent, this meant an interest rate reduction of 2 percent per annum for bank loans. In each case, the motive was long-term industrial planning and long-term strengthening of the local industrial base. For normal business purposes of respondents, vertical competition seemed to center on tax and procedural incentives.

Locality is a crucial element in marking the transition from the first stage of gradual privatization to the new stage of full-scale privatization. The transition to full-scale privatization is geographically uneven and depends on local privatization trajectories. The focus of local authorities is shifting from access to cash flow of enterprises to access to their profit through taxation. Enterprises find themselves in this new business environment faced by competition between local jurisdictions and locally varying incentives. The second generation of privatized enterprises is characterized by their increased mobility and the need to react to these localized incentives.

Corporate translocality

Respondents react to these incentives less with outright mobility, but rather through gradual territorial expansion of their activities and structural adaptation. In this way, they maintain benefits accumulated from long standing local links in their place of origin, while at the same time exploiting advantages to be gained from basing their business activities in different localities. The resulting forms of translocality are specific to the Chinese institutional environment and have a bearing on China's emerging corporate structures, in particular the preference for group structures over vertical integration.

Relocation to a different jurisdiction was the least frequent option chosen by respondents, certainly by those who had longstanding local links. Respondents who had recently relocated had mostly done so because of the availability of land for new or expanding activities at a new location. There were frequent indications that local administrations make efforts in the course of privatization to accommodate demands for more land by relocating enterprises within their jurisdiction to sites in newly established development or industrial zones. In one township south of Suzhou the local Party secretary had attracted settlement of new industries by offering land and options for future expansion to specific enterprises he wanted to attract. These enterprises were offered land at reduced rates about 10 percent below the standard price that the township could have achieved. Land prices and options for further expansion were major points of negotiations with prospective investors from neighboring Zhejiang who demanded guarantees that the favorable conditions they had secured with one office holder would be maintained by successors in his position. Here land was used to attract new entrants to a location, but also as a way to reduce the likelihood of exit by established enterprises.

A specific adaptation to horizontal competition between local authorities is translocal expansion through subsidiary companies. While expansion through branches would have been the most obvious and easiest choice for geographically expanding business activities, it does not seem to be the preferred option. Respondents indicated that local authorities have a preference for independently registered companies in their jurisdiction, because unlike branch offices, these companies contribute to their local tax revenue. Local authorities at the target location exert pressure by either offering or withholding various incentives, such as access to land, improvement of infrastructure or procedural support. This at least partially explains the ubiquity of groups or holding structures (*jituan*) among small enterprises. The spread of independent subsidiary companies under a joint holding can be seen as a response to local discrimination against the establishment of integrated branch offices by enterprises which are tax-registered in other jurisdictions.

The structure of subsidiary companies is dictated by commercial needs as well as administrative demands. Group shares in local subsidiary companies range from full ownership to minor controlling shares or even minority shares in spin-offs. Respondents with fully owned subsidiary companies emphasized the need for control and protection of market and technical know-how. At the other end of the spectrum, a decreasing share by the mother company allowed it to draw in local investment and share its risk. The point to note here is that commercial considerations are only one factor in deciding spread and structure of subsidiary companies. The other important factors are the structure of the market and the ability to access local incentives. Enterprises which depend on allocation of land or access to scarce input for their local operations are more likely to include local investors in their subsidiaries, as these enjoy better access to local administrations.

For example, a soft drink producer in Hangzhou, who had started off as a honey supplier to Wahaha, the nationally operating soft-drink company, set up independent subsidiary companies for the different types of drinks he was producing in different localities. His preferred structure was to hold a controlling share of over 50 percent and to give shares between 3 and 20 percent to technical investors and a maximum of 25 percent to local financial investors.

Vertical competition between levels of administration also produces demand for holding structures. In one case, a local production enterprise near Hangzhou decided to convert to a holding structure in order to register in one of the tax-free zones of Hangzhou City. The actual production enterprise (a bakery) remained in its original township location, while the holding structure's office with some newly added activities (baby milk formula) was registered in Hangzhou. By splitting its tax burden between the two locations, the holding structure enabled the entrepreneur to benefit from the tax-exempt status that came automatically with registration in Hangzhou.

Conclusion

This report focuses on institutional aspects of translocality. Some recent developments in the wake of local full-scale privatization are an indicator of a structural and material translocality at village and township level and above that differs from the ideological aspects of translocality or mobility that are reflected in many policy statements. This structural form of translocality is also not be confused with operational mobility of private enterprises. While most private enterprises face open domestic and international markets, they are constrained by jurisdictional barriers and limited access to certain industries. While access to industries is a macro-issue that requires a political solution, the jurisdictional barriers can be overcome at local level by specific forms of translocality. At this stage it seems that China's administrative environment of "soft institutional constraints," which gives localities the option to define their own industrial policies, has led to inter-jurisdictional competition between local authorities. In these localities enterprise are able to cross jurisdictional borders and to respond to incentives offered by other localities. There would be nothing remarkable about their mobility if these enterprises operated in a nationally unified institutional environment. They could be expected to be mobile and capable of consolidating and centralizing their various local operations through the establishment of local branches. Instead, among the new private enterprises in Zhejiang and Jiangsu we observe a preference for geographical expansion through legally independent subsidiary companies. This translocal expansion links one specific location to another on the basis of their specific institutional characteristics and without creating a spatial hierarchy. This structural—as opposed to operational—translocality enables enterprises to exploit different local incentives without losing their original basis. It is a conservative form of expansion that is likely to increase their internal transaction costs. It may not reflect an optimal solution in economic terms, but it is a sure way to expand institutional security at local level. The wider social benefit might lie in the spread of local entrepreneurship and the deepening of transition know-how and professionalization of local administrations.

In more general terms, and coming back to the introduction to this volume, the translocality discussed here results from local inequality and the need to better allocate and exploit local resources. This institutional translocality contests the institution-building monopoly of the state by isolating its local components. This translocality testifies to the resilience of the local as an institutional space that can link enterprise and state activity to overcome the institutional weakness of the central state and create its own specific responses in form of administrative procedures and corporate practices. Translocality can be seen as a response to and escape from the confines of local embeddedness. The mobility it entails induces some of the restructuring observed in contemporary developed market economies, such as flexible management structures, urbanization effects, weakening local control, local state competition, and changes in labor markets (Soja 1989: 157–189). Unlike general geographical mobility which presupposes a unified institutional environment, translocality emerges gradually and in horizontal and vertical direction to create new institutional spaces in which entrepreneurial activity can take place.

Note

1 The major participants in this project are Barbara Krug, Rotterdam School of Management, Erasmus University, Rotterdam; David D. S. Goodman, University of Technology, Sydney; Yao Xianguo, Zhejiang University and Wan Jieqiu, Suzhou University. The author is grateful for support from Faculty of Arts and Social Sciences and the Goldstar Grant Scheme of the University of New South Wales and from "Shifts in Governance" project of the Dutch Research Council (NOW).

References

Duckett, J. (1998) *The Entrepreneurial State in China*, London and New York: Routledge.
Findlay, C. (ed.) (1992) *Challenges of Economic Reform and Industrial Growth: China's Wool War*, Sydney: Allen & Unwin.
Forster, K. and Yao, X. (1999) "A comparative analysis of economic reform and development in Hangzhou and Wenzhou cities," in J. H. Chung (ed.), *Cities in China: Recipes for Economic Development in the Reform Era*, London: Routledge, 53–104.
Goodman, D. S. G. (2000) "The emerging public sector in Shanxi," paper presented at the UNSW-UTS Centre for Research on Provincial China Workshop on Social Change and Enterprise in China's Provinces, Taiyuan, October.
Guthrie, D. (1999) *Dragon in a Three-Piece Suit: The Emergence of Capitalism in China*, Princeton, NJ: Princeton University Press.
Hendrischke, H. (2004) "The role of social capital, networks and property rights in China's privatisation process," in Barbara Krug (ed.), *China's Rational Entrepreneurs: The Development of the New Private Business Sector*, London: Routledge, 107–114.
Hu, Z. and Cao, X. (eds) (2001) *Zhejiang suoyouzhi jiegou biange yu jingji fazhan* (Changes in Ownership Structure and Economic Development in Zhejiang), Hangzhou: Zhejiang University Press.

Huang, M. (ed.) (2003) *Zhongguo minying jingji fazhan baogao* (The Development Report of Non-State-Owned Economy in China), Beijing: Social Sciences Documentation Publishing House.

Huang, Z. and Fu, X. (eds) (2002) *Zhejiang nongcun gufen hezuozhi: zhidu chuangxin yu shijian* (The Cooperative Shareholding System in Rural Zhejiang: Renewal of the System and its Practice), Hangzhou: Zhejiang University Press.

Kornai, J. (1986) "The soft budget constraint," *Kyklos* 39(1): 3–50.

Krug, B. (2002) "The emergence of firms with Shanxi characteristics," *Provincial China* 7(1): 35–56.

Krug, B. and Hendrischke, H. (2003) "China incorporated: property rights, networks, and the emergence of a private business sector in China," *Managerial Finance* 29(12): 32–44.

Lefebvre, H. (1974) *La production de l'espace*, Paris: Anthropos.

Lieberthal, K. and Lampton, D. (1992) *Bureaucracy, Politics, and Decision Making in Post-Mao China*, Berkeley, CA: University of California Press.

Nee, V. (1992) "Organizational dynamics of market transition: hybrid forms, property rights, and mixed economy in China," *Administrative Science Quarterly* 31(1): 1–27

—— (2000) "The role of the state in making a market economy," *Journal of Institutional and Theoretical Economics* 156(1): 66–88.

Nolan, P. and Dong, F. (eds) (1990) *Market Forces in China: Competition and Small Business—The Wenzhou Debate*, London: Zed Books.

Oi, J. (1999) *Rural China Takes Off: Institutional Foundations of Economic Reform*, Berkeley, CA, Los Angeles, CA, London: University of California Press.

Shi, J., Jin, X., Zhao, W., and Luo, W. (eds) (2004) *Zhidu bianqian yu jingji fazhan: wenzhou moshi yanjiu* (Change of System and Economic Development: Research on the Wenzhou Model), revised edition, Hangzhou: Zhejiang University Press.

So, B. W. Y. (2000) "Chinese private enterprises at the close of the 1990s: their growth and legal protection," *China Review 2000*, Hong Kong: Chinese University Press, 307–330.

Soja, E. (1989) *Postmodern Geographics: The Reassertion of Space in Critical Social Theory*, London: Verso.

Sun, L. (2000) "Anticipatory ownership reform driven by competition: China's township-village and private enterprises in the 1990s," *Comparative Economic Studies* (Fall) 42(3): 49–75.

Sun, L., Gu, E. X., and McIntyre, R. J. (1999) *The Evolutionary Dynamics of China's Small and Medium-Sized Enterprises in the 1990s*, World Development Studies Series WDS 14, United Nations University, WIDER, Helsinki, Finland.

Unger, J. and Chan, C. (1995) "China, corporatism, and the East Asian model," *Australian Journal of Chinese Affairs* 33: 29–53.

—— (1999) "Inheritors of the boom: private enterprise and the role of local government in a rural south China township," *The China Journal* 42: 45–74.

Vermeer, E. (1996) "Experiments with rural industrial shareholding cooperatives: the case of Zhoucun district, Shandong province," *China Information* 10(3/4): 75–107.

Walder, A. (1995) "Local government as industrial firms: an organizational analysis of China's transitional economy," *American Journal of Sociology* (September): 263–301.

Wan, B. (ed.) (2001) *Zhejiang gaige kaifang 20 nian de lixing sikao* (Reflections on 20 Years of Reform and Opening in Zhejiang), Hangzhou: Zhejiang University Press.

Wank, D. (1995) "Private business, bureaucracy, and political alliance in a Chinese city," *Australian Journal of Chinese Affairs* 33: 55–71.

Wank, D. (1999) "Producing property rights: strategies, networks, and efficiency in urban China's nonstate firms," in J. Oi and A. Walder (eds), *Property Rights and Economic Reform in China*, Stanford, CA: Stanford University Press, 264–267.

Wong, C. (2002) *China—National Development and Sub-National Finance: A Review of Provincial Expenditures*, World Bank Report No. 22951-CHA.

Xin, K. R. and Pearce, J. L. (1996) "Guanxi: connections as substitutes for formal institutional support," *Academy of Management Journal* 39: 1641–1658.

6 Urban transformation and professionalization

Translocality and rationalities of enterprise in post-Mao China*

Lisa Hoffman

Introduction

In 1996, Dalian's Free Trade Zone published several investment brochures to distribute to potential foreign investors. As cultural texts, these brochures offer interesting material for understanding reform-era representations of urban coastal spaces and the emergence of urban subjects. Located at the end of Liaodong Peninsula in Liaoning Province, Dalian has become an important year-round, ice-free port in northeast Asia, making its coastal location an important "asset" in post-Mao times. This is reflected on the cover of one brochure with the image of Dalian positioned in both national and non-Chinese networks of capital and culture (Figure 6.1). The cover's background is light blue, highlighting two main images and the words "Free Trade Zone Investment Guide" in pink. The first image appears to be a globe, set in stark blues and greens and bearing an imprint of China's coast opposite North and South America. The globe is situated so that Liaodong Peninsula is conspicuously placed in the center of the page. Hovering just above this imprint are several colorful lines that loop around the globe and congregate at Dalian city, suggesting both the city's translocal connections and its relevance to the global economy. The second image is a picture of a ship, steaming along one of the looping networks, aiming for the hub that is Dalian. In another brochure, also printed in 1996, Dalian is again at the center of the map image with lines, which represent nautical distances to major ports around the world, radiating out from it (Figure 6.2). Just below this image is another picture that also represents the hub-like qualities of Dalian, with similar networked lines emanating from the city. Interestingly, in this second picture, the outline of China disappears in the background (Figure 6.3). It is as if the city exists on its own, a freestanding center for business and leisure that could serve not only northeast Asia, but also the world.[1]

I begin with these images to emphasize that the social and spatial transformations I address here have much to do with a shift in Dalian's status from a place within the socialist nation's landscape of production and politics to one that is enmeshed in national and non-Chinese networks and spaces of global capital. In contrast to high socialist practices which embedded cities and citizens in central, provincial, and municipal level production plans, the re-spatialization of coastal centers highlights global networks and translocal imaginaries. Although this does

Figure 6.1 Cover of the Dalian Free Trade Zone investment guide (1996).

not negate the significant role state organs and actors play in this process, it does narratively reposition Dalian in the region. This reterritorialization of Dalian from a Chinese industrial city to a strategic global site attempts to present the city as a center of trade, finance, and tourism for northeast Asia and the Bohai Rim Economic Area. Also in marked contrast to the high socialist era when Dalian was well known for its concentration of state-run heavy industry units in power generation, oil refining, shipbuilding, and chemical and machinery production,

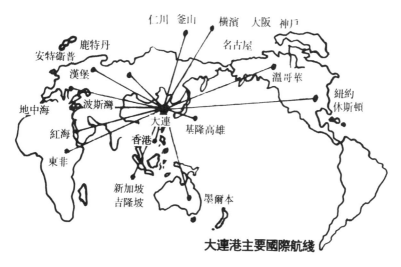

Figure 6.2 Major international shipping lines from Dalian (1996 investment guide).

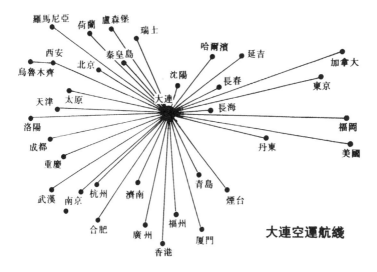

Figure 6.3 Airlines from Dalian (1996 investment guide).

recent policies have prioritized "non-polluting" processing, such as pharmaceuticals, textiles, consumer products, and fish processing. These investment brochures, aimed at potential investors from abroad, including Taiwan and Hong Kong, are important means for conveying an image of the city as modern, developed, and having the potential for future growth. Yet they also gloss over attendant problems of urban poverty and unemployment, discounting the effects of dislocations generated by this urban transformation.

Intertwined with the refiguring of this urban space is the emergence of post-Mao professional subjects who imagine and experience their lives in new ways that incorporate these translocal geographies. While the planned economic system assigned workers and quotas to units, reforms have phased out the job assignment system and guarantee of a steady and stable salary for college graduates. Instead of receiving a state directed assignment, college graduates now go to job fairs, write resumes, and compete for positions in a marketplace that privileges quality (*suzhi*), efficient human capital, and connections (*guanxi*). These new policies posit university officials as *guidance* counselors (rather than plan implementers) who foster the conditions to nurture and employ these knowledgeable and competitive subjects. The officials work closely with work-units and companies hiring their graduates, for instance, asking them what the potential employers need and how the schools can best meet these new market demands. All of these changes are important factors when assessing the new urban narratives of global attractiveness, the construction of central business districts (see Gaubatz 2005), and the emphasis on enticing those with higher education and credentials to settle in Dalian.

Based on fieldwork in Dalian (1993–2003), I suggest here that Dalian's "new urban form" and reform-era professional subjects are mutually constituted through discourses of self-development and enterprise in late-socialist China. Rationalities of self-enterprise and improvement, which shift the site of decision-making and responsibility from planning bureaus to specific localities and individuals, permeate discourses of cities and their citizens in contemporary China.[2] People I met while doing fieldwork, such as city planners, university officials, company personnel officers, and young professionals engaged rationalities of enterprise and expressed themselves in corresponding narratives, informing urbanization strategies as well as resume writing. These certainly were not the only ways people expressed themselves, as I also heard about employment insecurities and nostalgia for "stability" (*wending*). Yet the prevalence of narratives of self-propelled development and market-based success used by both city officials and college graduates draws our attention to how neoliberal rationalities and the proliferation of an "enterprise culture" are emerging forms of governmentality that connect subjectivity and spatiality—*for specific populations in urban places*—in late-socialist China.[3]

A central concern of this paper is then, identifying narratives and vocabularies that help constitute both places and people as translocal subjects imbued with responsibility for their own individualized improvement in the global marketplace. Plans to make Dalian a center of global exchange in northeast Asia, for instance, connect the city with this "vocabulary of enterprise" and market ethics where the city goes from being a site of needs fulfilled by the state to a "source of energies" and potential growth (see Dean 1999: 152). Cities also find themselves competing against each other for foreign direct investments (FDI) and like state and private companies must "calculate for their own advantage, [drive] themselves hard, and [accept] risks in the pursuit of goals" (Rose 1998: 154). Concomitantly, young professionals seek jobs that can provide them with opportunities for advancement and personal self-realization, placing a new emphasis on individual "acts of choice" handled responsibly (ibid.: 151; see Hoffman n.d.). Governing through these practices and rationalities of enterprise specifies subjects "who can become an actively seeking factor of production, rather like a mineral resource with an attitude" (Olds and Thrift 2004; see also Jessop 1997, 1998; Jessop and Sum 2000).

Grounding this argument is the idea that vocabularies and rationalities of enterprise are forms of power and regulation that enable places to refigure their symbolic and material spaces in certain ways and enable college graduates to plan their own careers, imagine futures of material success, and take risks while also bearing responsibility for the consequences themselves. This line of inquiry clearly builds on Foucault's notions of governmentality (1991), as well as analyses of the techniques of governing in advanced liberal regimes and the kinds of political reasoning and subjects they produce (e.g. see Burchell *et al.* 1991; Barry *et al.* 1996; Dean 1999; see also Butler 1993, 1999). Practices of enterprise and individual choice are not, in other words, outside the bounds of national power and governing, but rather are the effects of specific mechanisms and techniques of rule.

This is a particularly important point when discussing late-socialist governmentality, for it exhibits both neoliberal rationalities and new state techniques. Arguing that governing occurs through a stress on self-enterprise and entrepreneurialism does not mean I am suggesting that in late-socialist China there is a duplication of advanced liberal forms of rule, as Nikolas Rose calls practices in Britain and the United States. While there is an emphasis on individual choices and enterprise, these techniques of rule do not push governing into the *non*-state realm as we see in the US. Rather, the state remains an important participant in late-socialist neoliberalism through a premium on nation-building, patriotism, and the legacy of a system that redistributed goods and services to urban citizens. In other words, at the same time there is a growing emphasis on individual entrepreneurialism as a way to govern, the state not only posits itself as a promoter of these rationalities and practices, and thus as a supporter of national economic growth, consumer satisfaction, and social mobility, but it also remains materially and symbolically important in people's everyday lives.

In the following sections I highlight three regimes of truth that emerge through these forms of governing, constituting new kinds of places as well as people. First, I argue that city administrators have promoted Dalian as a kind of "outward-looking" location and that this perspective resonates with how many young professionals imagine their current and future lives. The very practices that shifted specification of subjects from revolutionary cadres to globally oriented professionals, for instance, also have informed municipalities' competitive strategies of place-specific urbanization and hub-based reterritorializations. Second, I discuss how vocabularies of enterprise permeate urban identities, leading to new forms of marketization for both places and professional subjects. Place-specific urbanization and competition for investments leads to the commodification of place itself and employment markets lead to processes of "neoliberal commodification" for young professionals where college graduates experience markets in terms of "fulfilling their potentials" through individual choices. Yet state desires for prosperity also regulate these marketization processes, suggesting that late-socialist techniques of governing draw on neoliberal as well as state-specific methods. In the third section I review the various models of urbanism used to promote Dalian in recent years, considering how urban planning aims to civilize both places and people, while also ignoring new social and economic inequalities.[4]

"Outward-looking" cities and citizens

The brochures described above suggest that a "new urban form" is emerging in the place called Dalian (see Dirlik 1999; Forbes 1999; Jessop 1999; Friedman 2002). Linked with this re-spatialization, I argue here, is the emergence of political and economic subjects whose sense of self, understandings of competition, and dreams of the future are informed by these new, "outward looking" geographies, illustrating that place-making and people-making are "intertwined," and that "geography matters" in the constitution of subjectivity (Massey and Allen 1984; Gupta and Ferguson 1999: 4).

The reterritorialization of Dalian has much to do with the city's coastal positioning, which has taken on a new significance in the reform era. Post-Mao reforms of the planned economy included accepting foreign direct investments, promoting export processing, and developing the eastern seaboard to enhance international trade. Maoist strategies of national self-reliance have given way to a more direct engagement with the international community through economic, social, and political exchanges. Special Economic Zones (SEZs) in the southeast were the first geographic-based experimentation of this modernization strategy. After their success, the central government designated fourteen harbors along the east coast, including Dalian, "Coastal Cities."[5] This designation, along with a decision to allow Dalian to surpass the provincial government and report directly to the central government on economic and administrative matters, promoted locally sanctioned management and municipal development.[6] Official and popular documents also referred to SEZs and Coastal Cities as "catalysts" for the development of interior regions, "classrooms" for learning new skills, and "corridors of development." Scholars and planners have used images of "mouths," "windows," and "hinges" extensively in Dalian as well, where the mouth represents both foreign access to the resources of the northeast and domestic access to things foreign, creating a "hinge" between national and international markets and cultures (Phillipps and Yeh 1989; Yeung and Hu 1992; Sum 1999; Gu and Tang 2002; Sassen 2002).

The transnational perspective embedded in the new representations of this Coastal City is reminiscent of the symbolism in the widely popular and controversial 1980s Chinese television series *Heshang*.[7] Many argued that in this show the Yellow River depicted a country landlocked, stagnant, and traditional, while the blue ocean represented modernity, outward exploration, and democracy (Su and Wang 1991). The narrator claims the "yellow soil and this Yellow River" are no longer enough "to give birth to a new culture, for they no longer possess the nutrition and energy they once had" (ibid.: 212–213). The "sea-breeze of 'blueness' " was identified as a source of future strength in the narration, "bring[ing] new life to the vast yellow soil plateau" (ibid.: 213). The writers depicted China as a place and culture that must not fear the outside world, but rather, should engage it and gain from it. This more internationally oriented route of modernization remains controversial in China. In fact, when the program aired in 1988 it provoked heated debates and many considered it scandalous, requiring support from Zhao Ziyang to be broadcast (see also Wang 1996).

By the mid-1990s, however, it was commonplace for municipal administrations to actively promote transnational and globally oriented urban geographies that embraced the "blue sea" and its (theoretically) energizing flows of capital, goods, and people. This refiguring of urban spaces and economies, from targets of state plans in the national economy to more individualized sites of global capitalism, created new spaces in the People's Republic of China (PRC), ones that were linked with non-Chinese networks of capital and culture in new ways. Yet it also created spaces of decline in the nation, such as the newly troubled "rust belt" in northeast China. Northeast China's industrial belt, unable to compete in the global marketplace and facing declining state support, began to experience serious social and economic dislocations in the reform era. During the Maoist era, Liaoning Province had the largest economy in China and was well-supported by the social-ist state. Yet by 2001 the three northeast provinces of Liaoning, Heilongjiang, and Jilin together approximated the economy of Guangdong Province in southeast China alone (Chow 2003).

Thus, by the end of the twentieth century, Dalian's municipal leaders actively tried to distance Dalian from the provincial capital, Shenyang, a city that exempli-fied the "rust belt" region, with its numerous bankrupt enterprises, extremely high levels of unemployment among industrial workers, and regular labor protests. Instead, to attract investments, they created images and wove narratives of a city that was business friendly, environmentally pleasing, and well positioned in the larger regional economy. Visions of post-Mao Dalian included a re-figured urban landscape of European style buildings, modern consumer spaces, and re-established international connections.[8] One interesting way the contrast between Dalian and Shenyang was made was through gender distinctions. Mayor Bo Xilai's wife explained to me in 1996 that the city government wanted to capitalize on the nat-ural feminine beauty of the area. As a "beautiful young woman" (*piaoliang de guniang*), Dalian could take advantage of its natural scenery and geographic loca-tion in the region. In contrast, Shenyang, which she described as a strong young man, did not have the ability to "attract" investors or visitors.[9] These are bright and optimistic representations that look pretty while silencing the disenfranchised who bore the brunt of economic restructuring. The new geographies of "openness" and contact with the blue sea, in other words, also produced "rust belts" where official discourses of commodification and self-reliance conflicted with socialist guaran-tees of health care, retirement, and employment, especially for those who had devoted their working lives to the Maoist vision of modernization.

Building Dalian into a hub of finance, trade, and tourism in northeast Asia not only affected urbanization plans, but it also created a spatial framework in which new college graduates and young working professionals imagined their future lives. Moreover, a market-based system of employment and a less restrictive household registration system made it possible for graduates to imagine moving to other cities, and perhaps even abroad. A professor of sociology at Dalian University of Technology once explained that China used to be closed and people could not move around, so the place itself where a person lived was very important. "But now so many people are moving around and having contact with things outside. Their lives are not so spatially determined. Before, young people had to listen to their parents, leader, or the head of their department," he went on, "but now it is not necessary. They can leave ... they can compare where they are with other places."[10] The legitimate comparison of places and decisions to try moving to another place are important changes from the Maoist era, and suggest the specification of post-Mao subjects is not delimited to one particular place. People not only compared Shenzhen with Dalian, but they also compared Shanghai and San Francisco, effectively looking and living beyond the spatial confines of their household registrations and Maoist ordering of locality—a process I am connecting here with the reimagined geographies of Dalian city in recent years. Connections exist between the emergence of urban professional subjects and broader spatial networks of investments, trade, and even prestige.[11] Transnational labor markets, for instance, affect the types of jobs available and the avenues by which someone may mark himself or herself socially and economically. In other words, imaginations of future lives are grounded in a translocal space. In particular, I found that college graduates had an outward looking perspective that often coincided not only with the reform era emphasis on "opening" China to the "outside" world, but also with official representations of Dalian city as a place with great "potential."

The comments of Miss He, a senior at Dalian University of Technology (DUT) in 1996 exhibited this post-Mao imaginary that not only compared places within China, but also acknowledged that these very places are connected with *non-*Chinese networks. When we were talking about her post-graduation employment plans, she said she wanted to stay in Dalian rather than return to her hometown of Daqing. I asked her why and she explained, "I could have picked other places, but I like the city's atmosphere. There is good potential for development here and it is the best city in the northeast. It has better future potential." As we spoke, I came to realize that she conceived of Dalian within a spatial network that included not just the three northeastern provinces (an enduring national and historic geography), but also the development potential of these urban places—and herself—within global networks. This translocal spatiality, not merely a reorganization of existing geographes, informed Miss He's sense of personal options and understandings of competition, creating *"new horizons of action"* for her and her future family (Jessop 1999: 25, emphasis added).

One of her schoolmates at DUT imagined her future in similar non-local networks and exchanges, connecting her plan of action with a wider spatial matrix than that of her parents's generation. "I need to go out (of the university) to learn new things...I also want to go abroad in the future, if it is possible, to learn something," she said. Echoing this emphasis on an outward-looking perspective from a person situated in a reform era coastal city, a third senior said, "I remember when China just opened. People were talking a lot about training people. People started talking about how young people should go overseas to open their eyes, to study modern things, and then come back home to help build their own country. So, from when I was little I have had this hope, to go abroad, but also to return."[12]

These women, like the city planners, situated themselves in ways that shifted their foci from Beijing and government directives to other landscapes of power. Their spatial frameworks extended past their hometown, their household registration papers, and even China's national boundary, albeit not displacing the continuing legacy of the state system and enduring feelings of patriotism (*aiguo*). While self-development and career training rested on a translocal, outward-looking perspective in the post-Mao era, they did not necessarily require that a young professional actually moved to an unfamiliar place or worked outside the state system. Although new college graduates dreamed about opportunities in "other" places and lamented the lack of employment choices in Dalian compared with Shanghai or Beijing, many did not move. Some had familial responsibilities that required them to return home. Others simply would not go to a city where they had no connections and instead opted for places with relatives to whom they could turn if in trouble. Still, others either had contracts with the university that said they would return to their hometowns upon graduation or they returned home because they could not pay the fee to transfer their registration. In the mid-1990s, universities still had a responsibility to distribute talent in a "balanced" manner around the country. To do this, DUT had a policy that prohibited graduates from transferring their registrations to several major urban centers to avoid an over-concentration of talent in these places. A student with top marks or one who paid a fee could get around this restriction, however (see Hoffman 2001).

A new Web site promoting Greater Dalian acknowledges that "swift scientific and technological progress and economic globalization *have changed the spatial pattern* of economic activities, and the realization of industrialization has highlighted the cities' roles as centers in regional economic development" (emphasis added). These new spatial patterns emerged from state policies that designated places as SEZs and Coastal Cities, municipal governments' pursuit of foreign investments, and new understandings of the city's role in national and transnational relations. Miss He and her classmates understood this and how these new "spatial patterns" influenced the kinds of opportunities they could find in Dalian compared with other urban centers within and outside of China. In addition to this translocal perspective, the constitution of post-Mao spaces and subjects occur through practices of commodification, understandings of how places and people manage and develop themselves, and attempts to self-enterprise. It is to these processes I now turn.

Enterprising practices: marketization in
late-socialist China

As cities relied more heavily on foreign investments and leisure spending in the 1980s and 1990s to support their local economies, competition grew between cities to attract this capital. This created a situation in which Dalian's municipal leaders found themselves "marketing" Dalian to multinational corporations with translocal images of the "Hong Kong of the North," the "Northern Pearl," and an economic hub of northeast China and northeast Asia. As such, states engage in "glurbanisation," per Bob Jessop, wherein states "restructur[e] urban spaces to enhance their international competitiveness" (1999: 35). By emphasizing the specificity and distinctness of Dalian, these campaigns subjected "place" itself to commodification, essentially making it "a commodity to be marketed" (Dirlik 1999: 51). These processes also turned Dalian's specificity into a more generalizable form that capital markets understood and consumed, mirroring similar situations in cities across the globe. Not surprisingly, discourses of market competition's value for urban development also have permeated social life in contemporary China, commodifying aspects of life that were not subject to these rationalities under Mao. Recently established employment markets for college graduates, the use of competitive exams for promotions and advancement, and daily consumerism are all examples of these changes.

Much of the literature on commodification of place argues that place-consciousness has increased with the "dismantling of the welfare state" so that the "gradual abandonment by nation-states of the responsibilities they had assumed . . . has brought places face to face with capital without the intermediation of the state [and] set places against one another in the competition for attracting capital" (Dirlik 1999: 47, 51). While there is much evidence that the state socialist welfare system is being dismantled in China today, it is important to recognize the important role the state plays in this current commodification process in China. In other words, the state continues to play a significant intermediary role in late-socialist China. It does so through the continued legacy of the urban welfare system, familial strategies to access those benefits, campaigns to promote patriotism and selflessness amongst college graduates, and governmental policies that designate places as SEZs or Coastal Cities. In fact, Fulong Wu argues that the post-socialist entrepreneurial city is a *state project* in China (2003).[13] State legitimacy in many ways stems from opportunities for wealth and status accumulation, and thus Wu argues "the entrepreneurial project allows the state to tap the market to restore its role as the promoter of economic development" (2003: 1694). Identifying specific places as Special Economic Zones and Coastal Cities are examples of how the state actively engages and promotes this entrepreneurial process. More recently, central government directives to revitalize the northeast identify Dalian as playing a key role.[14]

Yet at the same time state organs and actors remained influential in daily life, decisions to develop Dalian as the "Hong Kong of the North" and the "Northern Pearl" also led to narratives of the city's increased localization of urbanization strategies. Like other cities around the world, to "become visible" to global networks and "pathways of capital," in the early 1990s, the mayor's office began advertising the city as a place with specific advantages (Dirlik 1999). In the 1990s, they used images of the Hong Kong of the North (see Bo 1993; Liu *et al.* 1994: 4; Yahuda 1994: 262), followed by Singaporean ideals and beautification visions in the late 1990s that prompted municipal investments in environmentalism, green space and a "garden city by the sea" image (*haiyuan chengshi*). And in 1999, the city's one hundredth anniversary, central government leaders and local promoters named Dalian the "Northern Pearl" followed by a campaign to build Greater Dalian (*Da Dalian*) in 2002.[15] All of these model images are what Forbes has called "consciously constructed 'imaginative geographies' " that work to convey images of modernity, beauty, and economic viability, especially in the face of painful urban poverty and unemployment (1999: 245).

Official and popular discourses identified the success of these models (and Dalian being able to play the role of a regional hub of looping networks) as depending on citizens who exhibited civilized and cosmopolitan behaviors and who were desirable to transnational investments. Terms like development (*fazhan*), future (*qiantu*), opportunity (*jihui*), and ability (*nengli*) were words that consistently appeared in conversations with the young professionals, echoing the way people commented on the city's hoped-for position in the global economy. Company directors, like municipal planners, said they needed talented workers for their projects to succeed. At job fairs and in interviews they boasted to job applicants that they knew how to use talent efficiently (vs. the Maoist era) and would value them in their enterprise. Deng Xiaoping in particular is credited with pushing for a greater reliance on *rencai* (talent). In 1984 he pronounced that people should respect knowledge and talent (*zunzhong zhishi, zunzhong rencai*) and that education, particularly scientific and technical education, would help the country develop (Deng 1994: 40–41). A young man from a state owned securities enterprise explained to me, "We need talented people for development. It doesn't matter what kind of enterprise it is. Everyone needs them. Talented people solve difficult problems. You can train them and they help guarantee an enterprise's future development." When I visited the new Rencai Dasha (Human Resource Building) in December 2003, I saw billboard-sized posters in the stairwells stating: distribute human resources perfectly; build the talented highland of the north (*youhua peizhi rencai ziyuan, gouzhu beifang rencai gaodi*, translated on the wall as "To dispose perfectly the intellects resources; To construct the intellect highland of the North"). Similarly, promotional materials for Dalian's new Software Park confidently proclaimed that "human resources are the fundamental source for sustained development."

Many young professionals also adopted the idea that they had talents that should be used and not "wasted," a new assessment of the Maoist era's relationship to certain workers. As new graduates who possessed high education and embodied a high "cultural level" (*wenhua shuiping*), many embraced the idea that they could experience social mobility and legitimacy because of their educational credentials. The fact that they hoped for this mobility did not mean they always found it, however, but it does signify a shift in the way they understood their working lives and their relationship with employers. The day I saw the signs in the Human Resource Building, I also spoke with a young woman who had recently returned from a failed attempt to start her career in Shanghai. While she identified Shanghai as a city with great potential where she would be able to grow and "develop herself," she returned to Dalian after feeling cheated by a boss and felt she had wasted her time and talents. "I will never trust another person so easily again," she said, clearly disheartened. Like other new graduates, she embraced the idea that she had valuable talents, at the same time she expressed anxiety over possible unemployment and being cheated by others. The stress on rationalities of self-enterprise does not erase feelings of insecurity or the reality of unemployment, but this form of governing does suggest it is a deficit in skills, ability, or quality, rather than the market itself, that the state must eradicate. Foreign investors also looked for a "talented labor pool" with language skills, technical knowledge, business acumen, and the ability to communicate cross-culturally. The hiring of such employees by foreign-based and transnational corporations in countries like India, China, and Ireland, has been termed "white collar globalization" by some and the emergence of white-collar sweatshops by others (see Engardo *et al.* 2003).

The concept of human resources as a source of place-based development expresses how making Dalian "visible" to the disciplinary gaze of capital not only marketizes the place, but it also brings professionals into the frame. Since the 1980s, for instance, the government has reformed the system of direct state job assignments for college graduates that prioritized equality and five-year plans, emphasizing an individual's skills and the market's exploitation of human resources. Rather than getting an often lifelong assignment in a state-owned unit, by the mid-1990s most graduates went to employment markets, met face to face with employers, and signed short-term contracts (e.g. 3–6 years). In conjunction with wider economic restructurings and the open door policy, more and more positions became available outside the state sector and in fields such as management, service, and trade.

Nevertheless, many graduates chose positions in state-owned units for reasons that ranged from security and access to benefits, to recognition of their patriotism (Hoffman 1999). A 1996 graduate of DUT, Mr Wei, was one such person.[16] After encouragement from his father, he applied for and won a coveted position in the Ministry of Foreign Trade and Economic Cooperation. During the interview process, he recalled they tested him on his oral English and his health. When they asked why he was interested in the position and what advantages he could offer, he said, "I told them I wanted this position because I wanted to get work experience in this big ministry and that my major included imports and exports and I wanted to do something related to my major. This is a high-level ministry so I will have opportunities to improve my abilities. In terms of my advantages, I told them I communicate with others well. I have been president of the student union in university and that is important, especially for a civil servant position." Although he ended up in the state sector, he did not arrive through state directed assignments. Rather, he talked with his father about his options, compared the different cities and types of jobs he could have, thought about his skills and career goals, and applied for the job. Similar to the way the site of governing for cities has moved from central-level directives to practices of commodifying place, employment markets create a site of what I call neoliberal commodification where young professionals experience the marketizing process through notions of individual choice handled responsibly and dreams of fulfilling their "talented" potentials.

Wei explained,

> In the last year of university, I started to think about my future and for a while I wanted to go back to my hometown of Shenyang and live with my family and be with my friends. But then I talked with my father and he told me I should choose a position in a high-level unit and Beijing is the capital so I should go there. We also decided that if I couldn't find a good job in Beijing then I would go back home...My father and mother encouraged me to study very hard and asked me to be a good student...They asked me to be a good student now and they will ask me to be a good employee in the future. [This means] I should do better than the others, and if I am the best they will be happy. Yes, I like competition because there is an equal chance for everybody and if you are better than others you can win.

At this point in the conversation, I asked him about the rampant use of connections and the pervasive worries of college graduates about finding jobs. Did he really think this last statement was true? He told me we should consider two factors. "First," he said,

> if you have a good background then you may win through connections (*guanxi*), but second, if you're good you also have the chance to do well. Not all positions can be occupied by those with good backgrounds [well-connected]. Ten years ago, it was worse. Others controlled your future. The boss ordered you to do this and that, but after Deng Xiaoping came into power, China changed a lot. Now we have reforms and policies about opening up.

While it is imperative that we recognize similarities with the Maoist era call for self-improvement, the meaning and result of desires to develop one's own potential (whether a city or citizen) in the post-Mao era are a distinct phenomenon. Striving to be a model worker like Lei Feng or a powerful Red Guard are acts of self-development, but the rationale is distinctly socialist, Party oriented, and rooted in ideals of selflessness. In addition, socialist mechanisms of governing identified collective goals and needs, fulfilling them through collective spirit and labor.

The norms of post-Mao subjectivity, however, resonate with (but do not duplicate) characteristics of advanced liberalism, specifically where individuals are encouraged to " 'enterprise themselves', to maximize their quality of life through acts of choice, according their life a meaning and value to the extent that it can be rationalized as the outcome of choices made or choices to be made" (Rose 1996: 57). Mr Wei deliberated with his family about where he should pursue his career and went through face-to-face interviews, an individualized process that associated the value of human capital with the individual and not just the state and its needs. Yet the state remained important both symbolically and materially in the young professionals' lives through political norms of patriotism and nation building and an emphasis on responsible choices, as well as the legacy of housing subsidies and work-place benefits. State dependency and direction, in other words, are giving way to what may be called a late-socialist "enterprise culture" that does not necessarily promote political and social diversity, but rather the "individual and local calculations of strategies and tactics, costs and benefits"(Rose 1992: 142).[17] These techniques of governing, I am arguing, produce particular kinds of subjects (outward looking, enterprising professionals) and spaces (entrepreneurial urban places). Young professionals like Mr Wei learn about and desire to make their own choices, about everything from where to work to what appliances to buy.

Although the possibility of "choice" is often glorified in the press, the marketization of labor allocation and the pulling back of state guarantees also rupture socialist ethics of labor security, basic health coverage, and retirement support after working for the state. Miss He, the DUT graduate mentioned above, explained that although she found her position in the employment market, her family was suspicious and worried about the unstable life she might face. In particular, they worried that she could not take care of such an important matter on her own and that the company would not honor the contract, leaving her with no job. Her first offer came immediately after an interview at the employment fair, but she did not accept the offer.

> They wanted me to do some marketing work, but I would not be able to use my major so I told them I would talk to them when I came back from vacation (Spring Festival). Before I returned, I got a call from another company and I went there for an interview. I signed a contract with them. If I break this contract I will have to pay 2000 RMB, but I won't break it. This company can help me settle my household registration in Dalian,[18] they may give me housing and the work is good. I can use English to communicate with them...My parents aren't really willing to let me go out, they want me by their side, but they support me because it is for my career, which is important. Still, they worry about this job. They worry that if I don't have connections to help me then I may have some trouble. They really can't believe that I can find a job on my own. A few days ago my mom called and said she is worried about the job because she still doesn't think the contract I signed is valid enough to get the job.

Her family, focused on security rather than these post-Mao rationalities of enterprise, worried about her ability to establish a stable life. Miss He, in contrast, felt comfortable in this setting of individual decisions, calculations about what would bring her future gains, and self-reliance. Later in our discussion, she explained she wanted to find a position where she could develop herself. "I don't know what the future will be for me. I have a lot to learn... I have no blueprint for my future. I want to test myself. I am not sure of my ability. I want to test myself in society and later I will decide." Miss He, in a sense, sees her individual self as an enterprise, a continuous project of developing her human capital; an extension of, as Colin Gordon states, "[t]he idea of one's life as the enterprise of oneself" (1991: 44).

This "care of the self" in late-socialist China, however, also incorporates state patterns of material life. Mr Chen's desires for his future are a good example. He was twenty-nine years old in 1996 when we met, and had high hopes for his life, which he approached as a kind of enterprising project in which he would acquire opportunities and "aptitudes" (ibid.) Although he had been working in a state-run unit for several years and felt depressed and frustrated in the position, he stayed because he could get "work experience" and an apartment, a legacy of the high socialist planned system. "I am like a slave here. I have responsibilities here but no power, which is not fair. I am more enterprising than others in this unit... People should be more enterprising here, but they are not. Trying to get people to offer quality service is no use; the staff handbook is no use. When the boss is here they work, when he's not here, they don't." Chen thought he was different from the "typical" state employee who depended on the state and felt no desire to improve. In contrast, he wanted to be enterprising, and to work with others more like himself, either in another unit as a general manager or vice general manager, in international trade, or as a foreign brand's Dalian representative. "I really should have my own business," he said, "because I want to be my own boss. That way you can have a kind of power, and I need to have more power than I do now." Yet he was willing to do so only after securing housing. It is this juxtaposition of state socialism and the official promotion of individual choice and enterprise that we may call late-socialist enterprise culture (vs. an advanced liberal enterprise culture).

Noting that decision making has moved from state planning bureaus to other, more individualized social actors, and that employment options extended beyond the state sector does not mean that governing itself is disappearing or that the state no longer plays an important role in space or subject formation. These acts of choice in late-socialist China, in other words, while leading to tangible change in people's lives, did not appear in a space where power and domination—or the state—were absent (Foucault 1991; Rose 1992, 1996, 1999). Rather, as I have argued elsewhere, governing occurred *through* these more individualized and localized acts (Hoffman n.d.).

For college graduates, the opening of human capital markets and the phasing out of post-graduation employment guarantees conceptualized them as social actors with a degree of choice not possible under the centrally planned system. In the 1990s, the Party no longer used forced relocations and job assignments to enforce compliance with national ideologies. Rather, distribution of college graduates worked through university attempts to guide (*zhidao*) them into certain types of jobs, fines for breaking employment contracts, rules about transferring household registrations, popular gossip about the kinds of people and places that were civilized (*wenming*), and desires to rely on and develop one's own abilities. Official discourses exhorted young people to extricate themselves from state dependence and the dream of state guarantees. Instead, they should learn not to depend on the state, to make their own responsible choices, and to promote their own career and skill development—while not necessarily leaving the state sector of employment (Hoffman n.d.). Young people like Mr Wei and Miss He understood they had to calculate the best way to get a job, secure housing (through state resources or private purchase), weigh self-development options, and be discerning consumers.

Young professionals and urban planners alike talked of potential, opportunity, and the desire to take advantage of one's, or the city's, special skills and characteristics—whether successful or not. The commodification of place and professionals in this late-socialist moment emerged alongside neoliberal rationalities of self-enterprise, producing a kind of neoliberal commodification experience. Differentiating oneself from other job applicants, differentiating Dalian from other places where foreign investors could take their money such as Tianjin or Shanghai, and differentiating educated employees from other workers also draw our attention to the fact that people experience these processes in differentiated ways.

Models of prosperity and the production of social inequalities

In a recent speech (2003), Dalian mayor Xia Deren noted that

> The twenty-first century is the century filled with opportunities and challenges. The trend of economic globalization and regional economic integration makes the individual development of different nations become more and more inter-related with each other, the complementarities of economic cooperation and technical cooperation are strengthening... The opportunities of Dalian are the opportunities of us all, the development of Dalian will provide a broad range of development scope for the world enterprises. We will greet our domestic and foreign investors with a better infrastructure, a better service, and a better environment. Dalian will become our investors' pioneering paradise and beautiful homeland.[19]

The Mayor's comments make the translocal and transnational character of Dalian explicit. They also sound like a tourist brochure that depicts a model city with little poverty and unemployment, and with well-trained citizens who have few complaints. While often positive for the privileged college graduates, new urbanization strategies and economic restructuring also produced employment insecurity, dissatisfaction, and marked economic hardship for many. The official, tourist-like models of urban development never address this issue. In fact, they tend to silence them, at least momentarily.

As mentioned earlier, since the early 1990s, a number of "consciously constructed 'imaginative geographies' " (Forbes 1999: 245) have emerged in Dalian that built on idealized models of urbanism. This process, I have argued, has enhanced the commodification of place while also producing new spaces in which, and through which, subjectivity is constituted. In addition, the use of non-local models for urban transformation (e.g. the Hong Kong of the North) embodies a rationality of enterprise that localizes planning and evaluates decisions not just through Party doctrine, but also through increasingly "commonsense" notions of market and enterprise values. These models also build on the elaborate use of models by the Party in post-1949 political rituals. Dazhai commune, for instance, was a model of "peasant virtue and self-reliance in the 1960s" and Wenzhou city was well known for its entrepreneurial spirit when reforms began (Parris 1994; Zhang 2001).[20]

An early and well-known model was the Hong Kong of the North. According to academics and planners, building the Hong Kong of the North required a diversification of the local economy, promotion of trade, finance, and tourism, and more direct connections with the international economy. In the context of these plans, Hong Kong represented a successfully diversified economy as well as a good model of how to merge the domestic and international economies. Cities and towns in the Pearl River Delta region looked to the British colony as a mentor, partner, and liaison to other parts of the world economy in the early reform era. Dalian was similarly positioned as a "catalyst" for the development of its hinterland with the 1984 Coastal City designation. Yet in the mid-1990s and in the face of the approaching handover of British colonial Hong Kong to Beijing, I was told Hong Kong was a limited model for Dalian. "Hong Kong only talks about money" one man assured me, "they only do business, so it is a limited model of development for the city." Dalian, in contrast, would offer a wider array of benefits, "raising the quality" of the citizens (*tigao renmin de suzhi*), and beautifying the urban environment. The connection between the intended production of model cities and model citizens is important to recognize.

As the Hong Kong model came to represent commercially defined growth, and perhaps even colonialism, Dalian's municipal government looked elsewhere for visions of what it could become. Singaporean Prime Minister Lee Guan Yew's policies of population control and the lack of urban "chaos" were appealing, and Singapore became an important symbol of an urban area that maintained control and was orderly. Also Lee Guan Yew was well known for his emphasis on green space and the garden city model. Mayor Bo Xilai drew on this and promoted sustainable development and environmentalism, receiving numerous awards for his efforts.[21] Singapore was appealing because the city-state had successfully circulated a representation of itself in government documents and scholarly articles "as a world city and hub of an evolving megaurban region" that was a clean and controlled site where one found neither spitting nor labor protests (Forbes 1999: 241).[22]

Emulating these principles, in 1995 Mayor Bo adopted the policy "strive not to be the largest, but to be the best" (*buqiu zuida, dan qui zuijia*). Rather than growing in size and population as Beijing and Shanghai had, Mayor Bo decided he would establish strict limits on growth and pursue sustainable development. This model coincided well with reform era imperatives to improve the "stock and quality" of the population, to maintain control over urban population growth, and Dalian's new planning objectives to "humanize" (*renxinghua*) the city. Economists frequently upheld the improvement of the "stock and quality of human resources" as an indicator of how governments prepared for new engagements with the global economy, particularly in Asia's newly industrializing economies (NIEs) (Chowdhury and Islam 1993; Siu and Lau 1998; Xiao and Tsang 1998). This was made explicit in an article in *Dalian Daily* in which Professor Liu Zhongquan pointed out that while the economy is the first key element of any modern, international city, human resources (*rencai ziyuan*) are a key factor (*guanjian yinsu*) (Shi 2000). These official pronouncements say nothing of those whom the new market values identify as lacking talent and quality (see Anagnost 1997, 2004; Yan 2002, 2003a,b) or the new forms of discipline that support multinational investments (Pun 2004).

Narratives of civility (*wenming*), culture (*wenhua*) and quality (*suzhi*) framed public conversations about the urban setting as well, linking the renovation of public squares (*guangchang*), the building of newly stylized high-rises (e.g. *dasha*), and the beautification (*luhua*) of the downtown area with attempts to produce proper citizens for a global city. Discourses of humanism identified the built landscape as a means for transforming residents into civilized and cosmopolitan urbanites as well as shifting the relationship between citizens and the government.[23] Mr Chen's comments illustrate this link. "The atmosphere is good here," he said. "Things are fair, civilized, the environment is good and the buildings are nice. There is a lot of greenery around town and people know they should stay off the grass." Two months prior to this conversation, I heard the city's then Mayor, Bo Xilai, commend his citizens for knowing they should respect the new pieces of grass at People's Square and not walk on them—an example of how civilized (*wenming*) the city was, he said. A hair stylist working at a large international hotel reiterated this sense of Dalian as a civilized city. "Why would I want to live anywhere else in China?" he was quoted as saying. "It's a beautiful city and I do my best to be civilized here because I want to keep it that way" (quoted in Cheng 2003, see also Yan 2003a: 585).

Yet not all college graduates had positive opinions of Dalian or positive experiences in the human resource markets, drawing our attention to the fact that these campaigns often failed and/or did not coincide with people's experiences. When I asked one chemical engineering senior why he did not want to stay in Dalian he said "I don't like Dalian because I don't think the people are polite. Some of them are rude. People who live in Dalian just care about money and don't know about other things. For example, the New China bookstore here is very, very small. I don't know if people in Dalian read books, but Beijing is different. There are many famous universities." This young man was criticizing the "cultural level" and quality (*suzhi*) of Dalian and its residents. Cultural level refers to formal educational attainment, but people also commonly used it to reference less tangible notions of civility and character, an increasingly popular phenomenon in reform-era China.

These official and popular pronouncements not only produce a dissonance for those who critique the city's "low level" and the new elite's conspicuous consumption, but they also mask new social inequalities that emerge with these imaginative geographies. Intellectuals as well as popular culture, Dai Jinhua argued, have ignored the "widening gap between rich and poor" in China and the fact that class divisions are now a central organizing force of contemporary life (2002). Moreover, in contrast to rural areas and those associated with them, the city itself has been "renewed as the privileged space of modern civilization and civility (*xiandai wenming*), gesturing toward elusive capital and development. In this discourse, it appears that *modernity* and progress, which themselves are the ideological effects of post-Mao modernist imaginary, are given their permanent residency in the city" (Yan 2003a: 585). One young professional whose family had been sent to the countryside during the anti-Rightist campaign called Deng Xiaoping his family's "savior" because of policies that allowed them to return to the city. It was this same man that turned to me with sincere excitement and said, "The twenty-first century will be the century of leisure!"

The renovation of Zhongshang Square (*zhongshan guangchang*), a round park in the middle of a large traffic circle in the center of town, is a good example of how the remaking of city spaces exhibits not only the influx of multinational capital and market logics, but also the reconstitution of urban political and economic subjects. Originally built by Japanese urban planners, Zhongshan Square remained a focal point of the city through the years. In 1995, construction crews cut down the trees, removed most of the low-lying bushes, paved a large raised area in the center, and built little fences to keep people off the grass. The paved section in the middle became a platform for official functions such as educational campaigns and patriotic school performances. Most evenings, waltz music was broadcast over the loudspeakers and people gathered for dancing and chatting in the newly renamed Zhongshan Music Circle (*zhongshan yinyue guangchang*) (Figure 6.4). Previously the plaza was filled with retired men playing cards and letting their caged birds sing to one another, especially under the shade of the trees when the summer sun beat down. After this renovation, however, all the trees were gone and with them went the shade. At the same time, mounted police appeared on the streets, patrolling this now very open and easily surveyed public gathering space. Writing about the redesign of plazas in San Jose, Costa Rica, Setha Low argues that "[a] public space that is valued ostensibly as a place for people to sit, read, and gather becomes a way to maintain real estate values, a financial strategy for revitalizing a declining city center, and a means of attracting new investments and venture capital" (2000: 180). Zhongshan Guangchang went from a social space at the end of Stalin Road to a more class specific site of leisure activity along the renamed People's Road. Young people flocked to the area for evening strolls and dancing, while some elderly people were not afraid to say how disappointed they were with the changes.

Dai Jinhua also notes the complexity and contradiction inherent in the use of the term *guangchang* (square or plaza), which is "firmly associated with the

Figure 6.4 Zhongshan Square/Zhongshan Music Circle (photo by Lisa Hoffman).

memory of revolution and the politics of various historical eras," for places with commercial value and activity, "signifying to the nation the gradual metamorphosis from socialism to a capitalist market economy" (ibid.: 215–216).[24] As in other cities around China, planners in Dalian prioritized the creation of spaces where "leisure, shopping, and consuming" mobilized and organized urban social relations, rather than the revolutionary rallying spaces or the generalized or proletarianized spaces of the socialist urban model (ibid.: 221; on generalized spaces see Gaubatz 1995; on proletarianized spaces see Hubbert 2002).

Another renovation of a plaza, the area across the street from People's Square (*renmin guangchang*, previously known as Stalin's Square) that houses the city government, occurred in the late 1990s. The new design uprooted the monument to the Russian soldiers who had lost their lives fighting in Dalian and shipped it out to Lushun, the former site of Port Arthur and currently a naval base. In its place was a large, stone fountain in a semi circular shape facing the municipal building (Figure 6.5). While music played the water sprayed up in the main round section and people walked behind the water, remaining relatively dry. Families, friends, and young couples screeched and pushed as they made their way along the wall, beaming when they came to the other side. The rest of the lawn remained the same, and still no one trod on the grass of "the first lawn square in Dalian" (*di yi ge coaping guangchang*). When I asked friends about this

Figure 6.5 People's Square (photo by Lisa Hoffman).

new construction, they explained Dalian was becoming a modern and beautiful city, just like the phrase in large characters at the port's entrance. The implications of this particular transformation—the removal of a statue of soldiers for a "leisure" fountain—are significant, and not innocent (Dai 2002: 220). These commercialized and humanized urban spaces remain in tension with the revolutionary memories of high socialism, obscuring, but not being able to erase what Dai calls the "brutal" reality of social inequality in contemporary China. This is apparent in the marked forms of inequality between coastal cities and inland provinces like Shaanxi, or even Jilin, that create geographies of booming coastal zones and declining rust belts. Within cities we also see both upward and downward social mobility, creating possibilities for wealth accumulation and painful poverty.

   These social inequalities become tangible not only with the renovation of places, but also in attempts to control population growth through policies about who could settle their registration in Dalian. Sustainable development, forcefully supported by Mayor Bo Xilai, for instance, meant not only enacting environmentally friendly policies such as increasing the amount of per capita open green space, but also the management of who would be able to become a permanent resident of the city. Dalian's municipal government adopted three policies to make sustainable development possible. The first was population control and improvements in the "population quality." These improvements would come about through disciplinary measures of birth control and through more pastoral methods of trying "to encourage middle-level or senior technical talents to settle in Dalian." The other two actions were limiting capital construction and improving its quality, and only accepting high tech and low pollution industries (Liu 2000). Those with bachelors, masters and doctoral degrees received preferential treatment when they applied to settle their household registration in Dalian. Starting in 2002 in Dalian, all four-year college graduates (*benke*) who could find a job (in any type of unit or company) could settle their registration in the city. By 2003, this privilege was expanded to include graduates with three-year degrees (*zhuanke*), although with some restrictions about settling in the city center. If the employer had the resources to manage the household registration, it stayed there, and if not, the employees could leave it at the Human Resource Market (*rencai shichang*). An administrator at the market told me that "highly talented personnel are especially important for building Greater Dalian. We have to compete with cities like Beijing and Shanghai and Shenzhen," she continued. "Salaries are lower here and many people move on to these other cities after staying here for a few years and getting experience. We have trouble keeping talent (*liubuzhu rencai*)."

In contrast, migrant workers from rural areas and without degrees still faced restrictive policies that provided temporary rather than permanent registrations. The loosening of household registration policies coincided with the strategy to build a Greater Dalian. Provincial Party Vice-Secretary and Dalian City Party Secretary Sun Chunlan promoted this strategy with the intention of extended city government control over a greater administrative area and expanding the economic functions of the city (see Zhou 2003). Similarly, a new registration policy in Beijing allows those who are employed in Beijing, have at least two year's work experience, and have graduated from college to obtain a Beijing registration. The deputy director of the Public Policy Center at Chinese Academy of Social Sciences noted that this move is behind other cities like Shanghai, Guangzhou, and Shenzhen and that "the new policy would help Beijing attract more talent" (Hu 2003).

Conclusion: the mutual inflection of subjectivity and spatiality

In the past several decades, Dalian's redevelopment has affected its built environment, its economy, its workforce, and its positioning *vis-à-vis* Beijing and the world. Images of the city as a hub of looping networks, as seen on the cover of the investment brochure, reflect Dalian's new border-crossing spatialization as well as the need for particular kinds of political and economic subjects who will be able to manage these global processes while also maintaining national stability. The Hong Kong and Singaporean models, the promotion of window and catalyst functions, and the renovation of the city's public squares all indicate an urban geography that significantly alters the imagined and material spaces in which people live and work. All of the models and urban development strategies rested on a spatiality that extended beyond the Beijing–Dalian relationship, expressing new urban identities of place and people. The shift from a Beijing/planned economy/heavy industry/revolutionary focus to a hub/market/global/talent focus has restructured how people experience social mobility and capital accumulation. Subject formation of young professionals, this paper has argued, should be analyzed in reference to this refigured, translocal city space. Concomitantly, analysis of the rise of these new geographies should consider the very subjects who are seen as making them "successful."

Recognizing connections between subject formation and the emergence of places that have a translocal character offers concrete and situated examples of how state and market rationalities—here of self-management, entrepreneurial ethics, and professional ambition—are integrated into people's material and symbolic worlds. The same rationalities of marketplace competition and now commonplace assumptions about post-Mao development that position cities as competitors in global networks inform subject formation processes. Specifically, there is a late-socialist enterprise rationality that links the production of subjects and spaces in contemporary coastal China. Both young professionals and cities are being positioned as new kinds of social actors with greater degrees of individualization and responsibilization than during high socialism. Yet we should not think of this independence from state planning bureaus as the arrival of freedom after state domination under "high" socialism. Rather, self-enterprise and self-development are late-socialist forms of regulation that support post-Mao open door development strategies, while also producing subjects amenable to the watchful eye of global capital. As such, we see geographies of prosperous coastal zones and declining rust belts, musical squares and dilapidated housing. Along with these spatial transformations, we see new valuations of the citizenry that uphold the worth of talented human capital and urban consumers, while degrading that of the poor and temporary migrant workers.

Notes

* The research for this article was generously funded by the Committee for Scholarly Communication with China, Foreign Language and Area Studies, and Berkeley's Center for the Study of Higher Education. An earlier version of this paper was published in *Provincial China* and I thank the anonymous reviewer for comments. Previous versions were presented at the Association for Asian Studies in 1999 and 2003 and I am grateful for the comments received there. I also received helpful comments from participants in the Shanghai workshop on Social, Cultural, and Political Implications of Privatization in the PRC in 2004. I also would like to thank Jennifer Hubbert and Monica Dehart for their multiple readings and support, and for the comments from Aihwa Ong, Li Zhang, and the editors, Tim Oakes and Louisa Schein. In addition, I would like to express my gratitude to Professor Liu Zhongquan of Dalian University of Technology for his insight and for our continued conversations about Dalian, as well as Dalian's Municipal Government and especially Mr Li Huimin of the Free Trade Zone for providing information and agreeing to share the images published here.
1 In a discussion of how states engage in "competitive bidding" to attract investments, Peter Dicken comments that "it is amazing how many places project themselves as being at the 'centre' of the world" (1998: 273).

2 Arguing that cities and citizens are mutually constituted through these social and power relations builds on the work of geographers who have argued that space is not just a thing, a closed system, or a place, but is the product of and also produces social relations (e.g. see Pred 1990; Lefebvre 1991; Massey 1994). Anthropologists also have critically examined assumptions about the connections between place and culture, arguing these two social fields are not synonymous, but rather that "associations of place, people, and culture are social and historical creations to be explained" (Gupta and Ferguson 1999: 4).

3 As a social class-specific study, this paper also is part of an emerging anthropological literature on professionals, managers, and the middle class in China. See, for example, Ong (forthcoming 2006), Rofel (2004), and Zhang (2004).

4 See Dai (2002). I also would like to thank Louisa Schein for emphasizing this point.

5 David R. Phillipps and Anthony G. O. Yeh argue that the Coastal City designation was an extension of the initial successes of the SEZs while also trying to "redress[s] the southerly bias of the SEZs"(1989: 116). Three SEZs, Shenzhen, Zhuhai, and Shantou were approved in 1979. Xiamen was added in 1980. The other Coastal Cities are: Qinhuangdao, Yantai, Qingdao, Lianyungang, Nantong, Ningbo, Fuzhou, Guangzhou, Ahanjian, and Beihai. By 1986 the government had selected four port cities as priority areas for the central government (Dalian, Shanghai, Tianjin, and Guangzhou). The 1984 push for more open areas came on the heels of Deng Xiaoping's visit to the SEZs in that year, but by 1985 "doubts were being expressed by some about the SEZ experiment" (e.g. costs were too high, they attracted the wrong kind of investments, little focus on exports), which led to the further central government concentration on only four cities (ibid.: 121–127).

6 In 1984 Dalian was granted the right to report directly to the central government for economic issues rather than going through the provincial government. This, Goodman explains, made the city "in effect [an] economic province" but notably only in economic matters, political ones still reported to the province (1989: 24). That same year Shenyang, Harbin, Xian, and Wuhan gained the same status. In 1983 Chongqing was included, in 1985 Qingdao and in 1986 Ningbo (ibid.). See also Schueller (1997).

7 *Heshang* is popularly known in English as River Elegy. It has also been translated as Deathsong of the River (Su and Wang 1991). I want to thank Jennifer Hubbert for suggesting this citation.

8 In Dalian's case this is primarily with Japan and Russia. On this issue, see Faure and Siu (Chapter 2, this volume).

9 Dalian's use of the feminine subverts the more typical representation of the north as industrial and masculine, which people often oppose to feminine images of southern China, its commercial success, and its minority populations. See also Cartier, Chapter 7, this volume; Schein (2000); Gladney (1994). I thank Tim Oakes for noting this north–south contrast.

10 Professor Liu Zhongquan, now retired from teaching, is in the sociology department at Dalian University of Technology. His insights were invaluable during fieldwork.

11 I would like to thank Tim Oakes for these comments.

12 Yet while young college graduates are expected to engage the global economy and "outside" world, they also are expected to *remain patriotic* during this "rescaling of…strategic territories" (Sassen 2002: 1). Thus, the very subjects who emerge in this new border-crossing space are expected to be *both* outward looking professionals and nation-focused patriots, what I call *patriotic professionals*. See Hoffman (n.d.).

13 This line of analysis also offers interesting parallels with Ferguson and Gupta's argument about how states are spatialized (2002). See also Ong (1997) for a discussion of how Chinese modernity is a state project.

14 In a recent speech, Mayor Xia Deren said "Because of Dalian's solid material foundation, perfect urban function, strong comprehensive economic strength, and huge development potential, the central government attaches great importance to Dalian especially in its pioneering role in the northeastern revitalization."

15 As part of the anniversary celebration, Jiang Zemin wrote "*Bai nian fengyu xili, beifang mingzhu sheng hui*" (translated as "The centennial test has baptized the North Pearl into its shining age," in *Zhongguo beifang mingzhu*, 2001).
16 The names of all interviewees are pseudonyms. The names of government officials, such as Mayor Bo Xilai and Mayor Xia Deren, have not been changed.
17 For more on the specificity of post-Mao experiences of choice and enterprise, see Hoffman (n.d.).
18 Miss He was allowed to settle her registration in Dalian because she had six scholarship points, an academic requirement for registration changes. If students did not have the required six points, obtained through top class rankings from exam scores during their college tenure, they had to pay 1000 RMB for each missing point for a maximum of 6000 RMB. Miss He did say, however, that "there are many policies like that but you can also get around them because they want talent to be able to flow (*rencai liudong*)." On the scholarships, see also Hoffman (2001).
19 Xia Deren "Dalian Municipal Symposium on the Implementation of Revitalizing the Northeast Industrial Base Strategy" 2003. I received an English version with no details about the time or location of Mayor Xia's speech. It was near the end of 2003.
20 People and households also have been recognized by the Party. Officials often identified, honored and paraded model workers around the community for emulation, see Anagnost (1992).
21 On the increasingly significant role of urban environmental governance, see Boland (2003). The awards Dalian has accumulated in this field include: the United Nations Environment Programme Award in May 2001, a state award for "Sanitary city, the Model City in Environmental Protection, the Advanced City in Green-Making, the Garden-Like City, the Advanced City in Water Saving, the Excellent Tourist City, and the Model City for Environment Improvement in the Asian-Pacific Region." Mayor Bo Xilai was awarded the UN Habitat Scroll of Honor Award in 1999. Dalian's urban environmental construction project was awarded the Best Practice Award in Dubai International Human Settlements Development of the Year 2000. Dalian was elected as one of the Ten Best Habitable Cities in China at the National Advanced Forum for Real Estate on July 1, 2000 (Liu 2000).
22 Forbes notes that the "metaphor of the hub" is "central to Singapore's world city status … and is a very prominent feature of the public face of the Singapore government," the kind of face that Dalian's planners wished to present as well (1999: 243). Singapore also used a three-part approach to its development that highlights the non-local networks in which it is embedded. First, the city-state promoted "the Singapore growth triangle" (similar to Dalian's hinterland relationship), second, it highlighted investments in non-local places like China, and third it offered itself as a "regional tourist hub" (ibid.: 244–245).
23 Interestingly, in a study of plazas in San Jose, Costa Rica, Setha Low quotes a brochure about the new Plaza de la Cultura, which was rebuilt according to governmental and banking visions of what a modern and economically prosperous Costa Rica would be like. It says, "This Plaza de la Cultura that we inaugurate today unites the forces of Costa Ricans interested in *humanizing* the city, embellishing it, preserving the National Theater, and giving it the space required" (2000: 197, emphasis added). For more on the intentionality of modernist planning, which presents the city as a site of experimentation and transformation, see Rabinow (1989) and (2003) and Holston (1989).
24 I thank the anonymous reviewer for Provincial China for suggesting this work.

References

Anagnost, A. (1992) "Socialist ethics and the legal system," in J. Wasserstrom and E. Perry (eds) *Popular Protest and Political Culture in Modern China: Learning from 1989*, Boulder, CO: Westview Press, 177–205.

Anagnost, A. (1997) *National Past-Times: Narrative, Representation, and Power in Modern China*, Durham, NC: Duke University Press.

—— (2004) "The corporeal politics of quality (Suzhi)," *Public Culture* 16(2): 189–208.

Barry, A., Osborne, T. and Rose, N. (eds) (1996) *Foucault and Political Reason: Liberalism, Neo-Liberalism and Rationalities of Government*, Chicago, IL: University of Chicago Press.

Bo, X. (1993) "Dalianshi shizhang Bo Xilai zai yantaohui shang de jianghua," seminar speech by Dalian Mayor Bo Xilai, reprinted in Beijing, May 5.

Boland, A. (2003) "Environmental governance in urban China: natural competition and the rescaling of the local," paper presented at the International Conference on Globalization, the State, and Urban Transformation in China, Hong Kong Baptist University, December.

Burchell, G., Gordon, C., and Miller, P. (eds) (1991) *The Foucault Effect: Studies in Governmentality*, Chicago, IL: University of Chicago Press.

Butler, J. (1993) *Bodies That Matter: On the Discursive Limits of "Sex,"* New York: Routledge.

—— (1999) *Gender Trouble: Feminism and the Subversion of Identity*, New York: Routledge.

Cheng, A. (2003) "Dalian is shining like no other city," *South China Morning Post*, July 29, reprinted in *China Study Group News Archives*, Online version: www.chinastudygroup. org/newsarchive.php?id=1988 (accessed November 9, 2003).

Chow, C.-y. (2003) "Rust-belt giants striving for a future," *South China Morning Post*, October 19, reprinted by the *China Study Group News Archives*, Online version: www.chinastudygroup.org/newsarchive.php?id=2888 (accessed September 10, 2003).

Chowdhury, A. and Islam, I. (1993) *The Newly Industrializing Economies of East Asia*, London: Routledge.

Dai, J. (2002) "Invisible writing: the politics of mass culture in the 1990s," trans. J. Zhang in J. Wang and T. Barlow (eds) *Cinema and Desire: Feminist Marxism and Cultural Politics in the Work of Dai Jinhua*, London: Verso, 213–234.

Dean, M. (1999) *Governmentality: Power and Rule in Modern Society*, London: Sage.

Deng, X. (1994) *"Da Yidali jizhe Aolingaina-Falaqi wen,"* (Responding to Italian reporter's questions), August 21 and 23, 1980, in *Deng Xiaoping Wenxuan*, Vol. 2 (Deng Xiaoping's Selected Works), Shenyang: People's Publishing, 344–353.

Dicken, P. (1998) *Global Shift: Transforming the World Economy*, third edn, New York: The Guildford Press.

Dirlik, A. (1999) "Globalism and the politics of space," in K. Olds, P. Dicken, P. Kelly, L. Kong, and H. W.-c. Yeung (eds) *Globalisation and the Asia-Pacific*, London: Routledge, 39–56.

Engardo, P., Bernstein, A., and Kripalani, M. (2003) "The new global shift," *Business Week*, February 3, reprinted in *China Study Group News Archive*, Online version: www.chinastudygroup.org/newsarchive.php?id=224 (accessed November 9, 2003).

Ferguson, J. and Gupta, A. (2002) "Spatializing states: toward an ethnography of neoliberal governmentality," *American Ethnologist* 29(4): 981–1002.

Forbes, D. (1999) "Globalisation, postcolonialism and new representations of the Pacific Asian metropolis," in K. Olds, P. Dicken, P. Kelly, L. Kong, and H. W.-c. Yeung (eds) *Globalisation and the Asia-Pacific*, London: Routledge, 238–254.

Foucault, M. (1991) "Governmentality," in G. Burchell, C. Gordon, and P. Miller (eds) *The Foucualt Effect: Studies in Governmentality*, Chicago, IL: University of Chicago Press, 87–104.

Friedman, J. (2002) *The Prospect of Cities*, Minneapolis, MN: University of Minnesota Press.

Gaubatz, P. (1995) "Urban transformation in post-Mao China: impacts of the Reform Era on China's urban form," in D. S. Davis, R. Kraus, B. Naughton, E. J. Perry, and L. H. Hamilton (eds) *Urban Spaces in Contemporary China: The Potential for Autonomy and Community in Post-Mao China*, Cambridge: Cambridge University Press and Woodrow Wilson Center Press, 28–60.

—— (2005) "Globalization and the development of new central business districts in Beijing, Shanghai, and Guangzhou," in F. Wu and L. Ma (eds) *Restructuring the Chinese City: Changing Society, Economy and Space*, London: Routledge, 98–121.

Gladney, D. (1994) "Representing nationality in China: refiguring majority/minority identities," *Journal of Asian Studies* 53(1): 92–123.

Goodman, D. S. G. (1989) "Political perspectives," in D. S. G. Goodman (ed.) *China's Regional Development*, London: Routledge, 20–37.

Gordon, C. (1991) "Governmental rationality: an introduction," in G. Burchell, C. Gordon and P. Miller (eds) *The Foucualt Effect: Studies in Governmentality*, Chicago, IL: University of Chicago Press, 1–51.

Gu, F. R. and Tang, Z. (2002) "Shanghai: reconnecting to the global economy," in S. Sassen (ed.) *Global Networks, Linked Cities*, New York: Routledge, 273–308.

Gupta, A. and Ferguson, J. (1999) "Culture, power, place: ethnography at the end of an era," in A. Gupta and J. Ferguson (eds) *Culture, Power, Place: Explorations in Critical Anthropology*, Durham, NC: Duke University Press, 1–31.

Hoffman, L. (1999) "Becoming a professional in 'late-socialist' China: social mobility, state welfare, and subject making," paper presented at Society for Cultural Anthropology Meetings, San Francisco, May.

—— (2001) "Guiding college graduates to work: social constructions of labor markets in Dalian," in N. Chen, C. D. Clark, S. Z. Gottschang, and L. Jeffery (eds) *China Urban: Ethnographies of Contemporary Culture*, Durham, NC: Duke University Press.

—— (forthcoming) "Autonomous choices and patriotic professionalism: on governmentality in late-socialist China," Urban Studies, University of Washington, Tacoma.

Holston, J. (1989) *The Modernist City: An Anthropological Critique of Brasilia*, Chicago, IL: University of Chicago Press.

Hu, Y. (2003) "Permit reform offers 'drifters' in Beijing first-class benefits," *South China Morning Post*, July 8, reprinted in *China Study News Archive*, Online version: www.chinastudygroup.org/newsarchive.php?id=1681 (accessed November 9, 2003).

Hubbert, J. (2002) "Consuming the nation, legitimating the state: theme parks in late-socialist China," paper presented at American Anthropological Association Annual Meetings.

Jessop, B. (1997) "The entrepreneurial city: re-imagining localities, re-designing economic governance, or re-structuring capital?" in N. Jewson and S. MacGregor (eds) *Realising Cities: New Spatial Divisions and Social Transformation*, London: Routledge, 28–41.

—— (1998) "The narrative of enterprise and the enterprise of narrative: place marketing and the entrepreneurial city," in T. Hall and P. Hubbard (eds) *The Entrepreneurial City*, Chichester: Willey, 77–99.

—— (1999) "Reflections on globalization and its (il)logic(s)," in K. Olds, P. Dicken, P. Kelly, L. Kong, and H. W.-c. Yeung (eds) *Globalisation and the Asia-Pacific*, London: Routledge, 19–38.

Jessop, B. and Sum, N.-l.(2000) "An entrepreneurial city in action: Hong Kong's emerging strategies in and for (inter)urban competition," *Urban Studies* 37(12): 2287–2313.

Lefebvre, H. (1991) *The Production of Space*, trans. D. Nicholson-Smith, Oxford: Blackwell.

Liu, C. (2000) "Urban environment construction and protection, Dalian, China," paper presented at Hangzhou International Seminar on Best Practices: UN Local Leadership Programme on Sustainable Development, October, Online version: www.sustainabledevelopment.org/blp/Hangzhou/Presentations/dalian.html (accessed September 12, 2002).

Liu, Z., Ji, X., and Chang, B. (1994) *Dalian xiandai chenzhen tixi yu jiasu quyu chengshihuade zhanlue xuanze* (Dalian's strategic choices for city and town systematization and rapid urbanization), Dalian: Dalian Urban Economy Working Group.

Low, S. (2000) *On the Plaza: The Politics of Public Space and Culture*, Austin, TX: University of Texas Press.

Massey, D. (1994) *Space, Place, and Gender*, Minneapolis, MN: University of Minnesota.

Massey, D., Allen, J. with J. Anderson, S. Cunningham, C. Hamnett and P. Sarre (eds) (1984) *Geography Matters! A Reader*, Cambridge: Cambridge University Press.

Olds, K. and Thrift, N. (2004) "Cultures on the brink: re-engineering the soul of capitalism— on a global scale," in A. Ong and S. Collier (eds) *Global Assemblages: Technology, Politics and Ethics as Anthropological Problems*, Oxford: Blackwell, 270–290.

Ong, A. (1997) "Chinese modernities: narratives of nation and capitalism," in A. Ong and D. Nonini (eds) *Ungrounded Empires: The Cultural Politics of Modern Chinese Transnationalism*, London and New York: Routledge.

—— (forthcoming 2006) *Neoliberalism as Exception: Mutations in Citizenship and Sovereignity*, Durham, NC: Duke University Press.

Parris, K. (1994) "Reinventing local identity in Wenzhou," paper presented at University of California at Berkeley, Center for Chinese Studies Symposium on Chinese Identities, February 25–26.

Phillipps, D. R. and Yeh, A. G. O. (1989) "Special economic zones," in D. S. G. Goodman (ed.) *China's Regional Development*, London: Routledge, 112–134.

Pred, A. (1990) " 'In other wor(l)ds' fragmented and integrated observations on gendered languages, gendered spaces and local transformation," *Antipode* 22(1): 33–52.

Pun, N. (2004) "The myth of capital: transnational corporate codes of conduct in the Chinese workplace," paper presented at the Workshop on the Social, Cultural, and Political Implications of Privatization in China, Shanghai, June 27–29.

Rabinow, P. (1989) *French Modern: Norms and Forms of the Social Environment*, Cambridge, MA: MIT Press.

—— (2003) "Ordonnance, discipline, regulation: some reflections on urbanism," in S. Low and D. Lawrence-Zuniga (eds) *The Anthropology of Space and Place: Locating Culture*, Oxford: Blackwell, 353–362.

Rofel, L. (2004) "The twenty-first century silk road," paper presented at the Workshop on the Social, Cultural, and Political Implications of Privatization in China, Shanghai, June 27–29.

Rose, N. (1992) "Governing the enterprising self," in P. Heelas and P. Morris (eds) *The Values of the Enterprise Culture: The Moral Debate*, London: Routledge, 141–164.

—— (1996) "Governing 'advanced' liberal democracies," in A. Barry, T. Osborne, N. Rose (eds) *Foucault and Political Reason: Liberalism, Neo-Liberalism, and Rationalities of Government*, Chicago, IL: University of Chicago Press, 37–64.

—— (1998) *Inventing Our Selves: Psychology, Power, and Personhood*, Cambridge: Cambridge University Press.

—— (1999) *Powers of Freedom: Reframing Political Thought*, Cambridge: Cambridge University Press.

Sassen, S. (2002) "Introduction: locating cities on global circuits," in S. Sassen (ed.) *Global Networks, Linked Cities*, New York: Routledge, 1–38.

Schein, L. (2000) *Minority Rules: The Miao and the Feminine in China's Cultural Politics*, Durham, NC: Duke University Press.

Schueller, M. (1997) "Liaoning: struggling with the burdens of the past," in D. S. G. Goodman (ed.) *China's Provinces in Reform: Class, Community and Political Culture*, London: Routledge, 93–121.

Shi, J. (2000) "Zuojin guoji mingcheng" (Becoming a famous international city), *Dalian Daily*, May 19.

Siu, N. Y. M. and Lau, C. P. (1998) "Training and development practices in the People's Republic of China," *China Report* 34(1): 47–67.

Su, X. and Wang, L. (1991) *Deathsong of the River: A Reader's Guide to the Chinese TV Series Heshang*, trans. R. W. Bodman and P. P. Wan, Ithaca, NY: Cornell University East Asia Program.

Sum, N.-l. (1999) "Rethinking globalization: re-articulating the spatial scale and temporal horizons of trans-border spaces," in K. Olds, P. Dicken, P. Kelly, L. Kong, and H. W.-c. Yeung (eds) *Globalisation and the Asia-Pacific*, London: Routledge, 129–146.

Wang, J. (1996) *High Culture Fever: Politics, Aesthetics, and Ideology in Deng's China*, Berkeley, CA: University of California Press, 118–136.

Wu, F. (2003) "The (post-) socialist entrepreneurial city as a state project: Shanghai's reglobalisation in question," *Urban Studies* 40(9): 1673–1698.

Xiao, J. and Tsang, M. C. (1998) "Human capital development in an emerging economy: the experience of Shenzhen, China," *The China Quarterly* 157: 72–114.

Yahuda, M. B. (1994) "North China and Russia," in D. S. G. Goodman and G. Segal (eds) *China Deconstructs: Politics, Trade, and Regionalism*, London: Routledge, 253–270.

Yan, H. (2002) "Self-development of migrant women: production of Suzhi (quality) as surplus value and displacement of class in China's post-Socialist development," paper presented at Association for Asian Studies Annual Meetings.

—— (2003a) "Spectralization of the rural: reinterpreting the labor mobility of rural young women in post-mao china," *American Ethnologist* 30(4): 578–596.

—— (2003b) "Neoliberal governmentality and neohumanism: organizing suzhi/value flow through labor recruitment networks," *Cultural Anthropology* 18(4): 493–523.

Yeung, Y.-m. and Hu, X.-w. (eds) (1992) *China's Coastal Cities: Catalysts for Modernization*, Honolulu, HI: University of Hawaii Press.

Zhang, L. (2001) *Strangers in the City: Reconfigurations of Space, Power, and Social Networks within China's Floating Population*, Stanford, CA: Stanford University Press.

—— (2004) "Intersecting space, class, and consumption: a cultural inquiry of a new *Jieceng* formation in the neoliberalizing China," paper presented at the Workshop on the Social, Cultural, and Political Implications of Privatization in China, Shanghai, June 27–29.

Zhongguo beifang mingzhu: Dalian (The Northern Pearl, Dalian, China) (2001) Beijing: People's Fine Arts Publishing House.

Zhou, D. (ed.) (2003) *Da Dalian: xin shiji tou 20 nian de zhanlue jueze* (Greater Dalian: Strategic Choices the First 20 Years of the New Century), Dalian: Dalian Renmin Chubanshe.

7 Symbolic city/regions and gendered identity formation in south China

Carolyn Cartier

Introduction

In China under reform, mobility has become a leitmotif of social and economic change. Rural migrants have surged into cities, *hukou*-for-investment policies have fueled sales of upscale private housing, tourism has become a major leisure time activity, and seeking a passport is becoming an urban trend. Geographical mobility, social mobility, travel, and imaginaries about these possibilities—all in relation to the pace of industrialization, at least for some of China's cities and regions, the fastest in world history—have made movement a central processural theme of transformation and identification in contemporary China. These new mobilities reflect dynamic economic transformations under reform, and, most basically, renewed opportunity to travel and relocate. Socio-economic mobility wrought by reform is symbolized by millions of rural migrants, and the new ties formed by migrants between small towns and large cities. Moving up this urban hierarchy and the economic ladder are widely held goals if not imaginations, as representations of the new rich—typically residing in China's major cities— circulate in media and society. International linkages are also increasingly evolving between regions and cities of rapid growth in coastal provinces and major source countries of foreign direct investment in China. As Wanning Sun (2002) has discussed, China's new media technologies, especially television, have brought images of not only Beijing, Shanghai and Hong Kong to the village, but also those of New York, London and Tokyo.

This chapter examines implications for the new mobility through translocal ties produced and forged in the context of travel and migration, and in imaginaries about such possibilities of mobility. These ties, and ideas about them, must take both material and symbolic forms, in ways that desires to migrate and travel have economic motivations and results, which in turn influence identity formation and subjects of popular culture. The perspective of the translocal I seek to explore stresses the simultaneity of ties to diverse places gained through mobility, imaginaries about replacing oneself in distant sites of desire and, consequently, the possibility of multiple place attachments as a basis for complex identity formation. Such new mobilities must impinge on ideas about the importance of place (*difang*) in Chinese society, as the important historic notion of being from a particular place or hometown begins to give way to more complex spatial lifepaths. While the time-space implications of "lifepath" suggest a linear unfolding—a mapped line of one's location and residence across the decades—I am alternatively interested to portray the translocal lifepath as one that embraces the multiple possibilities of place awareness and consequent place-contextualized identity formation, in terms of the increasing number of places and enhanced awareness of places a person experiences: places a person resides in, visits, gets connected to (as a consequence of personal and professional ties), detests, and desires.

While such expansions about the experiential and contextualized meanings of place are in flux, we can approach understanding them through perspectives on how meanings of place are changing in both popular and official realms, and ways these two arenas are imbricated in contemporary society. Thus I shall argue that one way of understanding the contemporary translocal is through popular expressions of place and their implications for identity formation, and in relation to the increased, state-sanctioned mobility and its reflection of changes in the spatial administrative hierarchy. Conjoining these arenas bridges the ideational and the material, reaching broadly to emplace a semiotic reading of popular culture, in textual representations of places, in the context of state transformations in China's spatial administrative hierarchy.

I depend on using examples of signifying practices, especially fragments of language and popular texts as place images, for their potential to tell us something about dynamic ideas of identity formation concerning cities and regions of high mobility. These examples include the language of "othering" between "locals" and migrants, and place images found in contemporary Chinese magazines and trade books, which rely on the established tradition of expressing regional differences in stock terms of place-based "traits" (as unchanging) and characteristics. But how should we attempt to read such stereotypic "trait" geographies in an era of "process" geographies, processes of rapid change, and globalizing cultural-economic influences? The following assessment works through three lines of inquiry. Based on a preponderance of images from cities and provinces of the south, the analysis treats the example texts as representative of southern regionalisms in an era of imagining and romanticizing the stratospheric economic rise of "the south." With regard to negotiations of migrant identity, the signifiers are categorical, essentializing names for migrants, including the notion of the mobile woman as prostitute. The textual examples from popular writings are especially gendered, emphasizing subjects like "southern beauties," "Shanghai masculinities," etc. Such popular expressions of "hot" places in terms of femininities and masculinities underscore personalized imaginaries about place accessibility and the new mobility. The discussion suggests how these images might be read. Two, since the texts concern places and regions of high mobility, the analysis treats them as representative of ideas about possibilities for migration to places at the top of the now crumbling "*hukou*-hierarchy." Such ideas about cities, and especially southern cities leading the reform experience, have been encoded in popular imaginaries as places of particular interest if not desire. Three, the political economic analysis considers changes in the spatial administrative hierarchy, especially how the state has "scaled up" numerous counties to become cities, thereby emphasizing the urban scale as the primary site of contemporary political/economic/culture interest, and promoting desire for the urban scene as a basis of identity formation. I develop this framework first, in the next section.

Local origins, urban desires

In China studies, the typical "center–local" dyad makes "local" stand in for any subnational geographic scale, from the province to the village, and so we may think of "translocal" as relations between different "locals." But we should probably consider a more nuanced scale dynamic that recognizes the different scales of local in the Chinese administrative hierarchy, and for two reasons: decentralization of power under reform, and loosening of the *hukou* system. Together these forces are restructuring the state spatial administrative system in terms of which places possess which kinds of political economic power and who can live in them. From small-scale hometowns to major cities, the contemporary migrant or traveler makes a journey across this spatial administrative hierarchy. Relocation between major urban centers among the professional class is also becoming increasingly common. Thus the new mobility often represents moving "up" and "down" the urban hierarchy or across spatial scales, from town to county to city, or "jumping" scale, say from village to city, or making lateral scale moves, from city to city.

What are the implications of the new, scaled mobility on identity formation? The trends of contemporary reform have arguably placed more intensive focus on the city as the leading scale of opportunity and place of desirable identification. The intensity of these trends is uneven and more characteristic of the eastern provinces; in some central and western provinces the county continues to serve as the pivot of political economic life and identity formation (e.g. Goodman 2002). Nevertheless, the urban shift holds significance for the country at large, for translocal identity formation, as the new mobility allows people to transcend the historic, more fixed character of scale possibilities, and instead begin to weave threads of common experience between people in, and tied to, diverse places. I have elsewhere discussed the relationship between scale and identity formation terms of dialectical scale relations as a set of translocal processes, and the translocal as "multiple places of attachment experienced by highly mobile people" (Cartier 2001: 26). Here I expand this perspective to include the realm of images and the ideational, I suggest that the translocal need not depend on actual person mobility but may be imagined through mindful engagement with place images and their forms of representation.

The central state's decentralization of power has been the outstanding trend highlighting the urban scale. Decentralization of state power is often described in terms of "to the provinces" or to "local governments." But it more realistically refers to giving over a wide range of political and economic decision-making powers to cities at different levels, which facilitates economic growth. In addition to the special economic zones and open cities, cities in general have greater power, for example, to contract foreign investment and develop land. In this transforming system, the state has extended power from the center down the hierarchy. Like the spatial metaphor of a telescoping cup, prefecture-level cities, for example, have absorbed or oversee lower level administrative centers (Tang and Chung 2000). Complementing the general trend of decentralization of power to cities, is the scaling up of numerous counties to the status of city: the *shixiaxian* (cities leading counties) policy, made counties come under the economic administration of cities; the *chexian gaishi* policy (abolishing counties and establishing cities) created new county-level cities. In 1993 and 1994, more than 700 counties each year came under the jurisdiction of cities, more than any other previous year under reform. In the process, counties widely vied to be reclassified "urban," which the state approved at higher rates after 1992 and Deng Xiaoping's southern excursion. In 1993 and 1994, fifty-three counties each year were redesignated as cities, over twice the average rate of previous years (Zhang and Zhao 1998: 338–339). In addition to creating more cities, reform policies have also increased designation of towns. Thus from two "directions," "up" and "down," the state has rescaled its spatial administrative hierarchy with a focus on cities.

Of course this hierarchy is also reflected in the spatial logic of the *hukou* system, in creating a hierarchy of settlement assignments in a pyramidal order, from villages at the bottom to the centrally-governed municipalities at the top. Each higher level of settlement has represented higher status and greater opportunities for its residents (Mallee 1996). Thus the *hukou* system has enhanced material and symbolic values about major cities as the most desirable places to live and work. The increasing gap in income distribution between rural and urban areas through the second decade of reform has arguably underscored perceptions about urban bias (Khan and Riskin 1998)—or urban desire. So whether we are thinking about "temporary" migrants, tourists, or relocated professionals, they all have faced a spatial imaginary of mobility laid out across the Chinese nation-space, in which traveling or toiling to reach the central municipality is represented as the height of place attainment if not personal achievement.

Gendered sites of urban imagining

The cultural side of the pro-urban policies manifests in what we might call a cultural economy of the new mobility, in an evolving urban commodity culture with distinct spheres of representation. These spheres include struggles between state and society over legitimate moral and economic positions, as nearly everything becomes open to market interpretation. On one hand, the state is interested to influence popular culture and leisure activities through its ongoing spiritual civilization campaign, by encouraging "appropriate" activities such as going out to movies and learning to use computers (Wang 2001). Such activities also promote the commodity economy through increased household consumption. But the spiritual civilization campaign is also promoted to counter the more chaotically popular sphere of sexuality in popular culture; this arena includes a male-gendered culture of entrepreneurialism (Barlow 1994: 347–348), in hyper-masuculinized competitive practices geared to the global economy (Rofel 1999: 240). The female-gendered counterpart to the culture of entrepreneurialism is found in the commodification of the female body, witnessed in the *qingchunfan* or "rice bowl of youth" phenomenon, signifying the basis of young women's economic opportunity in their physical capital (Zhen 2000: 94). Evidence of the *qingchunfan* idea is emerging even in the revival of legendary accounts, such as the story of Yang Guifei, the Tang dynasty imperial consort, whose beauty and liaisons with powerful men, ultimately the emperor, were the source of her family's success. As Susan Mann (2000: 857) writes in regard to the Yang Guifei revival, "In today's China, where men of wealth and power demand the sexual services of beautiful young women, families recognize that one fast track to upward mobility in the 'sea' of Chinese commerce is a pretty daughter who can work as a prostitute." The popularization of such representations also symbolizes how alternative sexual relationships, from affairs to prostitution, have been constructed within the realm of rational behavior on economic terms.

In China's contemporary cultural economy, the body is the fundamental site of expression and political economic negotiation. The new economy of consumption is apparent everywhere, and especially in urban centers where shopping centers define the new leisure culture. The "portable" imaginary of shopping takes form in a wide variety of women's fashion and lifestyle magazines; some are Chinese versions of Western ones, like *Elle* or *Cosmopolitan*, others are domestic products, like *Shanghai Style* (Shanghai Fushi, lit. Shanghai dress and accessories) and *Metropolis* (Dadushi). All focus on defining aspects of lifestyle for the new urban woman and many are literal guides to consumption—if just for visual pleasure—sometimes focusing entire issues on particular types of clothing, offering page after page of dresses or lingerie. Other layouts take the diurnal approach, showing pajamas and home-lounging clothes, work clothes, leisure outfits, what to wear for a date, or how to dress for a formal dinner. Above all, accessories proliferate. Seeing these texts as part of a semiotic system of consumption... theorizing the new global consumer society, Jean Baudrillard (1998: 87–98) has observed this tendency, what he calls the "smallest margin of difference" in personalized consumption. It "*ushers in the reign of differentiation*" in which products are apparently tailored for the individual, promoting especially embodied consumption and as a basis for notions about unique identity formation (ibid.: 89). Articles in these magazines typically concern guidelines for developing personalized style of comportment, from distinguishing yourself at work by wearing a series of different colorful scarves to adopting a distinctive walk. Of course, like during the early twentieth century, these kinds of images of the contemporary woman get centrally mapped on to ideas about national identity (Andrews and Shen 2002).

The body is also the essential material vehicle of mobility (given force of speed by technological conveyance). Agency of movement, combined with new political economic and technological possibilities to be mobile, makes individual movement both an opportunity and a potential project, embraced by both men and women under reform. Imaginaries about the body and one's potential mobility bind the mind and the sensible body into a dialectic: the seduction of mobility begins with imagining oneself along the way, a process of sensory imagining and desire, decision, movement, detour, and—perhaps—ultimate arrival. Such preparatory geographies of imagination are also about envisioning bodily emplacement: one's appearance, comportment, gestures, interactions, mindfully playing out the possibilities of encounter. The semiotic potential and suggestive power of such imaginary routes, though, is marked by obstacles and political and economic barriers, combined with limiting effects of the resurgence of traditional gendering practices and regionalisms, often in new forms.

In south China, Guangzhou serves as the new shopping mecca—if you can't get to Hong Kong. For the new mobile woman who has migrated to Guangdong, the export-oriented sector of factory compounds has been a primary scene of experience. In Shenzhen especially, the first city with the greatest number of special privileges and migrant workers, differentiation based on place of origin—regionalism—plays out in the workspace, as everyone sorts each other out on the basis of place of origin and spoken dialect. The workers form social groups based on such ties, and act as intermediaries for engaging in translocal practices like bringing relatives and friends into the workplace (Ngai 1999). In this case, translocality is not so much about transcending scale as maintaining local power structures, in the way that Emily Honig (1992) defined ethnicity based on hierarchies of place difference. Locals refer to inter-provincial migrants in general as *waisheng ren* (people from outside the province), and then by their province or region of origin, such as Guangxi *mei* (Guangxi girl) or *beimei* (northern girl) and so forth. In another way, the migration regime is giving rise to new translocal households: Guangdong and Fujian have the highest rates of mainland women marrying men from Taiwan or Hong Kong (Ye and Wen 1996). In addition, untold numbers of investors from Taiwan and Hong Kong have taken so-called second wives in the region—the historical concubine, characteristic of the successful man in China's imperial patriarchal social formation (Tam 1996). Such male-gendered explanations for the "secondary household" phenomenon reflect how historic tropes are used to contextualize contemporary practices in a commodity culture of hyper-masculinity.

Prostitution, and fears raised by anxieties about it, also reflect translocal conditions. Under reform, sex work has expanded substantially (Hershatter 1997), and it too is often represented in *nei/wai* (inside/outside) symbolisms to cast prostitution as a geographically "othered" problem (Ho 1998). In the first years of reform, the official Chinese press blamed Hong Kong and Macao as sources of prostitution. In the early 1990s, based on arrest records, official statistics reported that Guangdong, Fujian, and Hainan had the greatest numbers of prostitutes from other provinces, and that fully over 90 percent of prostitutes in Shenzhen, Guangzhou, Xiamen, and Hainan were from "outside" provinces (Dong 1996). The othering of mainland women from bordering and distant provinces suggests consideration of what Louisa Schein (1996) has observed as internal boundary-making in desires to maintain identity differences among different regions within the same nation-state. The degree to which *waisheng* prostitutes are held responsible for prostitution in general parallels anxieties about the mainland migrant woman in Hong Kong and Taiwan, where the arrival of the single mainland woman has ignited interpretations of the women in symbolic terms of invaded territory. In Hong Kong, people have feared the "invasion" of hundreds of thousands of mainland children born to mainland mothers and Hong Kong fathers (Tam 1996). In Taiwan, media accounts of single mainland women or *dalumei* (mainland girls), largely informal migrants, have represented them symbolically in terms of the prostitute, as women who would seek economic gains through practically any means possible and especially sex. Reports have gone as far to suggest that *dalumei* might have been sent to Taiwan to work as agents for the Chinese government (Shi 1999: 290), purposefully working to compromise both "man" and nation. These symbolic qualities constructed around the mobile migrant woman as prostitute reflect the patriarchal market economy, and how, as a signifier foregrounding sexual relations, the idea of the prostitute marginalizes the importance of the women's labor contributions to the regional economy, thus facilitating low wage labor and maximum surplus appropriation.

These discursive constructions of identity in spatial and geographical terms represent ways of reasserting Chinese traditions of place origin as a primary marker of ethnicity and difference. No doubt some of these formations also represent a class element of antagonism toward rural *hukou* holders and resistance to their mobility. By contrast to accepted ideas about globalizing identity formation in major cities worldwide, identity formation for new arrivals in the south China coast cities is not reliably taking place in terms of hybridity—that would require substantial international migration—but rather through preliminary encounter, resistance to norms, and local boundary keeping. Local populations in the south China coast cities regularly "other" domestic migrants, which can positively affects migrants' needs to maintain translocal ties with places of origin. At the same time, migrants desire to maintain familial ties for diverse reasons, and, in the process, urban residents are brought into contact with such translocal systems of place. So far, the *hukou* system has broken down far enough to encourage formation of translocal ties, comings and goings, but its ideological effects, as a system of hierarchical places, arguably continue to limit more open possibilities of identity formation.

By contrast to informal migrations, relocations of the new rich in China have been increasingly based on the relatively instant acquisition of urban citizenship rights. Major cities have structured an economic relationship between urban desirability and the stalled property market by offering *hukou* in exchange for relocation or local housing purchase. This started in Zhuhai in 1992, which, in seeking to compete with other major cities, innovated an employment system to recruit professionals from all over China by offering high salaries, housing benefits, and Zhuhai *hukou* (Qin and Ni 1993: 514). In 1994 Shanghai introduced the blue chop *hukou* policy, which provided local residency rights in exchange for local investment or for purchasing an expensive private flat, especially in Pudong (Wong and Huen 1998). Shenzhen introduced a similar blue chop *hukou* system in 1995. Thus the *hukou* system in China's leading cities became more flexible on class terms, and reinforced limitations on real and social mobility generated by uneven income distribution in society. The *hukou*-for-sale scheme actually originated in the 1980s at lower scales in the settlement hierarchy, first at the township level in Anhui and Henan provinces (ibid.; see also Chan and Zhang 1999). Thus from both ends of the settlement hierarchy, the local state formally commodified legal mobility strategies and affirmed the ascendant system of upward mobility culminating at the scale of major cities.

City/regions of the south

The rise of the cities of the south coast has been one of the great transformations in the urban system under reform. Shenzhen and Zhuhai are entirely new major cities in Guangdong province. Shanghai has emerged from reform as a city reconstructed, its planners literally building the city to command position on the world scale. Hong Kong holds the preeminent role in international finance for the country at large, and its property market elite has dominated the development of the city's Guangdong hinterland in the Pearl River Delta. The rise of the south China coast led the reform movement, and its growth, at least in the 1980s and 1990s, has represented a kind of regional reversal over the historically dominant north, yielding new perspectives on the role and meaning of regions in the national order (Qin and Ni 1993). Southern imaginaries have accompanied this shift, and have inflected popular culture and ideas about places and people in the region.

Ideas about the rise of the south have been negotiated in diverse print media, including popular books, magazines, and more literary accounts of regional life. Most of these print materials concern new urban lifestyles, and especially focus on lifepath stories, relationships, and gender identities. The balance of this paper discusses examples of these accounts to assess ideas about gender identities circulating in the contemporary region and how they work as a basis of geographical imaginaries and thus translocal possibilities. I suggest that images and representations about the dynamic southern city/region may work to both advance and deflect popular interest in experiencing its regional realities, which, in producing contradiction and tension, serve both to propel and check mobility. Meanings of such representations must be polysemic, contradictory, ambiguous, just as people's interpretations of them take different positions of engagement and resistance. Still, as the reform city is the setting of many such stories, these images advance attention on the city/region. The narrative form of many accounts about experiencing the southern city/region is chronological, describing people's journeys and arrivals, but often circular rather than linear in structure as the accounts commonly reference home or returning home. Such accounts suggest ideas about coping with the rapidity of social transformation under reform and diverse translocal experiences and circulating ideas about them in the era of new mobility.

Other narratives about the southern city/region are revisiting longstanding ideas about local cultural traits and characteristics. Ideas about place characteristics and regional stereotypes have a history of distinctive usage in China, serving as a basis of practical ethnic differentiation among the Han population (Young 1988; Honig 1992). Though the use of regional stereotypes and regional tropes is widely known and practiced within China, it is not commonly a subject of scholarly analysis. But such idiomatic forms are elements of popular culture as is writing that depends on these forms. Some recent popular writings on gender identity have made generous use of regionalisms, to the degree that authors of such writings treat them as so much truth and do not move to identify or question their essentialist characteristics. How should we interpret the continuing use of such regional images in the contemporary era? Some writings in this genre, such as *Southern Beauties* (Nanguo jiali), discussed later, at first read, appear in the style of guides to knowing and differentiating among women in the south. *Ah, Shanghai Men* (Ah, Shanghai nanren) suggests similar treatment for men of Shanghai. However, the descriptive style of such regionalist or "placist" writing just barely papers over their symbolic value. Apparently stereotypical in content and style, such narratives can work to reaffirm transhistorical notions about culture and place, even as those places experience wrenching change. The contemporary use of regionalist gender narratives appears to suggest traditions of familiarity or even nostalgia in an era of intensive social transformation. Similarly, they can offer a way of negotiating change in the context of known traditions. In this way, writing, talking about, and resisting gender identity through regional stereotypes is also a way of having symbolic discussions about place.

On January 16, 2002, the *Liberation Daily* (Jiefang ribao) ran an article under the headline "Shanghai men are not strictly controlled by women anymore" (Shanghai nanren bu zai "qi guan yan"). The article reported that a survey conducted by the Shanghai Academy of Social Sciences concluded that only 5.3 percent of Shanghai families interviewed depend on men to do housework, mostly for shopping and washing dishes. Women do most of the housework in 57.6 percent of Shanghai families, and in the rest, men and women are co-responsible for housework. As far as consumption is concerned, 29 percent of men acknowledged that they spend more money than their wives, and 78 percent said they did not feel any lack of freedom in using money. The article explained

> Because most Shanghai wives have stronger capabilities than their husbands for managing their household responsibilities and families, this gave the first impression that wives dominated in decision-making among Shanghai families (Youyu duoshu Shanghai qizi dui jiating zerenxin he chejia nengli bi zhangfu geng qiang, keneng shi Shanghai jiating gei ren yi qizi zuozhu de diyi yinxiang).
>
> (Ibid.)

It is reasonable that the Shanghai Academy of Social Sciences carried out research on the gender division of labor within the household; but the hypothesis implied at the basis of the study strikes at the heart of "placist" gender stereotyping in China: strong Shanghai women had resulted in domesticated men. Where gendered place images spur social science research, we have an interesting issue at stake. The article cited an "expert" who recalled that ten years ago when the "apron husband" (*weiqun zhangfu*) was appraised on Shanghai TV, in most places in China women did most of the housework. That Shanghai men had been known to do housework spawned the saying "big Shanghai small men" (*da Shanghai xiao zhangfu*). Explaining the results of the new survey, the expert observed that as the status of women has improved, more and more men across China have begun to share household tasks. Thus, as the survey also demonstrated, Shanghai men were really not doing all that much housework. On both local and national scales, Shanghai men could now take off their aprons and *qi guan yan* (strictly controlled by wife) hats.

In the way that a semiotic analysis works to reveal meanings that are ambiguous or contradictory (e.g. Hebdige 1979), this explanation seems to take an existing gender stereotype and positively reinterpret it in terms of increasing gender equality and Shanghai's role as a place of leading social trends under reform. The research also reveals the Shanghai househusband to be a constructed image, a national stereotype. How does this portrayal square with the new cultural economy of hyper-masculinity pervading the urban sphere? The Shanghai Academy's research results on local men suggest that they have never been "domesticated" per se, and on the contrary, concluded that Shanghai men have been relatively advanced in beginning to contribute to household labor. This signifier of the man from Shanghai, as ahead of his countrymen at large, can reflect the image of the city, renewed after 1990 and the opening of Pudong, as the country's leading center of economic and cultural change. On these terms, the masculinity of Shanghai men is at the forefront of leadership and national style.

But the portrayal of Shanghai masculinities though unchanging stock traits is pervasive. In *Southern Beauties* (Nanguo jiali), which otherwise concentrates exclusively on the characteristics of women, we find this characterization of Shanghai men:

> Shanghai men are gentlemen with "anemia." They appear neat, soft, sweet and submissive. They are fragrant. They are introverted and tender. They look slim and lacking *yang*. In life, Shanghai men have many nicknames such as *ma dasou* (sister-in-law Ma) [Shanghai dialect, *ma*—buy; *da*—wash; *sao*—cook] and "apron husband."

> (Zhou 1997: 62)

This image of Shanghai men is also at the center of a hotly debated essay by Long Yingtai, a noted Taiwanese author in diaspora. Her book, *Ah, Shanghai Men*, is a collection of articles and responses to them by her readers, and the essay, "Ah, Shanghai men!," originally published in *Wenhui Daily* (Wenhui bao) (Long 1997), has drawn especially intensive interest. Self-described as cosmopolitan and world-traveled, Long (1998: 11) writes in the opening lines of the essay, "she thought nothing in the world could surprise her until she met men of Shanghai":

> The Shanghai man is so lovely. He will not feel it is beneath him if he buys groceries, cooks, and cleans the floor. He will not feel low even if he washes his woman's underwear. He speaks softly without thinking that he lacks manly mettle. He will not feel weak if his woman is strong.
>
> (Ibid.: 14–15)

Readers of *Wenhui Daily* wrote to contest and correct Long's interpretations, complaining in general that Shanghai men are actually *da zhangfu* (big men) (ibid.: 16). One respondent wrote to explain his ambivalence over bringing his son to the first Shanghai Boys Festival in 1998, which "aimed at changing weaknesses such as softness and timidness among boys by attempting to remold their masculinity and social responsibility" (ibid.: 48).

Shanghai itself is a city populated by migrants, yet intensity of debate over the idea of the Shanghai man must reflect a long-term resident population, as ideas about gender-specific local cultural traits must accrete in place even as they also reflect distant views of that place. Ideas about Shanghai masculinities circulate widely within China, and in Taiwan, where people's fascination for the rapid transformation of the mainland is especially apt to be portrayed in terms of new twists on traditional "placisms." The translocality of such place images lies in their wide circulation and repetition in diverse regions, as ways of both linking knowledge about distant places and differentiating among them. Thus we can assess that the following claim must represent a northern vantage: "If you categorize Chinese cities according to traditional Chinese thinking of *yin/yang*, Shanghai is a *yin* city. In other words, Shanghai is a city that belongs to women, and woman-ization (*nüxinghua*) is its main characteristic" (Zhou 1997: 39). From a northern perspective, Shanghai is a city of the south and so the evolution of notions about "Shanghai masculinities" suggests a historically based complicity with a northern discursive project—a project with longstanding contradictory interest in Shanghai's comparative status, especially as the city rises again under reform. Recent interest in such gendered regionalisms likely also reflects the influx of new migrants to Shanghai, both formal and informal, and especially the arrival of the new rich—representing the hyper-masculinity of the commodity economy—who are able to buy local *hukou*, and who must contend with such images of "manliness."

In *Southern Beauties*, which portrays traits of women from Shanghai, Hangzhou, Changsha, and Guangdong, we find the Shanghai man's counterpart: "Shanghai girls, like calendar girls, are *dia* [Shanghai dialect, 3rd tone] sweet, tender, and glutinous. At the same time, they are famous in China for being competent and practical, with resolution, tenacity, and independence" (ibid.: 1).

> We can use one word to generalize Shanghai women, *dia*. *Dia* is the vividness of voice, gesture, and expression among Shanghai women. It is a comprehensive description and evaluation of their charms. It includes a woman's sweetness, gentleness, interest, style of conversation, posture, family origin, upbringing and

skills. ...It includes the image of the pretty and soft Jiangnan beauty over hundreds and thousands of years. It also reflects women's awareness of gender qualities combined with commercial sense in order to gain social sympathy and acknowledgement in the modern commercial civilization of Shanghai.

(Ibid.: 48).

By contrast to the gender images of Shanghai, *Southern Beauties* describes Guangdong women in less flattering but nevertheless upwardly mobile terms:

Guangdong girls are not pretty. It is not easy to find a local beauty in Guangdong. Guangdong girls are very practical in love and marriage. They do not know what is a bachelor, master's or doctoral degree. They pay more attention to a man's business network and his financial ability. They are conservative and love their families. They are kind and capable. They can cook very good soup. They do not like to divorce. Even if the husband has a new lover, a Guangdong woman will tolerate him. Guangdong women feel close to Hong Kong and seek fashion and ways of speaking from Hong Kong and look down upon northerners.

(Ibid.: 167)

In these quotations, women's bodies and lifepaths are foregrounded: their appearances, their modes of embodiment, and their values over the life course. Their successes are bound to their gender identities in relation to men and male-gendered perceptions. Ideas about their characteristics are formed against a national backdrop of regional comparisons. But here Shanghai has no peer or model, whereas Guangdong, likely in its southern differences, looks even further south to Hong Kong for leading urban trends. These ways of talking about gender identities and the city must also reflect attempts to capture in familiar terms the unprecedented emergence of gender and sexuality in the public sphere, as well as attempts to maintain traditional humanist discourses about the city and urban life even as people find the urban scene thrust chaotically into twenty-first-century modernities. That these popular discourses about gendered identities in the city are really about the city is underscored in the following terms:

It is true that in the thirty years after liberation, Shanghai was always the symbol of wealth, prosperity, fashion, civility, and excellence. Shanghai women were very proud everywhere they went in China and spoke distinctively in Shanghai dialect. And the outsiders (*wai di ren*) from all over China had traditional respect, humility, and envy for Great Shanghai (*da Shanghai*). Shanghai girls were the image of privilege, fashion, and the *avant garde*.

(Ibid.: 37–38)

However, since the coastal cities were opened, the city of Shanghai and Shanghai women began to feel confused and irritated. Facing rapidly changing Beijing and newly rising Guangdong, they felt the sadness of an aging beauty. Resulting from the weakness of the city, Shanghai women became more sensitive, stronger, and emotionally volatile. They were faced with the dilemma of having both pride and self-contempt.

(Ibid.: 38)

Place traditions in China, including place-based identities, regionalisms, and the spatialities of the state system itself, in the organization of the administrative hierarchy and *hukou*, are enduring forms of human-environment relations reworked over time. Discourses about comparisons and competitions among cities, represented as agents, are part of these place traditions and ideological attempts of empire and state has knit itself into a coherent whole. Thus Shanghai only falters in the face of the rise of Beijing and Guangdong—in the latter case where a province is named instead of a single city, as the Pearl River Delta beyond Guangzhou has morphed from fields to factories to a phalanx of new towns and cities in less than a generation.

The wildly rapid transformation of city/regions in south China leaves seductive images scattered across the landscape of everything that is new. People are faced with thinking about the consequences of change whether they want to or not, which generates contradictions and tensions about experiencing the contemporary city. Living with the new city, combined with the new mobility, has thrust people together in new places and into new and untested arrangements. After leaving behind an era in which personal movement and space was more tightly controlled, experiencing the contemporary city is available to anyone who is willing to take the journey. Access to personal space is available to anyone who can pay the premium. Travel to the new city is everything from a voyeuristic opportunity and touristic adventure to an economic opportunity and necessity. The latter position especially is the experience of migrants.

Narratives of migrant journeys to south China represent migrants' naiveté, shock, and fascination in the face of the new city. Many of these stories are about women who find their needs and values compromised by encounters with men, which symbolizes the male-gendered entrepreneurial culture of the commodity economy. Other stories establish how women test and accept aspects of urban modernity. The following adapted account symbolizes how men and women alike can be compromised by the city.

Bai Ling was a pretty village girl from Hunan; she had a handsome and intelligent boy friend. After he failed in the college admission exam, she encouraged him to remain in high school for one more year and take the exam again. But he said his mom was old and his brother and sister-in-law were on their own, and he wanted to make money. He went to Zhuzhou and started working as a porter. Meanwhile, when Bai Ling's cousin and her husband came back from Guangzhou, they were well dressed in Hong Kong style. They left their son and daughter in their hometown, returned to Guangzhou, and mailed home a lot of money every month. Bai Ling's cousin worked as a waitress in a hotel in Guangzhou and said Bai Ling could make money there too. They invited Bai Ling to come to Guangzhou, and Bai Ling thought it would be good if her boyfriend worked in Guangzhou too. She decided to go. When she arrived, her cousin introduced a Hong Kong boss who gave her a birthday gift and slept with her. Since she was a virgin, the Hong Kong man paid 1,000 *yuan* to her cousin and another 200 *yuan* as bonus.

(Adapted from Ni 1993: 214–220)

In this vignette, Bai Ling's female cousin pimps her to an acquaintance, representing how all bets are off after entering the city: bonds of solidarity and protection from family or among women evaporate in the sexualized commodity economy in which anything or anyone has a price. Thus translocality is no guarantee of security. Along the journey, Bai Ling thinks of her ties to her boyfriend and the possibilities of new monetary resources. Her journey is a translocal experience as she travels to be with people she knows, easing the transition. But the story's conclusion sends the larger message of migration narratives collected in *Nanxia nüren chao* (Waves of Women Migrating South) (Qiao 1993): migration is a fraught and contradictory experience in which women become subject to the forces of the patriarchal economy.

In an account of group labor migration to Shenzhen, women in the Hunan–Jiangxi border area are encouraged to migrate as a result of seeing the modern transformation of their counterparts.

In 1987, upon the request of officials from Jinggangshan [Mao's revolutionary base], local girls were recruited to factories in Longgang, Shenzhen. On the second day that girls were transported to Longgang, half of the girls that had gone there returned to Jinggangshan with the bus. Those who stayed mailed money back. They learned new values and began a life different from those of their mothers and grandmothers. They wore stylish clothes, imitating Hong Kong and Taiwan stars. After they returned home, the other 100 girls that originally fled on the second day returned to Shenzhen. Then hundreds of other girls in the counties around Jinggangshan wanted to go to Shenzhen as well.

(Adapted from Chen 1993: 138–146)

This story repeats the common experience of migrants' "demonstration effect" on their counterparts at home, thereby encouraging further out-migration. The migrations have translocal effects that bind the women and their journeys into a set of chain migrations from hometowns and home counties to Shenzhen, the new city of the south. Their returns home have profound impacts on local women and society, substantiating the judgment of officials who foresaw in the women's labor remittances an important new resource for the local economy. Thus women are encouraged to enter the migration stream for their earnings potential. Hometowns and counties have substantial interests in maintaining ties with these women, and the resulting translocal connection is both cultural and economic as the women's needs for social support are mirrored in their economic support for their places of origin.

Conclusions

The rise of the new city in China, both in the south and in the country at large, as hundreds of counties have been upgraded to city status, represents both ideas and realities about how the urban scale is being substantially inscribed in the cultural economic landscape. Combined with the new mobility, the extension and reworking of urban space has resulted in new spatial opportunities—spaces to occupy, buy, experience, work in, and avoid—and new place contexts with gendered dimensions. The new commodity economy has created places where men and women test boundaries of gendered identities and sexuality. The glittering built environments of the development zones and streetscapes of new cities, as instant environments of commodity desire and cultural blankness, invite alternative interpretations. In their newness and difference, these can be spaces of liminality where especially recent migrants experience alternative practices.

In modern Chinese historiography, many scholars have noted the relationship between nation formation, national identity and representations of the modern woman. As Prasenjit Duara (1998: 296) has written, perspectives on women have been "a very significant site upon which regimes and elites in China responsible for charting the destiny of the nation have sought to locate the unchanging essence and moral purity of that nation." Against this historical backdrop, it is possible to suggest that, instead of the primacy of nation, contemporary gender images reflect the rising significance of the scale of the city, as the vortex of change in China under reform. Though certainly the nation remains at stake, what we may be seeing are ways in which a contemporary city-nation dialectic is under formation. From the extremes of migration experience, in the image of the mobile woman as prostitute, we may draw conclusions similar to those of Duara, that is, that such imagery reflects the contemporary state's exhortations for women to accede to the interests of the patriarchal nation: for male heads of households to get jobs in this era of substantial urban unemployment and for the mobile woman (as prostitute) to abandon her search for paid employment and go home (Liu 1997; Howell 2000). Yet concerning cities and regions of economic success, images of women more likely code positive values, represented especially in terms of the contemporary woman's capacity for sophisticated embodiment. This urban woman—urban in style and form if not place—is assessing the city's new opportunities for leisure/consumption (another interest of the national state), remaking herself in ways that symbolize translocal urban linkages. The worth of the imagery of the Shanghai man may be its potential to serve as antidote to the commodity culture's hyper-masculinity, serving to check ideas about resurgence of patriarchal manliness, as China's leading city of the early twentieth century poises itself for that role renewed in the twenty-first.

Many popular writings about the new city/region reflect more traditional forms of expression, and ways of assessing the present in the language of the past. Such narrative strategies renew conventions as they transcend historical space, recalling the city of familiarity in times of extraordinary transformation. They also encompass the new mobility in terms of translocal ties, seeking to make sense of the differences in everyday life between places of origin and destination, and places of the imagination.

The evolving intensity of translocal connections will ultimately rework long held ideas about meanings of place in Chinese society, and in the shorter term will anchor people to diverse places of experience and sites of meaning along the way.

Acknowledgments

I am ever grateful to David Goodman and the Centre for Provincial China Studies for sponsoring my participation in the Translocality Workshop, and to Tim Oakes and Louisa Schein for inviting my participation and encouraging development of ideas in the paper. Thanks especially to Louisa for careful reading of the paper and critical comments that guided me in making the final revision.

References

Andrews, J. F. and Shen, K. (2002) "The new Chinese woman and lifestyle magazines in the late 1990s," in P. Link, R. Madsen, and P. Pickowicz (eds) *Popular China: Unofficial Culture in a Globalizing Society*, Lanham, MD: Rowman and Littlefield, 137–162.

Barlow, T. (1994) "Politics and protocols of *funü*: (un)making national woman," in C. K. Gilmartin, G. Hershatter, L. Rofel, and T. White (eds) *Engendering China: Women, Culture, and the State*, Cambridge, MA: Harvard University Press, 339–359.

Baudrillard, J. (1998) *The Consumer Society*, London: Sage, 87–98.

Cartier, C. (2001) *Globalizing South China*, Oxford: Blackwell.

Chan, K. W. and Zhang, L. (1999) "The hukou systems and rural–urban migration in China: processes and changes," *The China Quarterly* 160: 818–855.

Chen, B. A. (1993) "Laizi 'nü'er guo' de baogao" (Report from the "Kingdom of Women"), in H. Qiao (ed.) *Nanxia nüren chao* (Waves of Women Migrating South), Guangzhou: Huacheng chubanshe, 120–158.

Dong, X. (1996) *Nüxing weifa fanzui jieshi* (An Analysis of Female Criminal Offenses), Chongqing: Chongqing chubanshe.

Duara, P. (1998) "The regime of authenticity: timelessness, gender, and national history in modern China," *History and Theory* 37(3): 287–308.

Goodman, D. S. G. (2002) "Structuring local identity: nation, province and county in Shanxi during the 1990s," *The China Quarterly* 172: 837–862.

Hebdige, D. (1979) *Subculture: The Meaning of Style*, London: Methuen.

Hershatter, G. (1997) *Dangerous Pleasures: Prostitution and Modernity in Twentieth-Century Shanghai*, Berkeley, CA: University of California Press.

Ho, V. K. Y. (1998) "Whose bodies? Taming contemporary prostitutes bodies in official Chinese rhetoric," *China Information* 13(2/3): 14–35.

Honig, E. (1992) *Creating Chinese Ethnicity: Subei People in Shanghai, 1850–1980*, New Haven, CT: Yale University Press.

Howell, J. (2000) "Organising around women and labour in China: uneasy shadows, uncomfortable alliances," *Communist and Post-Communist Studies* 33(3): 355–377.

Khan, A. R. and Riskin, C. (1998) "Income and inequality in China: composition, distribution and growth of household income, 1988 to 1995," *The China Quarterly* 154: 221–253.

Liberation Daily (Jiefang Ribao) (2002) "Shanghai nanren bu zai 'qi guan yan'" (Shanghai men are not strictly controlled by women anymore), January 16, Online version: http://www.zaobao.com/special/newspapers/2002/01/jfdaily160102.html

Liu, B. (1997) "A summary of issues in women's employment," *Chinese Sociology and Anthropology* 29(3): 7–51.

Long, Y. (1997) "Ah, Shanghai nanren!" (Ah, Shanghai Men!), *Wenhui Bao* (Wenhui Daily) (Shanghai), January 7.

—— (1998) *Ah, Shanghai Nanren* (Ah, Shanghai men), Shanghai: Xuelin chubanshe.

Mallee, H. (1996) "Reform of the hukou system," *Chinese Sociology and Anthropology* 29(1): 4–5.

Mann, S. (2000) "Presidential address: myths of Asian womanhood," *The Journal of Asian Studies* 59(4): 835–862.

Ngai, P. (1999) "Becoming *Dagongmei* (Working Girls): the politics of identity and difference in reform China," *The China Journal* 42: 1–19.

Ni, Y. (1993) "Xiandai jinu pian (Report on modern prostitutes)" in H. Qiao (ed.) *Nanxia nüren chao* (Waves of Women Migrating South), Guangzhou: Huacheng chubanshe, 214–235.

Qiao H. (ed.) (1993) *Nanxia nüren chao* (Waves of Women Migrating South), Guangzhou: Huacheng chubanshe.

Qin, X. and Ni, J. (1993) *Nanbei qunqiu: Zhongguo huibuhui fenlie?* (The history of the north and the south: will China disintegrate?), Beijing: Renmin Zhongguo chubanshe.

Rofel, L. (1999) *Other Modernities: Gendered Yearnings in China after Socialism*, Berkeley, CA: University of California Press.

Schein, L. (1996) "The other goes to market: the state, the nation, and unruliness in contemporary China," *Identities* 2(3): 197–222.

Shi, S.-m. (1999) "Gender and a geopolitics of desire: the seduction of mainland women in Taiwan and Hong Kong media," in M. M.-h. Yang (ed.) *Spaces of their Own: Women's Public Sphere in Transnational China*, Minneapolis, MN: University of Minnesota Press, 278–307.

Sun, W. (2002) *Leaving China: Media, Migration and Transnational Imagination*, Lanham, MD: Rowman and Littlefield.

Tam, S. M. (1996) "Normalization of 'second wives': gender contestation in Hong Kong," *Asian Journal of Women's Studies* 2: 113–132.

Tang, W.-s. and Chung, H. (2000) "Urban–rural transition in China: beyond the *desakota* model," in S.-m. Li and W.-s. Tang (eds) *China's Regions, Polity, and Economy: A Study of Spatial Transformation in the Post-Reform Era*, Hong Kong: The Chinese University Press, 275–308.

Wang, J. (2001) "Culture as leisure and culture as capital," *Positions* 9(1): 69–104.

Wong, L. and Huen, W.-P. (1998) "Reforming the household registration system: a preliminary glimpse of the blue chop household registration system in Shanghai and Shenzhen," *International Migration Review* 32(4): 974–994.

Ye, W. and Lin, Q. (1996) "Fujiansheng shewai hunyin zhuangkuang yanjiu" (A study of marriage with non-mainlanders in Fujian province), *Renkou yu jingji* (Population and Economics) 2: 21–27.

Young, L.-c. (1988) "Regional stereotypes in China," *Chinese Studies in History* 21(4): 32–57.

Zhang, L. and Zhao, S. X. B. (1998) "Re-examining China's 'urban' concept and the level of urbanization," *The China Quarterly* 154: 330–381.

Zhen, Z. (2000) "Mediating time: the rice bowl of youth in fin de siècle urban China," *Public Culture* 12(1): 93–113.

Zhou, Q. (1997) *Nanguo jiali* (Southern Beauties), Taipei: Jieyou chubanshe.

8 "Net-moms"—a new place and a new identity

Parenting discussion forums on the Internet in China

Wang Gan

Discussion forums, also called Broadcasting Bulletin Boards (BBS), are an important means of sharing ideas, opinions, and information on the Internet. Often specified according to certain themes, they attract people of similar minds. In recent years, there have emerged some active parenting discussion forums on the Internet in China. Whether professionals, pink-collars, or home-makers, most of the participants in the discussion forums are young mothers with higher education and income so as to have access to the Internet. Through the discussion forums, they share information important to themselves and their children, exchange experiences in their new lives, make friends of similar minds, and organize various kinds of activities in real life.

Ever since the emergence of the Internet, there have been discussions about identity issues on the Internet. In previous face-to-face interactions, people infer others' identities from physical features, clothes, body language, accent, or other cues. But on the Internet, many such cues can be easily hidden or changed. Therefore, it would be difficult for people to guess others' identities in conventional ways.

In the earlier years of the Internet, the possibility of identity play in virtual space was highlighted, exemplified by Peter Steiner's popular cartoon: "On the Internet, nobody knows you are a dog" (Steiner 1993: 61). Identities on the Internet were seen as malleable, with unlimited possibilities. But later commentators pointed out the danger of cutting off online identities from their offline context. Agre called our attention to "the Internet's embedding in the social world." He argues that

> so long as we focus on the limited areas of the Internet where people engage in fantasy play that is intentionally disconnected from their real-world identities, we miss how social and professional identities are continuous across several media, and how people use those several media to develop their identities in ways that carry over to other settings. Just as most people don't define their activities in terms of computers, most people using Internet services are mainly concerned with the real-world matters to which their discussions and activities in the use of those services pertain (Agre 1999: 4; see also Escobar 1994; Turkle 1995; Burkhalter 1999; and O'Brien 1999).

Between December 2000 and March 2002, I conducted my fieldwork by participating in parenting discussion forums in China. Throughout the time, I found that the Internet could provide a place where people concerned with "real-world matters" met and communicated. For many young mothers who surfed the parenting discussion forums everyday, the Internet offered not only information they needed, but also a place to belong to. Through networking and community building in cyberspace, these young women were negotiating and producing their new identities: being new mothers in the wake of the revolutionary era and in modern times.

Focusing on parenting forums in China, this chapter tries to answer the following questions: what kind of space is being made on the Internet by the parenting forum participants? In what way does the Internet facilitate the formulation and expression of their new identity? How does the on-going process of globalization affect the views of motherhood of this young generation of Chinese women? Are the social relationships in virtual space copying the relationships in real life, or they are making any differences? What is meant by "being in the center in a fast-changing world" in which childrearing practices in Beijing are influenced by ways in New York, and in turn, are influencing ways in other provinces in China?

"Net-mom" is a word coined by the parenting website surfers themselves to designate those young mothers who frequent parenting websites either to maintain their babies' homepages or participate in discussion forums, or do both. In Yaolan, the website this research is based upon, participants also refer to themselves as "Yaolan Moms." In December 2000, I registered in Yaolan and became a "Yaolan Mom." I made a baby's homepage for my then three-year-old son, and participated in discussions as a "net-mom." From December 2000 to 2002, I surfed Early Education Forum everyday, reading postings, reviewing different opinions, and sometimes participating in the discussions. I took my child to several offline gatherings organized by Yaolan website, and participated in many weekend outings organized by the net-moms. In this process, I met many net-moms, most from Beijing, but also some from other cities. I also met several young mothers during my trips out of Beijing. I interviewed key informants as well as sysops (operators of bulletin boards). At the same time, through spending time with net-moms, exchanging ideas through the Internet as well as by phone, taking children on weekend and holiday outings, shopping and dining together without children, participating in life event celebrations as friends, I had the chance to understand the influence of the Internet in these women's lives offline.[1]

The construction of a community

Yaolan is one of the most popular parenting websites in China. Formally established on December 15, 1999, Yaolan attracted more than 150,000 registered members in five months.[2] By March, 2002, registered membership reached 450,000, and homepages have been made for 18,000 babies in Yaolan. Among the registered members, about 15 percent lived in Beijing, 4 percent lived in Shanghai, and 7 percent lived in Guangdong Province.

In March 2002, there were nine discussion forums in Yaolan, that is, Pregnancy Forum, Childrearing Forum, Early Education Forum, Family Relations Forum, Husbands Forum, Flea Market Forum, Net-Friends Forum, Women's Feelings Forum, and Twins Forum. This chapter is mainly based on participant observation in the Early Education Forum. I also browsed the postings in other forums by my main informants.

Most people who frequent Yaolan forums have one thing in common: they have young children, usually under 6 years old. As one informant explained to me: "Raising a young child is a lonely thing. You often have problems so that you need to seek help, you also have special emotions and feelings you want to share. It's hard to find the right answer for your specific question, and many people around you are not patient enough to listen to a new mother's babble. After I found Yaolan, I found that many mothers offer their precious guidance when you need help, and we have so many feelings in common!"[3]

Many young parents come to Yaolan forums for information on baby caring and feeding, nutrition, health, and early education. Questions with the words "SOS" or "Help needed" in the title fall into this category. They also exchange opinions. For example, one young mother asked: "There are always strangers who want to hold and kiss my baby. I just want to stop them from doing so for sanitary reasons. But it's embarrassing to say so. What would you do in such a situation?" Some sought support from others on issues ranging from dealing with a mother-in-law who was against breastfeeding to coping with an upcoming divorce. Sometimes they share their feelings and life events with others. Baby's first steps, parent's passing away, are all issues that can gather commenting postings. They also share amusing baby anecdotes with other participants in the forums.

Unlike discussion forums on many other topics, the degree of anonymity in Yaolan discussion forums is not very high. One important reason is that many forum participants have made homepages for their children on the website. This is a feature provided by the website to attract more participants. Choosing from several ready-made formats on the website, anyone who can input Chinese will be able to make a homepage for her child. With some computer knowledge or following instructions provided by some Yaolan mothers, one can make the link to her baby's homepage into a "signature," appearing under every message she posts. If you are interested in a certain forum participant, you can go to her baby's homepage by clicking on her signature.

A baby's homepage includes the following information:

- basic information about the baby: name, nickname, gender, blood type, birthday, birth weight, birth place, city, parents' net-names
- wishes for the baby from the parents
- the newest activities of the baby
- name story of the baby
- birth story of the baby
- baby's photo album

- baby's family photos
- baby's works
- baby's diary
- baby's funny words
- baby's best friends
- message board for the baby.

If a parent is willing to invest more time, she can put photos of the baby and the family on the homepage. She can also write entries on baby's birth and naming, and keep a diary on baby's development. Through browsing a child's homepage, one can often gather background information of the family, such as the parents' professions, education, residence, and values.

There are designs on the children's homepages that can enhance the social interactions among the participants. There is an area called "Baby's Best Friends," where one can gather links to other babies' homepages. Using this function, with a click one can visit a friend's baby's homepage on Yaolan.

Young mothers talk about Yaolan as if it is in real space. For example, Yaolan babies' homepages are called "babies homes," and the links in the "Best Friends" area are "small sofas in the home," because sofas are supposed to be occupied by visiting guests. After meeting someone interesting in the discussion forums or chat room, they exchange their babies' "home addresses," invite each other for a visit, and often remind each other to "set a little sofa for my baby in your home."

There is a message board in each baby's "home." It is polite to leave greeting and congratulation messages on your friends' babies' homes during the holiday seasons or when babies' birthdays come. After examining the birth dates, mothers soon clarify the birth order and start to address each other's babies as "elder brothers" or "little sisters," as the Chinese etiquette requires. Some people also feel it important to leave thank-you notes or comforting messages when their friends have supported them in a debate or have been "attacked."

Yaolan mothers not only visit each other's "home" on the web, they conduct conversations in the forums as if in real space. Frequent writers begin to know each other well. They exchange email addresses, or even phone numbers. After a vacation or business trip, some might come to the forum and greet people warmly with words such as "Long time no see. I miss all of you so much!" They also offer positive comments on each other's babies or their own appearances.

Many Yaolan mothers have a strong feeling of belonging to the Yaolan community. In messages and articles reminiscing about Yaolan experiences, many Yaolan mothers admit that they visit Yaolan discussion forums almost everyday. This is confirmed by an online poll conducted by Yaolan, in which more than half of the people investigated stated that they surfed Yaolan everyday. Yaolan BBS or their babies' homepages are set as the first page of the Internet browsers on many computers. It becomes a morning ritual for many Yaolan mothers to browse the forums after they turn on the computers in their offices, although they might not have enough time to write messages until lunch time. For those who work in less disciplined offices, they often keep the forum page open and refresh it now and then.

Although stay-at-home mothers are growing in numbers, it is still not a prevailing phenomenon in China. In my impression, there are more working mothers in the discussion forums. Most of them work with computers during the daytime. Lawyers, computer engineers, teachers, and accountants are common professions. The obsession with Yaolan becomes a problem for many professional women working in the offices. One woman suggested in the forum that Yaolan should have two kinds of backgrounds for its discussion forums, one pink as the current background for stay-at-home mothers, the other grayish, for working mothers so their boss would not notice that they were browsing a parenting website!

After the birth of children, many working women express their wish to be with their young children at home for the first several years. As one young mother noted in the forum:

> [N]ow we only have one child, and all parents hope their children will have a good environment to grow up. But both parents have to go to work. Except for eating together and talking for a little while, children are mostly taken care of by grandparents or even nannies. When the mom goes out, baby doesn't want her to go, and mom doesn't want to go either. But we have to work. It would be wonderful if mothers can be with their children for the first two or three years. That's the wish of both the mothers and the children. But the current social conditions do not allow such practice. First, fathers cannot get double payment to allow mothers to stay at home. Secondly, there are no such laws to protect mothers without economic independence.[4]

Missing their children at home but confined in the office, these young mothers "talk" to other women in similar situations in virtual space, "visit" each other's "homes," and admire each other's babies. While the office is identified as the place of work, the Internet is associated with their new identity: young mothers.

The construction of an identity

Every registered user in Yaolan discussion forums has a net-name. There were a few who used their own real English names, if they have one, or Chinese names in pinyin. Some others made up new names. But the most common format of the net-names for Yaolan mothers are "so-and-so'(child's nickname)'s mom." Many young women who meet on the Internet do not quite remember each other's real names, while some others prefer the net-names even if they remember the real names. They explain that the net-names make them feel "more amiable" and "closer." When Yaolan mothers meet each other, the first sentence they say to each other would be: "Whose mom are you, please?" It also happened, more than once, that when one woman called another net-mom in her office, she couldn't say her real name, but had to describe the latter's baby's name and age to her colleagues in order to locate the mother.

Addressing a woman as the mother of her child is a custom considered "old fashioned." During the revolutionary campaigns of women's liberation, it was emphasized that women were oppressed so much that they even did not have their own identities. While peasants still address women as somebody's wife or somebody's mother in the countryside, it is impolite to address a high-status woman (e.g. a woman teacher) this way. Then, why do so many highly educated young mothers prefer such "old fashioned" titles?

CV-Mom, an enthusiastic Yaolan mother, explained in her interview with Yaolan that being a mother helped her find "the real feelings of being a woman." JE-Mom, another young woman active in Yaolan discussion forums, gave up her position and promotion opportunities in the overseas branch of her company and returned to Beijing because of her baby. She believed that being a good mother was as important as a successful career. At present, her young baby is more important than her career.

CV-Mom and JE-Mom represent some highly educated young women who have begun to contemplate motherhood. In a series of political campaigns after the CCP came to power, motherhood and private life were considerably undermined and subordinated to a political party/state. After the Maoist era, things began to change. Some women now choose to stay at home after their babies are born, if the fathers' income can support the families. Although stay-at-home mothers are still not too prevalent, in some people's minds, they become a status symbol.

Whether staying at home or working in offices, many Yaolan mothers celebrate their motherhood in cyberspace, although their chorus is not always in harmony. The new identity is being negotiated and produced in cyberspace.

Happy motherhood

Some young women in Yaolan believe that it is no longer fashionable to boast of the bitterness of motherhood. Their opinion is revealed by the titles of the postings in the forums: "Mothering is an Easy Thing" or "Mothering is a Kind of Spirit."

One net-mom wrote in her posting

> After my daughter was born, it seems to me that I've found my source of joy finally. Loving my daughter is not a burden but my happiness and enjoyment. People always ask me whether I feel exhausted raising the child. I always reply that you should ask me whether I feel happy raising the child. Many young mothers around me cannot understand why I do not feel exhausted and why I am so happy.... I like Yaolan, because there are many mothers here who, just like me, regard child-rearing as happiness, instead of a burden![5]

Some net-moms state clearly that their highlight of the happiness of motherhood is the reaction against the traditional emphasis on the bitterness of motherhood. At the same time, some people also realize that over-romanticizing child-rearing ignores the differences induced by education, class and income.

Significance of mothering

Some young mothers regard mothering as no less important than careers, especially in the earlier years of children. Many emphasize their sacrifice in their profession in favor of their children's development. They make the sacrifice not because of pressures from family or friends. To the contrary, highly educated women face pressures and misunderstandings when they give up professional development, even temporarily, in favor of their young children. In facing these pressures, these young women celebrate their modernity and independent thinking, and find support in Yaolan.

JE-Mom told me about her experiences after she decided to give up her overseas position. She said

> My supervisor cannot understand me. He always reminds me that I graduated from one of the top schools in China, and shouldn't shame my school in giving up my future. This really makes me feel disheartened in my office. But after I met some net-mom friends through the Internet, I found that there are many top school graduates who share my thoughts. Now I can raise my head and walk in the office. I am as happy as an underground party member who finally found her organization!

Seeking a balance between profession and mothering

Although many young mothers wish to spend more time with their children, most of them have to remain in the office. They justify their choice by the argument that with rational and clever planning, professional women can still make great mothers through quality time.

There is advice on how to find more time to accompany children during meal time, sleeping time, and bathing time. Some mothers drive their children to school in order to talk on the way, instead of sending them on the school bus. There are others who often travel with their children. Many hire house helpers to do the housework in order to spend more time with children. They also encourage other working mothers not to feel guilty, because "to raise a healthy child, the amount of time spent with the child is not the most important thing. The most important thing is to have a happy, peaceful, serene, and confident mother."[6]

Affectionate parent–child relationship

Some new mothers hesitate to show affection toward their children because they worry that would spoil the children. But some others believe that loving parents would benefit the development of young children. They also discuss the attachment children have toward parents, especially mothers. One mother suggested that over-attachment revealed that the emotional needs of the child were not met by the parents. This view made many forum participants contemplate their own experiences.

Mothering as a learning process and life enrichment

Some assert that reading and sharing more about early childhood development is a great way to help the children and be great mothers. Many also emphasize that being mothers provides them opportunities to develop themselves further, to study more things, and to meet new friends of similar minds on the Internet.

Some amateur writers suddenly find a place where they have enthusiastic readers of their works. Yaolan mothers are never stingy in giving lavish praise to someone who writes about feelings they share. Popular messages are selected and marked as "the best messages" and kept on the website. Some are also published by the Yaolan magazine on the website, and the writers are very proud of their electronic publication, especially when their professions have little to do with writing. Parenting magazines and television programs search for good writers, stories, and good ideas in the parenting websites. At least one Yaolan mother already published a book based on her postings on Yaolan.

Breastfeeding: New York, Beijing, and small town

Internet as a technology facilitates interaction among people who would otherwise have little chance to meet and communicate on issues as personal as child-rearing. In Yaolan, the most popular net-moms are those who put in time and energy to share with others their professional knowledge (such as medical doctors) or experience (such as mothers of older kids). Their postings are read by more people and welcomed with more replies. These popular net-moms often live in big, modern cities, such as Beijing, Shanghai, Guangzhou, and Shenzhen. Some informants believe that the easy access to information and more diversity and experimentation in early childhood education enable the net-moms living in these cities to contribute more to the discussion forums. One informant also pointed out that in those big cities there were more net-moms and more off-line activities, therefore stronger networks among the net-moms. The familiarity among the net-moms encourages greater contribution and participation.

As the biggest Chinese parenting website, Yaolan attracts some young mothers who have overseas experiences and enjoy sharing their experiences with other Chinese mothers. They bring new information to readers geographically dispersed. For the first time, many young women hear about the culturally different ways of postpartum care, child-rearing, and many new concepts in early childhood education.

Internet complements traditional channels of information flow. As one mother put it: "I read in translated books about Western ways of child-rearing, but it's much more impressive to hear somebody telling you her own personal experiences, often in a Chinese perspective. And you can ask questions!" Many young women said that when they learned new concepts from the discussion forums, they asked for references, and found the books for further reading. For example, in discussions on Montessori education, on cultivating young children's financial awareness, or on physical punishment, Yaolan mothers distributed book titles on the forums, and then discussed the contents.

The West often represents modernity and cultural capital. It is noticeable that the western ways are often described as more "scientific," humanistic, and therefore, right ways. For example, in the debates on natural birth versus C-section, or on breastfeeding versus bottle feeding, foreign doctors (whether German,

American, or French) were quoted as persuasive evidence. Successful examples from abroad—foreign colleagues, Chinese young mothers who have lived abroad—were also mentioned.

In a debate on breastfeeding versus bottle feeding, both sides sought support from the west. The breastfeeding promoter, WW, a Chinese woman with American citizenship, cited a La League brochure and talked about her foreign friend's surprise over Chinese women's unwillingness to breastfeed. Her argument was widely accepted by Yaolan mothers until one day, a bottle feeding supporter argued that it was no longer fashionable in the US to breastfeed the babies. Her evidence was that nursing in public was ridiculed in an American sitcom. Several days later, in a lunch meeting of some Yaolan mothers, WW was asked by several Yaolan mothers about the sitcom. She briefly described the sitcom and assured the others that the certain sitcom ridiculed almost everything. The next day, another Yaolan mother, WW's friend, posted a message in the discussion forum to support WW. Having given birth in the United States, she used her own experiences to confirm that nursing in public was promoted and practiced by middle-class women in the US.

However, the use of the West has to be tactful. Generously spending time and energy promoting breastfeeding on Yaolan, WW had been respected by many Yaolan mothers. But a later message brought her trouble. In the message, she criticized those Chinese doctors who made a profit in helping baby formula companies sell their products in hospitals. She was not cautious enough in her wording when she said "The conscience of the Chinese doctors is eaten by the dogs!" And she criticized Chinese hospitals for not providing necessary information. Her generalization offended some Yaolan mothers who started to criticize WW. One wrote: "What WW said is not true. I gave birth in Beijing and the doctors did persuade me to breastfeed. Although what you described might be true in some small cities and remote areas, breastfeeding is being promoted in the good hospitals in big cities!" Another mother criticized WW as "regarding all Chinese mothers as so ignorant!"[7] They agreed on WW's goodwill, but expressed dissatisfaction with her tone when she talked about the west, and her undifferentiated use of "China."

Internet, new mothers, and translocality

As more and more people have access to the Internet, pessimistic views have been expressed about its impact on our social life. According to Victor Nee, the more time Americans invest in online interactions, the less time they spend with their families and friends. Therefore, the Internet has a detrimental impact on people's social life.[8]

However, the parenting discussion forums provide a case of contrary evidence. The communities built by forum participants in the virtual space not only promote interactions online, but also improve interactions offline in real space. Starting from sharing information online, many forum participants develop long-term and strong relationships among themselves through both online communication and offline social activities.

With the one-child policy and the popularization of nuclear families in the urban areas, first-time mothers often feel isolated during a time when they need to share experiences and seek support. The Internet discussion forums become a place where geographically dispersed young parents can get together at times and locations convenient to them. For them, the Internet is a gathering space.

For young mothers, the Internet also provides a place where they negotiate and construct their new identities, after their private life had been suppressed for several decades. In the 1950s, women were motivated to go out of their homes and work in the public arena. In later political propagations, women were considered equal to men when they could do the same things as men. Motherhood was rarely mentioned except when it was subordinated to the revolutionary cause. Things began to change at the turn of the century. More significance was attributed to the early years of childhood in children's development. The economic situation of many families can afford the arrangement of one parent staying at home. In the early years of the twenty-first century, many young women begin to contemplate whether they deserve the same respect even if they do things differently from men. Sitting in the office but "talking" about child-rearing with other net-mom friends online, they identify themselves not only as career women, but also as mothers. They air their grievances in the difficult task of balancing work and life, share information and experiences, and encourage one another with examples from other places.

As some parents actively experiment with some new child-rearing practice from the outside, they also seek confirmation and support from other parents on the Internet. People who are living abroad or have overseas experiences become references for them in their pioneering experiments. Montessori education, Orff music education, and other notions from the outside are communicated and debated in the discussion forums. Located in China but absorbing ideas from the outside, these young women identify themselves as modern and scientific-minded parents.

Notes

1 In this paper, all names and net-names are pseudonyms, where I try to keep the original format when the real name is XX-Mom. When both oral interview and Internet postings are available to verify an informant's opinion, I use the Internet postings instead of the interview. The quotes from discussion forum postings have filing codes in the endnote.
2 http://www.yaolan.com
3 All communications are in Chinese, and the translations are mine.
4 ID6SY.
5 ID1PPM.
6 ID3QQ.
7 BF2.
8 http://www.stanford.edu/group/siqss/Press_Release/internetStudy.html

References

Agre, P. (1999) "Life after cyberspace," *EASST Review* 18: 3–5.
Burkhalter, B. (1999) "Reading race online: discovering racial identity in usenet discussions," in P. Kollock and M. Smith (eds) *Communities in Cyberspace*, London and New York: Routledge, 60–76.

Escobar, A. (1994) "Welcome to Cyberia: notes on the anthropology of cyberculture," *Current Anthropology*, 35: 211–232.

O'Brien, J. (1999) "Writing in the body:gender (re)production in online interaction," in P. Kollock and M. Smith (eds) *Communities in Cyberspace*, London and New York: Routledge, 77–104.

Steiner, P. (1993) "On the Internet, nobody knows you're a dog," *The New Yorker*, July 5.

Turkle, S. (1995) *Life on the Screen: Identity in the Age of the Internet*, New York: Simon & Schuster.

9 The village as theme park

Mimesis and authenticity in Chinese tourism

Tim Oakes

The village as a replica of itself

In 1994, while traveling across Hainan Island, I visited the Li minority villages of Fankong and Fanmao. They had recently been transformed into small theme parks. Having contracted with a local tourism development company, founded by an entrepreneurial Li from the same region, the villages had been turned into displays of themselves for a 5 yuan entry fee. They featured elaborate front gates resembling water buffalo horns, and model houses displaying the collected everyday objects of village agricultural and ritual life (crude farming implements, woven baskets, textiles and other crafts, and culinary tools). These objects—clearly labeled and displayed under track-lighting along the interior walls of the model house—had been donated by the villagers themselves, as had the clothing articles that were available for rent in case tourists were inclined to step into the display and go native for the duration of the visit. An additional 80 yuan would buy an on-demand song and dance performance in which tourists were also welcome to actively participate. The highlight of both villages, though, was the cockfighting arena, where 50 yuan purchased an actual cockfight (gambling during fights, while officially illegal, was an additional aspect of tourist participation that was clearly encouraged by the villagers).

What strikes me about these villages was how they were not just making themselves accessible for tourists, but were self-consciously *displaying* themselves in a very particular way. It was as if the villages were encasing themselves as objects, much as one might expect to find dioramas in a natural history museum, and the effect was to perceive these villages as "typical" according to some unspecified but implicit and assumed broader frame of reference. Tourists were invited to view village artifacts, for instance, in a museum-like display which was itself located in a "model" show-house. This kind of display would be expected within a large urban museum or theme park, but tourists making the journey all the way to the mountainous interior of Hainan Island might expect a more unmediated version of village life. Villagers did, after all, continue to live and work there, going about their daily agricultural tasks whenever they were not called upon to sing and dance or march their roosters to battle. It clearly did not occur to them, however, that tourists would find their daily lives particularly interesting or worthy of a visit. Instead, the villages had been set up with the intention of providing an experience very similar to that which a tourist might expect in a modern urban museum or theme park. The founder of the company that developed the villages later confirmed as much to me. He had grown up in one of the villages, but had traveled extensively throughout China and had been impressed by the tourist sites in the urban centers of Beijing and Guangzhou. He had modeled his villages on these tourist displays. Displaying village traditions was, perhaps, one way of making villages seem more modern.

Indeed, through the 1990s, this kind of display could increasingly be found at ethnic village tourist sites throughout China's peripheries.[1] After several years of informally receiving an increasingly steady stream of tourists, for example, the Dai village of Manchunman, in Yunnan's Xishuangbanna Autonomous Prefecture, began in 1993 to construct displays replicating their own houses for tourists to view (Yang *et al.* 2001). By 1995 they had turned their village into a stock-sharing corporation, were charging an entrance fee, had built archways to various cultural and scenic displays throughout the area, created a public market for the sale of ethnic goods, and built a large Bamboo Exhibition Hall, where song and dance performances could be arranged upon request. They were so successful—with each household earning between 1,300 and 3,000 yuan from tourism annually—that they attracted the attention of a company from Guangdong which negotiated to transform the whole area, including several surrounding villages, into a vast ethnic leisure resort. Manchunman's villagers became employees of a tourism industry they no longer controlled, displaying themselves for a small share of the company's profits.

Meanwhile, in Guizhou, the Bouyei village of Huashishao, just downstream from China's largest waterfall, was petitioning the local tourism authorities in vain to turn itself into the kind of theme park Manchunman had initially established for itself. The villagers had already secured funds to build a small museum (though they had not yet established a collection of objects to display), and they wanted to start charging tourists an entrance fee for the privilege of strolling through the village's picturesque stone lanes and admiring its ancient and sprawling banyan trees. Huashishao's scenery and charming layout, as well as its proximity to the falls, had inspired the provincial Nationalities Affairs Commission to declare it an "open air museum," Guizhou's "first preserved Bouyei village." But the villagers' request to be allowed to charge visitors an entrance fee was repeatedly denied by the local authorities on the grounds that villagers lacked the necessary skills to develop the site as a modern theme-park style attraction. The local authorities sought to model the village's development specifically on the successful China Folk Cultures theme park in Shenzhen. As the director of the tourism administration told me, "You go (to Shenzhen), you buy a ticket, you go in and you get to see all sorts of activities, songs, dances, demonstrations. *That's* what Huashishao will be like once we develop it."[2]

This is an essay about the translocality of tourist villages like Huashishao. Such villages replicate (or *hope* to replicate) across space the urban theme park model of what is often regarded in China as advanced or modern tourism. In doing so, they have become places where the newly acquired mechanisms of tourist display have generated a self-consciousness about identity conditioned by the broader networks of travel to which locals are now linked. Travel, in other words, fundamentally shapes the ways places are made and remade by encouraging villagers not just to welcome and perform for paying visitors but to *replicate* themselves in newly self-conscious ways. I see this replication as part of a more general translocal imaginary, in which villagers view themselves quite clearly as objects—or sites— within a much broader canvas of the Chinese nation. Replication makes possible the simultaneous performance of traditional local ethnicity and the more distant modernity of urban-based tourist attractions. It thus allows for a kind of performance that enables villagers to demarcate—and thus control—the boundary between tradition and modernity. This is a performance of translocal imagination, because it results from mobilities which have linked village identities to far-away places and enabled villagers to objectify themselves in new, translocal ways. Their performances of display illustrate an ability to view themselves in terms of *spatial relationships*, as locals relative to other localities and, more broadly, relative to the modern Chinese nation itself, the nation being that implied frame of reference which authorizes claims of authenticity.

The analysis that follows seeks to interpret village tourism as the display and performance of a particular translocal imaginary in which modernity figures prominently. Because of its centrality as a marker of both modernity and of the larger canvas of the nation in relation to which such villages view themselves, the concept of authenticity also plays a critical role in my analysis. Rather than simply consider the extent to which travel leads villagers to display and perform their unique place-based traditions, I suggest that such performances be viewed as the mimetic replication of a specific tourism model that carries with it associations of distant modern and urban civilizations. This approach echoes Schein's (1999: 372) focus on the Miao as reflexive performers of modernity, and implies a similar project of challenging the assumption that those who perform their traditions in China do not reflect upon the greater social context that constructs such performances as boundary markers between modernity and tradition (see also Adams 1996b). Thus, although the theme park model carries with it strong associations of the fake and inauthentic tourist attraction, I resist evaluating village theme parks in terms of an unreflexive loss of authenticity. Rather, the theme park model is viewed here as an *authentic replica*, in which the yardstick of authenticity is consciously wielded to both mark the originality of tradition and the replicability of modernity. Although visitors might lament the loss of "originality" in theme park villages, for villagers themselves tourism allows for a self-conscious act of replication which is no less "authentic" or meaningful. And it is this quality of replication that most defines the translocality of ethnic village tourism. Theme park villages perform and display replications of touristic modernity as much as they do their place-bound customs and traditions. They have, as such, become translocal places—identified not simply as "ethnic" localities but also as national "tourist sites" with all the standard features that such a designation would entail. But while networks of travel and tourism have generated the mimetic proliferation of theme parks throughout China, it would be wrong to suggest a loss of meaning or place as the end result of this process. Villages continue to be remade as meaningful places when locals engage the currency of authenticity in self-conscious ways. In doing so, they construct a translocal subjectivity in which distant, urban-based identity as "modern" articulates with the rural identification of "ethnic," or "traditional."

My analysis is based on a combination of archival and secondary source readings along with data acquired during several visits to six theme park villages in Hainan and Guizhou provinces between 1993 and 2003. In two cases, I merely visited villages as any tourist would, noting my observations and casually interviewing visitors and villagers alike. In two other cases, I made repeated visits over the course of several months and conducted more extensive and repeated interviews with key villagers. And in two more cases, I stayed in the villages for several weeks conducting interviews and observing repeated tourism performances. My research was primarily focused on the ways villagers sought to attract tourism development for economic gain and cultural or ethnic prestige.

The authentic replica

Elusive authenticity

It is a well-established assumption that ethnic and cultural tourists are motivated by a search for authenticity (e.g. MacCannell 1976; Cohen 1988; Culler 1988; McIntosh and Prentice 1999; Wang 1999; Cohen 2001). In this vein, Erik Cohen has proposed a model for analyzing ethnic tourism development throughout Southeast Asia in which authenticity plays the key role in marking a shift from the daily life activities of ethnic communities prior to tourism's arrival to a "tourist culture" in which daily life and tourist-related activities become practically indistinguishable (Picard 1997). According to Cohen (2001), as the tourist's desire for an authentic experience begins to penetrate daily life in ethnic communities, a separate "tourist sphere" begins to emerge in which authenticity becomes "staged" by villagers for tourist consumption (MacCannell 1973; Silver 1993). As this "tourist sphere" becomes increasingly separate from the daily life of the community, staged attractions become increasingly contrived. It is at this point that the "theme park" label is often used to indicate the implicitly inauthentic nature of staged display. It is also at this point, however, that the obvious separation of the "tourist sphere" begins to dissolve as the community itself becomes thoroughly transformed by tourism; the "tourist sphere" becomes absorbed into an ethnic culture that is now better understood as a "tourist culture" in which the difference between the authentic and the touristic disappears. Cohen's model therefore maps a progression from a landscape of unselfconscious places to one of consciously staged sites that have lost the authenticity of uniqueness and originality.

After spending more than a decade watching the expansion of the ethnic tourism industry in Guizhou, it is clear to me that there is a development cycle resembling Cohen's model, in which tourism flows across the countryside like a wave, crashing over increasingly remote communities and allowing villagers to briefly enjoy and profit from their "15 minutes of authenticity," as it were. The problem with the model, however, is that it rests upon a concept—authenticity—which defies any single definition or interpretation. Underlying the assumption that authenticity explains the tourist's motivations is an unproblematic association of authenticity with "the original." While there is much to say for this assumption in the context of Western European and North American tourists, it is perhaps more difficult to sustain when considering the increasingly numerous east Asian tourists (Nyiri forthcoming). Such an assumption marks the replica as a "fake," the opposite of the authentic or "real." This, in turn, marks the theme park model of ethnic village tourism as a commercial fake, a "tourist-trap." Such a dualism leaves little room for interpreting the translocality of village tourist sites as anything but meaningless imitation, reducing translocality to the equivalent of modernity's destructive and homogenizing diffusion: each locality just the same as the next.

A recent appraisal of the tourist village of Zhouzhuang, written by Jasper Becker and published in *The Observer*, illustrates these assumptions clearly (Becker 2004). Noting at the outset that as China modernizes and becomes more and more popular among tourists, there is "less and less to see," Becker portrays the reconstruction of Zhouzhuang into a "traditional water town" on the Changjiang Delta as something of a heritage scandal. Although the mayor of the village was persuaded to adopt a heritage preservation plan for tourism development, after taking a tour of Europe, he ended up bulldozing half the town, relocating most of the residents, and building new traditional buildings from "carefully disguised concrete." That Zhouzhuang is now a replica of a traditional water town is viewed by Becker as a kind of deception; China is "faking it" in order to entice heritage tourists:

> Closer inspection reveals that the most attractive and picturesque old build-ings are modern fakes, including a 800-year old "Yuan dynasty" Buddhist temple. The building has ochre yellow walls and green tiled roofs and sits on Luoxi Island surrounded by a lake. Only when you get there do you discover that no temple has existed here for 300 years and even now it is still not a place of worship.
>
> (Ibid. 2004)

By assuming authenticity can only be tied to the original, and by assuming that tourists only want to see originals, Becker misses the possibility that replication might itself be regarded as authentic, while failing to explain why Zhouzhuang is so spectacularly successful as a tourist site for Chinese tourists themselves.

What are we to make, then, of this term that repeatedly comes up in Chinese tourism, both in villages and in theme parks: the "authentic replica" (*zhenshi zaixian*)? At first glance, the notion of an authentic replica strikes one as oxymoronic. Becker's view of Zhouzhuang illustrates how most Euro-American thought associates authenticity with the original. The very idea of authenticity, as it is commonly understood, appears to be precisely the *opposite* of the replica. There is a particular history which explains why this is so. Walter Benjamin (1968) has famously argued that industrialization, and mass production in particular, created a distinctly modern *need* to recognize and valorize the original over the copy, as a mark of distinction and bourgeois class ideology. It became an important quality of social differentiation, in other words, to recognize a true "work of art," and such recognition depended upon that work's *originality*. In the age of mechanical reproduction, John Berger (1972) has written, "the uniqueness of the original now lies in it being the original of the reproduction." Value, Berger continues, is thus based on an art object's rarity, rather than on any intrinsic qualities of the work itself. It is in this context that Brian Spooner (1986: 200) has called authenticity a modern *need*, driven by what Bourdieu termed *distinction*. The only way to approach authenticity, then, is not to clarify any absolute or essential *quality* to which it refers, but to delineate the social processes that condition its construction in any given place or time. Thus, Edward Bruner (1994: 408) has written that authenticity is not "a property inherent in an object... [It is] a struggle, a social process in which competing interests argue for their own interpretation."[3] Writing in the context of nationalism, Duara (1998: 294) has defined authenticity as a "regime of power" authorizing an unchanging subject as the locus of the nation's core values and identity. Following from this, any claim of authenticity could thus be construed as a claim of national authority—that is, a call for the right to represent the nation.

Dydia DeLyser's (1999) study of the "authentic ghost town" of Bodie, California illustrates both the constructedness of authenticity and its importance to the nation. A former mining town in which a principle of "arrested decay" is employed to preserve the weather-beaten and decrepit structures in a frozen state of dilapidation, Bodie is recognized by most tourists as more authentic than commercial "ghost towns" such as Virginia City, Nevada and Tombstone, Arizona. Employees of the Bodie State Historical Park characterize their approach to preservation as one of "keep it standing but make it look like it's still falling down." What is preserved, in other words, is not "the original," but an arbitrarily selected moment of decay, a moment tourists have come to expect in their imagined idea of a "real" ghost town. Preserved Bodie is certainly *nothing* like the original Bodie of the nineteenth century mining era. Indeed, it is no doubt *less* like the original Bodie than today's Virginia City, with its lively commercialism and unappealing vulgarity. Yet Bodie is authentic where Virginia City is not because it fulfills the tourist's expectations of authenticity; it *reminds* them of a nostalgic ideal which is nevertheless informed by the idea of the original even if it bears no resemblance to that original. Indeed, "the original" itself must be an arbitrary moment in the long life of Bodie, from its earliest few shacks to its current "frozen" state. And while DeLyser does not push the argument into the realm of nationalism, it is hard not to suggest that the arbitrary moment of Bodie's "arrested decay" is precisely the most mythic of moments in terms of a broader national narrative of western frontier expansion, pioneer struggle, and plucky determination. Bodie's authenticity, in other words, is legitimated by a regime of power which authorizes the myths of the American west as an authentic core of national identity and consciousness (see Truettner 1991). The importance of that myth requires creative constructions of authenticity, like "arrested decay," in order to maintain its power.

Authenticity—as a regime of power—may also be claimed by groups seeking legitimacy within the broader frameworks of nationalism, civilization, or modernity. Such claims can be made through replication or mimesis, the creative act of imitation. Recognizing that any examination of "touristic culture" needs to problematize authenticity as a framework of analysis, Adams (1996a) deploys mimesis as a kind of creative and virtual construction of identity. Mimesis defines "a process of identity construction—the imitation of what is taken to be one's 'natural' self by way of the Other, through whom one's constructed identity is made visible to oneself" (ibid.: 17). Here, Adams argues, the construction of "natural," or authentic, Sherpa identity is a creative imitation of Western expectations and representations of those expectations. But it is not simply that Sherpa identity mimics Western expectations of authentic "Sherpaness." Rather, mimesis marks a shift in ontology, where imitation creates a "virtual" Sherpa more "real" than reality itself. Adams cites specific virtues in Buddhism and Shamanism, in addition to those offered in Western representations, to which Sherpa identity aspires, in order to point out that this mimesis is not simply a passive *response* to Western expectations, but a creative working with and blending of those expectations within a much broader set of cultural resources for identity construction. In this context, the authentic replica suggests a kind of alternative ontology, one which can be quite meaningful.

As Duara (1998) also points out, authenticity not only has a special relationship to nationalism, but to capitalist modernity as well. It marks a realm of the "real" within a world where relentless commodification threatens all that is sacred with fetishism. And here we should remember the affinity in meaning between the real and the sacred.

> Authenticity is a conceptualization of elusive, inadequately defined, other cultural, socially ordered genuineness. Because of our social expansion recently we have been needing more and more of it, and it has become necessary to alter our criteria in order to be able to continue to satisfy our needs.
>
> (Spooner 1986: 225)

Thus, "realness" becomes a kind of modern longing, and authenticity takes on the qualities of any particular social context in which the need for the real expresses itself. But what happens when the modern longing for the real is recast from an implicitly nostalgic urban and cosmopolitan look back to a rural and parochial look forward to material wealth, sophistication and style? What happens when that longing is expressed in very different social and cultural settings than the "western" contexts in which it has predominantly been theorized? In China's village theme parks, authenticity is appealed to *both* mark the "originality" of place and custom *and* to replicate, and thus capture a "real" distant world of modern prosperity and national prestige. Authentic replication becomes a claim of national authority and representation. Indeed, there is something about theme parks as a *genre* of cultural display and performance that answers a schizophrenic modern longing for the original as well as a particular kind of *representation of the original*, one that confirms the modernity and evolutionary advancement of the nation in which the theme park is built.

Authenticity and mimesis in theme parks

How is it that theme parks can be thought of as authentic in any sense of the term? Part of the answer comes from interrogating the assumed distinction between theme parks and other formats of cultural display. For example, authenticity has long played the crucial role in distinguishing museums—as curators of national origins and values—from "less serious" attractions like theme parks and traveling freak shows. And this distinction clearly rests upon an authenticity confidently tied to "the original thing itself." Before moving on to a discussion of theme parks in China, this section will briefly explore a more general understanding of authenticity in relation to theme park type cultural displays.

Museums are, almost by definition, collections of original things: "A building, place, or institution devoted to the acquisition, conservation, study, exhibition, and educational interpretation of objects having scientific, historical, or artistic value" (AHD 2003). As Berger (1972) would remind us, the "scientific, historical, or artistic *value*" of things in museums is based precisely on their *originality*. Yet, the current trend in which museums are increasingly being asked to transgress their solemn mission with "edutainment" suggest that the distinction between museums and more entertaining ventures that we might today call theme parks is in fact rather difficult to maintain (MacDonald and Fyfe 1996; Macdonald 1998). It is also suggestive of the "altering" of the meaning of authenticity suggested by Spooner's quote in the previous section. Both museums and theme parks offer versions of authenticity which reveal this altering in significant ways.

If museums can be thought of as shrines of authenticity in terms of making the original sacred (in what Berger (1972) called a kind of "bogus religiosity"), then theme parks might be shrines of authenticity in terms of a kind of mimetic sacralizing of the copy. This also offers an interesting point of comparison between contemporary theme parks and their spectacular nineteenth-century precursors: the great exhibitions. At the 1889 Paris Exposition Universelle's Egyptian exhibit, for example, a panoramic model of Cairo had been built so that it surrounded its viewer, offering a sensation of actually standing at some vantage point in the center of the city and gazing at the spectacle of it in all directions. An Egyptian writer commented at the time that the effect was a representation "not differing from reality in any way" (Mitchell 1988: 8). A better testimony to the authenticity of the replica could not be found.

Like museums, the great exhibitions of the nineteenth century offered collections of originals displayed in such a way as to emphasize the historical evolution of mankind (Impey and MacGregor 1985; Greenhalgh 1988; Mitchell 1988, 1–33). Yet rather than isolating the objects of display in the neutral container of science, the exhibitions also offered elaborate displays which sought to replicate as faithfully as possible the far flung places of empire. The "authenticity" of these replicas was insured not only by the exquisite craftsmanship and original materials used for the construction of model buildings and streetscapes, but also by displaying actual people from the places represented. The presence of "natives" reinforced the theme of social evolution while at the same time enhancing the authenticity of the replicas exhibited. Indeed, the presence of actual humans confused the distinction between the real (original) and the fake (replica), creating the sensation of a "living display" which was in fact promoted as a key attraction of London's Great Exhibition of 1851 (Briggs 1979: 398). Timothy Mitchell (1988: 12) has argued that the world itself was for nineteenth-century European metropolitans a kind of exhibition, objectified and displayed before them to gaze upon:

> Outside the world exhibition ... one encountered not the real world but only further models and representations of the real. Beyond the exhibition and the department store, ... the theatre and the zoo, the countryside encountered typically in the form of a model farm exhibiting new machinery and cultivation methods, the very streets of the modern city with their deliberate facades, even the Alps once the funicular was built ... [e]verything seemed to be set up before one as if it were a model or the picture of something.
>
> (Ibid.)

What this speaks to is the possibility that the great exhibitions drew upon another kind of a modern longing, one that desired not so much *the original itself* as a particular kind of *representation of the original*, one which faithfully met certain expectations or needs. In fact this need for a kind of mimetic authenticity cannot be limited to a modern or European social context, but has been a significant aspect of Chinese cultural display for centuries. Villagers thus draw upon a cultural precedent for mimetic authenticity when they reproduce themselves as translocal sites of modern theme park tourism.

Mimesis, then, is a more meaningful framework than "originality" for under-standing questions of authenticity in theme parks. Certainly, as Joy Hendry (2000: 162) has argued, mimesis has been a significant feature of theme parks in Asia. Hendry points out, for instance, that Japanese theme parks need to be understood as taking authenticity very seriously, but in terms of the "faithful replica" rather than the "original thing." In fact, she argues, this can be said, to a certain extent, of Japanese museums as well, noting that in the National Museum of Ethnology, the real object is no more highly valued than a good replica. More significant, perhaps, is Hendry's argument that any collapse in the distinction between theme parks and museums in Japan needs to be understood in a specifically Japanese context, rather than assuming that the same forces of "global postmodernism" are impacting the nature of cultural display in the same ways throughout the world. This is an important claim because it introduces a culturally-specific dimension for interpreting the ethnic village theme park. That is, the simulacra and "hyperreality" of theme parks need not be tied to a single narrative of (Western) (post)modernity but instead might have other cultural antecedents depending on where they develop. Village theme parks in China might be seen, then, as less the triumph of a standardized global tourism than a culturally mediated negotiation between villagers and global tourism, a negotiation mediated by the nation and signified by performative replication of the nation's standard markers of modern identity.

In Japan, Hendry notes, mimesis has long been part of a deeper spiritual process of renewal. Mimesis, in this sense, refers not simply to the acts of imitation or replication, but also a kind of sacredness of the idol, as a kind of substitute for something too vast or powerful to grasp in a single view. It entails a replication that deliberately confuses the distinction between the sign and the thing. This is something more creative than what the typical understanding of "imitation" allows; mimesis "enhances and enchants the act as more than an expression of technical expertise" (Cox 1998: 106; cited in Hendry 2000: 183). Hendry refers to the idea of *mitate*, which has been translated by Masao Yamaguchi as the "art of citation," whereby the image of a mundane object is extended to stimulate a broader range of meanings and feelings in the viewer. "*Mitate* is a technique of using a mundane object to evoke images of mythology or classical reference, so that in a scene from the *Pillow Book* of Sei Shonagon a snow-covered mound in a garden is named after a mountain in China, known to be particularly beautiful after a snowfall" (Hendry 2000: 187). The *mitate*, she writes, "is always a simulacrum, or a pseudo-object, quite in the way that Baudrillard first used the term, Yamaguchi asserts, 'not as a fake, but as a positive process' " (p. 190). Along similar lines, Hendry also refers to the periodic rebuilding of Shinto's Ise Jingu Shrine as an ongoing process of spiritual revival. The cultural power of mimesis is such that preserving "the original" structure is irrelevant to the fact that the meaning of the shrine lives in its continuously reconstructed image. The kind of "frozen preservation" and "arrested decay" practiced at Bodie, California would, it follows, be quite foreign to Japanese sensibilities.[4] Indeed "frozen preservation" (*tōketsu hōzon*) has become something of an epithet describing the inability of inhabitants to reconstruct or remodel buildings that have been selected for UNESCO's World Heritage List (Hendry 2000: 167; see also Herzfeld 1991). Hendry also cites the example of the Maruyama Shakespeare Park, a "careful copy" of the original house at Stratford-Upon-Avon. The park's promoters tellingly claim it to be "more authentic" than the English original because theirs was restored to how it looked during Shakespeare's time. They have, in other words, mimetically recreated an image of Shakespeare's time, and therein lies his power to stimulate the imaginations of tourists.

Other observers have noted the mimetic qualities of Asian theme parks and tourist attractions more generally. Ellen Schattschneider (1996: 24) noted of the Tsugaru Earth Village in Morita Mura, Japan—a collection of replica models of the world's "sacred stone sites"—that the organizers "strove to reproduce a visible ritual icon of translocal space." Like the nearby Akakura Mountain Shrine, a Shinto temple devoted to making visible the hidden forces of the cosmos, "the Morita culture brokers hoped to make visible the hidden forces of the new global economy" by reproducing the icons of global civilization in one concentrated space. John Pemberton (1994: 247) has likewise noted something similar at the "Beautiful Indonesia" in Miniature Park outside Jakarta, where the replicas have been invested with such sacred "realness" that the distinction between the replica and the thing represented, that is, the original, has in effect collapsed. Where Pemberton interprets this collapse in a decidedly postmodern fashion, Hendry proposes examining such confusions of categories (real, fake, authentic, replica, original, etc.) as more culturally-specific problems of translation. There may be, in other words, more geographically and historically specific reasons for the mimetic qualities of theme parks than the globalization of postmodern sensibilities (Hendry 2000: 17). And it is precisely this that suggests the theme park as a translocal (as opposed to, say, transnational) phenomenon in Chinese ethnic tourism. The theme park mode of display and performance generates a new sense of identity that is translocal—at once steeped in the uniqueness of the village while asserting a belonging to a distant, more modern, nation.

Theme parks in China

Cosmological mimesis and empire in China

If the dominance of mimetic authenticity in Asian theme parks suggests, as Hendry argues, specific historical and cultural contexts more than a kind of generic global postmodernism, then we might explore the possible contexts for understanding the mimetic qualities of China's theme parks. Chinese modernity and nationalism are the most significant in this regard, but it is also revealing to first explore how the authentic replica might offer an insightful reading of China's earlier imperial imagination as well. If, as Faure and Siu (Chapter 2, this volume) argue, a translocal imaginary emerged as part of late imperial China's "earth-bound ideology," then we can also identify a cultural precedent of mimesis and authentic replication for this imaginary.

Benjamin (1978: 334) suggested that the earliest human acts of mimesis focused on the cosmos, the copying of that which was unseen or too vast to comprehend in a glance: "allusion to the astrological sphere may supply the first reference point for an understanding of the concept of nonsensuous similarity." René Barthelot was identifying something similar with his concept of "bio-astrale," translated by Paul Wheatley as "astrobiology." For Barthelot, mimesis was a way of making the profane sacred. As Wheatley (1971: 457) put it,

> Sacrality (which is synonymous with reality) is achieved through the imitation of a celestial archetype, as a result of which such religions can be powerful transformers of landscape... Throughout the continent of Asia, where this latter category of religious dramatization was strongly represented, there was thus a tendency for kingdoms, capitals, temples, shrines, and so forth, to be constructed as replicas of the cosmos.
>
> (Ibid.)

In China, Needham (1971: 73) claimed, principles of astrobiology informed the Zhou ideal of the square city. There was "a strong cosmological element in the tradition [of square walled cities]... connected no doubt with the ancient and widespread idea that the heavens were round while the earth was square." In fact, the connection went far beyond this familiar geometry; the ideal royal city, or *Ming Tang*, was itself a mimetic rendition of a calendar which governed the appropriate time and place for ritual observance (Feuchtwang 2001: 29–31). This ideal informed imperial capital plans, culminating in the late-imperial layout of Beijing (Sit 1995; Knapp 2000). But county capitals could also be conceived as replicas of the imperial capital, itself a replica of the cosmic cycle (Chang 1961). The placement of walled county capitals, particularly along the frontiers of the empire, was, in turn, a means of sacralizing the space of empire through mimesis. The creative, empowering, and sacralizing aspects of mimesis also seem to be at the heart of Sima Qian's remark that, "whenever Ch'in Shih Huang-ti conquered territory, he gave orders that the plan of the palace should be copied and the structure then recreated in the imperial capital at Hsien-yang. In this way he apparently sought to focus and concentrate at his own capital the vital forces that had previously been channeled through rival capitals" (Wheatley 1971: 464).

Michael Dutton (1998: 194) has likewise commented on the mimetic qualities of Chinese spatial organization. Elaborating on the ideas of architectural theorist Zhao Dongri, Dutton rebuts the common observation that Chinese cities lacked religious symbols like the dominant cathedrals of European cities:

> Chinese did not lack spirituality but lacked display and, in place of this "embedded" the spiritual in daily life practices. The hierarchised family order of Confucianism was both a spiritual and practical world and this was embedded in the spatial ordering of the compound house. Traditional China, then, was the land of a million churches, all of which were called home.
>
> (Ibid.)

While Dutton goes on to call China a "walled culture," it might be more accurate to call it a "mimetic culture" in which the world was "made real" through the on-going replication of the key symbols of empire, family, and faith, and the reenactment of rituals associated with these. For the imperial state, these replicas were, as Dutton and others have pointed out, intensely hierarchical and nested (see Wu 1999: 65–101).[5] Traditional Chinese state space was an exquisite hierarchical ordering of nested replication: house, town, capital, and empire. Mimesis, as a creative act of ritually replicating a broader meaning and authority at each level of this hierarchy conjured what Stephen Feuchtwang terms "the imperial metaphor."[6] As Ron Knapp (1999: 10–11) observes, the traditional (particularly northern) courtyard-type dwelling was "a functioning microcosm of the state itself." Knapp and Dutton identify a translocal quality to dwelling in China, in which houses are always linked—through replication—to broader scales and more distant places of identity. Drawing on Bachelard's *Poetics of Space*, Mueggler similarly refers to houses among Yi communities in Yunnan as representing multiple scales of being that "double, enfold, and invade one another" in "an intimate immensity" (Mueggler 2001: 41). Thus, the intimate space of the house "becomes the center of all space" (Bachelard 1994: 203).

178 Tim Oakes

Exhibiting the modern nation

By the twentieth century, authentic replication would be actively called upon to not just identify China's place in the cosmos, but to assert its place among the pageant of modern nations as well. Here, the international exhibition-theme park model was called upon for the work of mimetic citation. Again, Japan's experience is instructional in several ways. By 1910, Japan's participation in London's Festival of Empire marked its claim to be a modern imperial power; it too exhibited "natives" from its various colonies, including Formasan and Ainu village displays. Japan's exhibits were noted for "their tremendous ability carefully to copy what they observed" as the most significant markers of modern Euro-American technology (Hendry 2000: 60). Japan's participation in the great exhibition game was one in which it excelled in mimesis, for this was perhaps regarded as the most effective means of capturing the modernist magic of the exhibitions for Japan itself. The Europeans, however, seemed rather put off by what they saw as Japan's "aping" of the West, a choice of terms revealing a prevalent European tendency to associate the mimetic faculty with more "primitive" peoples in less advanced stages of evolution. By the time of the industrial age and its obsession with "the original," European pundits had apparently forgotten that mimesis had once been highly valued in European civilization itself. During the Renaissance, imitation "embraced a spectrum of meanings that our own narrow and pejorative usage of the term no longer suggests" (Lowenthal 1985: 80). The Japanese ability to appear, in a sense, more western than the West itself was clearly both a source of fascination and unease for Euro-American audiences.

Japan was also active in hosting its own international exhibitions, which tended to represent Japan's own East Asian imperial influence rather than any respect it commanded among Euro-American powers. For example, at the 1903 Osaka Trade and Industrial Exposition, seven Asian races were displayed in exhibits created by the Japanese themselves: Ainu, Ryukyuan, Formosan aboriginals, Korean, Chinese, Hindu, and Japanese. The Chinese were humiliated to find that their exhibit was sadly devoted to the well known Chinese "customs" of foot binding and opium smoking (Young 1996: 2–3). This experience was apparently one of the motivations for Nanjing's governor-general Tuan Fang to open China's own World's Fair in 1910—the Nanjing South Seas Exhibition (*Nanjing Nanyang Chuanyehui*)—and for the Chinese to represent themselves at the 1915 "International Celebration to Commemorate the Discovery of the Pacific Ocean and the Construction of the Panama Canal" in San Francisco.

According to Michael Godley (1978: 506), Tuan Fang had recently toured Europe and America and felt that "the secret of foreign wealth and power was to be seen in the trade fair." His Nanjing exhibition was held at the same time, and as a kind of alternative to, London's Festival of Empire Exhibition, being held at the Crystal Palace. Fourteen Asian nations participated in the Nanjing exhibition, thanks to Nanjing's vigorous lobbying of the overseas Chinese business community. The governor-general's exhibition was both a deliberate effort to mimic the West, and an illustration of "essence-use" (*ti-yong*) ideology in practice. Replication worked two ways here. Along with the citation of the symbols of technological advancement was a conscious displaying of distinctive national essence. Visitors entered the grounds through a south-facing main gate, decorated in traditional Chinese style, and exited through a European-looking gate lined with commercial stalls and facing west. This was but one of many design features of the exhibition which illustrated how China's march toward modernization needed to be viewed in the context of China's own glorious heritage, rather than in the context of China's current state of international humiliation. This theme continued in 1915 when the Chinese delegation brought to San Francisco a scale model of the Forbidden City and filled it with the most technologically sophisticated products they could gather. The exhibition-theme park model, in other words, allowed its producers to perform—and thus control—the boundary between modernity and tradition. Duara (1998: 290) identifies this boundary as the "aporia of linear history" and sees it as vital to maintaining an authentic and timeless core of national identity amid the historical change that necessarily gives nations a past from which to draw heritage, and a future toward which to progress. In China, he further notes, this split between the atavism of the nation and the telos of modernity was often expressed in terms of a dichotomy between East and West, or more specifically in terms of the *ti-yong* construction (Duara 1995: 29). It is a split which apparently continues to inform today's ethnic village theme parks, where local tradition and ethnicity are likewise performed in a highly modern and national genre.

Authentic replication in China's theme parks

In a 1993 inventory of theme parks in China, Bao Jigang (1995: 7–8) catalogued a total of 95 major parks, with 40 of these based on Chinese folk legends (23 of which were devoted to the classical tale *Journey to the West*), 34 parks based on ethnic folk culture, and 8 based on historical re-creations. But this was merely the beginning of a "theme park fever" which swept China during the latter half of the 1990s and which was inspired by the remarkable early success of Shenzhen's "Spendid China" (*Zhenxiu Zhonghua*) and "China Folk Culture Villages" (*Zhongguo Minsu Wenhua Cun*) parks (Anagnost 1993; Young 1996). According to Yang Zhengtai, some 2,000 theme parks opened between 1995 and 1999, with "more than 80 percent" of them soon losing money (Faison 1999). Most metropolitan areas were quickly saturated with far more parks than the market could bear. More than 100 parks opened on the outskirts of Chengdu alone, and most had shut down by the end of the decade. Nevertheless, the China Association of Amusement Parks and Attractions reported that by 2000, about 350 Chinese "amusement parks" were receiving a total of about 350 million annual visitors and earning revenues of some US$544 million (*China Daily* 2000).

These parks represent a full spectrum of amusements, from leisure parks featuring rides and other thrilling diversions—such as Shanghai's "American Dream" park—to ethnic and cultural themes that sometimes question the very definition of a tourist attraction. A brief description of a few parks illustrates their mimetic ability to authentically replicate both tradition and modernity simultaneously while enabling a kind of easy transgressing of the boundary between the two. In Shenzhen, a "China Food Culture City" was planned (*Beijing Review* 1996). The park would include four divisions: a China Food Culture Center, featuring numerous restaurants representing regional cuisines from throughout China and decorated in traditional regional styles; a Liquor Culture Center, where a "liquor culture street" would feature "wine-brewing shops of past dynasties"; a Tea Culture Center, featuring "replicas of famous teahouses and markets"; and a Medicine Culture Center, including a "modern traditional Chinese medicine research institute, restaurants serving medicinal food, TCM workshops, a sanatorium and market." In the medicine center, tourists would also be able to consult with TCM practitioners and even receive treatments. The center would include its own plots for the cultivation of traditional Chinese medicinal herbs.

In Hangzhou the Orient Culture Park recently opened, built around the restored Yangqi Buddhist Temple (*China Daily* 2001). This park was simultaneously designated a "Buddhist Culture Exhibition Center of China" by the Chinese Religious Society, and features exhibits of Buddhist cultural heritage from throughout Asia. It also features Confucian and Taoist sections as well. The majority of the park's visitors have been Buddhist pilgrims, as opposed to more conventional tourists. Indeed, the seriousness with which religious beliefs are mimetically replicated in some theme parks is illustrated in Kunming's Yunnan Culture Village, where a replica Dai Buddhist temple has been done so authentically that visitors are asked to remove their shoes before entering and are admonished to refrain from photography while inside.

Other parks more brashly replicate China's position in the world of global modernity, but do so, again, by citing national (traditional) essence in the built landscape. Probably the best known instance of this would be Shenzhen's Window of the World, which features 118 exquisitely detailed miniature replicas, of various scale, of the world's "best sites." A more extraordinary example was recently suggested in Beijing, where Nanmaofang Town is planning to build a World Currency Park, displaying "currencies from around the world, reconstructions of famous ancient and modern financial streets, and theme park rides based on the pursuit of money" (Jia 2001). The park apparently emerged as a result of the Town's plans to develop a block of office towers which were thwarted by the city's new zoning restrictions. Instead of attracting the Beijing's international white-collar class through real estate speculation, the town shifted gears and thought that this same wealthy market could be tapped for tourism.

What the above examples suggest is a mimetic tendency in theme parks in which replicas are often promoted as conveying more meaning than simple leisure and entertaining diversion. Concerning Splendid China in Shenzhen, Ann Anagnost (1993) has noted how both the miniature size and the attention to detail invested in the attractions serves to replicate the Chinese nation itself, as a complete and viewable object. This theme, along with the broader political economy of "reflexive accumulation," is explored by Ren Hai (1998), who argues that the commodity form turns the nation into an object allowing images of cultural difference to mask the potentially divisive social differentiations within the nation. And Jennifer Hubbert (2003) sees Chinese theme parks as sites which displace older venues of national political ritual; they offer opportunities where the modern subject—the Chinese citizen—can be consumed. These arguments point to a role for mimesis in many of China's cultural theme parks to convey not simply entertainment and pleasure but also the on-going "renewal," as Hendry (2000) has called it in the case of Japanese parks, of China as a nation, a culture, a modern society, and a legitimate member of the international pageant of nations.

China Folk Culture Villages

Next door to Splendid China, China Folk Culture Villages park (FCV) can be similarly interpreted as reflecting a complex variety of cultural and nationalistic concerns through its devotion to replication. On one level, the park, which features authentic replicas of twenty-four folk villages, conveys the modernist theme of social evolution applied to a specifically Chinese context. The villages represent a range of *minzu* groups which have been classified according to principles of evolutionary development in which all groups have been confidently placed on a linear time line of progress, with the Han not surprisingly occupying the most developed, civilized, and modern end of that line (see Harrell 1990, 1995; Brown 1996). But as Hitchcock *et al.* (1997) point out, there is much more to FCV than this display of official nationality ideology. FCV offers a display of a more timeless and authentic multinationalism in which replication of specific styles and forms becomes an important principle in and of itself. It is a theme park devoted to the display of Duara's (1998) "aporia of linear history." The "authentically replicated" villages, in other words, seem to leave one not just with an impression of which rung a particular group temporarily occupies on the tall ladder of social evolution, but also of the mosaic of China as a culturally diverse nation-state of many place-based traditions. FCV is a space of display, of performance and "edutainment"; it replicates China in a way complementary to Splendid China which, as Anagnost notes (1993), presents no temporally-defined "narrative" of the Chinese nation, just a timeless space of repeatedly instantiated national identity.

But "authentic replication" must be interpreted in the broader terms of performance to capture all that is happening at FCV. While *zhenshi zai xian* is the defining principle in terms of the actual village architecture—with native materials, artisans, and equipment employed in its construction—the costumes of village "inhabitants" and the songs and dances they perform have been adjusted for entertainment value. The objectification of display is also confused somewhat by the fact that—like my own experience in the Li villages of Hainan—visitors to FCV can themselves become performers in rented ethnic costume. Walking around the park, it is sometimes difficult to tell who is a working performer and who is a tourist. This fact, along with the "living" aspect of each village, where natives of each *minzu* group represented are employed, confuses the distinction between the replica and the real. This confusion allows for the active manipulation, perhaps, of what suddenly appears to be a rather arbitrary boundary (between the real and the fake, the traditional and the modern, timeless authenticity and linear history). Visiting Beijing's Nationality Customs Park (*Minzu Fengqing Gongyuan*) in 1994 while it was still under construction, I encountered a group of Dong workers from Guizhou who were in the midst of building the park's drum tower and "wind and rain" covered bridge. Giving me a tour of the site, they were clearly proud of their work and its high quality, and they spoke highly of the park's managers who had provided them with building materials from Dong regions of Guizhou and Guangxi. The replicas would be built just as they would have been in a Dong village, the men pointed out, only here they would be "even better." Clearly, the conventional distinction between "real" and "fake" does not easily apply in such cases of replication.

The blurring of real and replica is deepened, however, when we also consider the impact that displays like FCV has had on the places and groups its villages represent. As FCV replicates "ethnic China," the "original" is also changed in the process. As alluded to in the villages introduced at the beginning of the chapter, this change is one in which the "original" villages start replicating the theme parks in terms of displays, programs, and routines. As is discussed in the final section below, much of this occurs because of the villagers employed by FCV, most of whom work at the park for a couple years and, unless they're able to find other more lucrative employment in the Special Economic Zone, return to their home villages where they become important agents of village ethnic tourism development.[7] They, and others who travel from the villages to the distant urban centers for work, bring the model back home with them. In this sense, the translocal imaginary of modern national theme-park cultural display is carried as part of the "baggage" one brings back home. The translocal imaginary is not, then, so much an abstract force of vast scale, a frequency to which localities "tune in," but something that is purposefully transported along particular instances of connection between places.

The mimetic village

And so we return to the villages that opened this chapter. It is at the village level that the mimetic qualities of Chinese tourism reveal themselves most profoundly. That ethnic villages predominantly *replicate* themselves, creating theme park attractions at the actual site of "the original" itself, speaks to the power of mimesis in defining for villagers the nature of tourism development itself. Villages rely on an essentially mimetic model in their efforts to develop attractions. Replication in terms of performance and display works in a dual sense for villagers. On the one hand it allows for a conscious identification with distinct ethnic and place-based traditions (timeless authenticity), while on the other hand allows for the "capturing" of more distant modern urban places where theme park tourist attractions signify development and civilization (the linear history of the nation). This is both a replication of "the original" (the "traditional village") and of the modern nation as represented by the theme park; the "authentic replica" is a means of reproducing the modern nation within the remote and unique place of the village itself. As such it conveys a translocal imagination at work. While village theme parks could be viewed simply as the result of tourism's apparently universal need to standardize its product, what I am suggesting here is that this need is met by villagers with a more culturally specific willingness to "be displayed" that has its roots in the deeper significance of mimesis and, consequently, in different notions of "authenticity."

We already have seen this kind of mimesis in some of the opening vignettes. Local tourism authorities at Guizhou's Huangguoshu Falls, for example, sought to develop Huashishao village with explicit reference to FCV as a model.[8] But mimesis is perhaps most clearly seen in the villages which have already been contracted to receive tourist groups with welcoming ceremonies and song and dance routines that both cite "original" village traditions and, at the same time, allow villagers to perform their modernity and make claims of national authority. These performances reproduce villages as translocal spaces, where a replicated theme park model informs the remaking of places according to a broader network of travel.

The Miao villages of Heitu and Changlinggang, in central Guizhou have received substantial investments from Guizhou's largest travel agency, Overseas Travel Corporation (OTC), to create comprehensive, on-demand ethnic cultural experiences for tourists. In cooperation with the county's *Nationalities* Affairs Commission, which was interested in developing tourism as an instrument of poverty-relief, OTC selected these villages according to a set of criteria including proximity to the provincial capital, proximity to a major highway, scenic setting, ethnic "purity," and enthusiasm of the villagers themselves.[9] Villagers were far from passive in this process; many local leaders throughout the region actively promote their villages to their local nationalities affairs authorities or to travel agencies. In Heitu and Changlinggang, OTC and the county nationalities affairs office had invested in parking lots, new toilets, improved performance squares, "traditional" village gates, and costumes for performing villagers. Along the highway signs were installed: "Heitu/Changlinggang Miao Stockade Ethnic Customs Tourist Site" (*Heitu/ Changlinggang miaozhai minzu fengqing lüyoudian*).

At each village a fairly standardized reception routine had been established, which included a procession into the village, with occasional enforced drinking of "road-block wine" followed by a song and dance performance. While some of the songs resembled those which might have been sung during festivals, there were many more songs that conveyed a more worldly attitude among villagers. With the guidance of OTC personnel, dances were based on the adjusted, entertaining dances developed at FCV; songs were for the most part contemporary ones that tourists would recognize. Indeed, the performance included a "nationalities karaoke" singing competition between the tourists and the villagers. Guides typically prepped tourists prior to their arrival, encouraging them to practice their songs on the bus as they approached the villages, so they would be ready to join in. As in FCV, where visitors could rent ethnic costumes and join in the various performances, participation was expected of visitors to Heitu and Changlinggang.

In addition to the karaoke competition, this included various games (in which the losers were forced to drink yet more wine), and a chance to pick up a wooden mallet and pound away at a tub of hot sticky glutinous rice, the kind used for making the new year's rice cakes. For the tourists, the experience was, in all respects, equivalent to going to FCV, but on a smaller scale and in a more attractive setting.

In fact, it seems clear that creating an FCV-type experience was OTC's primary objective. Even the county nationalities affairs officers saw the theme park as the ultimate stage in the villages' development. "In the future," the county nationalities affairs director told me, "you won't even have to make arrangements ahead of time, but will just be able to show up, buy a ticket, and get treated to a Miao cultural feast." When queried, OTC guides admitted that they rarely brought Western tourists to these villages. Westerners, they said, were interested in the "more authentic" villages in the more remote southeastern region of the province. Chinese tourists, however, including those from Taiwan, Hong Kong, and Singapore, tended to enjoy the theme park villages. Guides suggested that this was partly due to a basic cultural affinity between the Miao and the Chinese; the tourists enjoyed the opportunity to participate in a fun afternoon with their "Miao cousins." In this sense, guides were affirming that exotic otherness was less the attraction than the desire to affirm a kind of inter-ethnic solidarity. Such a message is indeed confirmed by villagers who went so far as to express the nationalist ideology imbedded in the theme park model, that contrived activities such as "nationalities karaoke" were a means of performing the unity of nationalities in China (*minzu tuanjie*). When asked if they enjoyed singing Taiwan pop songs and performing karaoke, villagers responded simply that it was good to support the unity of China's nationalities, a response they had probably learned from the guides themselves.

But while an ideology of national unity is being performed here, there is also a different kind of authenticity at work which helped villagers and tourists meet in a somewhat more meaningful way than would be the case if tourists felt they were simply being fed a dose of propaganda. Comments tourists made to me during village song and dance performances made it clear that they evaluated the villagers according to the quality of their singing and dancing, that is, how well it replicated their idea of an entertaining performance. Seldom did Chinese tourists comment on the "inauthenticity" of these performances compared to their expectations of the songs and dances of actual Miao festivals and rituals. While tourists had no trouble admitting these villages were clearly *Hanhuale* ("Hanified"), they tended not to view this as a corruption of the village's "authentic origins." This attitude made it more feasible for villagers to envision national modernity as attainable merely according to the *quality* in which it is replicated. Karaoke is a *modern* kind of performance, after all.

It is perhaps ironic that it was in southeastern Guizhou, the region OTC guides claimed to be regarded as "more authentic" by western tourists, that the village theme park model got its start in Guizhou. The pioneer village in this regard was Langde, recognized in the 1980s as an "open air museum" for the investigation and preservation of Miao culture. This already distinguished it from villages like Heitu and Changlinggang, which were selected by a travel agency primarily for their potential for tourism. Yet as previously noted, the distinction between a museum, and especially an "open air" one, and a theme park is a difficult one to sustain, and while Langde may have initially been recognized by the provincial Nationalities Affairs Commission as a "cultural relic" (i.e. an authentic "original"), it has since become just as much of a theme park as the OTC's more recently developed tourist villages. This is, in part, due to Langde's exceptional exposure within China's broader ethnic tourism industry. Youth from Langde were among the first recruited by FCV to work in Shenzhen as performers, and Langde villagers have also performed with song and dance troupes in Beijing, Guilin, Guiyang, Shanghai, and Kunming. They have traveled as far as the United States and France to participate in cultural festivals, and have been heavily recruited as staff in large hotels and other resorts seeking a bit of "ethnic flavor." In fact, by the mid-1990s, villagers were lamenting the decline in talent in village performances since most of the talented youth had been recruited for more lucrative jobs elsewhere. When the National Tourism Administration (NTA) began promoting their ethnic tourism theme for the year 1995, the village head's daughter was featured in nationally distributed promotional posters. But Langde's central role in China's ethnic tourism development is most succinctly symbolized by the village's performance arena itself. Funded by an investment from the NTA, it features an inlaid stone rendition of the NTA's logo; China's tourism industry is literally imbedded into the very bedrock of the village.

This has not been a one-way relationship by any means. Langde has benefited financially from its role as one of China's quintessential ethnic tourist sites, and its approach to hosting tourists has likewise been influenced by the villagers who return from working in places like FCV with clearer ideas about modernity, the nation, and tourism. Not surprisingly, Langde's song and dance routine bears numerous similarities with those performed at FCV. In some cases the villagers doing the performing are the sisters and brothers of those doing the same thing in FCV. In Langde, I was able to witness the different reactions of Chinese and Western tourists because the tourists typically saw me as a fellow metropolitan with whom they could relate. As in Heitu and Changlinggang, the Chinese tourists recognized Langde as "Hanified." However, they tended to judge their tourism experience not on this fact but on its entertainment value. Most commented on how happy the villagers made them feel, particularly when copious amounts of wine were involved. But the theme park atmosphere of the routine was not lost on the Western tourists who go to Langde. They tended to regard the performances with a kind of bemused charm, but to me they invariably asked about the "real" Miao villages that they were not being allowed to see. What were the Miao *really* like, the ones who had not become "spoiled?"

As for the villagers themselves, there was a conscious acknowledgement that their performances should not be regarded as replicas of traditional welcoming ceremonies, but rather as a something like what tourists might see in Shenzhen, only better. Villagers stressed to me many times that their routine reflected Han influences, but that this was a mark of how "modern, developed, and civilized" (*xiandai, fazhan, wenming*) Langde was compared to other Miao villages (see Oakes 1998). Thus, their mimetic reference to theme park tourism need not be interpreted as the simple response of "primitives." Such was, as we have seen, the reaction of Europeans to Japan's forays into the great exhibition game, and historical hindsight tells us that these accusations of "aping" revealed more about the parochialism of the Europeans than the supposed primitivism of the Japanese. Langde's villagers felt they were actively engaged in a project of modernization in which their imitation of that quintessentially modern institution, the theme park, offered a gateway to the legitimacy of the Chinese nation. As with the villages of Heitu and Changlinggang, one way of performing this was by turning a traditional "bronze drum dance" into a dance of national unity by inviting tourists to participate. This dance was a standard festival dance which had been adjusted as a means for villagers to express their unity, in time and space, with their visitors. As such it was a performance of translocal modernity as much as placed tradition.

But it was also recognized that entirely new songs and dances were needed; innovation in the reception routine was thought to keep Langde a step ahead of a growing field of competing villages. For instance, songs from the Cultural Revolution era had been added to the routine, to the consistently great applause of the Chinese visitors. Innovations like this were necessary not only for keeping tourists happy, but for keeping villagers themselves interested in performances. It was an important opportunity, the village head once told me, for villagers to learn new songs and dances, something he regarded as valuable in and of itself.[10] In more general terms, though, the performances before an audience of "modern outsiders" (*xiandai de waidiren*) gave villagers a momentary opportunity to display their own modernity, turning their village into a translocal space where the space of the nation was gathered and claimed. Most importantly, it was a translocal space where the hardness of the traditional–modern divide—that aporia of linear history normally wielded against the Miao with discrimination—was controlled by the villagers themselves.

This is not to say that an ideology of authenticity as "the original" did not also inform tourism development in Langde. As a "regime of power" rather than an essential quality, authenticity allowed for the translocal replication of local origins even as it enabled the claiming of the modern nation. Periodic visits by high-ranking Miao officials, state cultural officials, state nationalities affairs officials, and leaders of the NTA itself, all served to convey this power to villagers by reminding them of their crucial role as *preservers* of Miao and Chinese heritage. This message had been internalized by some of the villagers, and was integrated into the theme park approach to tourism development. But the idea of preservation perhaps offered villagers a more problematic path toward modernization and national integration; many of them complained about being unable to "modernize" the village with newer-looking structures, or reap greater tourism revenues by building some souvenir shops or a large guesthouse because such changes would violate the terms of Langde's status as an officially recognized "preserved cultural relic" (*wenwu baohu danwei*). Like their counterparts in Huashishao, village leaders wanted to charge tourists directly for entering the village; they also sought to develop various leisure diversions, including a proposal to dam up the river in front of the village to create a fishing and boating pond. These efforts were denied by prefectural and provincial tourism and cultural officials on the grounds that they would compromise the authenticity of the village, reminding us again that, as a "regime of power," authenticity invited contests over whose authority would determine its meaning.

Ultimately, then, villagers received—and themselves conveyed—the mixed and even contradictory versions of authenticity that traveled back and forth across the traditional–modern boundary. Such a boundary is maintained by a regime of power, but when authenticity takes on the diverse meanings that such a regime requires, that boundary comes to be recognized—by villagers themselves—for the arbitrary construction that it is. While their official status invested in them a responsibility for maintaining a kind of "frozen preservation" for the sake of the nation, they also sought to embrace modernity. Having learned a great deal from the broader tourism industry in his various travels as promoter of China's premier ethnic tourist village, Langde's village head was explicit in his opinion that these were not contradictory objectives. He stressed that Langde was the most scientifically advanced village in the area; it had adopted high-yield variety seeds earlier than any other and had embraced the new commercial economy of tourism. Langde's farmers, he claimed, were the area's most productive, despite their busy schedule of tourist receptions. There was a difference between being a stubborn peasant locked into traditional ways, and being a peasant who understood the importance of heritage and preservation. These latter ideas are, after all, *modern* ideas (see also Wu 1991). Langde for him was a *performer*, a model for the rest of the Miao to emulate. Langde's engagement with the arbitrary nature of authenticity (both "original" *and* replica)—marking the divide between timeless local village and modern nation state—made it a translocal space. Through the replication of a theme park model of performance and display, Langde was continually remade as a place infused with the ideas of authenticity and change.

Coda

During the Cultural Revolution a teacher from Shanghai was "sent down" to the village of Fanpai, not far from Langde. He was amazed at the wild and uninhibited style of dance practiced there. Instead of returning to Shanghai after the reforms began, he stayed in the region, became the prefecture's tourism director, and organized and promoted Fanpai's dance troupe to begin touring and performing for tourists. So successful was the troupe that they eventually even performed for China's leaders in Zhongnanhai. Though Fanpai itself never emerged as an ethnic tourist theme park like Langde (it was far too difficult to reach), it exported what became a standardized and ubiquitous model of Miao dance performance, a modified version of which is still regularly performed at FCV today. To help attract tourist audiences, Fanpai's dance troupe was labeled the "Oriental Disco" (*dongfang disike*), and the dance was altered in a number of ways to make it amenable to contemporary music with a disco beat. Costumes were made more exotic and risqué until tourists were watching a completely new form of dance performance which fulfilled their expectations of the authentic Miao (wild, promiscuous, and sexual) while at the same time allowing, through replication of "modern" forms, a kind of sympathetic affinity to develop ("they're just like us after all"). Performing in Beijing was the ultimate confirmation that the key to modernity was how well it could be performed and replicated. There is more to the *dongfang disike* than the unsophisticated "aping" of a passing Western fad. At the same time, it is too easy to dismiss it as inauthentic, for reasons which by now should hopefully be apparent. The modern currency of authenticity travels through China, creating translocal spaces in unexpected ways. Its meaning is far from fixed, and its outcomes, like modernity itself, far from predictable.

Notes

1   Theme-park display is by no means *limited* to China's periphery, however. Village theme parks have existed for some time in Hong Kong's New Territories, and have been set up near Beijing and Shanghai, since the late 1980s. They have been growing rapidly throughout China's key tourist destinations, such as Huangshan in southern Anhui. See Knapp (2004) for details on the Huangshan region.
2   When I visited Huashishao again in 2003, it had indeed become a theme park, with a new highway having been plowed right through the center of the village. Access for tourists into the village was controlled by a gate with a ticket window; carts were available for tours, accompanied by serenading village girls, and song and dance shows could be conjured in a matter of minutes. Some individual households were earning their own tourist-related incomes from the sale of souvenirs, while others had managed to establish restaurants or cafes. Only a portion of the village entry fee, however, was actually retained by the village itself.
3   Bruner (1994: 400), in fact, identifies at least four types of authenticity often at play in tourism. First there is the "historical verisimilitude" of representation, in which the idea of an "authentic replica" becomes plausible if it resembles the original in what tourists regard as a convincing manner. Second is a similar notion of authenticity as historically accurate and genuine, with the criteria for evaluation being whether a person from the actual historical period represented would recognize it as true and believable. The third type Bruner identifies is the more familiar "original, not a copy," which by definition negates the possibility of the first two. Finally, there is the more legal sense of the term, in which an authority certifies and legally validates authenticity. The slipperiness of the term, of course, is simply an indicator of its socially-constructed and situational nature. And if authenticity is socially constructed, then any examination of authenticity in Chinese village tourism must account for the social context in which constructions of authenticity occur.
4   "Frozen preservation" is, however, being practiced in some of China's theme park villages. In the southern Anhui village of Qiankou—which claims to be China's first "open-air museum"—preservation is regulated according to a policy of *xiujiu rujiu*, or "repairing the old to appear old; maintaining the original appearance" (Knapp 2004: 16). This is remarkably similar to the "arrested decay" noted by DeLyser (1999) in Bodie, California.
5   The reference here to a "nested hierarchy" is not meant to be a reference to Skinner's use of this idea in his regional-systems analysis of Chinese social space (Skinner 1964). Rather, it identifies the interrelated systems of popular and official ritual and

spatial ordering. Although Sangren (1987) argues that regional space hierarchies constructed in popular territorial cult rituals do match Skinner's regional-systems hierarchy, the lack of reference in either case to the hierarchy of state administration seems to be a glaring absence. For a sustained critique of Skinner's approach, see Cartier (2002). For a relevant critique of Sangren, see Wang (1995).

6 Though it is clearly privileged in this analysis, the hierarchical ordering of state space in China was not, of course, the only structuring element in the spatiality of everyday China. As Feuchtwang (2001) and Wang (1995) have observed, popular territorial cults produced their own spaces via mimetic referencing of official space. While neither Feuchtwang nor Wang deploy mimesis as a conceptual framework for analyzing local cults as alternative popular spaces, their analyses lend themselves well to such an approach.

7 FCV employs about 7,000 workers, most of whom come from one of the 24 *minzu* groups represented. Originally, each employee underwent a rigorous 294-hour training program, later reduced to a still-substantial 161 hours. According to Hitchcock *et al.* (1997: 204), ten areas of study are included in the training: (1) The Party's direction and the initial stages of socialism; (2) The Party's open-door reforms and the creation of Special Economic Zones; (3) The development of Overseas Chinese Town (where FCV is located); (4) Tourist culture; (5) Public relations; (6) Folklore and ethnology; (7) Language training in Mandarin, English, and Cantonese; (8) Music training; (9) Personal presentation; and (10) Performance training.

8 Other examples of the model are also readily available on the Internet, to which theme park villages throughout China are increasingly becoming linked. Many of the tourist villages in southern Anhui, for instance, have their own Web sites, as do the heavily traveled canal towns of the southern Jiangsu—northern Zhejiang region, five of which (Zhouzhuang, Tongli, Luzhi, Wuzhen, Xitang) recently won a UNESCO heritage award of distinction for their preservation efforts (Knapp 2004: 25).

9 This final criteria is debatable. In most cases officials just assumed villagers would support their inclusion in tourist itineraries, and for the most part my observations confirmed this assumption to be true. Official attitudes were revealed in this telling exchange between myself and a provincial cultural official: When I asked him whether or not they take into account the unity of villagers in support of tourism development, he told me that this was unnecessary. "*Of course* they support it; who wouldn't support it? All these villages around here, they all wish *they* had been chosen. Being selected means a big boost in income for the villagers."

10 It is interesting to note, however, that in contrast to the village head, Langde's tourism director made it a point to emphasize the authenticity of the songs and dances performed for tourists. This was, of course, true for *some* of the performances. But his attitudes illustrated the sharp differences of opinion within the village itself over the merits of replicating theme park type performances versus maintaining the integrity of actual festival and ceremonial performances. The village head and the prefectural tourism officials tended to have the final say, however, and they advocated the more "modern" approach.

References

Adams, V. (1996a) *Tigers of the Snow and Other Virtual Sherpas: An Ethnography of Himalayan Encounters*, Princeton, NJ: Princeton University Press.
—— (1996b) "Karaoke as modern Lhasa, Tibet: western encounters with cultural politics," *Cultural Anthropology* 11(4): 510–546.
American Heritage Dictionary of the English Language (AHD) (2003), Fourth edn, Online version: http://www.bartleby.com/61/32/MO493200.html

Anagnost, A. (1993) "The nationscape: movement in the field of vision," *Positions* 1(3): 585–606.

Bachelard, G. (1994) *The Poetics of Space*, trans. M. Jolas, Boston, MA: Beacon.

Bao, J. (1995) *Zhuti Gongyuan de Fazhan jiqi Yingxiang Yanjiu: Yi Shenzhen Shi Wei Li*, PhD dissertation, Department of Geography, Zhongshan University, Guangzhou.

Becker, J. (2004) "Faking it: Chinese burn their bridges with the past," *The Observer* (April 2).

Beijing Review (1996) "Shenzhen's China food culture city," *Beijing Review* 39(46) (November 11—November 17), Online version: http://www-cibtc.ceic.go.cn/bjreview/november/96–46–14.html

Benjamin, W. (1968) "The work of art in the age of mechanical reproduction," trans. by H. Zohn, in H. Arendt (ed.) *Illuminations*, New York: Harcourt, Brace & World, 217–252.

—— (1978) "On the mimetic faculty," in P. Demetz (ed.) *Reflections: Essays, Aphorisms and Autobiographical Writings*, New York: Harcourt, Brace & Jovanovich.

Berger, J. (1972) *Ways of Seeing*, Harmondsworth, MD: Penguin.

Briggs, A. (1979) *The Age of Improvement, 1783–1867*, London: Longmans.

Brown, M. (ed.) (1996) *Negotiating Ethnicities in China and Taiwan*, Berkeley, CA: University of California Institute for East Asian Studies China Research Monograph No. 46.

Bruner, E. (1994) "Abraham Lincoln as authentic reproduction: a critique of postmodernism," *American Anthropologist* 96(2): 397–415.

Cartier, C. (2002) "Origins and evolution of a geographical idea: the macroregion in China," *Modern China* 28(1): 79–143.

Chang, S.-D. (1961) "Some aspects of the urban geography of the Chinese hsien capital," *Annals of the Association of American Geographers* 51(1): 23–44.

China Daily (2000) "China's amusement industry booms," July 20, Online version: http://chinadaily.com.cn

—— (2001) "Theme park features different cultures," *China Daily*, February 28, Online version: http://chinadaily.com.cn

Cohen, E. (1988) "Authenticity and commoditization in tourism," *Annals of Tourism Research* 15(3): 371–386.

—— (2001) "Ethnic tourism in SE Asia," in C.-B. Tan, S. Cheung, and H. Yang (eds) *Tourism, Anthropology, and China*, Bangkok: White Lotus Press.

Cox, R. (1998) *The Zen Arts: An Anthropological Study of the Culture of Aesthetic Form in Japan*, PhD Dissertation, Dept of Anthropology, University of Edinburgh.

Culler, J. (1988) "Semiotics of tourism," *American Journal of Semiotics* 1(1–2): 127–140.

DeLyser, D. (1999) "Authenticity on the ground: engaging the past in a California ghost town," *Annals of the Association of American Geographers* 89(4): 602–632.

Duara, P. (1995) *Rescuing History from the Nation: Questioning Narratives of Modern China*, Chicago, IL: University of Chicago Press.

—— (1998) "The regime of authenticity: timelessness, gender and national history in modern China," *History and Theory* 37 (October): 287–308.

Dutton, M. (1998) *Streetlife China*, Cambridge: Cambridge University Press.

Faison, S. (1999) "Even if you build them...the Chinese may not come to theme parks," *New York Times* (August 3).

Feuchtwang, S. (2001) *Popular Religion in China: The Imperial Metaphor*, Richmond, Surrey: Curzon.

Godley, M. (1978) "China's world's fair of 1910: lessons from a forgotten event," *Modern Asian Studies* 12(3): 503–522.

Greenhalgh, P. (1988) *Ephemeral Vistas: The Expositions Universelles, Great Expositions and World Fairs, 1851–1939*, Manchester, NH: Manchester University Press.

Harrell, S. (1990) "Ethnicity, local interests, and the state: Yi communities in southwest China," *Comparative Studies of Society and History* 32(3): 515–545.

—— (ed.) (1995) *Cultural Encounters on China's Ethnic Frontiers*, Seattle, WA: University of Washington Press.

Hendry, J. (2000) *The Empire Strikes Back: A Global View of Cultural Display*, Oxford: Berg.

Herzfeld, M. (1991) *A Place in History: Social and Monumental Time in a Cretan Town*, Princeton, NJ: Princeton University Press.

Hitchcock, M., Stanley, N., and Chung, S. K. (1997) "The south-east Asian 'living museum' and its antecedents," in S. Abram and M. Waldren (eds) *Tourists and Tourism: Identifying with People and Places*, Oxford: Berg, 197–221.

Hubbert, J. (2003) "Consuming the nation, legitimating the state: theme parks in late-socialist China," paper presented at the Annual Meetings of the American Anthropological Association, Chicago, IL.

Impey, O. and MacGregor, A. (1985) *The Origins of Museums: The Cabinet of Curiosities in Sixteenth and Seventeenth Century Europe*, Oxford: Oxford University Press.

Jia, H. (2001) "New park aims to rake in dough for Beijing," *China Daily* (October 16), Online version: http://www1.chinadaily.com.cn/bw/2001–10–16/38706.html

Knapp, R. (1999) *China's Living Houses: Folk Beliefs, Symbols, and Household Ornamentation*, Honolulu, HI: University of Hawai'i Press.

—— (2000) *China's Walled Cities*, Oxford: Oxford University Press.

—— (2004) "(Re)presenting rural heritage: the preservations of China's vernacular landscapes," paper presented at the Symposium: "The Persistence of Traditions: Monuments and Preservation in Late Imperial and Modern China," Columbia University, New York (April 2–3).

Lowenthal, D. (1985) *The Past is a Foreign Country*, Cambridge: Cambridge University Press.

MacCannell, D. (1973) "Staged authenticity: arrangements of social space in tourist settings," *American Journal of Sociology* 79: 589–603.

—— (1976) *The Tourist: A New Theory of the Leisure Class*, New York: Schocken.

Macdonald, S. (ed.) (1998) *The Politics of Display: Museums, Science, Culture*, London and New York: Routledge.

Macdonald, S. and Fyfe, G. (eds) (1996) *Theorizing Museums: Representing Identity and Diversity in a Changing World*, Oxford: Blackwell.

McIntosh, A. and Prentice, R. (1999) "Affirming authenticity: consuming cultural heritage," *Annals of Tourism Research* 26(3): 589–612.

Mitchell, T. (1988) *Colonizing Egypt*, Cambridge: Cambridge University Press.

Mueggler, E. (2001) *The Age of Wild Ghosts: Memory, Violence, and Place in Southwest China*, Berkeley, CA: University of California Press.

Needham, J. (1971) *Science and Civilization in China*, 4(3), London: Cambridge University Press.

Nyiri, P. (forthcoming) *Scenic Spots: The Construction of the Chinese Tourist Site and the Question of Cultural Authority*, Seattle, WA: University of Washington Press.

Oakes, T. (1998) *Tourism and Modernity in China*, London and New York: Routledge.

Pemberton, J. (1994) "Recollections from 'Beautiful Indonesia' (somewhere beyond the postmodern)," *Public Culture* 6(2): 241–262.

Picard, M. (1997) "Cultural tourism, nation-building, and regional culture: the making of a Balinese identity," M. Picard and R. Wood (eds) *Tourism, Ethnicity, and the State in Asian and Pacific Societies*, Honolulu, HI: University of Hawai'i Press, 181–214.

Ren, H. (1998) *Economies of Culture: Theme Parks, Museums, and Capital Accumulation in China, Hong Kong, and Taiwan*, unpublished PhD dissertation, Deptartment of Anthropology, University of Washington, Seattle, WA.

Sangren, S. (1987) *History and Magical Power in a Chinese Community*, Stanford, CA: Stanford University Press.

Schattschneider, E. (1996) "The labor of mountains," *Positions* 4(1): 1–31.

Schein, L. (1999) "Perfoming modernity," *Cultural Anthropology* 14(3): 361–395.

Silver, I. (1993) "Marketing authenticity in Third World countries," *Annals of Tourism Research* 20: 302–318.

Sit, V. (1995) *Beijing: The Nature and Planning of a Chinese Capital City*, New York: Wiley.

Skinner, G. W. (1964) "Marketing and social structure in rural China," *Journal of Asian Studies* 24: 3–43, 195–228.

Spooner, B. (1986) "Weavers and dealers: the authenticity of an oriental carpet," in A. Appadurai (ed.) *The Social Life of Things: Commodities in Cultural Perspective*, Cambridge: Cambridge University Press, 195–235.

Truettner, W. (ed.) (1991) *The West as America; Reinterpreting Images of the Frontier, 1820–1920*, Washington, DC: Smithsonian Institution.

Wang, M. (1995) "Place, administration, and territorial cults in late imperial China: a case study from south Fujian," *Late Imperial China* 16(1): 33–78.

Wang, N. (1999) "Rethinking authenticity in tourism experience," *Annals of Tourism Research* 26(2):349–370.

Wheatley, P. (1971) *The Pivot of the Four Quarters*, Chicago, IL: Aldine.

Wu, D. (1991) "Minzu chuantong wenhua de shuaitui yu duice," in *Zouxiang Shijie Dachao*, Guiyang: Minzu Chubanshe, 53–59.

Wu, L. (1999) *Rehabilitating the Old City of Beijing: A Project in the Ju'er Hutong Neighborhood*, Vancouver: University of British Columbia Press.

Yang, H., Liu, C., Liu, Y., and Duan, Y. (2001) "Man-chun-man village at the crossroads: conservation and vicissitudes of ethnic cultures during the development of tourism," in Tan C.-B., S. Cheung, and H. Yang (eds) *Tourism, Anthropology, and China*, Bangkok: White Lotus Press, 167–178.

Young, M. (1996) " 'Splendid China': virtual reality," *Papers of the British Association for Korean Studies* 6: 2–3.

10 Flows of heroin, people, capital, imagination, and the spread of HIV in southwest China

Weng Naiqun

Globalization describes the exaggerated tendency toward time–space compression that Marx and Engels identified in the *Communist Manifesto* as characteristic of the capitalist mode of production (see Chakrabarty 1992). That is, globalization implies a radical acceleration of the flows of images, people, money, technologies—subjects and objects, in short—across the face of the globe (Appadurai 1990). These flows move increasingly quickly along routes of increasing distance. But the network of flows is not fixed; nor is it symmetrical. There are blockages: not everything flows everywhere (see Hannerz 1996). As Lash and Urry (1994:12) put it: "Indeed the flows are highly specific to particular times and particular spaces. And these certain times and certain spaces, through which labor, capital, and signs flow, are determined by very specific sets of institutions. These latter, which are initially institutions of economic regulation, figure at the same time as institutions of spatial regulation." Not only are the flows particular to particular times and places; particular times and places are themselves the contingent outcome of these flows.

(Robert J. Foster 1999: 141–142)

Strikingly patterned outbreaks of HIV, tuberculosis, and even Ebola—and the social responses to these outbreaks—all suggest that models of disease emergence need to be dynamic, systemic, and critical. They need to be critical of facile claims of causality, particularly those that scan the pathogenic roles of social inequalities. Critical perspectives on emerging infections must ask how large-scale social forces come to have their effects on unequally positioned individuals in increasingly interconnected populations; a critical epistemology needs to ask what features of disease emergence are obscured by dominant analytic frameworks. Such models must strive to incorporate change and complexity, and must be global in scope, yet alive to local variation.

(Paul Farmer 1999: 5)

Over the past two decades, AIDS has accompanied the flow of people and commodities (such as polluted blood products and heroin) spreading over the face of the globe. Paradoxically, many current epidemics and diseases show that globalization includes not only "the radical acceleration of the flows of images, people, money, technologies," but also diseases, particularly contagious diseases (between human and human, human and animal, and animal and animal). In recent years, the HIV/AIDS epidemic in China is becoming more real than ever before. However, the spread of HIV/AIDS accompanying the flows of people, commodities, capital, technologies, and information, is highly specific to particular times and particular spaces. And these particular times and spaces are determined by very specific sets of political-economic and sociocultural institutions. In other words, these particular times and spaces are the contingent outcomes of these flows that encounter very specific sets of political-economic and sociocultural institutions. The spread of HIV/AIDS in China, in some sense, as the spread of HIV/AIDS in the world, implies specific political-economic inequalities and socio-cultural institutions.

In addition to providing a sketch of the HIV/AIDS epidemic in China, this chapter focuses on the HIV/AIDS epidemic in three specific localities in Yunnan based on a very short-term field project conducted by a research group led by the author. The discussion and analysis of the spread of HIV/AIDS in the first two villages and the emerging risk of HIV/AIDS epidemic in the latter township are put in the context of the uneven translocal flows of drugs, people, capital, and information, including imaginaries produced by media. However, some of the flows including drugs and people, do not end within the state boundary, but spill over to neighboring countries, mainly Myanmar and Thailand. In other words, the HIV/AIDS epidemics in southwest China discussed here will be associated with different forms of translocality that include rural to rural and rural to urban migration, cross-border heroin and women trafficking, tourism and sex tourism, capital and translocal imaginaries produced by and in media.

A sketch of HIV/AIDS epidemic in China, especially in southwest China

According to an updated Chinese government estimate released on April 11, 2002, by the end of 2001, 850,000 people have been infected with HIV, an increase of 30 percent from the number of HIV infected people by the end of 2000 (Rosenthal 2002). According to a Health Ministry Report, China found its first HIV case in 1985. By June of 1998, HIV infected cases have been found all over the thirty-one administrative regions including provincial, autonomous regional level, and municipalities directly under the Central Government in China. By the end of September 2000, 20,711 HIV/AIDS cases were reported in all Chinese provinces, autonomous regions, and municipalities directly under the Central Government (阿水 2001). Among the HIV infections mentioned there were 741 cases of AIDS and 420 deaths. By June of 2001, China identified a total of 26,058 HIV infections; 1,111 AIDS patients; and 800 deaths (刘元亮等 2001; 刘元亮、姜荣生 2001; 中英性病艾滋病防治合作项目 2001b). According to the most recent statistics, by the end of 2002 the cumulative number of HIV cases found in China was 40,560. Among them, 2,639 cases have developed AIDS resulting in 1047 deaths. In 2002, 9,824 new cases were reported, representing an increase of 32 percent between the end of 2001 and 2002 (中国新闻网 2003). However, the rate of increase has slowed; between the end of 2000 and 2001 the rate was 36.5 percent. Between 1985 and 2001, China reported 30,736 HIV cases comprised of 28,453 adults (age twenty and above), 5,547 women, and 241 children (age below fifteen). In 2001, the new HIV cases totaled 8,291 with 7,857 adult cases, 1,866 women, and 93 children. According to the estimation made by Chinese experts at the end of 2000, HIV cases totaled 600,000 at the time. Indeed, by the end of 2001, the estimated number of HIV infections in China increased over 40 percent from the number estimated one year ago. The new estimate also reported that 200,000 people might already have full-blown AIDS (Rosenthal 2002). A Chinese official news release shows that 63.7 percent of China's HIV cases were caused by needle sharing among intravenous drug users, 8.1 percent by unprotected sex, and 9.3 percent the result of collecting blood through unhygienic methods (中国新闻网 2003).[1] It is quite important for epidemiologists to understand the different percentages of the three different modes of HIV/AIDS transmission in China. However, it may be more important for a researcher in social sciences and humanities, such as an anthropologist like me, and other personnel who are in charge of HIV/AIDS prevention and care projects to know who, in terms of socioeconomic and sociocultural status, are more likely to be infected by HIV. And why? In addition, they would also like to know why the distribution of HIV/AIDS infection was spatially and temporally uneven and why the major mode of HIV/AIDS transmission in a particular place or time has social, economic, and cultural significances.

The spreading course of HIV and the uneven geographic and temporal HIV prevalence in China since the mid-1980s implies significant socioeconomic and sociocultural meanings. The socioeconomic and sociocultural status and institutions of a country, region, or community may strongly affect the situation of HIV prevalence there. The spreading course of HIV in China happened simultaneously with the unprecedented large-scale "translocal" movement in terms of laborers as well as the merchant migration induced by economic and political reforms since the late 1970s. However, the translocal movement happened under the Chinese socioeconomic structure of urban–rural binary. Hundreds of millions of rural people have been on the move especially since the 1990s. The majority of them, both men and women, are young and middle-aged people. Leaving their home villages and families behind, they are confronted by an unfamiliar and new sociocultural environment. They are situated in an environment without social support or moral surveillance. The change of sociocultural environments might induce them to indulge in risky behavior, including the use of drugs, practicing unsafe sex, or working as sex workers. However, in the era of AIDS, these risky behaviors might make them vulnerable to HIV.

Peter Piot, Executive Director of UNAIDS, argues that "with the movement of people, HIV moves. These changes are not unique to China—across the world, the story is the same" (Piot 2001). It is quite easy to generate a long list of similar stories that can be used as supporting cases to Peter Piot's statement. Paul Farmer saw many HIV infected rural Haitians who had experiences of leaving their home villages to work as servants in Port-au-Prince, Haiti's capital city (Farmer 1990, 1992, 1995, 1999). He illustrated the early stage of HIV transmission in Haiti as a linkage between tourists from North America—urban residents in Haiti (especially Port-au-Prince)—truck drivers and soldiers—to rural Haitians. Many young women of Akha, Hmong, and Lisu, three hilltribes in northern Thailand, were infected by HIV when they were traded to lowland urban centers as commercial sex workers and then became major transmitters on the track of HIV transmission from lowland urban centers to the mountain rural areas of the northern Thai periphery of their home villages (Kammerer *et al.* 1995). People can easily find a similar transmission pattern of HIV/AIDS between urban and rural areas in China as well.

It has been eighteen years since China found its first case of HIV infection in 1985. According to Chinese epidemiologists, China has experienced four stages of HIV/AIDS transmission. First, the introduction stage (传入阶段输入阶段) (1985–1988) during which HIV/AIDS was introduced to mainland China from outside its territory. Second, the spreading stage (扩散阶段传播阶段) (1989–1993) in which HIV/AIDS infection spread mainly in specific regions of Yunnan, a southwest province bordering the Golden Triangle located in the border area of Myanmar and Thailand. Third, the stage (增长阶段) (1994–1998): in which HIV/AIDS infections spread all over China's thirty-one administrative regions including provinces, autonomous regions, and municipalities directly under the Central Government and the annual increasing rate reaching 30 percent. Fourth, the stage of HIV/AIDS infection increasing in high gear (快速增长阶段) (1999–) in which HIV/AIDS cases in China has annually reached over 30 percent (中英性病艾滋病防治合作项目 2001b: 13). Before 1994, most of the HIV/AIDS infected people were found in Yunnan. Within less than four years, all of China's thirty-one provinces, including autonomous regions and municipalities directly under the Central Government have reported HIV/AIDS cases. One of the most important nodes of HIV/AIDS infections has been parallel with the traffic routes of illegal drugs, namely heroin, from Yunnan to Xinjiang (新疆) passing through Sichuan (四川), Shanxi (陕西), Ningxia (宁夏), and Gansu (甘肃). Currently, the highest rates of HIV/AIDS infections are found in Yunnan, Xinjiang, Guangxi and Guangdong.[2] It is very important to note that both the majority of estimated 600,000 HIV/AIDS cases in the summer of 2001 and that of 850,000 HIV/AIDS cases estimated in April of 2002 were rural registered populations (中英性病艾滋病防治合作项目 2001b: 13). According to the statistics of HIV infection in Yunnan, 93.8 percent of HIV cases found in 1989 were *nongmin* (peasants) (中英性病艾滋病防治合作项目 2001a: 76). Although the percentage of *nongmin* among the HIV cases found in Yunnan has dropped gradually between 1989 and 1994, and dramatically since 1995, the percentage of *wuyerenyuan* (men without employment in cities) among the HIV cases found has risen rapidly since then. The *nongmin* percentage of HIV cases found in 2000 was only 32.9 percent. By contrast, the percentage of *wuyerenyuan* among the HIV cases found in 1995 was 26.2 percent, up to 47 percent in 1999, and slightly down to

44 percent in 2000. I would like to suppose that a large proportion of HIV infected *wuyerenyuan* were migrants of rural origin living in cities. Thus, the total percentage of rural population among the HIV cases in Yunnan must still be very high in 2000. Among the HIV cases found in Sichuan between 1987 and 2000, 76.44 percent are rural population (ibid: 8).

According to the most recent official report mentioned above, 63.7 percent of the HIV/AIDS infections found in China were transmitted through the sharing of non-sterile syringes and needles among intravenous drug users. However, the highest rate of these HIV infected IDUs were found in Yunnan, a province in southwest China that borders Myanmar, Vietnam, and Laos, and next to the Golden Triangle, one of the largest opium producing regions in the world which is located on the border area between eastern Myanmar and northern Thailand. In Thailand and Myanmar more than 2 percent of the total adult population is HIV infected (Piot 2001). Over the past two decades, most of the illegal drugs, including heroin and opium, were trafficked into China through the border between Yunnan and Myanmar. Yunnan has become not only the first transferring stop of the illegal drug traffic, but also the province to have the largest number of drug users in China since the 1980s, particularly the 1990s. Moreover, many are IDUs. As a result, the bordering region of Yunnan, Liangshan Yi autonomous prefecture and Panzhihua in Sichuan, and Baise in Guangxi are the most serious regions of HIV/AIDS prevalence in their respective provinces and autonomous regions.

According to the current cumulative total of HIV cases in China, 82 percent are male and 18 percent are female. The male to female ratio of HIV/AIDS infections between 1990 and 1995 was 9:1. It successively dropped to 7:1 between 1996 and 1997; 5:1 between 1998 and 1999; 3.4:1 in 2001; and 2.9:1 in 2002 (王英 2003). But this ratio in different provinces may be very diverse. In Yunnan, the proportion of males among the HIV/AIDS cases found was higher than the national average male ratio. The ratio between male and female cases found in 2000 was 6:1 (中英性病艾滋病防治合作项目 2001a: 77). But in some rural areas of Henan where HIV/AIDS cases resulted mainly from unsanitary practices while selling blood, the male–female ratio among the cases showed the number of females infected is slightly higher than males.[3] However, with the passage of time, the ratio of women among HIV/AIDS infections nation-wide is increasing rapidly, particularly in recent years. It is a strong sign that sexual transmission of HIV is going to become more important than it previously had been in China since the sexual ratio among the IDUs hasn't changed in recent years.

Between October 2001 and May 2002, together with three other scholars from Yunnan and Beijing, I conducted a research project entitled *A Study of HIV/AIDS Prevention and the Reconstruction of Rural Health Care System in Yunnan* in two villages and one township in Yunnan.[4] This research project was funded by China–UK HIV/AIDS Prevention and Care Project. The two villages are respectively located in Dehong Dai and Jingpo Autonomous prefecture and Xishuangbanna Dai Autonomous prefecture in southwest "Yunnan, bordering Myanmar". The township is located in Lijiang Region in Northwest Yunnan adjacent to Liangshan Yi Autonomous prefecture in southwest Sichuan. The two villages and the township cannot be considered economically impoverished in rural China, but the economic situation of different households within the villages and the township are very diverse.

The flow of heroin and HIV/AIDS epidemic in a Jingpo village

The Jingpo village in Dehong that we visited is already experiencing a severe local HIV epidemic.[5] The village contains about sixty households and 284 villagers. The ethnic identities of most households in the village are Jingpo. Only two households are Han, and one is Hui.[6] By early March of 2002, thirty-nine villagers were infected with HIV. Most of them got the infections through sharing unsterilized syringes and needles with other IDUs. Of these, twenty-one have died. While some of the deaths probably resulted from drug overdose, six of the deceased died of AIDS. There are four women among the thirty-nine infected, of which one has died; one recently went to Myanmar with her husband; one left the village after her husband died without letting other villagers know where she went, and one still lives in the village.

The village was formed in 1956. At the time, fourteen Jingpo households from four different villages in mountainous areas were successfully pursued by the government to move down to the plain areas where the village is located now in voluntary relocation. The Jingpo's name of the village means "being one mind." It implies the first fourteen households came from different villages in mountainous areas, and had prepared to work together for the prosperity of the village. The village used to be a model production team of *NongyexueDazhai* (the agricultural campaign for studying Dazhai) during the Cultural Revolution. The production team owned more than 200 water buffaloes and cattle at that time. Before the late 1950s, some elderly villagers used to smoke opium when they became sick. Opium smoking was later eradicated. By the late 1970s, drug users reemerged after they had been eliminated in the area for more than a decade.[7] It began with a couple of elderly villagers, who had quit smoking opium decades ago, and started to smoke it again. The communist party secretary of the administrative village told us that "The village had been a quite good Jingpo village since 1965 until the late 1970s. The production team of the village had money to buy a Dongfanghong tractor with 75 horse power and a couple tractors with 35 horse power during the period. Grain produced from their land was plentiful as sand in the river bank that could never be exhausted. The villagers didn't need to worry about starving and owed nothing in year-end. There weren't many such villages during that period. However, the situation was ruined by the entering of drugs to the area since the 1980s." The situation has been getting worse since the late 1980s and early 1990s with the increase in heroin use. By March 2002, there are, in cumulative total, 86 drug users in the village since the late 1970s, of which 13 are female. Among them, 37 have died. Two-thirds of the households in the village have a least one drug user.

There are twenty-six female villagers who were married to men outside Dehong prefecture, most of them outside Yunnan province even as far as Shandong and Inner Mongolia Autonomous Region since the early 1990s. A small number of them were widows whose husbands died of AIDS before they got remarried. A couple of them were also drug users or HIV infected persons. Most of the men whom they married are Han who came to the area as laborers, small construction contractors, or small venders. Many rural Han who came to the area occupied special niches as house and road construction workers and small construction contractors since most of the local people in the area lack the skills to construct roads or buildings made of bricks and tiles, with multiple stories. With high bride cost and lack of accessible women in their home villages due to many of the women in their villages having hypergamous marriages, or leaving for coastal areas to seek jobs, many Han sojourning laborers in the area find themselves brides and take them back to their home villages. The worsened situation of drug abuse among the male population in the area over the last decade, on the other hand, has caused many young female villagers to leave the area through marrying men from afar to avoid becoming wives of local men who may abuse drugs or contract HIV. An increasing number of young female villagers have migrated to other rural areas away from Yunnan. Beside those who married out of Yunnan, there are about 13 villagers, including 10 females and 3 males, working outside the village as migrant laborers. Two of the men are drug users who went to Myanmar to get off the habit since it is said that a much stricter punishment is imposed there on drug users.

I asked some heroin abusers that I met in the rehabilitative center for drug users run by the township in Dehong why they consumed heroin through intravenous injection instead of smoking it. They told me that it was because they could get an instant and better feeling and that they spent less money through intravenous injection than through smoking. The dose of heroin they need per intravenous injection is less than that for smoking.

Most of the drug users in the village have sold drugs in the past in order to get cash for buying drugs. Many of them became thieves, stealing whatever they could get from households or fields in the area, including their own or those of neighbors. They become people condemned and hated by others, including their own relatives. As rural and minority residents, they were marginalized by mainstream society. Their lack of skills or training needed in the market economy, both inside and outside agricultural sectors, places them in a non-competitive position in current Chinese society. As a result, some villagers are tempted by the illegal trade of drugs. They go to a nearby small market right on the border between China and Myanmar to buy a tiny amount of drugs for trade. Some of them have experienced being caught by police and detained for a short-term period.

An epidemiological study showed that there is a close link between the spread of HIV-1 and the outbreak of IDU along the three routes of illegal drug trafficking between China and Myanmar. Two of these cross-border illegal drug trafficking routes are from the eastern Myanmar border to Yunnan province in China and beyond, and the other one is from Myanmar through Laos, northern Vietnam to

China's Guangxi province and beyond (Beyrer *et al.* 2000). However, Dehong prefecture which borders Eastern Myanmar is the most affected area in terms of drugs as well as HIV in China.

The flow of people, capital, and HIV/AIDS epidemic in a Dai village

The second of our village research sites is in *Xishuangbanna Dai* Autonomous Prefecture. It is a Dai village located just next to the border between China and Myanmar.[8] A port at provincial level was set up right in the village in the early 1990s. Before then, the Chinese frontier inspection station was by the bank of the further side of a river to the north of the village. The village used to be in a transition zone between the China–Myanmar borderline and the Chinese frontier inspection station that was dismantled in the early 1990s.

There are 74 households and 317 people in the village. Among them, there are 6 Han people, 2 women and 4 men. All of them married Dai villagers and moved into the village after they got married. One of the Han men is a member of the village committee and has worked as the village's accountant because he is one of the two villagers who have completed a high school education. The rest of the villagers, ethnically, are Dai.

The village was founded around 1920. There were only about four households at the outset. The founder of the village was a Dai man who was in charge of feeding elephants owned by the Zhaomeng.[9] During the Second World War, the villagers often moved back and forth between the neighboring villages around the area due to chaos caused by the Japanese invasion. The Chinese People's Liberation Army garrisoned the area in 1950, and all the households there moved to the Burmese territory. The villagers were persuaded by the PLA to move back shortly thereafter. The number of households in the village increased to fourteen in 1955. In 1960, the survey of the boundary between China and Burma was completed, and the boundary tablets were set up along the borderline. All villagers living along the both sides of the boundary were no longer being allowed to cross the border freely. However, this regulation has never been strictly enforced by the authorities of either side. Cross-border mobility of the villagers has never stopped because there is no natural barrier or artificial obstacle set by the governments of either side along the borderline that is covered by dense forest or paddy fields next to the village. Many small trails can easily lead to either side of the border. The villagers living on both sides are mainly Dai who consider that they belong to the same cultural community and endow each other with qualities that make for a feeling of mutual belonging. Cross-border reciprocities, marriages, and sexual activities are quite common. Most of the families in the village have relatives near Myanmar and many elderly villagers have experiences of living there.

Almost half of the villagers' paddy fields have been gradually turned into a development area by the township government since the early 1990s. The local government has attracted and encouraged outside private developers to turn the land into a tourist spot through developing entertainment industries there.

Zhifu (being rich) has become a general goal and tenet of many Chinese under the market economy. Sex and gambling industries have no longer been excluded by many Chinese, including some officials, from their list of means to reach the economic goals of individuals or a local government though both industries are illegal in accordance with Chinese law. Gambling houses and brothels with legal fronts had become major industries that were developed in the development area of the village under direct administration of the township between 1995 and 2001. The gambling houses were banned and forced to close by the local government under the intervention of provincial government in the summer of 2001. The number of tourists who stay overnight there sharply declined soon after. The number of establishments with commercial sex aimed at tourists has also been reduced significantly. Meanwhile, a booming tourist town with many big gam-bling houses and erotic entertainment resorts has been rapidly developed just on the other side of the border. However, all the tourists and gamblers are mainly Chinese that come from all over China. Tourists, gamblers, laborers, sex workers, and money have flowed to the town since then. There were ten young women and four young men from the village working in the tourist town near Myanmar when we conducted our field research there. They work in the gambling house as waiters or in *renyao* theaters as assistant keepers of performers' costumes.[10]

Most of the villagers still grow paddy as their subsistence agriculture. Every household in the village owns rubber plants. Some households grow watermelons and vegetables for sale in the market. However, all these agricultural products only comprise a small portion of their annual income. The village collectively owns a park and a couple of commercial buildings in the development area. All the commercial buildings owned by the village have been leased to outside busi-nessmen to run stores, restaurants, or hair salons. The park is a famous scenic spot with the exotic look of one of its banyan trees, namely *Dushuchenglin* (a forest made by a single tree). The annual earnings of the park are quite considerable. However, with the rising income of the local people and the allure of sex services, many local men, including those from the village, are no longer excluded from the hoardes of sex customers since the beginning of the industry. Indeed, local people rather than tourists, including villagers, merchants from all over China who run small businesses in the town, and staff members of various local gov-ernment organizations comprise the majority of customers of these entertainment industries. Most of the sex workers come from outside the county, even the province. Their mobility is very high.

According to a physician in the township hospital as well as some villagers, between 1998, the year of the initial AIDS-related death in the village, and February 2002, there were three adults and one baby girl in the village who died of AIDS. Among the adult deaths, there were two men and one woman. The baby girl died when she was only about 1-year old. The first man and woman who died of AIDS in the village were a married couple. The husband was the only Blang villager in the village before he died.[11] It was said that he had married three times and had opportunities to visit Myanmar to do various kinds of jobs there when he was alive. His first marriage was with a Dai woman of the village. It was the reason that he, as a Blang, could move into the village. His first wife died several years after they were married. He remarried with a Myanmar woman who was ethnically Dai as well. They got divorced years later. His third wife was also a Dai woman from Myanmar. She went back to her home village in Myanmar after her husband died of AIDS. She also died of AIDS in her own home village soon after she returned.

The other man and the baby girl who died of AIDS were father and daughter. Some informants in the village told my colleague that the father had an opportunity to work for a *renyao* as the latter's servant and sexual mate when he was in his late teens in the Myanmar town. He married a Dai woman from Myanmar and moved back to the village later on. It was said that his wife and both the second and third wives of the Blang man had experiences of being sex workers in Thailand before they were respectively married to this man. The third wife of the Blang man went back to her own home village in Myanmar after her husband and daughter died of AIDS. But no one in the village knows whether she is still alive.

Most of the villagers believe that it is women from Myanmar or Thailand, who have had experiences of being sex workers there, who transmit AIDS to other people. Thus, only those men in the village who have had the opportunity to go to Myanmar or Thailand and work there, and at the same time behave promiscuously (*feichangluan*, the Chinese word used by the villagers), or play with many girls (*wanguniang*, the Chinese word used by the villagers to characterize the need for multiple female sexual partners) can get AIDS. They have associated HIV/AIDS with the cross-border mobility of the villagers from both sides of the border, but further extend the mobility to the territory of Thailand. Such an understanding has led the villagers to reduce their awareness of the possibility of sexual transmission of HIV among themselves, something which has already been a reality for many years.

The flows of tourists, imagination and, the risk of HIV/AIDS epidemic in a tourist township

The third field site of our AIDS research project is a township located in a county under the administration of Lijiang Region. Upto now no HIV/AIDS infection has been found in the township. Although through compulsory HIV tests taken in the rehabilitative center for drug users in the county, several HIV infected cases have been found among the drug users in the county since the late 1990s, none of them are a resident of the township. This might not be the reality of HIV/AIDS epidemic situation in the township since there is a lack of knowledge and awareness about HIV/AIDS among even the health care workers in the township as well as county levels. This might also reflect the nature of HIV/AIDS surveillance in China that functions better in confronting the epidemic among the illegal drug users than the one among the people who practice unsafe/unprotected sex. Once I asked a gynecologist of the township hospital whether they had ever found any HIV/AIDS case. "No, never (没有。从来没有见过。*meiyou. conglai meiyou jianguo*)," she answered. Continuing our conversation, I found she even did not know that there is no unique syndrome among AIDS patients. She also didn't know that most AIDS patients die of various kinds of opportunistic infections caused by deficiency of the immune system in their body. It is obvious that there was no ground for me to take her answer as a truth that there was no HIV/AIDS case in the area. It is not because she wants to cheat me, but rather she lacks information about the epidemic as a result of the inequality of distribution of medical knowledge. I met with a similar situation when I asked the same question of a rural doctor, who was also in charge of epidemic prevention in an administrative village of the township when I visited there late last year. "It is impossible. Such kinds of contagious disease can only be found in urban areas where many people have promiscuous behavior (这不可能。这样的传染病只可能发生在城市里。因为城市里比较多人性乱。 *zhe bukeneng. zheyang de chuanranbing zhikeneng fashengzai chengshili. yinwei chengshili bijiaoduoren xingluan*)," he said. Like the gynecologist in the township hospital, he also knows very little about HIV/AIDS.

The township, particularly a couple of villages that are situated near a famed highland lake in the middle of the mountains, has become one of the hot tourist attractions in the Lijiang region since the mid-1990s. The annual volume of tourists has dramatically increased simultaneously with the continuous improvement of motor roads that reach these villages. According to statistics provided by the County's Bureau of Tourism, between 1995 and 2000 the volume of tourists has tripled, from around 80,000 to 240,000.

The attraction of very few villages of the township for tourists is not only the natural beauty of the lake and its surrounding mountains, but the "exotic others," especially the matrilineal society and the practice of *tisese* of the Na people who have inhabited the area for more than a thousand years.[12] In defining tourism as a pillar industry in Yunnan since the reform era, especially since the 1990s, the township has been no exception. Like other tourist sites in China, the local government, people, and migrant businessmen have marketed not only the scenery and wildlife, but also "exotic culture" to tourists. However, such an "exotic culture" has never been real, but a hybrid of the existing culture and the one being newly created or produced to cater to the tastes of tourists (McKhann 2000; Weng 2001; 翁乃群 2001).

Tisese is a sexual institution that has prevailed among the Na people for centuries (詹承绪等 1980; 严汝娴等 1983; Shih 1993; Weng 1993; Cai 2001). Under this sexual institution, the two parties of a sexual relationship do not cohabitate. It was translated into Chinese as *zouhun* (literally meaning "visiting marriage") by some Chinese scholars, journalists, writers, as well as the local people (詹承绪等 1980; 严汝娴等 1983; 杨二车拉姆 1997, 1998; 和钟华 2000; 周华山 2001). The Chinese term *zouhun* has since been broadly accepted and used by the Na, particularly when they talk with non-Na people referring to the *tisese* practices.

It is their sexual institution of *zouhun* that has amazed many others. *Zouhun* has become the hottest attraction of the Na culture depicted by scholars and non-scholars in their writings. Nevertheless, with the influences of their own culture as well as the cultural bias of the mainstream, many authors who have written about the Na *zouhun* have distorted this institution with or without intention. Although some of the distortions have made many Na angry and insulted them in the past, they have been accepted, even welcomed to some degree, by the Na since the late 1990s when the development of tourism in the area increased (周华山 2001). Moreover, individual Na people deliberately involved themselves in fantasizing and confusing their culture, particularly *zouhun*.

In her several published autobiographies, *Yang Erchelamu*, a native Na girl, has vividly described her multiple sexual relationships with western men, seven in total, and attributed all her sexual experiences to her biological cultural trait as a Na woman (杨二车拉姆 1997, 1998; 周华山 2001: 220–227). "Most of my boyfriends were foreigners. I mixed well with them. This must be related to the Mosuo blood flowing inside my veins (我的男朋友多是外国人，我和他们相处得很好，这和我血脉里流动、蕴藏着摩梭人的血液有关。 wo de nanpengyou duoshi waiguoren, wo he tamen xiangchu de henhao, zhe he wo xuemaili liudong, yuncangzhe mosuoren de xueye youguan)"[13] (杨二车拉姆 1997: 353). "Concerning the matters of love and marriage, I have been deeply influenced by the Mosuo's tradition. The blood of Mosuo is flowing inside my vessels, and my bones are filled with Mosuo's marrow. (我在恋爱婚姻的问题上，是深受我们摩梭人的传统影响的。我的血脉里流着摩梭人的血 骨子里积存着摩梭人的精髓，... *wo zai lianai hunyin de wentishang, shi shenshou women Mosuoren de chuantong yingxiang de. wo de xuemaili liuzhe Mosuoren de xue, guzili jicunzhe Mosuoren de jingsui*)" (ibid.: 354); "There is no ethnic group that can match the obduracy and indulgence of Mosuo in courting lovers of the opposite sex (我们摩梭人追求异性的执着和放荡不羁的劲头，是别的民族不能比的。*women Mosuoren zhuiqiu yixing de zhizhuo he fangdangbuji de jintou, shibiede minzu bunengbide*)" (ibid.: 355).

In a recent visit to the hottest tourist village of the township, I witnessed many times that, when tourists curiously asked their hosts about *zuohun*, some of the latter often responded in a disingenuous way. Local hosts deliberately told them either a fake and fantasized story or a confused one. Once I saw a tourist guide (a Na girl) of a Na culture museum owned by two village households standing outside the gate of the museum's inner court and, pointing to a window right above the gate, telling her guests how a Na man furtively visits his *A xia* (sexual partner, an intimate term that was rarely used in public in the past) at night. It is always a question that many tourists curiously would like answered and ask their hosts again and again when they visit the village. "By climbing up to the window right above the gate and getting into the room (which is supposed to be a girl's bedroom) through the window, a Na man can visit his *A xia* at night," said the guide to the tourists. In fact, there is no window in Na traditional house buildings. Tourists who visit the museum will be led to *Yimi* first. (*Yimi* is a main building of a Na household where the family members gather, cook and eat, worship their ancestors, and entertain guests. It is also a sleeping room for the elderly female members and young children of a household.) They will be seated around a hearth in the room, and served with home-made liquor and butter tea. The guides will tell the tourists about how the liquor they serve is a home-made one that is known to the local people as *Guangdangjiu* (吮当酒), and suggest it will be more precise if it is named *Zhuangdanjiu* (壮胆酒). The name suggested means liquor that can boost one's courage. It implies that you have to drink the liquor for boosting your courage before you visit a girl in her room at night. Similarly, they name *zhubiaorou* (猪膘肉), the traditional bacon of the Na, as *zhuangyangrou* (壮阳肉) (meat for boosting masculinity). A strategy to make their culture look sexy has been chosen by the local people, including cadres, commoners, and migrant businessmen, as a way to promote their tourism industry. Charles F. McKhann also observed a similar cultural practice when he visited the village in 1999 (McKhann 2001). In the global era, eroticizing culture often constitutes an important strategy of commercializing culture in tourism industries worldwide. It has been used as a means of market promotion. However, the sociocultural practices as such can no longer be understood from the spatial scale of the local, but instead must be understood at a translocal or global one.

With the development of the tourism industry in the village, like many other tourist sites, the sex industry has gradually emerged since the mid-1990s. It began with the opening of salons run by migrant women from Hunan and Sichuan who initially provided haircuts and hairdressing. By getting familiar with the sociopolitical environment of the village and the villagers, they moved into providing sex services. Not too long after the opening of those salons in the village, a couple of karaoke houses had also emerged. With the intervention of prefecture government concerned about protecting the "authenticity" of the Na culture in order to make the tourism industry in the area sustainable, and because of the complaints made by elderly villagers about the noise coming from those karaoke houses and the worsening living environment of the villagers, an administrative regulation of the village's tourism industry was issued by the County Committee of Tourism Administration in early 1999. Karaoke houses and salons were banned in the residential area of the village, but allowed to move to a special area by the road from the county city to the township about 1.5 kilometers away from the residential area of the village. Later on, the local people called the special area *hongdengqu* (the red light district).

In the beginning, all the brothels were run by migrant people. They rented buildings owned by the villagers or had a contract with the owners of hotel buildings to run the hotels. With the ending of the lease and contract term one to two years later, many of these lease holders and contractors successively left for other places. Many of these brothels began to be run by the local villagers with more and more Na girls joining the large numbers of sex workers. But all of them come either from the hinterland villages of the township or from villages of neighboring townships in both Yunnan and Sichuan. None of them are from the villages where the tourist sites are located.

The demand for Na sex workers is higher than that for the non-Na ones because the tastes of customers are catalyzed by fantasizing about the Na culture, particularly their sexual institution of *tisese*. All practices of commercial sex in the village are labeled as *zuohun* by many personnel who are involved in the business. By doing so they are trying to legitimize their activities and make them look morally correct in the local context. It may also increase the appeal for tourists. Many hotel hostesses in the red light district of the village always tell their male customers that they may practice *zouhun* with Na girls at night if they stay there. As a result, sex workers who are Na tend to have better business than the non-Na. Over the past two years, more and more non-Na sex workers have left for other places.[14]

However, there are also many sexual activities without exchange of money between villagers, particularly young male villagers and young female tourists. Over the past decade, the flow of fantasized stories of the Na culture spread nationwide through various kinds of media: TV, journals, newspapers, publishing houses, Internet Web sites etc., in the form of reports, travel notes, fiction, and TV movies, has been arousing many fantasies about the Na people and their culture. With the successive introduction of VCRs, TVs, VCDs and Karaoke to the township in the last decade, the fantasies of the Na people about other cultures have also been aroused, especially sexual cultures of the urban life that fill the media. The encounter of different fantasies respectively imagined by the Na villagers and tourists based on the flow of sociocultural constructed information included in images, sounds, and letters, have shaped the forms of sexual activities both in the village and the red light district. However, all these happen in the era of HIV/AIDS and under the condition that most of the people, especially the local people (both the Na and non-Na) involved in the activities, lack knowledge about HIV/AIDS and its prevention. Thus, all sexual activities mentioned above, and the lack of knowledge about HIV/AIDS and its prevention, have put the people involved at risk of being infected with HIV. With two of the neighboring regions in Sichuan—Liangshan Yi autonomous prefecture and Panzhihua city—as well as the Dali Baizu Autonomous prefecture of Yunnan all severely hit, the risk for the township being affected by HIV might be more real. All these situations, along with the practices of the specific sexual institution of *tisese* among the local Na, may also ultimately put the township and its neighboring township on the Sichuan side in a dangerous situation of HIV/AIDS prevalence.

Conclusion

The spread of HIV in China has been closely associated with the translocal flows of people, goods, capital, and information in particular space and time. The translocal flows are shaped by a specific set of institutions, including political, economic, and cultural ones. Indeed in Yunnan, one of the severest HIV-hit provinces in China, the particular flows have gone beyond the border.

The political, economic, and social changes that occurred over the last decade in China, Myanmar, and Thailand have caused the governments of the three countries to establish trade, tourism, and service industries as priorities in their border areas. It has brought the improvement of roads, transportation, communication, and infrastructure to these previously remote and isolated areas. Although, in the past, the border communities consisted of minority populations involved in many cross-border activities, such as trading, reciprocal activities, including labor exchanges, attending various ritual activities between relatives and friends scattered about the mountainous areas along the borders, the lack of modern roads, transportation, and communication limited all their movement within their immediate surroundings. The improvement of infrastructure in border areas has significantly increased cross-border trade, people mobility, capital, and information flows in the border areas of the three countries (Caouette 2001: 8–13). The growing economic activities in the border areas have also attracted the flow of migrants from other parts of China to these border areas for tourism, trade, and employment in southwest Yunnan. During the past decade, the borders between China, Myanmar, and Thailand have observed the largest flow of migrants in history. Although there are no available statistics on the numbers of migrants as many of them are without travel documentation, the estimated numbers are in the millions. They are moving between these borders for tourism, trade, business, refuge, employment, and other opportunities. According to the estimation of the Myanmar government, 74.1 percent of the population migrating out of the country crosses the border into Thailand. Almost 18 percent of the migrants from Myanmar cross into China. Most of these migrants stay along the border area, but increasing reports show migrants from Myanmar throughout China (Save the Children 2001: 2). Some studies have confirmed that the number of Chinese people transiting through Myanmar to Thailand and beyond increased throughout the 1990s, though we lack precise data. The Thai Immigration Detention Centers, which hold significant and consistent numbers of detainees from China, has also noted the influx of Chinese migrants into Thailand at the end of the last century (Caouette 2001: 2–3). Many of these migrants were traveling with false or no documentation. Fewer jobs and trade opportunities, limited profits caused by the 1997 economic crisis in Thailand, and stricter border restrictions imposed by Chinese and Thai authorities diminished or stabilized the number of migrants from China. However, the demand for cheap migrant labor in Thailand remains. Some assessments made in the three countries have identified mobility, particularly along the border, as an indirect factor lubricating the spread of AIDS (ibid.: 14; Asian Research Centre for Migration 1997; Wrigley 1998). According to the country epidemiological fact sheets of 1998, the epicenter of HIV in Asia was a complex area comprising northern Thailand, Myanmar, Laos, and southern China (UNDP South East Asia HIV and Development Project 2000: 4). Dehong Dai and Jingbo Autonomous Prefecture, District of Lincang and District of Simao of Yunnan that are located in the border with Shan and Kachin States in Myanmar are the severely hit areas of HIV in China. In Myanmar, the highest rates of HIV infection have been found along the border with Thailand and the town of Mandalay in the north (Min Thwe *et al.* 1995; Caouette 2001: 14). The findings correspond with the distribution of HIV epidemics in Thailand in that some of the highest rates of HIV/AIDS there occur along its border with Myanmar (Asian Research Centre for Migration 1997; Caouette 2001: 14).

These mountainous border areas are mainly populated by minority people of their respective countries. With the economic, political transformations that happened in recent decades in the three countries, trade, tourism, and the service industries have become government priorities in these border areas. These changes have brought improved roads, transportation, communication, and infrastructure to these previously remote and isolated areas and further facilitated translocal mobility within each country as well as transnational mobility between the three countries. With the improvement of roads, transportation, communication, and infrastructure in the last decade, the agrarian society of some border areas with over a thousand-year history are being supplemented or replaced by aspects of non-agricultural economy such as trade, tourism, and service industries. The changes that occurred in the Dai and Jingpo villages described above in the recent decade have also revealed such a trend. However, the result in terms of translocal as well as transnational flows has shaped the mode of HIV transmission there.

The ethnographies mentioned above indicate that particular translocal modes produce particular sorts of HIV transmission. The HIV epidemic found in China, as those around the world, show that uneven flows of drugs, migrants, capital, and information produce different vulnerabilities of locals and social groups as well as uneven rates of HIV infection. These rural or registered rural people with ethnic minority identity who are situated in the social margin tend to be more vulnerable to the epidemic than their urban and ethnic majority counterparts who are situated in the social center. Their vulnerabilities become more salient when they encounter the expanded and accelerated translocal flows in terms of space and time mentioned earlier.

The identities of the Na and their homeland have been recreated or redefined by the interaction between the Na and the non-Na, especially tourists, in the process of various translocalities, including the flows of description and imagination of the Na made by scholars, journalists, writers, and tourists. The imaginations of their sexual institution of *tisese* and matrilineal system which result in the translocal flows have made them and their homeland to be seen by outsiders as a very exotic people and place. They in turn condition the imaginings of villagers.

The encounters between the flows of population, commodities, information, and diseases and local socioeconomic and sociocultural institutions has changed the spatial and temporal scopes of local people, both in mind and in practice. They compose an important element of new translocal sociocultural environments that induce social agents of the locale to redefine or readjust their identities away from their previous ones. However, the change of the spatial and temporal scopes of the local people, in mind and in practice, has also affected the models of HIV/AIDS epidemic and peoples' health there.

Acknowledgments

I am pleased to acknowledge a deep debt to Du Juan, Jin Li Yan, and Hou Hong Rui for their painstaking efforts and intelligence. We conducted participant observation field research together in the three villages mentioned in this chapter. I greatly thank Louisa Schein and Tim Oakes for the opportunity to present a version of the chapter in June, 2002 at the Eighth China's Provinces in Reform Workshop held in Haikou, Hainan China, and their very useful comments on the chapter. I also appreciate

Carolyn Cartier and Elanah Uretsky for their valuable comments on the chapter. I am very grateful to Feng Yi for helping me edit this chapter.

Notes

1 The breakdown of the statistics seems to imply the nature of epidemic surveillance of HIV/AIDS in China. Most of the HIV/AIDS cases found were through non-Voluntary Counseling Testing (VCT) undertaken nationwide in rehabilitation centers for drug users. The difficult nature of surveying HIV/AIDS cases produced through sexual transmission and the lack of VCT and comprehensive nationwide survey has tended to make the statistics less precise. In addition, the statistic figures of HIV/AIDS infections among the Chinese gay community are also unclear.
2 I cannot find an official report concerning the number of HIV/AIDS infections in Henan.
3 This information was obtained through personal communication with a friend who is an epidemiologist. He has provided medical services for many years in some rural areas of Henan where HIV/AIDS is prevalent.
4 The three other members in the research group are Du Juan, Jin Liyan, and Hou Hongrui. Both Du Juan and Jin Liyan are from the Institute of Ethnology, Yunnan Academy of Social Sciences in Kunming. Hou Hongrui is from the Institute of Ethnology and Anthropology, Chinese Academy of Social Sciences in Beijing. Our cooperation has been very successful. I am indebted to them for their painstaking efforts and intelligence.
5 Jingpo are referred to as Kachin in Myanmar. According to the 2000 census, there are 132,143 Jingpo who live mainly in mountainous areas of Luxi, Ruili, Longchuan, and Yingjiang of the Dehong Dai and Jingpo Autonomous prefecture in Yunnan. A small number of them live in the Pianma of Lushui county in the Nujiang Lisu Autonomous Prefecture, and in the Gengma Dai and Va Autonomous County of the Lincang District. There are two branches of spoken language among Jingpo. One belongs to the Jingpo branch of the Tibetan–Burmese group of the Chinese–Tibetan language family, the other, including Zaiwa, Leqi, Lang'e and Bola dialects, is affiliated to the Mian branch. The two branches of spoken language are mutually unintelligible. There are also two written languages. One is Jingpo script which was created in late nineteenth century. The other is Zaiwa script which was created in 1957. Both are Latinized systems.
6 Han are an ethnic majority in China. They are referred to as Chinese by Westerners. Hui are an ethnic minority in China. Most of them are Muslim.
7 Before the second half of the 1950s, Jingpo who lived in mountainous areas used to plant opium, and some elderly villagers, especially when they got sick, smoked opium without getting addicted. Both planting and smoking opium were forbidden in those areas after the late 1950s.
8 Dai are referred to as Shan in Myanmar. According to the 2000 Chinese census, Dai's population is 1,158,989. They dwell in compact communities in the Xishuangbanna Dai Autonomous Prefecture, Dehong Dai-Jingpo Autonomous Prefecture, the autonomous counties of Gengma, Menglian, Yuanjiang, Xinping, Jinping, Jinggu, and Shuangjiang. Small numbers of Dai live dispersed in the cities and counties of Baoshan, Zhenyuan, Lancang, Wuyang, Mile, Maguan in Yunnan, and in Panzhihua City in Sichuan. The Dai language belongs to the Zhuang-Dai branch of the Zhuang-Dong group of the Chinese–Tibetan language family. It has two dialect districts: the Xishuangbanna dialect and the Dehong dialect. The Dai have their own scripts with four kinds of writing, namely, the Daile, the Daina, the Daibeng, and the Daiduan. All these writings are derived from the Sanskrit writing system.
9 Zhaomeng was a title of the Dai chief before the founding of the People's Republic of China and is usually assigned by a Dai King (Zhaopianling).

10 *Renyao* are men who transform their bodies into a female form by taking hormones when they are still young and work as entertainment performers later on. They are very popular in Thailand.
11 Blang is referred to as Palaung in Myanmar. Blang have a population of 91,882 in 2000 in China. About 60 percent of them live in the counties and autonomous counties of Shuangjiang, Gengma, Yongde, Yunxian, Fengqing, Lancang, and Mojiang in southwest Yunnan. Others dwell in the mountainous areas of the Menghai County of the Xishuangbanna Dai Autonomous Prefecture, including Blang mountain and mountainous areas around Bada, Xiding and Daluo townships. Blang language belongs to the Wa-De branch of Mon-Khmer group of the Austo-Asiatic language family. It has close ties with the Va, the Deang, and Kemu languages. The Blang have no writing system.
12 The Na is identified as a subgroup of the Naxi by the People's Congress of Yunnan Province, but as Menggu (Mongol) by the People's Congress of Sichuan Province. Na or Naze is the group name that they use to identify their own ethnicity. The Na inhabit mainly the lacustrine area of the Lugu Lake which is located in the border between Ninglang County of Yunnan and Yanyuan and Muli Counties of Sichuan provinces. There are no official statistics of the Na population since they are identified differently by the governments of Yunnan and Sichuan mentioned above. They are included in either the Naxi census of Yunnan or the Mongol census of Sichuan. According to my rough estimation, the Na population was about 40,000 in 2000. Their spoken language is considered as a dialect of the Naxi language which belongs to the Yi branch of the Tibetan–Burman group of the Han-Tibetan family. The Na do not have a written language.
13 This quote and the following ones are translated from Chinese to English by the author.
14 Hou Hongrui, my colleague who just returned from the Na village tourist hot spot at the end of September, 2004, told me that with the opening of several new hotels in the red light district of the village this year, the number of non-Na sex workers is increasing again.

References

English language materials

Appadurai, A. (1990) "Disjuncture and difference in the global cultural economy," *Public Culture* 2: 1–24.

Asian Research Centre for Migration (1997) *The Second Technical Consultation on Transnational Population Movements and HIV/AIDS in Southeast Asian Countries*, Bangkok: Chulalongkorn University.

Beyrer, C., Razak, M. H., Lisam, K., Chen, J., Liu, W., and Yu, X. F. (2000) "Overland heroin trafficking routes and HIV-1 spread in south and Southeast Asia," *AIDS* 14(1): 75–83.

Cai, H. (2001) *A Society Without Fathers or Husbands: The Na of China*, trans. by A. Hustvedt, New York: Zone Books.

Caouette, T. M. (2001) *Small Dreams Beyond Reach: The Lives of Migrant Children and Youth Along the Borders of China, Myanmar and Thailand*, London: DFID & Save the Children.

Chakrabarty, D. (1992) "The death of history? Historical consciousness and the culture of late capitalism," *Public Culture* 4: 47–65.

Farmer, P. (1990) "AIDS and accusation: Haiti, Haitians, and the geography of blame," in D. Feldman (ed.) *AIDS and Culture: The Human Factor*, New York: Praeger, 67–91.

——(1992) *AIDS and Accusation: Haiti and the Geography of Blame*, Berkeley, CA: University of California Press.

—— (1995) "Culture, poverty and the dynamics of HIV transmission in rural Haiti," in H. ten Brummelhuis and G. Herdt (eds) *Culture and Sexual Risk: Anthropological Perspectives on AIDS*, New York: Gordon and Breach, 3–28.

—— (1999) *Infection and Inequalities: The Modern Plagues*, Berkeley, CA: University of California Press.

Foster, R. J. (1999) "Melanesianist anthropology in the era of globalization," *The Contemporary Pacific: A Journal of Island Affairs* 2(1): 140–159.

Hannerz, U. (1996) "The local and the global: continuity and change," in *Transnational Connections: Culture, People, Places*, New York: Routledge, 17–29.

Hyde, S. T. (2001) "*Chi Qingchun Fan: Jinu and Meirongting* in Jinghong: The Wedding of Qualitative Research and Public Health Policy," in *Symposium Papers of Social Science for STI and HIV/AIDS Prevention and Care in China*, Beijing: China–UK HIV/AIDS Prevention and Care Project, Department of Sociology, Tsinghua University, and School of Public Policy and Administration, Tsinghua University.

Kammerer, C. A., Hutheesing, O. K., Maneeprasert, R., and Symonds, P. V. (1995) "Vulnerability to HIV infection among three hilltribes in northern Thailand," in H. ten Brummelhuis and G. Herdt (eds) *Culture and Sexual Risk: Anthropological Perspectives on AIDS*, New York: Gordon and Breach, 53–75.

Lash, S. and Urry, J. (1994) *Economies of Signs and Space*, New York: Sage.

McKhann, C. F. (2000) "Mass tourism and cultural identity on the Sino-Tibetan frontier: reflections of a participant–observer," unpublished manuscript.

Min, T., Kywe, B., and Goodwin, D. J. (1995) "HIV surveillance in Myanmar, 1985–1995," paper presented at the Third International Conference on AIDS in Asia and the Pacific, Chiangmai, Thailand.

Moore, H. L. (1996) "The changing nature of anthropological knowledge: an introduction," in H. L. Moore (ed.) *The Future of Anthropological Knowledge*, London and New York: Routledge.

Piot, P. (2001) Speech at the First Plenary Session of National AIDS/STD Conference, Beijing, November 14.

Rosenthal, E. (2002) "China raises HIV count in new report," *The New York Times*, April 12.

"Save the Children" & the British Department for International Development (2001) *Breaking Through the Clouds: A Participatory Action Research Project with Migrant Children and Youth Along the Borders of China, Myanmar and Thailand*.

Shih, C. K. (1993) "The Yongning Moso: sexual union, household organization, gender, and ethnicity in a matrilineal duolocal society in southwest China," unpublished PhD dissertation, Stanford University, CA.

UNDP Southeast Asia HIV and Development Project (2000) *ASEAN Workshop on Population Movement and HIV Vulnerability*.

Weng, N. (1993) "The mother house: the symbolism and practice of gender among the Naze in southwest China," unpublished PhD dissertation, University of Rochester, NY.

—— (2001) "Naxi cultural reproduction and tourism development," paper presented at the Annual Meetings of the Association for Asian Studies, Chicago, IL.

Wrigley, O. (1998) *HIV/AIDS Prevention and Care in Myanmar: A Situation Analysis and Needs Assessment*, Myanmar: United Nations Press.

Chinese language materials

阿水 (2001) 艾滋病例我们有多远? 载于《时代潮》2001/21: 28–29.
和钟华 (2000)《生存与文化的选择—摩梭母系制及其现代变迁》, 云南教育出版社.

刘元亮等 (2001) 艾滋病危机报告。载于《时代潮》2001/21: 26.

刘元亮、姜荣生 (2001) 中国艾滋病防治任重道远: 中国艾滋病防治协会副 会长戴志澄访谈录。载于《时代潮》2001/21: 32–33.

王英 (2003) 与艾滋病有关的社会性别问题, 载于中英性病艾滋病防治合作项目办公室, 清华大学人文社会科学院社会学系, 清华大学公共管理学院社会政策研究所编印《社会科学与中国艾滋病防治工作研讨会论文集》.

翁乃群 (2001) 全球化背景下的文化再生产—以纳西文化与旅游业发展之间关系为例。载于中国社会文化人类学年刊《人文世界》Vol. 1, 华夏出版社.

严汝娴、宋兆麟 (1983)《永宁纳西族的母系制》, 云南人民出版社.

杨二车拉姆 (1997)《走出女儿国: 一个摩梭女孩的闯荡经历和情爱故事》, 中国社会出版社.

—— (1998)《走回女儿国》, 中国青年出版社.

詹承绪、王承权、李近春、刘龙初 (1980) 《永宁纳西族的阿注婚姻和母系家庭》, 上海人民出版社.

中国新闻网 (2003) 我国公布 2002 年艾滋病疫情, 疫情仍呈上升趋势, www.sina.com.cn, 2003 年 2 月 21 日.

中英性病艾滋病防治合作项目 (2001a) 四川省及云南省性病艾滋病形势分析。北京, 七月。.

—— (2001b) 对艾滋病感染者和病人关怀服务的起点—中国艾滋病治疗及关 怀服务文献检索报告。北京, 九月.

周华山 (2001)《无父无夫的国度?—重女不轻男的母系摩梭》, 香港同志研究社.

11 Negotiating scale

Miao women at a distance

Louisa Schein

It has become a banal commonplace to note that people in China are on the move. This chapter undertakes to query what specific translocal effects and social formations might be charted as a result of the burgeoning of mobilities across China. The inauguration of Dengist reforms after 1978 could be depicted as a gradual unraveling of the caste-like character of the rural–urban divide that had so dominated the Chinese landscape. The internal migration that exploded with the diminishing of state regulations on mobility and residence revivified and intensified an urbanizing trend that had begun with the industrialization of the 1950s. The enormity of the population shift toward the urban invites a portrait of a unidirectional flow of persons and resources out of a relatively static sending zone that is the rural, and toward a dynamic and expanding destination zone that is comprised of the cities, special economic zones and new towns. To complicate this sense of directionality, I want to look instead at the flows, networks, and linkages *between* migrants and home sites and to ask what such connections mean for Chinese spatiality.

The reform era, especially the 1990s, has also seen an unprecedented movement of women out of the Miao highland villages that represent some of the most remote regions of China. In a volume and type of mobility that the Miao mountains have never seen, women, and of course men, are leaving villages to find wage income and other opportunities within and beyond their regions. Some are typical "*dagong*" laborers, either in manufacturing, agricultural production, or service jobs such as waitressing or domestic work. But some occupy special niches as performers and entertainers, or as craftswomen, in work that exploits what are perceived as particular Miao skills. Others are highly successful professionals and entrepreneurs, most of whom got their starts much earlier with patronage by the Maoist or post-Maoist state. An increasing number are married off to men from Han regions where the birth planning policy and economic upheavals have created a demand for "diligent" and affordable brides. This chapter presents a sample of such Miao women—whether those who are living outside or those who have returned to their villages—not as an aggregate under the rubric "internal migration" but rather to explore the particularities of the long-distance *practices of translocality* that their sojourning at a distance entails.

To this end, I inquire as well into the spatial subjectivities of these Miao women—whom I have interviewed since 1999 in various sites across China, including in their rural homes to which some have returned. Through attending to the life narratives of women in crafts sales, factory work, performing work, and pyramid marketing, as well as village returnees and those who have married out to Han villages, I develop some senses of the "translocal" that might supplement if not substitute for models of "migrants" and their purportedly more singular relocation. Accordingly, I take a cue from Basch *et al.*'s notion of the "transmigrant," that is, persons who "take actions, make decisions, and develop subjectivities and identities embedded in networks of relationships that connect them simultaneously to two or more nation-states" (1994: 7). Hence, I frequently use the term "translocals" in place of "migrants" to emphasize the mobile quality of their strategies and subjectivities. Translocals within China, then, are characterized by being identified with more than one place at the same time.

Scales, hierarchies, and social practice

China's urban and rural zones, in the parlance of contemporary human geographers, may be thought of as scales, in a schema in which the "local" is positioned in relation to urban, provincial, national, and global scales. If these scales were to be vertically ordered, ranked as in the metaphor of rungs on a ladder, they would approximate the longstanding spatial hierarchy that has held sway both socially and administratively in China.[1] The relationship between the urban and the rural as two discrepant and ranked scales was, in the latter half of the twentieth century, fixed in place by state policy that bifurcated the Chinese population into agricultural and non-agricultural personnel (*nongye* and *feinongye renkou*), with the latter as the prestige designation and the locus of power. This vertical formation persists in conditioning the contemporary era.

Recent discussions in geography contain an elaborated treatment of what has been called by some the "social production of scale." Following the constructionist framework of Henri Lefebvre, especially in his groundbreaking *The Production of Space* (1991) scholars have argued that "scale is not necessarily a preordained hierarchical framework for ordering the world—local, regional, national and global. It is instead a contingent outcome of the tensions that exist between structural forces and the practices of human agents" (Marston 2000: 220). Neil Brenner has been one of the most adamant contributors to the notion that static hierarchies cannot describe the social dynamism of scale: "The relation between global, state-level and urban-regional processes can no longer be conceived as one that obtains among mutually exclusive levels of analysis or forces" (1997: 159). In Marston's exegesis on Brenner: "Scales are not unilinearly ordered—with the global theoretically and empirically superior to the local—but rather they interpenetrate and are superimposed through a 'scaffolding of spatial scales' " (2000: 227).

An attention to social actions and competing forces in producing particular scale configurations, then, has produced a burgeoning literature on the social construction and contestation of scale. In existing studies, however, the scales under scrutiny have tended to be restricted to those of the state versus the global (capital), or of the state in relation to localities. It could be argued, at the risk of appearing nihilist, that an emphasis on such macro social agents, even on organized social movements as sites of locality, cannot avoid perniciously reinscribing and privileging a fixed set of ranked scales—the global, the state, the local. Meanwhile, much less attention has been paid to the enormously socially consequential scale practices that link the rural, the provincial, and the urban *within* states, to say nothing of the potential for apparently horizontal translocal strategies to ultimately contribute to the generation of scale hierarchies.

Rural–urban migrants such as those in China might be rethought in this light. Alternative to conceiving of migrants as flowing upwards in an already fixed and static hierarchy, we might read their moves as constituting a form of participation in the actual social production of scale. One potential formulation would be that migrants are, in geographer Neil Smith's words, "jumping scales" in their mobility practices, in effect acting to "dissolve spatial boundaries that are largely imposed from above and that contain rather than facilitate their production and reproduction of everyday life" (1993: 90). In terms of prestige, their strategies would defy their imposed confinement to the banality of the rural scale as they proactively move from a smaller, more parochial level to one higher and more associated with social and economic power. Through attending to what Alan Latham (2002: 116) has called "the skein(s) of relationships between bodies, materials, and information through which society is built and unbuilt," any spatial hierarchy that organizes China could be conceived as more dynamic, even contested, though never power-free. Following Erik Swyngedouw:

> Spatial scale is what needs to be understood as something that is produced; a process that is always deeply heterogeneous, conflictual, and contested. Scale becomes the arena and moment, both discursively and materially, where sociospatial power relations are contested and compromises are negotiated and regulated. Scale, therefore, is both the result and the outcome of social struggle for power and control.
>
> (Ibid. 1997: 140)

If scale is always in process, "under construction," as it were, then what does this mean for the shift from envisioning one-time unidirectional moves "up" the social-spatial ladder from villages to cities to envisioning the production of translocal connectedness across China? One possibility is that migrants may be renegotiating the ranking of scales, potentially (though not necessarily) remaking the relation between urban and rural into something more horizontal.

Migrants' strategies, then, would have to be empirically analyzed in specific scenarios for their social implications. One hypothesis here, is that migrant social and body practices may be contributing to a lateralization of scales within China. In other words, instead of simply jumping to higher-ranked scales in a clear-cut hierarchy, they may be renegotiating that hierarchy in such a way as to be less disempowered or diminished by it. This distinction is aptly expressed by Andrew Herod and Melissa Wright in their description of "rescaling":

> [T] the process of rescaling is often presented as one in which social actors in a sense "relocate" their operations from one scale to another through this practice of jumping scales. In other [work], the concern has been to analyze not how social actors jump from one scale to another but to explore how they negotiate their ways through different scales or how they operate on multiple scales at the same time. Practices of scale jumping and negotiation, then, can be interpreted as instances of social actors producing new scales of economic and political organization for themselves in a process of "becoming."
>
> (2002: 10)

Considerable research has been done on this ongoing social production of scale, or "rescaling." The focus has been thus far on more institutional bases for social action—political parties, labor unions, activist groups—and hence has focused on questions of labor and social policy.[2] What has received less attention is the domain of cultural politics, of the micro practices of socio-cultural life and their potential to impact constructions of scale. It may be objected that micro-practices in the cultural field are incapable of addressing the existing scalar terms through which persons' lives are structured. However, if, for instance, the scope of migrants' effects on China's overall landscape—even in sheer demographic terms—is taken as an example, it becomes conceivable that such an aggregate of quotidian practices could be consequential to scale as it is specifically con-structed within the space of China. For the purposes of this chapter, I will focus on such arenas as style, body, consumption, and translocal shuttling. I will show how embodied practices of place-making suggest reorderings of the localities and regions that Miao translocals connect.

To rephrase the problematic, then, what might migrant practices in these arenas *do* to scale? To be sure, they could be seen to affirm, or even to "perform" by "citation" (in Judith Butler's phraseology[3]), the vertical ordering of the rural and urban scales. Yet what Butler's performance theory has taught us is that wherever there is reiteration of social norms, there is also potential for their destabilization. Does the movement of migrants, and the formation of lateral networks across all China by peasants and minorities formerly more isolated trouble in any way the fixity of the rural and urban scalar relationship? Do practices of translocality, in effect, unbound the local? Or do they merely refigure the local as that place which is left behind precisely because its scale is so diminutive? Does labor migration, because of its complicity with the state design of generating capital accumulation through the planned—if not contracted—flows of cheaper workers out of less developed regions of poverty and labor surplus, do nothing but solidify the inequality that constitutes the binarized rural and urban scales?

The theme I want to emphasize here is that translocals form new, spatially dispersed communities which in turn stand to reconfigure the relations of scale that order Chinese society. Not only the presence of Miao people, especially young women, across all of China, but also the linkages, circuits and interconnections that they produce between regions, create the conditions for significant translocal networks and reconfigurations of space. Parallel to anthropologist Aihwa Ong's sense of trans*nationality* as "the condition of cultural interconnectedness and mobility across space—which has been intensified under late capitalism" (1999: 4), translocality connotes conditions of connectedness *within* as well as beyond the nation-space. How are space and belonging conceived among both migrants and those in home villages? Has the notion of "home" become plural or expanded? How does place, and/or the experience of being "out of place," get narrated in terms of bodies, cultures, languages, and style? Concomitantly, what new forms of place-making are emerging as artifacts of such dislocations? And how might spatial subjectivities be recast under translocal conditions? Is it possible that the transformative presence of Miao on the move also stands to destabilize that *ethnicized* scale hierarchy in which minority regions signify the most diminutive of localities while Han and urban areas invariably are ranked above them? Marriage migration, here, becomes an important analytical supplement to the dominant trope of labor migration. In what sense might minority migrant women be reconstituting scales through their newfound "belonging" to the Han, or to all China?

I will look first at Miao women's practices of place-making and their ways of describing the experiences of belonging and of being "out of place." Practices and strategies need to be analyzed in tandem with close readings of the way migrants produce places—and perhaps scales—through their speech acts to get at the subtleties of spatial subjectivity. These crafted places are akin to what Lefebvre has referred to as "representational space": "the dominated—and hence passively experienced—space which the imagination seeks to change and appropriate. It overlays physical space, making symbolic use of its objects" (1991: 139). I will look at the way strategies of spatial and social mobility end up recasting senses of belonging and at how these senses are in turn spoken. The embodiment of place, and the way in which narratives and practices of the body produce the identities of and the relations between places, emerge as major themes throughout.

The translocal shuttle

When translocals move out of rural villages, they assume the diacritic of being "out of place." This characteristic can be an official one, as denoted by the Chinese category of "floating population" or by the more generic categories of illegal or undocumented. For women, so long associated with domesticity, interiors, and immobility, their occupying of publicly mobile roles is always somewhat marked by anomaly. These are the persons that, as Saskia Sassen (1998) has pointed out, constitute the underbelly of globalization, the other and less visible mobilities that undergird the creation of global cities. In China, however, such migrants and women also suffer hypervisibility as never quite belonging (Yan 2002; Zhang 2001). Migrant status is regularly framed as temporary; rather than being emplaced, they become transients, sojourners who never quite fit in to their place of domicile. Home is by definition elsewhere, yet in practice it has lost its fixity. Typically, long term residence does little to change this essentialized feature of being "out of place." In contemporary China, ghosts of the *hukou* system haunt the movements of would-be translocals, tethering them to places that are fixed by official designation as permanent homes, while they live according to strategies of "flexibility" of the type described by Ong for transnational "flexible citizens."[4]

For certain Miao and other minority women, a particular niche has widened for them to circulate between the remotest villages and the most global cities of China: they work as collectors of ethnic handicraft. International tourist demand prompts them to traverse multiple scales in their entrepreneurial ventures. Some women in highly touristed regions go only as far as the nearest city, such as that of Kaili in the heart of the southeast Guizhou Miao and Dong Autonomous Prefecture. As switchpoints for tourists going on to village destinations, small cities such as Kaili, only a couple hours bus ride from many Miao villages, provide ready access to easy-spending travelers. Some Miao women have made their livelihoods around these intra-regional centers of commerce, but others have gone farther, "jumped scales" to sites where they hope to find less competition and higher returns for their goods.

A few such women live in the migrant ghetto adjacent to Panjiayuan, the weekend antique and handicraft market in Beijing. The Miao crafts they sell might be collected directly from the heirlooms of rural families, or acquired through contracting with individual artisans or small putting-out shops for tourist commodities (see Oakes 2002). They may travel back and forth to collect goods themselves, or they may be one node in a network of family and associates who collaborate to move the wares to Beijing. Unlike the paradigmatic *dagong* situation in which livelihood is derived from the availability of wage away from "home," here home is also an integral node in the production of livelihood, but only by virtue of its being proactively connected to other nodes. Two factors distinguish this system from any time-honored Chinese institution of merchant accumulation. First, it is often in a context in which the movement of persons that accompany the flow of goods is undertaken only semi-legally or unofficially rather than being a central driver of the economy. Second, it is primarily a practice of minority women who would not have been on the move across China in earlier eras.

Zhang (a pseudonym[5]) is an unusually prominent player in the handicraft scene in Beijing. She is older than most, in her mid-fifties when I meet her, and she comes from southeast Guizhou. When I visit her in 2000, her Beijing base is two rooms in the Guizhou strip of the single-storey structures near Panjiayuan thrown up to accommodate outsiders with peddler business in Beijing. Bathrooms are shared public facilities and the unpaved alleys between buildings run muddy with streams of cooking and washing water that has no place to drain. Zhang complains in confidential tones about the questionable morals of the Han guards at the gate, intimating that they might prey on outsider women.

With only a middle school education, Zhang got her start through a unique opportunity: being recruited as early as 1980 by the Guojia Minwei

(State Nationalities Affairs Commission) to help make a collection to sell to the Japanese. For two years she was salaried to do this work. From the late 1980s on she started living as a transient in Beijing and elsewhere as she was commissioned by a series of over twenty-five museums and institutes to do collections for their permanent holdings. Her employers were situated all over China, including Shanghai, Nanjing, Wuhan, Xi'an, Chengdu, Guangzhou, as well as her native Guizhou. From that springboard, she organized an independent family business. Its fluid structure exemplifies the network-type translocal strategy of accumulation of these new entrepreneurs. Her husband collects goods from Miao and other minorities in southern China. Her eldest daughter lives with her in Beijing to help with selling. Her second daughter is at "home" overseeing production of a line of products, and the third daughter, at the time I spoke with her, was working with a Malaysian on a collection.

Zhang decided to make a commitment to sojourn more continually in Beijing after her goods were stolen when she left them unattended for one of her collecting trips. Now she thinks of herself as residing in the capital, but traveling back home many times a year. She loves these trips, like any nostalgic returnee on a pleasure visit. She speaks of home now in the parlance of a Beijinger othering the ruggedness of the rural: "*Nongcun hen hao wanr*" (the countryside is so much fun) she exclaims, but it is also "*hen xinku*" (full of hardship). As might a Chinese from anywhere in the country, she also narrates another nostalgia, that for the Maoist era in which she came of age. Her wall is adorned with a Mao portrait next to which she poses for pictures. If she saves enough money, she says, she wants to buy a VCD player so that she can watch fragments from her past: history movies about liberation and music videos of Miao singing. In an interesting twist on the Maoist era institution of the *hukou*, she tenderly attributes her mobility to the Chairman himself: "*Meiyou Mao Zhuxi, wo bu lai Beijing*" (If it weren't for Chairman Mao, I would never have come to Beijing).

Zhang presents a complex subjectivity marked by multiple and rich senses of belonging. She exemplifies what anthropologist Roger Rouse so aptly described for a group of Mexican migrants, Aguilillans, living in a cross-border circuit that includes California: "Obliged to live within a transnational space and to make a living by combining quite different forms of class experience, Aguilillans have become skilled exponents of a cultural bifocality that defies reduction to a singular order" (1991: 15). For Zhang, no crossing of national borders occurs, but the Chinese economy has become so sharply uneven that her life ranges in class experience even within a single national space. Shuttling between glittering Beijing and the rugged Miao mountains, she had to cultivate a chameleonic "bifocality" to be effective in such disparate contexts. In doing so, her life course affirmed Massey's sense of places in articulation: "Instead of thinking of places as areas with boundaries around, they can be imagined as articulated moments in networks of social relations and understandings. And this in turn allows a sense of place which is extra-verted, which includes a consciousness of its links with the wider world, which integrates in a positive way the global and the local" (1993:66).

But while Zhang seemed to somehow revel in these differentiated places, others found the watering holes of their translocal lives to be much less inviting. Wu was a 35-year-old woman when I met her in Beijing at the apartment of another Miao friend. She had rushed over to her friend's home when she heard I was coming. Unobtrusively she brought along a huge bag of handicrafts, clearly hoping I would show an interest in acquiring some, but never asking me point blank to make a purchase. Before we talked, she insisted on changing clothes. She put on the characteristic fine costume from her native region—Songtao/Xiangxi on the Hunan–Guizhou border. Her jacket was of bright blue brocade with panels of homespun black cloth and embroidery trim. An apron, fastened at the neck with a silver clasp, was studded with silver alloy ornaments and adorned with more stitchery. Ten inches of dense embroidery ringed the bottom of her pants leg over shoes that were also covered with stitched patterns. A long strip of black cloth was wrapped and wrapped around her head to make a large turban. Now she was ready to tell me her story which, it became clear, she was very anxious to share.

From the outset, her narrative encoded a disavowal of place. She characterized her natal village in the tropes of the small and remote. Her village had no road when she was growing up. She only finished second grade because she had to walk 7 or 8 li to school. "I had nothing but dislike for the local people there" (*wo yidian bu xihuan wo difang de ren*). Her language revealed a paradoxical identity and distance. It was her place (*wo difang*) but she did not like it. The signifier *difang* evoked locality, the size of which was not specified, but which set up a sharp contrast to the urban destination to which her story would teleologically lead her. It was clear that what she repudiated was the imputed insularity and stasis of the Miao countryside, its lack of development, of worldliness. How was she to exit, to shift the scale at which she conducted her life?

Her father had been killed when she was only six and her mother had not coped with the situation. At the age of seventeen, as a young woman, she became the first person in her area to "*zuo shengyi*" (go into business). She took out a loan to start a small shop. With a hint of contempt, she characterized the locals' lack of comprehension of market mentality: "People thought I was mad. But I made six kuai the first day and I was so happy. My family still objected to what I was doing."

Despite her entrepreneurial spunk, she now narrated a distinctly gendered mobility scenario for patrilocal China. Unlike Zhang, she did not regard her business interests alone as sufficient to take her to another scale. "I had always had a dream, since I was small. I knew I didn't have a chance to study, but I had a chance to marry to Beijing." Notably, her sights were set high. She did not dream about a nearby city or town; she did not dream about Changsha or Shanghai; she dreamt about the nation's capital, an intimation that she wanted not only to move out and up, but that she wanted to jump scales to a pinnacle beyond the several intervening levels that might have been more readily accessible to her. Unwittingly participating in the production of what Tsing (2002: 472) calls "ideologies" or "rhetorics" of scale, she construed Beijing in terms of cultural capital, as the focal point for her transcultural desire for mainstreaming. Emphasizing language, which can be acquired, as opposed to ethnicity, which would be difficult to change, she adds: "*Wo tebie xianmu naxie hui Hanhua de ren*" (I really admired those people who could speak Han Chinese, i.e. Mandarin.) She now speaks it well herself.

One day some local men (*laoxiang*) came by her shop. They had returned from their tour of duty in the military. They had come from Beijing, and they did not look Miao at all. In Wu's eyes, that they might have been Miao did not matter. What mattered was that their bodies and manners performed a worldliness associated with Beijing, that precise worldliness after which she hungered. Interestingly enough, thanks to the market savvy demonstrated by her small shop, they reciprocally didn't believe that she was Miao. Somehow out of this parity, this mutual disavowal of locality and ethnicity, an attraction as marriage partners could grow. "The man who is now my husband said '*Wo xihuan ni*' (I like you). That night he stayed somewhere nearby. He couldn't sleep all night," she boasts.

His father objected to the marriage. Perhaps he hoped that since his son was working in Beijing as a *dagong* laborer for the railroad, he would be able to marry a woman with a bona fide Beijing *hukou*. The father-in-law still objects to this day. Nonetheless, the couple embarked on the type of translocal relationship that has become increasingly common as an artifact of the negotiability of the *hukou*. They got engaged in 1986, and she told him she wanted to stay behind and make money in her shop while he returned to Beijing to earn money there. Wu had still never left her region, but now she was to begin living a translocal life, in an expanded space. Her economic strategies as a member of this newly formed couple, it could be argued, were now at the scale of the nation, or at least of the Beijing-local axis.

In 1987 she visited for the first time, and complained bitterly of the hardship and disappointment. Prestigious Beijing failed to live up to her dreams. Her fiancé was only a laborer, and his humble abode was so tiny. The weather was frigid, and there was only *mantou* (steamed buns), no rice, to eat. The food was tasteless without her regional spicy chillies. Nonetheless, her drive did not diminish.

In 1988, two years after they'd become engaged, they finally got the paperwork approving their marriage. She was still living in Guizhou and an official resident of Guizhou. In 1989 she came to Beijing again, to live for a period of time. She got pregnant and had her first child, a girl. Her husband was disappointed that it was not a boy. She returned to Guizhou in 1990, her life having taken on a rural–urban shuttling quality as she balanced official constraints, such as her and her child's *hukou*, with her financial and marital needs. Still in disfavor with her in-laws, she went back to live with her mother in her natal village. In an attempt to establish an economic base according to patrilocal principles, she asked her father-in-law for land to support the family. But he refused.

She was living on her savings from her lucrative shopkeeping in the past, but her money was running out and she had but a few thousand left. She decided to go back to Beijing, to use her remaining cash to start another business. Near her husband's residence, she found a tiny space by a garbage dump and had a little building constructed for a shop. With pride, she reported that it had expanded every year, and now made 1–2,000 RMB a month. Still, she described her residence in vague terms, as the illegitimate space of a sojourner. "We don't have a home, we just stay with *laoxiang* (people from the same region)."

Her second child, also a girl, was born in 1996. Because Wu was still a Guizhou rural resident, and because she was Miao, she could get away with having another child. But in Beijing, she laments, this child is as good as undocumented. The presence of the second child increases her liminality, marking her as someone from a less populated, implicitly less desirable, region with a different economy of births. That she had borne two girls was intimated to be part of the reason for her husband's estrangement. She and her spouse do not really have feelings for each other any more (*bu tan ganqing*), she says. They are just struggling to bring the girls up as Beijingers. Because of the girls' outsider residence status, it costs, she claims, a monthly 3000 RMB each for schooling. Making this money is what their lives are now about.

Although Wu has realized her mobility dream and reached Beijing, she describes her life in an almost desperate tone, as unimaginably bitter. Her discontent and sense of powerlessness keep us mindful of Doreen Massey's caution about the power-geometry of mobility: "Different social groups have distinct relationships to this anyway differentiated mobility: some are more in charge of it than others; some initiate flows and movement, others don't; some are more on the receiving end of it than others; some are effectively imprisoned by it" (1993:61). Wu's translocal strategies, which have allowed her to base herself in Beijing, but to exceed the urban Han birth quota, and to live off the agricultural land of kin when she was strapped, are experienced in her account as the banal exigencies of a marginal life. Like Zhang, she too strives to capitalize on her Miao roots, taking part in the massive movement of handcrafted goods out of the countryside to domestic and international markets. Always on the lookout for every potential opportunity, she hoped that I might be a major purchaser of these treasures from Miao country, and bring her an unanticipated windfall of cash.

Wu's Miao roots are no longer a subject for the kind of unequivocal disavowal she had described for the period of her youth and courtship. This was demonstrated by the ardor with which she dressed up to speak to me. By the end of the visit, her friend, also Miao and married to an official Beijinger and living quite comfortably with a single child, had also put on ethnic dress. Such proud style practices were highly contextual, however, as I found out when the two women escorted me to the street still wearing their Miao attire. I asked them how they felt when they went out (*shangjie*) in Miao dress. "We've never done this before," they averred. "We only dressed this way in honor of your visit." I had not asked them to dress Miao, nor shown much interest in traditional style. Ironically, I was marked less as a foreigner than as connected to Guizhou. Somehow, the fact that I had specifically wanted to meet migrants who were Miao had made a space for them to indulge an aspect of their identity that otherwise remained submerged in their quotidian Beijing existence. This moment of transnational encounter, happening at the scale of a "global city," had prompted them to re-inhabit their ethnicized Miao bodies.

Bodies dislocated, emplaced, and re-placed

> Just as there are no places without the bodies that sustain and vivify them, so there
> are no lived bodies without the places they inhabit and traverse.
>
> (Casey 1996: 24)

That the two Miao women had never once worn their costumes on the streets of the capital until the moment that a white foreigner inspired them to do so speaks to the body discipline that quotidian life in Beijing exerted on them. Grooming practices and discourses, in a variety of micro-variations, are part of what produce places. They are a material part of what anthropologist Kathleen Stewart denotes in her eloquent depiction of the social density inherent in place-making: "The sense of place grows dense with a social imaginary—a fabulation of place contingent on precise modes of sociality and on tense, shifting social deployments of local discourses that give place a tactile, sensate force" (Stewart 1996: 137). Beyond simple conformity or assimilation, the dress and body practices of translocals in cities serve to reiterate the difference of those cities, the shifts that bodies have undergone in their spatial movements, the normativity of urban style. As anthropologist James Ferguson has suggested:

> The idea of style as a cultivated competence implies an active process, spread
> across historical and biographical time, situated both within a political-
> economic context and within an individual life course. Such a complex
> process involves both deliberate self-making and structural determinations,
> as well as such things as unconscious motivations and desires, aesthetic
> preferences, and the accidents of personal history.
>
> (Ferguson 1999: 101)

Miao women I met in Beijing crafted their urbanity on their bodies in multiple forms of style, from maxi skirts, jeans and parkas, to make-up and permanents, to platforms and athletic shoes. Each of these style performances accrued to make Beijing the heteroglot global city that it fashioned itself to be. But most also affirmed a particularity to the canons of "global" fashion to which translocals were subjected.

Places are not only constituted by their location and physical features, then, but by the specific, often regulated, forms of bodies that inhabit them. Bodies, further, can serve as dislocated signifiers of places. Note that Wu was initially attracted to her husband because he *didn't look Miao*. She encountered him in the Miao countryside but he looked like Beijing. Her place-desire was commensurate with his body practice so, as she told it, she pursued the marriage. Translocals perform their uneasy belonging by assuming urban style when they inhabit cities, and this complicity can solidify the distinction of the urban scale. But translocals also travel with their assumed urban style, taking it back to the countryside as cultural capital. Embodied place-making, then, is not stationary but mobile.

Styling places

In 2001, when I returned—as I do yearly—to walk the small commercial strip in the Miao community of Xijiang where I have done long-term fieldwork,[6] I noticed a new business: a beauty parlor with mirrored walls hung with sparkling garlands, posters of models in fashionable haircuts, and a painted white dressing table displaying an impressive array of beauty products. It was not the first such business in Xijiang, but its proprietor, a 19-year old whom I shall call Liang, had a special story. Liang was from an isolated Miao community one mountain ridge over from Xijiang, a large village that was still not connected to the world by road. She had lived as an orphan of sorts since her father had died, for her mother had remarried in a remote village and the new husband did not want to take responsibility for the children of the first husband. Moreover, she and her siblings wanted to stay where they were so they would have better access to school. Liang described her family as "*zhongnan qingnü*" (favoring boys over girls), so girls were barely supported to study. She had only completed first grade when she dropped out to devote herself to cultivating the family land and supporting her little brother in his ongoing education.

At the age of 12 she hit the road in search of income, making what ended up being the classic labor migrant's circuit of exit and return. She had come first to Xijiang, a move that was arguably scalar in local constructions, since Xijiang was an administrative seat, featured a road with public bus transport and a periodic market. Already, it was beginning to be peopled with translocal entrepreneurs whose presence generated other opportunities. Hers was that of serving as a nanny for a Han woman from Hunan who was busy running Xijiang's first salon and who was married to Liang's cousin. After watching that child for two years, she then took care of another child in Xijiang for about two more years. At 16, she networked a job with relatives in the provincial capital of Guiyang and moved there as a nanny for another one-and-a-half years. Through yet another relative, she was introduced to a restaurant manager in the southeast Guizhou city of Kaili and got a job as a waitress. Notably, since the waged work of waitressing was considered a move up in employment status, it didn't matter that she moved back from the provincial to the prefectural capital. Only two months into this work, she was burned horribly by boiling water over half of her body. Unable to work, she returned to Xijiang where her Hunanese first employer trained her in hairstyling for six months. Not with any savings of her own, but when her sister got married, she sensed an opportunity. Borrowing 800 RMB of the sister's wedding money, she set up her own salon right up the road from her original styling mentor. There she purveys luxuries almost unimaginable from the perspective of villagers, but services that, nonetheless, become consumables as translocals shift the consumption landscape. At the salon you can get a dry wash or a wet wash. The dry wash does not use water until after the shampoo has been worked into the hair and the scalp massaged for about ten luxurious minutes. It costs three times as much. Liang also offers hair dyeing, which is little used, and mostly by older men trying to look younger by concealing their gray. "*Shengyi*," she says, is "*keyide*" (business is pretty good), and she confesses that her mentor is not exactly happy about it.

Liang lives her whole life out of this one-room business, with a curtain hung in the back to conceal the bed she sleeps in at night. What she is able to earn, she sends back to her brother, now 12, who is living at home alone attending third grade.

Each day as I pass by the beauty parlor, I am struck by Liang's style. She does not look like Xijiang. Her shirt is tight-fitting, her skirt is maxi length, her shoes are 1.5 inch platforms. Mills has described these types of style decisions for Thai migrant laborers as follows: "As consumers, young women mobilized prestigious symbols and meanings to construct and contest identities and, at least momentarily, to assert their claims to a degree of status and autonomy from which they were more often excluded within the wider society" (1999: 164–165). It is clear that stylish grooming according to urban standards has become *de rigueur* for Liang. Perhaps her style is part of the allure that brings customers in seeking to model themselves after her returnee urbanity. I find out more about standards when I ask to see what make-up she uses. She and her close girlfriend, a young returned migrant who has opened a noodle shack down the street, exuberantly begin applying eyeliner and lipstick out of a large pouch filled with a variety of colors and brands. We decide to exchange, trying some of theirs on me while they test out mine. But when I go to apply the make-up, they intervene immediately. "You don't know how! You have to do it like this!," they pronounce. Apparently my technique is not so good, and they proceed to tutor me by making up my face for me.

In this moment of bodily encounter, beauty culture has become universalized, such that it does not come into question that these two rural Miao young women might possess superior knowledge as to how to modify my urban American face. Suddenly the respective scales with which we are identified become nullified, meaningless. Through their performance of style savvy, the young women placed themselves in a domain of cosmopolitan knowledge, marked only by its peripatetic character. To be sure, the display of beauty knowledges routinely serves as a form of distinction in rural settings, but in moments such as this one, what is affirmed is that such knowledges are, with a baseline of small cash, vehicles for the *re*-placing of bodies onto the cosmopolitan scale. Gupta and Ferguson have suggested

> The ability of people to confound the established spatial orders, either through physical movement or through their own conceptual and political acts of reimagination, means that space and place can never be "given" and that the process of their sociopolitical construction must always be considered.
>
> (2002: 75)

Through producing themselves as agents of the importation of urbane style to the countryside, these returnees also tamper with scales as indexed by body practices. Importantly, it is not only their move out, but their move back that accomplishes this act of renegotiation (Schein 2005).

To forfeit ethnicity?

Other beautification practices do not appear so liberatory, however. For many Miao women who leave home for labor, the extent to which their ethnic identities are effaced is uncomfortable, a form of constraint. The ethnic dimension of body discipline is often commensurate with the baseness of toil. Physical and other low-prestige laborers feel the most subjected to metropolitan normativities. Two sisters, whom I shall call Li and Xiao, had returned home from waged positions as factory laborer and performer respectively. I first met them at home in their parents' house. Li wore an orange top over red bell bottoms studded with metal, a white vest, and athletic shoes. Xiao wore black pants and a bold red shirt printed with the English word "CANDY" and a huge pair of blue lips. Her sleeves were ornamented with the words "LOVE" and "KISS" alternating with blue hearts. Neither wore make-up, and their hair hung in ponytails down their backs.

Li, only 16 at the time, seemed to have a permanently troubled furrow in her brow. She narrated the bitterness of her voyage out. She had left home at 15, angered because her parents said they were too poor to support her studying any longer. She had had not a cent and no *shenfen zheng* (identity papers). She borrowed money from Miao acquaintances in the nearby city and made her way to Zhejiang where she had the address of friends. There she found work operating a metal press to make car parts. Her hours were exhaustingly long, from 7.30 AM to 12 midnight with two breaks for meals and only two days off a month. She toiled there for a year, not even calling her parents to tell them her whereabouts until three months after she had left.

Why had Li eventually come home to visit? "It was so hard (*ku*) there. I missed my parents. I wanted to see how my home town had changed, and I wanted to see my parents." She then described the translocal shuttling strategy of so many seasonal migrants. "In December I will go back. I want to help my parents with the harvest first, and celebrate Miao New Year. Because I left a deposit there, they have to take me back to work." In the classic words of the filial and sacrificing *dagongmei* (young female migrant worker), she explained that she wanted to intensify her labor in exchange for that of her elders. "If I earn more money I can send it back to my parents so they won't have to harvest the rice themselves. It costs three hundred to hire five people for a two-day harvesting job. I also want to earn enough money to improve our house. And I want to support my brother to go to school. He is just entering middle school. But," she laments, "it's so hard to find money, and you earn so little; it's hard to get anything done."

Li had come to conceive of herself in translocal terms, based both at home and in her workplace several provinces away. At sixteen, she had taken on, in highly embodied ways, the cultural liminality that comes with such shuttling. She had learned a little Zhejiang dialect to use when she went out shopping on the street. She missed eating Guizhou's hot chillies, but had already accustomed herself to the rich food in Zhejiang: "over there we eat more oil." Her wardrobe had been purchased in Zhejiang, making her another of the returnees who stood out on the streets of Xijiang.

Li had also made the decision to cut her hair to shoulder length. Her parents thought it was a terrible shame but, she affirmed, it was necessary for her work. Yet even as Li asserts her autonomy from local norms and parental strictures, she recounts another form of pressure constraining her choice of style, and perhaps indicating a newfound sense of bashfulness about minority identity. An inch from her scalpline start streaks of reddish highlights in her black hair. Li characterizes the dyed look as a matter of social exigency for her life in Zhejiang: "Over there men and women all dye their hair blonde [*sic*]. It costs forty yuan, but if you don't do it they laugh at you. They say your hair is so black!"

Li's perceptions of grooming and style, however, are considerably more complex than the slavish emulation of Han norms. For the style to which she feels compelled to conform involves a dyed *reddish* hair color associated not with any racialized Han look, but rather with an altered, cosmopolitan, urbane image. What she is pressured by Han co-workers to emulate is, in fact, a form of grooming that could be characterized as a kind of "jumping scales" beyond that of the generic Han urbanite to the scale of globalized cultures of body modification that feature the looks of artifice and hybridity.

But even as she capitulates to style exigencies, she looks with reverence on the opportunity her sister has had to retain her Miao looks with dignity. Li's sister Xiao, now 18, also left home at 15 but under completely different circumstances. A Dong minority woman leader of a performing arts troupe had come to Xijiang to recruit new talent. The children had stolen away from school, not telling their teachers they were going to audition. After she was chosen, Xiao went off to be trained in the nearby city. She danced, sang, and even learned to play the *lusheng*, a characteristic Miao bamboo reed pipe rarely taught to young Miao women. The work in effect had hyper-ethnicized her in ways that would not have happened at home were she to have continued farming and attending school. From then on she had belonged to a series of multi-ethnic troupes both within the region and in Guangzhou and Chongqing.

Xiao exudes a distinct satisfaction with her accomplishments, a sharp contrast to Li's restless deliberations. She prefers, she says, to live in the nearby city of Kaili where she knows many people, over working in coastal cities. By performing her own culture, Xiao had avoided some of the intercultural strains that confronted so many other migrant Miao, working at generic forms of labor, adjusting themselves to the alien norms of Han urbanity. Instead, she intensified her own cultural identity, becoming expert at forms of music and dance that were marked as Miao no matter how much those styles had been processed for the customer's entertainment tastes. She wears her hair long, and dons Miao costume with pride for work. Her little sister envies her, listening longingly as Xiao describes the work with composure, even dignity. Bespeaking the pain of the debased manual laborer, Li exclaims, at the end of her interview: "My greatest wish is to find theatrical (*wenyi*) work, like my sister. I don't care if the pay is lower!"

Place-making and narratives of dislocation

In the previous instance, Li disavowed the style practice of coloring her hair as nothing but an uneasy capitulation to cosmopolitan norms of the fashioned body. The way that translocals narrate these bodily dislocations can also be seen as a form of place-*making*. In addition to energetically refashioning bodies to effect new forms of belonging, translocals also speak of the difficulties of doing just this. As we saw earlier, with Wu's discomfort upon arrival in Beijing, the familiar categories of cuisine and climate tend to be the two tropes through which bodily dislocation is recounted. Indeed some returnees told me that they terminated their wage-earning sojourns prematurely precisely because they could not tolerate the food, they never felt full, or there was no taste due to the absence of chillies. The weather, if they had gone north, was too cold in winter; if they had gone south, it was too hot most of the year. Guizhou, and other parts of southwest China, was in turn cast as a site of temperate comfort and culinary delight. Such discourses of inflexibility link the physical to the cultural at the site of the body in transformation.

For some translocals, on the other hand, transformation becomes another way to narrate re-placement. Wang Shouhua[7] had been a wide-eyed country girl performing for the Splendid China Folk Culture Villages when I met her in Shenzhen in 1993. Her skillful performances in the Chinese metropolis were to win her a special opportunity. Within the next year she was to go to Florida to entertain Disney tourists escaping to an orientalist interlude amid their sojourn with Mickey and Ariel. She and her troupe were set up at the Splendid China theme park near Orlando to offer a live dash of ethnic flavor amid the miniature reconstructions of Chinese landmarks and ethnic villages. She was to call me from Florida, with her cohort of a few other young men and women, to talk about how difficult things were, how they didn't understand the English language, and how it was hard to get used to the food. But she had survived the initial ordeal, had come to thrive there and then, when the managers realized that it was well nigh impossible to lure a clientele sufficient to support a live troupe of performers, she was sent back to her performing job in China.

By 1999, much had changed and Wang Shouhua had left her job at the park. She had transformed herself into the kind of model entrepreneur that the state was exhalting in its drive for speedy marketization. She had saved enough cash to be able to buy into a beauty salon business in the heart of the theme park district. Then, with the income that she and her husband—also a Miao, but from another region—had gradually accumulated, they had invested in a comfortable apartment nearby with a bathroom and two bedrooms. Their pride and joy was a 2-year-old girl, whom Wang's mother-in-law had come to help care for. Every day Wang Shouhua went to work, giving haircuts and facial makeovers, inserting herself with vigor into the mainstream economy from which so many Miao across China are excluded. She came on strong, dressed trendy and talked swiftly, with the kind of brusque savvy of a nouveau urbanite. Wherever she went, she did all her business on a cell phone.

When I went back in 2000, however, much had changed again. In keeping with the ever mobile nature of flexible accumulation, the Chinese Canadian with whom Wang had invested in the salon had decided to go home and had pulled out of the venture. Wang didn't want to be in business with strangers so she sold out of the business. She hadn't been able to find anything else to do. Between mortgage and child care costs, they were poor now, she lamented. She had set up to do beauty treatments at home and saw occasional clients in the evening. During the day, with what she recounted as great boredom, she embroidered Miao handicrafts for sale. She embroidered and embroidered. Her right forearm, she complained, was tired and thin from the work. She had begun to dream of home, of returning to set up a little shop in the countryside. But they could not leave, for all their earnings were invested in the apartment they had bought. Moreover, she had brought five of her six siblings to Shenzhen to work now. And, she confessed as she told of her last visit to see her parents, she was no longer able to live that rough life or to endure the cold of the Miao mountains. Her body had adapted to Shenzhen, and she didn't see it changing back. For Wang, narrating her "success" at life in Shenzhen was commensurate with fixing a portrait of that other place in terms of bodily unlivability—cold winters, rough living, and (ironically since so many of her fellow Miao were flocking to cities for assembly line labor), mind-numbing, arm-stiffening, repetitive toil in the form of embroidering.

In 2001, when I returned again, Wang had once again become exuberant. She had found another vocation, one that put her back in the vanguard of economic modernization. She had become one of the pioneers introducing Amway commodities to the Chinese market. She whipped out her catalogue and began to tell me with such passion about the beauty, household, and health products that for a moment I thought she was hoping to make a customer of me. But she was simply brimming with enthusiasm, convinced of the extraordinary quality of these imports, fully versed in the biography of the company founder, and inspired by the success of some fellow saleswomen whose volume had earned them trips abroad. Her customers were the women still coming to her home for beauty treatments. Although she was earning almost nothing yet, she was sure that with Amway income she would one day be able to send her 4-year-old daughter abroad to study. Twice a week she paid a few yuan to attend training classes to better understand the products. And she waxed rapturous about the ways that Amway had overhauled her own body, imparting better health to her skin, for instance, than she had ever experienced before.

In Wang's eyes, Amway stood to be transformative in several ways. First, she was deploying these imported products to remake her body once again, improving its quality and health. Second, she was supremely confident that her incipient economic success would eventually allow her to again jump scales, to parlay her earlier translocality into a life lived at a transnational scale through the trips she would earn to Australia or America, all expenses paid. Third, doing Amway, as she put it implicitly, had made her even more different from the locality from which she hailed. "I've tried to tell other friends about this, but my *minzu* (minority) friends don't understand what an opportunity this is. You don't need any money to start up and they train you as you go." In a poignant exemplification of the drastically uneven economy that increasingly divided China's regions, she explained that the products could never be sold where she came from in rural Guizhou, because people would find them way too expensive. Then in a more condemning sketch of the cultural fixity of her people, she distinguished herself from other closed-minded minorities who would never undertake Amway ventures: "They're just incapable of getting it (*lijie budao*); they could never have the patience [to gradually accumulate the customer base and the income]!"

Hot chilli peppers and other places

Wang Shouhua's narrative about transformation—the "can't go back" narrative—bespeaks a kind of bodily forgetting that long-term sojourners often chronicle. Typically such accounts are class-based discourses of place, marking the intolerability of the locality of origin as a humble home that has been transcended by the upwardly mobile. But at the same time a longing for home, a bodily memory that makes one ever experience the physicality of dislocation is also frequently narrated. As Casey has put it: "Moving in or through a given place, the body imports its own emplaced past into its present experience: its local history is literally a history of locales. This very importation of past places occurs simultaneously with the body's ongoing establishment of directionality, level and distance, and indeed influences these latter in myriad ways. Orientation in place (which is what is established by these three factors) cannot be continually effected *de novo* but arises within the ever-lengthening shadow of our bodily past" (1987: 194). The discourse of hot chillies so widely reiterated by translocals—whether Han or minority—from southwest China is one of these forms of bodily memory. The absence of chillies, that apparently trivial condiment, a mere supplement to food, becomes one of the most marked and embodied emblems of dislocation.

In a cluster of neighboring villages in the Han countryside between Shanghai and Nanjing dwell a handful of daughters-in-law that hail from halfway across China. They are Miao women, mostly from the rugged mountains of Guizhou province, and they were sought out by Han men whose family hardships meant their quest for brides took them beyond their immediate locality. Exploiting the disparities generated by China's uneven development, most grooms themselves traveled to China's interior, networking through contacts to seek out marriageable women at lower brideprices who would demand less in terms of living conditions. Such suitors choose minority areas in particular for these are regions where the implementation of the birth planning policy has not been so stringent as to already produce a population imbalance with a paucity of young women. Local officials tell me that in this *zhen* (administrative township), made up of 80 villages and a population of 36,000, there are 200 women from the southwest provinces of Guizhou, Yunnan, and Sichuan. Marriage migration here follows the chain pattern, with introductions by new brides eventuating in subsequent marriages. Sometimes the brides even travel home with the express purpose of making other matches for their relatives.

Family members, and the daughters-in-law themselves, assert with vehemence that these unions cannot be described by the much sensationalized inter-provincial traffic in women (*guaimai*) that has tricked many would-be wage earners into unwanted marriages with unchosen husbands. "I came here on my own!" one says to me. "They courted by themselves," affirms a father-in-law. The reason, almost without exception, that women give for having agreed to come is once again an embodied one, about the physical difference of spaces. What drew them to accept such distant marriages, they say, was simply the lure of flat land. Never until the recent era was it possible for Miao women to consider using marriage to escape the bitter labor on the steep terraced slopes of their home mountains. "At home, the moment you step out the door you are carrying something on shoulder poles. Here everything can be pulled by the tractors," they explain. The Han grooms whom they marry may be of lower status than they are, with less education, and with parents who are peasants rather than salaried workers and officials. Nonetheless, from the perspective of Guizhou natives, these were considered hypergamous marriages not because they were to Han, but for the sole reason of the level land.

Settled into villages surrounded by the sprawl of flat fields outside their doors, now toting the one child they are permitted to bear in this populous Han region, many of these women have become bitter about the move across China. In some cases, they assert that they were duped, that they'd been promised a life of leisure, of watching TV free of farmwork. Instead it usually turned out that their new families were especially short of labor and that their toil was ceaseless. In many cases, other sons had split off into separate households; the Miao bride and her husband were the ones designated to stay home and take care of aging parents. One woman discovered that, in addition to singlehandedly tilling the fields, she was expected to be the primary caretaker for a disabled adult sister-in-law who needed to be bathed and fed daily. Some described intense loneliness: they knew that their fellow Miao sisters were so nearby, yet their families would not release them from domestic duties so that they could visit with each other. Moreover, almost every husband sojourned most of the year away from home, traveling China to seek wage labor as has become the strategy of so many peasants everywhere.

Alone with strange villagers, whose dialect of Chinese was well nigh incomprehensible to them, these Miao brides passed their days as the perennial daughter-in-law, in meaningless work, taking delight in their only children. What they had not comprehended, or bargained for, was the sheer physicality of space that made home so far away. They narrated their desire for home and relatives with acute deprivation. For most, although they longed to more than anything, they could not go home, whether to visit or even to run away. In the Miao mountains, a bride had usually married within walking distance, even if it was a matter of a couple days' excursion. Thus her sense of space took shape as a larger regional community, in which she knew both language and specific people. There she had always lived a small-scale translocality, traveling between villages to market days and festivals. There was security in the awareness that should life with in-laws become insufferable, she might simply walk on her two feet out the door and go "home." But in this faraway province, the material distance of home constituted an unanticipated sense of immobility. Most brides did not have access to enough cash, or lacked permission from their in-laws, to travel home. In-laws protested that the women were not competent to undertake travel, that they would be vulnerable and helpless. Indeed, in some cases, the women did not have the literacy or other travel skills that would have been required for them to make the trip. Similar to a circumstance that has been described for brides who were duped and sold off to faraway villages whose geographical location was actually kept secret from them, these willing brides had likewise become disoriented in space; in a certain sense they did not know how to find their way home.

In lieu of home, the most fortunate had put their meager resources into the telephone, that instrument of time–space compression that could instantly connect them to the voices of their loved ones. Some paid for phone calls at local shops; others managed to afford phone hookups in their homes and in those of their parents back in Guizhou. The proliferation of telephone communications in the rural hinterland represents one concrete impact of translocal strategies that create instant linkages between remote areas and any part of China in the form of a web-like, lateral network. For the brides, the comforting physicality of home was supplanted by that instantaneous but one-dimensional substitute—the plastic headpiece that made talking to their kin a possibility across their agonizing separation. Yet, there was something about these disembodied voices that seemed to exacerbate the experience of distance, and I saw tears fall amply during phone calls home.

The brides still hungered for a more embodied sense of community. In the absence of blood kin, what they eagerly awaited were those brief, sometimes stolen, moments in the company of their co-ethnics. By their accounts, it was this tiny and fragile sub-community of women that they valued, not the attentions of the Han men with whom they cohabited. Some openly expressed repugnance for their husbands, and indicated that the only way they achieved a sense of belonging was among those who also came from "home." If their in-laws would free them, they would willingly walk as much as a few hours to visit their friends' villages. A few were envied as extremely fortunate for they lived in a large village where at least five Guizhou women had married in, making it possible for them to associate on a daily basis. When together, these women could use Miao dialects, or a more widely intelligible Guizhou dialect, to have private conversations free of the prying ears of their in-laws.

Other than issues of language comprehension, these women narrated most of their experience in terms of bodily disjunctions and fusions. It was through their bodies that they produced not only the mixed child, but also the hybridized lives they continued to live. Most had voluntarily cut their hair to sensible Jiangsu peasant lengths. To explain this style decision, they cited not any canons of coastal cultural discipline, but rather the suitability of short hair to the physical features of their peasant lives—the intensity of their labor and the ovenlike heat of the Jiangsu summer. In this narrative, home was portrayed as a site of greater cultural constraint from which they gained a degree of self-determination upon their exit. Nonetheless, they continued to embroider Miao-style hats to protect their babies' heads, and one woman who had been there several years said she had chosen to begin growing her hair long again so that she could wear it in proud Miao style for the rare occasion when she might visit home.

Significantly, the accounts of these women also contained fragments of testimony as to how their presence had impacted their new communities, altering them ever so slightly. That such impact would be noted at all on the part of these migrants may be readable in terms of the politics of scale. Interestingly, one of these fragments emerged when I asked about the hair decisions of a visiting Miao mother. Miao married women from her part of Guizhou typically wrapped a towel over their tied-up hair to protect it from dirt, creating a ubiquitous and distinctive look. I asked if the mother-in-law had removed her towel out of embarrassment when she visited the Han countryside. At first she had, I was told, but it bothered her because her head felt cold. She put it back on, and discovered that it didn't matter. Nobody stared. Local Han, I was told, had already become "*xiguan*" (accustomed) to the look because so many Guizhou Miao women had married in, altering the visual landscape. Such a tiny anecdote indicates a remarkable shift in place-identity. That the presence of Miao and their characteristic looks could become a matter of *xiguan* in the Han countryside suggests that, at least in this instance, what migrants' mobilities are doing is refashioning certain places—even rural villages—in terms of more polyglot identities that include more heterogeneous ethnicities, body practices, and cultural norms.

Food practices too revealed this narrative of impact. Brides spoke of how they'd taught their husbands and in-laws to eat spicy food. From home, they'd imported their cherished chillies—hallmark of China's southwest cuisine—and introduced them into the local Jiangsu dishes, actually persuading not only their children but also their husbands and in-laws to adjust their taste buds. And if spiciness was not enough, they also introduced the beloved flavor of sour. They lovingly transported huge ceramic pickling jars, so that they could get the right tangy taste for the vegetables they painstakingly cured in Miao style. When they met each other, they would exchange their delicacies, comparing notes on whose product best preserved the hometown flavor. With a mischievous glimmer in their eyes, these custodians of a rarified culinary knowledge seemed to take delight in the opportunity to purvey their flavors among a tiny few of those northern and coastal elite who have protested over history that the taste of spice is inedible. Here the politics of bodies could clearly be seen to intersect with those of sociocultural prestige.

Scale negotiations

How could such banal minutia as the taste of spice have bearing on the politics of scale? If we take scale to be socially produced, then each iteration of scale becomes a moment in which prevailing rankings and definitions might be reinforced or subverted, whether volitionally or not. As Tsing puts it

> Place-making is always a cultural as well as a political-economic activity. It involves assumptions about the nature of those subjects authorized to partic-ipate in the process and the kinds and claims they can reasonably put forth about their position in national, regional, and world classification and hierarchies of places.

(2002: 464)

As I have said, at the moment that they were contracted, the marriages of Miao women to Jiangsu Han were considered hypergamous. In other words, to the extent that marrying out to the flat Han countryside was considered desirable, it was framed as marrying *up* from a small and backward locality to a more prestigious scale of the purportedly more worldly and agriculturally efficient Han countryside, in proximity to such global cities and sites of *dagong* opportunity as Shanghai and Nanjing. It is possible to argue, then, that what brides were doing when they later critiqued the desirability of those places, complained about the difficult life and revalorized home, brought their chillies, their pickling jars, and their toweled mothers and accustomed local Han to them, was *in effect* asserting a more horizontal relationship between these places, one not organized by the ranking of scales but rather by the *lateral* movement of persons, goods, customs, etc. We might think of their negative recasting of hypergamous marriages as a kind of *descaling* of the relationship between the purportedly more insular Miao countryside and the ultimately ever-so-confining Han rural life. That the women narrated their sense of entrapment rather than liberation in the Han villages reveals not only their authorizing themselves as arbiters of scale hierarchy, but also their rejection of the notion that they had somehow moved up and out through their cross-ethnic, spatially distant liaisons.

The above argument, however, is premised on the assumption of a scalar relationship between two tiers *within* the Chinese countryside. What remains is to examine the effects of practices of translocal Miao women who moved between the country and the city. It may be argued, of course, that the ranked bifurcation of the country and the city is precisely what oppresses Miao and other rural women and men who have no alternative but to leave home because of the way in which state and capitalism have organized production for China within the global economy. It might be argued that their moving, in turn, only strengthens the hierarchical position of the urban over the rural scale. Their strategies become part of the overall process of flows canalized by the marketizing economy, by state neglect of the less developed regions, and by what Yan calls the discursive "spectralization of the rural" (2003). But we might also think of Smith's call for a more critical reading of such scale-making:

> How do we critically conceive of these various and nested scales, how do we arbitrate and translate between them? Further, how do we conceptualize such a translation in a way that centres social practices and politics designed to destroy the oppressive and exploitative intent of hierarchical space?
>
> (1992b: 73)

Put simply, this paper might be seen as part of the project of "centering social practices," of taking seriously the impact of agentive moves and of translocal linkages. Because such forms of connectedness across the space of China are so new for Miao women, they stand out in high relief as potentially socially consequential. Such consequentiality need not be assessed only in terms of such tangibles as dislocated persons or economic flows, but also can be found in the shifting subjectivities of translocals as they come to see themselves as occupying a higher scale—whether city, nation, or globe—than they previously had. Far from being ameliorations of space, shifts may have place-making functions, may be narrated as dislocations or relocations, and may be situated in the materiality of the (re)fashioned body. What they reveal is often the bifocality described by Rouse (1991: 15). In some cases we may even need to think in terms of multifocality, an orientation toward space that bridges distance and disparate sites.

At a political level, two effects of the new translocal practices seem most salient. First, translocals announce themselves to have *moved up* in social ranking if their moves are calibrated according to hierarchical scales. Such upward moves, such jumping of scales may effect "abrogation[s] of boundaries" (Smith 1992a: 66), such that translocals, through their own agency, come to operate at higher scales than their original social status might have scripted. They thus present a tacit challenge to the confinement of so many to a classed location in the stigmatized rural backwaters. They claim sociospatial mobility as available to them, and in turn as potentially transformative of China's entire social structure. With women this spatial "poaching" obliges migrants to confront the moral connotations of their mobility in terms of the gender order. Yan describes a

> notion of transgression and contamination [that] constitutes a vague source of shame for these women—vague because it is caught uneasily between the state ideology of women's liberation and the continued presence of patriarchal power that defines what a proper woman is through the spatial circumscription of her labor.
>
> (Ibid. 2003: 5)

Yet in laboring outside, they not only acquire a gender stigma, but also stand to trouble ranked spatializations of gender.

This suggests the second effect, which is that, in some cases, the horizontality of translocal strategies may actually stand to erode the existing scale structure of Chinese society. If linkages between city and country, between capital and provincial remote, between coast and interior, become more commonplace, it is conceivable that such lateral ties will, at the minimum, come to supplement the more stratified sense that Chinese hold of these scales. These spatial nodes, in other words, may become a little less fixed as scales, or alternately, they may become subject to "rescaling" in relation to each other. And these reshufflings would be taking place outside the rubrics of social movements or other forms of organized political contestation, as an accumulation of material micropractices and subjective dis- and re-locations. It is too soon to know whether this has begun to take place, but it is time to begin paying attention to the dynamics that have the potential to precipitate such shifts.

Notes

1 The rank-ordering of these scales in the Chinese social imaginary may be debatable. Specifically, if the "provincial" is a significant scale, does it rank above or below the urban?
2 In part it appears that it is the emphasis on macro scales that has, in turn, foregrounded these sites of social and political practices as pivotal.

3 For a review of Butler's works in relation to China's cultural politics, see Schein (1999).
4 Ong defines flexible citizenship in terms of the "cultural logics of capitalist accumulation, travel, and displacement that induce subjects to respond fluidly and opportunistically to changing political economic conditions" (1999: 6).
5 All names that appear in the text have been changed unless specified otherwise.
6 Fieldwork was carried out for short periods in 1999, 2000, and 2001 against the backdrop of extended research over four stays in Xijiang between 1985 and 1993. Research has also been conducted in Beijing, Jiangsu, Shenzhen, Guiyang, Kaili, Leishan, and other Miao villages. I am extremely grateful to the people of Xijiang and other sites for their ongoing participation in the project. I am also grateful to Rutgers University and to the Rutgers Research Council for support of ongoing research.
7 This is not a pseudonym. Wang Shouhua has told me specifically that she prefers that I use her real name.

References

Basch, L., Glick Schiller, N., and Szanton Blanc, C. (1994) *Nations Unbound: Transnational Projects, Postcolonial Predicaments and Deterritorialized Nation-States*, Langhorne, PA: Gordon and Breach.

Brenner, N. (1997) "Global, fragmented, hierarchical: Henri Lefebvre's geographies of globalization," *Public Culture* 24: 135–167.

Casey, E. S. (1987) *Remembering: A Phenomenological Study*, Bloomington, IN: Indiana University Press.

—— (1996) "How to get from space to place in a fairly short stretch of time: phenomenological prolegomena," in S. Feld and K. Basso (eds) *Senses of Place*, Santa Fe, NM: School of American Research, 13–52.

Ferguson, J. (1999) *Expectations of Modernity: Myths and Meanings of Urban Life on the Zambian Copperbelt*, Berkeley, CA: University of California Press.

Gupta, A. and Ferguson, J. (2002) "Beyond 'culture': space, identity, and the politics of difference," in J. X. Inda and R. Rosaldo (eds) *The Anthropology of Globalization: A Reader*, Malden, MA: Blackwell, 65–80.

Herod, A. and Wright, M. (2002) "Placing scale: an introduction," in A. Herod and M. Wright (eds) *Geographies of Power: Placing Scale*, Malden, MA: Blackwell Publishing, 1–14.

Latham, A. (2002) "Retheorizing the scale of globalization: topologies, actor-networks, and cosmopolitanism," in A. Herod and M. Wright (eds) *Geographies of Power: Placing Scale*, Malden, MA: Blackwell Publishing, 115–144.

Lefebvre, H. (1991/1974) *The Production of Space*, trans. D. Nicholson-Smith, Malden, MA: Blackwell.

Marston, S. A. (2000) "The social construction of scale," *Progress in Human Geography* 24(2): 219–242.

Massey, D. (1993) "Power-geometry and a progressive sense of place," in J. Bird, B. Curtis, T. Putnam, G. Robertson, and L. Tickner (eds) *Mapping the Futures: Local Cultures, Global Change*, London: Routledge, 59–69.

Mills, M. B. (1999) *Thai Women in the Global Labor Force: Consuming Desires, Contested Selves*, New Brunswick, NJ: Rutgers University Press.

Oakes, T. (2002) "Dragonheads and needlework: textile work and cultural heritage in a Guizhou county", *Provincial China* 7(2): 151–177.

Ong, A. (1999) *Flexible Citizenship: The Cultural Logics of Transnationality*, Durham, NC: Duke University Press.

Rouse, R. (1991) "Mexican migration and the social space of postmodernity," *Diaspora* 2(2):8–23.

Sassen, S. (1998) *Globalization and Its Discontents: Essays on the New Mobility of People and Money*, New York: The New Press.

Schein, L. (1999) "Performing modernity," *Cultural Anthropology* 14(3): 361–395.

—— (2005) "Ethnoconsumerism as cultural production? Making space for Miao style," in Jing Wang (ed.) *Locating China: Space, Place, and Popular Culture*, London: Routledge, 150–170.

Smith, N. (1992a) "Geography, difference and the politics of scale," in J. Doherty, E. Graham, and M. Malek (eds) *Postmodernism and the Social Sciences*, New York: St. Martin's Press, 57–79.

—— (1992b) "Contours of a spatialized politics: homeless vehicles and the production of geographical scale," *Social Text* 33: 55–81.

—— (1993) "Homeless/global: scaling places," in J. Bird, B. Curtis, T. Putnam, G. Robertson, and L. Tickner (eds) *Mapping the Futures: Local Cultures, Global Change*, London: Routledge, 87–119.

Stewart, K. C. (1996) "An occupied place," in S. Feld and K. Basso (eds) *Senses of Place*, Santa Fe, NM: School of American Research, 137–165.

Swyngedouw, E. (1997) "Neither global nor local: 'Glocalization' and the politics of scale," in K. Cox (ed.) *Spaces of Globalization: Reasserting the Power of the Local*, New York: Guilford Press, 137–166.

Tsing, A. (2002) "The global situation," in J. X. Inda and R. Rosaldo (eds) *The Anthropology of Globalization: A Reader*, Malden, MA: Blackwell, 453–485.

Yan, H. (2002) "Xiandai hua de huanying: shengchan he xiaofei de shuang ren wu" (A mirage of modernity: *pas de deux* of consumption and production), *Taiwan: A Radical Quarterly in Social Studies* 48: 95–134.

—— (2003) "Spectralization of the rural: reinterpreting the labor mobility of rural young women in post-Mao China," *American Ethnologist* 30(4): 1–19.

Zhang, L. (2001) "Migration and privatization of space and power in late socialist China," *American Ethnologist* 28(1):179–205.

12 The leaving of Anhui

The southward journey toward the knowledge class

Wanning Sun

Going south—an introduction

Popular narratives of mobility, if and when constructed in reference to Anhui, are usually framed within a discourse of rural poverty and economic hardship, and as such, tend to mobilise the trope of history. In fact, the mere mention of Anhui in China immediately conjures up, in most people's minds, the image of the domestic maid. As early as the 1960s and 1970s, Anhui, a largely rural province in eastern China, became the source of a seemingly endless supply of maids for middle class families in more prosperous regions such as Jiangsu, Zhejiang, Shanghai, and Beijing. This phenomenon therefore represents a particular form of gendered mobility in which rural, poor, and illiterate women from northern provinces travel to large cities like Beijing to perform domestic servitude. My preliminary research has found that the "Anhui maid" is seen as a metaphor for the gendered, unequal, and uneven relationship between Anhui and developed places such as Shanghai and Beijing (Sun 2005). Mobile, plentiful, and available at any time, she also embodies the enduring potency of such a metaphor. The Anhui maid is a national brand name, a product, whose cachet, authenticity, and desirability are made possible not in spite of, but precisely because of, the uniqueness of Anhui as a poor, backward, and un-modern place. In this sense, the association of Anhui with poverty operates as both a metaphor—Anhui is like a maid—and metonym—the maid stands for Anhui.

Even before "the Anhui maid" had emerged, Anhui already had a reputation for producing itinerant beggars, a phenomenon which arose in circumstances of poverty. During the Ming and Qing Dynasties, poverty and bad farming conditions turned many peasants in northern Anhui into *liumin*, or the "gypsies of China," who would leave their villages on annual begging tours. This economically driven cultural practice has transmogrified into a cultural phenomenon unique to the region. For many generations, leaving home in the winter and returning in the spring was thus known to be a collective regional habit which many peasants main-tained, even in those years of good crops (Chi 1996a,b). These itinerant beggars roamed around in more affluent provinces and cities, advertising Anhui's poverty like walking billboards. Their visibility is therefore credited with—or blamed for—the widespread association of Anhui with poverty in the popular imagination. The image of the wandering beggar from Anhui persists in the national consciousness, and Anhui has gradually become a mythical land of wanderers (*liumin*): "gypsies," tramps, vagabonds, drifters, and, of course, cheap laborers.[1]

The legendary figure of the Anhui maid is part and parcel of the narrative of rural migrants in the city, one of the two enduring tropes of mobility which have emerged in contemporary Chinese urban folklore: "going to the city" (*jincheng*) and "going abroad" (*chuguo*).[2] While both tropes result from the imbrication of social mobility and translocal practices, the former features villagers on the road to the urban spaces in China, whereas the latter centers upon city folks on their way to becoming transnationals. Central to the latter trope is "America," or any of the "global cities" in the West, for that matter. In the popular consciousness of the late 1980s and early 1990s, "America," or "foreign countries" embodied the promise of everything that China wanted but lacked—wealth, modernity, freedom, adventure, and above all, exotica—and was so imagined by both those who had access to mobility and those who did not. When such perceptions took a concrete form in the context of social relations in reform-era China, they manifested in the accumulation of social power and cultural capital by those who are either seen to have the means to migrate to America, or have some kind of connection with American people and things.

While such a national imagination with "America" as the object of desire continues to shape the experience of many would-be Chinese transnationals, I argue that increasingly during the past decade, "the south," and a cluster of places which I call the "internal global cities"—Shanghai, Shenzhen, Guangzhou, Hainan, etc., in southern China—have started to attract hundreds and thousands of Chinese from the inland and northern provinces. The emergence of the south as the desirable destination for hundreds and thousands of Chinese has resulted in a trope which is distinct from that of going to the city and going overseas, but which generates a similar degree of clout and social capital.[3] This is certainly the case with the group of people I am concerned with in this chapter. They are neither unskilled cheap labour forces from the villages eager to make some money doing whatever they can, nor the "flexible, deterritorialised and highly mobile" (Nonini and Ong 1997: 11) transnationals traversing Chinese borders. They are a group of people from less prosperous—mostly inland and northern—parts of China, but who are nevertheless urban, well-educated, and ambitious. Their technical knowledge and expertise no longer generate decent income or clout in their current places of work, while their experience and skills may bring both high income and professional identity in the prosperous south. The feeling of being stuck or even trapped in their current workplaces, combined with the prospects of becoming members of a "globalised capitalist managerial elite" (Nonini and Ong 1997: 11), has resulted in an infectious, if not feverish sense of restlessness, and to go or not to go south has become the perennial existential question.

The accounts of the individuals described in this chapter, who have been chosen from a range of interview subjects, are deliberately schematic. By offering a few slices of individual experience, I intend to sketch out the texture and layering of the "going south" narrative. I want to examine the changing notion of selfhood by considering the sense of hope, anxiety, uncertainty, ambivalence, and aspiration which colors the experience of mobility engaged in by this particular group of people, and in doing so, work toward a useful taxonomy of translocal practices at a conceptual level. I adopt the notion of translocality in order to ask an empirical question: what does mobility—of people, capital, and images—do to localities and to an individual's sense of place? Specifically, this notion of mobility refers first to the activity of travel, including departure, arrival, and return, and the circumstances in which decisions about these activities are made. Second, it refers to the relationship between a range of globally circulated images of places, and the ways in which travelers—and non-travelers—talk about places and space. This includes looking at how those who are immobile talk, speculate, and fantasize about certain places, and how those who have resettled remember experiences of familiar places about their lives prior to geographical displacement. Third, it refers to the ways in which the local intersects with global forces—economic, technological, and social—and how such intersection facilitates or inhibits the formation of a particular kind of mobile subjectivity.

In light of these methodological parameters, what are, for instance, some of the consequences of mobility in reference to the reworking of the identity and subjectivity of these individuals? Subsumed under this general line of inquiry is a cluster of related questions: how has mobility challenged the logic of place-identity and increasingly rendered the mobile self as a site for the contestation and negotiation of difference? Furthermore, in what ways is mobility in the spatial/geographic sense imbricated with travel and migration in the cultural sense? In other words, how has selfhood been transformed as a result of the individual moving not only from the inland to the coast, but also from, say, the state sector to the private sector? Finally, how has mobility produced, contributed to, or altered the spatial imagination of individuals, including both those who travel, and those who do not?

The Anhui intellectual and the fantasy of "the south"

In their study of the strategies and tactics of capital accumulation among diasporic Chinese, Nonini and Ong (1997) argue that this group necessarily need to confront the constraints of three regimes of power, namely, the family, the capitalist workplace, and the nation-state. Each regime, according to the authors, disciplines and controls the individuals so as to form acceptable subjectivities; and for this to succeed, each regime requires the subject to be locatable and defin-able. Such regimes, the authors further argue, become unstable and dysfunctional when individuals "elude the localisations" and "take advantage of the disjunctures in space, and therefore in power." Mobility and deterritorialization, therefore, conspire to render Chinese transnationalism "wild," dangerous, and largely a "guerrilla" phenomenon:

> With globalization there has been the appearance of new managerial, financial, legal, technical, and commercial service professionals, and of design professionals in architecture and advertising. These transnational

professionals and technocrats provide the managerial and technical innovations of flexibility...They have evolved new, distinctive lifestyles grounded in high mobility (both spatial and in terms of careers), new patterns of urban residence, and new kinds of social interaction defined by a consumerist ethics. These professionals have come to form what Weber...called "status groups," yet ones sharing common privileges as members of a globalized capitalist managerial elite.

(Ibid.: 11)

The high degree of mobility and flexibility of the transnational professionals described by Nonini and Ong can be best described as postmodern nomadism: they feel at home everywhere, are constantly (re)constructing their identities, and they adopt a cosmopolitan worldview and lifestyle.[4] Unlike the wandering beggars from Anhui who perennially wander away from home in search of food and survival, these nomads feel at home everywhere because they possess flexible capital (both economic and social) and deterritorialized professional skills. While the figure of the cosmopolitan nomad can be contrasted with that of the wandering beggar from Anhui, it is quite similar to the emerging group of professionals within China, whose lifestyles are increasingly befitting the description of "flexible, mobile, and deterritorialized managerial elites." Nonini and Ong's framework for studying transnational practices of diasporic Chinese is also useful when we consider the translocal practices of this emerging knowledge class. The circumstances under which many migrants and sojourners in China leave home, travel, arrive in a new city, or return home are equally unpredictable. Like their international/transnational counterparts, these intra-national travelers are also confronted with the family, workplace (*danwei*), and the government—regimes or forces which encourage or discourage, facilitate or inhibit, their decision to leave, stay, or return. Also like their transnational counterparts, their mobility has made it possible for internal travelers to "take advantage of the disjunctures in space, and therefore in power" (Nonini and Ong, 1997: 24) between these regimes. In addition, the particular point of subject formation at which individuals find themselves is also the result of these three forces intersecting, sometimes contradicting, sometimes reinforcing each other. Furthermore, the processes of the movement, sojourn, travel, or migration of these individuals are in one way or another marked by an array of tactics—of resistance, elision, avoidance, and the strategies of haggling and appropriation—either in confronting or playing with each or some of these regimes.

However, although it may well be the aspiration of some of the educated urban Chinese to join the membership of the globalized professional elites, circumstances confronting those actual and want-to-be translocals are more likely to be marked with constraint and inflexibility. In other words, although many indeed traverse the space between "home" and "away," few can be described as shuttlers or itinerants—nomads, like their transnational counterparts. In fact the difference between the two groups can be seen in a number of ways. Their stories of departure and arrival threaten to destabilize and even call into question—rather than reinforce—the clear delineation between these regimes outlined by Nonini and Ong. For instance, while it is possible to regard nation-states and capitalist workplaces as disparate processes which nevertheless work together to impact on the transnational practices of individuals, as evidenced in diasporic Chinese communities, the situation facing many mobile workforces—both skilled and unskilled—within China is quite different. Very often the *danwei* (workplace) is not separate from the nation-state. Instead, it may be the material embodiment of the nation-state per se. Moreover, unlike internal migrants, most diasporic Chinese communities do not need to negotiate a shift from a socialist workplace ethos to the work practices of the free market. In other words, internal migrants can less afford to "travel light," free of baggage from the history and memory of the collective era. Furthermore, much like diasporic Chinese transnationals, urban Chinese professionals contemplating or practising translocalism also need to come to terms with the status of being in a "foreign" country, whereby the mobile body, rather than the fixed place, becomes the site of power struggles and the negotiation of regional inequalities.

Anhui, a largely rural province still suffering from the legacy of a command economy, is a good example of the burden of history and memory which individual travellers have to carry. Unlike some provinces and regions which are endowed with plentiful resources for self-invention of place identity, Anhui's identity has been kept in its place by a history of poverty and slow economic growth. Its economic performance in the reform era has done little to change this impression. Largely associated with agricultural production, and to some extent, the manufacturing sector, it has attracted neither capital investment from outside the province nor preferential treatment from the central government. In spite of China's Science and Technology University in the capital, Hefei, and its cities hosting a number of research institutes under the direct management of various departments in Beijing, Anhui is seldom, if ever, associated with the lure of transnational capital, the high-tech information sector, the services and hospitality industries, or the finance and banking sectors. Anhui in the national imagination, as well as in its self-perception, is not only poor in economic terms but also conservative in a cultural and political sense. It is often cited as an example of those provinces inhabiting an "inland peasant mentality"; its organizations are infested with the malaises of state bureaucracy, particularly corruption, incompetence, and lack of vision, and its leadership is sapped by a "residual inertia of an old command economy." People from Anhui are generally perceived to be lazy, inward-looking, uninterested in change, and bereft of entrepreneurial, risk-taking, and dynamic qualities (Sun 2002a). Unlike some more prosperous provinces, Anhui provides little space for upward mobility within the province. The province has as many as 10,000,000 surplus workers in its labor force. However, in spite of the provincial government's *hukou* (residential permit) reform, which is designed to encourage rural–urban movement, Anhui ranks below the national average in terms of its speed of urbanization. By 2005, only 25 percent of its population is projected to live in the city and urban areas. Cities and townships in Anhui, due to their sluggish economic performance, high unemployment rate, and weak tertiary sector, do not have the capacity to absorb surplus labor forces.[5]

One of the major cities in Anhui is Bengbu, a medium-sized city with a population of around 530,000. Bengbu is hardly known to outsiders except as one of the big stops along the Beijing–Guangzhou railway line. During the socialist era, the largest employers in the city were in the manufacturing sector, comprising a large tobacco factory, a meat-processing factory, and a number of heavy machinery and other manufacturers, with the biggest state enterprise at that time being a manufacturer of air-compression machinery. Massive retrenchments during the subsequent enterprise restructuring has seen thousands of workers laid off, and stories of workers "sitting-in" in the courtyard of the city municipality are perennial in the social life of Bengbu. Of course, mass unemployment in the city also accounts for the city's incapacity to absorb internal migrants from rural areas. The bankruptcy of these state enterprises has also resulted in the redundancies of many engineers and workers with technical expertise. Once perceived to be the backbone of the state's modernization project, these state intellectuals (*zhi shi fen zi*) suddenly found themselves jobless, unable to translate years of education, training and professional experience into tangible social and cultural capital.

Bengbu, like many other cities in the province, has its fair share of government-assigned research and design institutes, a consequence of state-managed translocal practices common in the socialist era of a command economy and central planning.[6] Those familiar with the politics of the central–local nexus in this era would know that although these research and design institutes were located in peripheral cities and provinces, they were both separate from and above local economic life. The staff in such institutions and their families were relocated from Beijing, and their presence in the province was a result of Beijing wishing to dissolve its central presence for strategic security reasons. Funding for these research enclaves was centrally controlled and administered by the various departments in Beijing, since research productivity and output went directly back to the center. As a compensation for their compulsory relocation from Beijing, staff enjoyed a salary, benefits, and other employment conditions which were commensurate with their colleagues in Beijing. They and their families, once relocated to Bengbu, lived within a clearly delineated compound, and although they shopped locally and their children went to local schools, they nevertheless maintained their Beijing dialects, and enjoyed standards of living higher than the locals.[7] These institutes were walled compounds on the outskirts of the city, and the local public would need permits to enter. They signified power and prestige. The people living inside these walls were recipients of "royal privilege."[8]

Things started to change in Bengbu in the early 1990s. Once fully funded by their respective ministries and departments in Beijing, these research institutes were told to sever their ties with Beijing, and they were to become corporatized and self-funding. In return, Beijing was to give them full autonomy. As a result, these institutes started seeking income-generating possibilities by forging partnerships with local industries and businesses, as well as increasingly employing local university graduates. For a few years, corporatization seemed to have worked. Freed from the constraints of "the Centre," these newly configured business entities were able to translate the special knowledge and expertise of their staff into lucrative business opportunities. Researchers, engineers, and designers became their cash cows, earning a disproportionately high income. For many university graduates in Anhui, to work in one of these institutes indeed seemed a plum job. The clout of being affiliated with them persisted, although it was now the lucrative financial reward, rather than the patronage of the powerful state, which lent them social capital.

This prosperity, however, proved to be short-lived. From the mid-1990s, as downsizing and bankruptcies at many state enterprises in the city and the province has led to a steep drop in partnership and business opportunities, income has started to dwindle. The institutes have also stopped attracting high-calibre researchers. The staff—particularly those whose *hukou* is based in Beijing—have left in droves, leaving the locals and the retired scientists to fend for themselves. Beijing's laissez-faire policy, once profitable and generous, now seemed cruel. Many existing staff, particularly young people, have begun to see their professional future as lying in the southern cities, the more prosperous regions of China. Abandoned and disillusioned by Beijing, the institutes have been in crisis, their staff discontented and restless, and everyone is talking about leaving. The south beckons.

In discussing how regional meanings are produced, Carolyn Cartier argues that people produce regional meaning through "actions and experiences," through the "production" and the "use" of texts, which are useful in constituting "identity positions" (Cartier 2001: 38). This is certainly the case with the meaning of "south." "The south" is an imaginary space as well as a geographic location. Mass media, particularly advertising, diligently sell the idea of success by creating a range of seductive figures: the "new rich" (*xing fu ren*), the "successful people" (*cheng gong ren shi*), and the "white-collar" (*bai ling*) or "golden-collar" (*jing ling*) professionals. These people are constructed to be always on the move, dynamic, affluent, and traversing transnational spaces. The visualising of these figures in advertising and mass media in general—buying an apartment with their smiling family, closing a business deal with foreigners, or relaxing in secluded golf clubs—often use the south as a backdrop, and as a backdrop it invariably connotes modernity, freedom, and success. "The south" in these fantasies operates according to a social semiotics of space. It is, first, a global space inhabited by deterritorialized people, capital, and images, and as such, is marked by an absence of the towering figure of the nation-state and its ideological control. Second, as a global space, the south is forever looking forward, and is not burdened by, nor does it burden the people in such spaces with, nation- and culture-specific memory and history. Third, as a global space, the south is also contrasted with the rest of China—that is, the "global cities" in the south are also points at which transnationalism enters China, as well as markers separating transnational spaces in China from those which are not.[9] Last, but not least important, the south is a space that is defined mythically rather than literally, referring, tacitly, only to those prosperous cities and provinces that are in the south and excluding those—such as Guangxi, Yunan, and Guizhou—which are not. In a similar way and to the same extent that the emergence of the "new rich" and "successful people" is a consequence of the creation of such cultural symbols,[10] "the south" as we know it today—modern, affluent, and full of successful people—is a result of the construction of the south as a fantasy space in consumer culture.

Such is the conundrum facing my interviewees and many other people from Anhui whom they come to represent. They are the most educated sector of the population, having obtained their tertiary education from the state-funded universities that were perceived to be crucial to the realization of the state modernization project. They also have considerable experience—both specialist and managerial—from working in the state sector, where they have honed their skills, and where many of them have occupied, or are still occupying, middle-level administrative, managerial, or technical positions. While to the rest of the population in the province, theirs may still be an enviably "cushy" existence, the appeal of a secure job in the state sector has started to lose its lustre. The things that once attracted them to the job have now turned into their reasons for wanting to leave. Security has begun to spell stagnancy, and their stability is becoming imprisoning. The success stories from the south, through daily exposure to both images from the mass media and urban myths and folklore, fill my interviewees, and people like them, with an increasing sense of urgency, and fuel both a dissatisfaction with the status quo and a desire for change. Their prospects of starting a brand new life, reinventing a new identity, and cashing in on the economic boom of the south seem irresistible, and all the more so, because they seem real enough. "Restlessness" (*zaodong*) hangs over their world like an invisible shroud, and particularly susceptible to such sentiments are those whose desire to change their life—through changing jobs and/or leaving for the south—is as strong as the forces which frustrate such a desire. During my conversations with many educated urban Chinese over the last few years, both in big cities such as Shanghai and small and medium cities like Bengbu, many people describe the mood of the city and the people around them as "restless" (*zaodong*). This restlessness, according to many, is a psychological state which results from a growing rate of social and physical mobility.

Indeed, the choice of focusing on the experience of going south of a number of people—engineers, doctors, and managers formerly from the state sector in Anhui—is intended precisely to reveal the disjuncture between the imagination of a certain place ("Anhui," "the south," etc.), on the one hand, and the actual geographic location, on the other. Also, it is intended to demonstrate the unequal, complex, and variegated nature of China's translocal practices. By focusing on a group of people who do not comfortably fit the image of poverty, I wish to de-essentialise Anhui as an imaginary place which is productive of little else but poverty and the discourse related to it. Having said this, I also want to stress the power of such a spatial imagination, and to consider how successful this group has been in resisting the dominant conception of Anhui. In doing this, I implicitly juxtapose and contrast the Anhui intellectual with two disparate social groups well-known for their mobility: the Anhui maid and the transnational professional elite. This, I hope, will serve as a local reminder of the unequal and stratified nature of the nation-wide journey of leaving home, moving upwards, and becoming modern.[11]

The question of how individuals negotiate with each of the three regimes—family, workplace, and the nation-state—helps to delineate the experiences examined here. However, what will emerge is not an account of the strength or the weakness of these regimes (although implicitly that will be unavoidable) but a description of the process of subject formation experienced by the individuals as a result of having to negotiate with each of these regimes. From this I hope to point to a paradox embodied in the everyday life of these translocal subjects: the inflexibility and the rigidity associated with the state, *danwei*, on the one hand, and the promise of an array of flexible, mobile, and deterrotorialised ways of life practised by transnational managerial elites on the other. What follows is a series of vignettes depicting the departures and arrivals of these people who are either travellers or contemplating travelling to the south, who thereby hope to become members of the much touted "knowledge class."

"We are the new Hakkas"

Haiyang[12] is 35 years old. Both his parents are retired senior engineers at the Design Institute for Glassware, a research institute under the direct management of the Ministry of Mechanical and Industrial Manufacturing of China. Haiyang and his parents moved to Bengbu from Beijing in the mid-1970s, when he was still a young boy. Although he spent his formative years in Bengbu, Anhui, and in spite of the fact that his parents are both natives of Anhui, he has always spoken perfect Mandarin, with a Beijing ring to his accent. Before their retirement, Haiyang's parents were not only senior scientists in the Institute, but they were also loyal members of the Communist Party. They were what the state considered to be model intellectuals, being both "ideologically sound" and "competent in their area of expertise" (*you hong you zhuan*).

When I interviewed Haiyang in early 2002, he had worked for the previous couple of years in the advertising department of *Nanfang Daily* in Guangzhou, the most influential press and publication conglomerate in China. He had recently been married, bought an apartment in Guangzhou, and secured a Guangzhou *hukou* (residential) permit. Although he was vague about how much money he earns, he indicated that his salary was more than his parents' and his sister's (a doctor) put together. In other words, Haiyang has come to possess the index of "success" of a migrant, with a local *hukou*, a high-income job as a professional, and an apartment to his name. As a result, Haiyang believes that he fits the description of the "new Hakka" (*xin ke jia ren*), apparently a common word in the local media to refer to the migrants from the north (mainly Shandong, Henan, and Hebei) who have migrated to the Pearl River Delta and who contribute to the prosperity of the region. In Haiyang's lexicon, "new Hakka" is a compliment, since "by comparison, Hakkas are culturally more sophisticated and better educated than the locals." Like the Hakkas, Haiyang sees himself as "here to stay."

Among my interview subjects, Haiyang is the youngest, and the earliest to leave Bengbu. Upon finishing his degree in business management from a university in Bengbu at the age of twenty-four, he did not even wait around for a job in Bengbu.

He and a few like-minded friends who grew up within the Institute's residential compound[13] went south in 1991. They were not clear what they were going to do, nor where exactly they were going. They simply headed south. Haiyang started as a storeman in a shoe factory owned by a Taiwan businessman, which was located in Longgang, on the outskirts of Shenzhen, where he was earning a meagre income of 300 yuan a month (US$30–40). From there, he started a roller coaster ride of job-hopping (*tiao cao*). He worked as an accountant, a factory foreman, and a salesman selling everything from insurance and health foods to club membership.

Haiyang proudly claims that he has never worked for the public sector. His initial decision to leave Bengbu was based on his deep-seated aversion to the state sector, and his desire not to repeat what his parents had lived through (all quotes from interviewees are translated from interview transcripts):

> I witnessed on a daily basis what my parents had to put up with in order to survive in that cocoon. Being in the public sector making a living from the state meant putting up with office politics and ideological clap-trap. There was so much back-stabbing (*gouxin doujiao*), arse-licking (*pai mapi*), and endless lies. These things filled me with disgust. I wanted to run away from it as soon as I could.

One may regard Haiyang's decision to avoid the fate of his parents, who were state intellectuals, as some kind of inchoate expression of a yearning for freedom of action, autonomy, and agency of the individual. In other words, his present translocality was inseparable from and, in fact, conditioned by, the historical translocalities of his parents as state professionals. It may well be due to this historical factor that, among my interviewees, Haiyang has been the most successful in refashioning himself. He was young (24), had no institutional baggage or public sector mentality, and thus was able to "travel light"—without the burden of historical memory. "The south" promised a clean slate on which he could invent a self-determined political identity. For Haiyang and his friends, the decision to leave home and create their own future had a necessary spatial dimension. By the early 1990s, particularly after the well-touted trip to the south by Deng Xiaoping, and infused with newly released political freedom and economic incentive, "the south" started to capture the imagination of young people from across the country. The power relation in the north–south spatial imagination started to shift in the national consciousness, and "the north," once the seat of power of the center, started to become associated with the weight of tradition, inertia, over-politicization, bureaucracy, inefficiency, and the burdens of the public sector. The south, once perceived by northerners to be barbarian and peripheral, began to be associated with dynamism, flexibility, risk-taking, economic vibrancy, the private/commercial sector, and personal freedom. Haiyang's departure from Bengbu was motivated by a desire to resist and elide the power of the state and to avoid the entrapment of being a state intellectual—a desire conditioned by history—and it took place at the cusp of such a sea change. The move "south" in this sense was both a spatial and political decision. A choice about the political and professional identity of the self was necessarily a choice about space and place.

Compared with the Anhui maid, whose place-specific identity follows her mobile body and becomes her trademark, Haiyang and skilled migrants like him are able to negotiate an identity with more ease in the host city. What they do not have—a native's claim to the place[14] and economic capital—they compensate for with what they do have: a good education, a cosmopolitan outlook, and a refined cultural and aesthetic taste. What we see here is a desire of a deterritorialized class to privilege one type of social capital—a cosmopolitan view—over another type of social capital—a native claim to place. Haiyang more than once pointed to the "peasant-like" qualities of some local Guangzhou residents, who, until only a decade ago, were peasants living off the land: "Urbanisation may have turned these villagers into urban residents overnight and they may have made a fortune selling their land, but deep down they are still peasants. And that's why we called them residents of 'villages in the city' " (*cheng zhong cun*).

The story of Haiyang points to an interesting paradox lived by the want-to-be knowledge class in China in the Reform era. Haiyang may consider himself flexible, mobile, and deterritorialized—the trademark of the knowledge class—but his success in professional development does not mean that he feels completely at ease in his new city. He has not mastered—nor does he want to master—the southern accent, which seems to give one the unquestionable sense of belonging. The fact that he speaks Mandarin suggests that he is not local. (Note that once upon a time in Anhui, Mandarin was a sign of power and prestige, whereas now it is a sign of foreignness.) Even when he tries to speak Cantonese, his accent betrays him. He is acutely aware of the fact that local residents in Guangzhou do not like migrants like him, calling them *lulao*[15] (someone from the mainland), *lao zai* (for male), and *lao mei* (for female).[16] The locals constantly remind migrants of their foreignness because they (the migrants) are not making enough money or do not think fast enough. Haiyang quoted to me a saying which circulates in China and encapsulates the new spatial imagination of the nation: "One does not realise how low the rank of his office is till he arrives in Beijing, and one does not realise how thin his wallet is till he arrives in Guangzhou."[17]

The hierarchical spatial configurations inflicted upon Haiyang by the locals are not flexible and are indeed territorially determined. Likewise, Haiyang's reactions as a subaltern[18]—as evident in his self-definition as the "new Hakka," and in his description of the Other as "villagers in the city"—are equally reliant on and contribute to socially determined spatial metaphors. Thanks to their agility and flexibility,[19] Haiyang, and many young professionals like him, are able to escape the state bureaucracy, with its attendant work ethos and organizational culture; but they are nonetheless confronted with a new set of social relations, delineated not so much by the state bureaucracy but by the power of the social imagination. Confronted with the xenophobia of the local, the nomad reacts with parochial disdain for—rather than cosmopolitan readiness to embrace—the other.[20] In this reconfiguration of the social, a new politics of the body has emerged, inscribing individuals like Haiyang himself with new inequalities negotiated along the line of "where you are from" instead of "which institution do you work for." Although mobile and deterritorialized, the self continues to be a site of resistance and negotiation between these not so flexible differences. Haiyang's desire to symbolically locate the unfriendly locals as the "villagers in the city" is indeed poignant: in pursuing a lifestyle of a global citizen, the mobile body, when confronting the locals, betrays the parochialism of "the villager" rather than the cosmopolitanism of the global citizen.

"There are a lot of things to adjust to"

Xueyan[21] is an associate principal doctor with more than fifteen years' experience specializing in lung-related diseases in the Hospital for Contagious Diseases in Bengbu, Anhui.[22] Like other hospitals in the city, hers is a state enterprise. She is married to an engineer who is head of his research unit at the Research and Design Institute for Glassware (the same one as Haiyan's parents retired from). When I first interviewed Xueyan at the beginning of 2002, she had just left Bengbu and started working for a private hospital in Guangzhou, on a trial basis. The hospital, owned by Peng Lingji, a wealthy businessman from Hong Kong who also owns a considerable portion of the real estate in Guangzhou, boasts to have the best medical facilities in the world (not just in the country). Xueyan's salary (6,000 yuan per month) is six times as much as her salary back in Bengbu. Now more than one month into her new job, Xueyan had not informed her *danwei* back home of her new job in Guangzhou, giving them the impression that she had been taking her long service leave in order to finish her postgraduate studies. She explained to me that this was because she was not sure if the new job would work out. What also added to Xueyan's desire to keep it quiet was the uncertainty surrounding her husband's job. He had also been contemplating moving, either to Shanghai or Shenzhen, but had been indecisive, and for a good reason. True, his salary was pitifully low compared with what he could earn in the south, and opportunities for professional development in Bengbu were scarce, but he was doing reasonably well at work and he was not sure if he could "hack it" in the south. Also, he did not want to live too far away from his parents, who were growing increasingly frail and dependent. Xueyan's departure from her home(town) had the endorsement of neither her *danwei* nor her husband.[23] Xueyan's leaving Bengbu may be partly a result of her less than fulfilling relationship with her husband. However, his reluctance to go with the flow—after all, everyone in his Institute was either thinking about changing jobs and going south or actually doing it—may contribute further to the strain in her marriage. Xueyan's story—and indeed the story of my other interviewees—points to an important fact seldom acknowledged: when people engage in translocal practices, they are not just leaving a place, they are often leaving their families, relatives and friends. What they stand to produce is not simply a translocal lifestyle of their own, but a translocal network, dispersed across space and embodying various shapes and contours of translocal imagination.

Although she was still in her trial period, her supervisor has already clearly indicated that her professional experience would be an asset and that the job would be hers should she choose to stay. To stay or return is indeed a difficult decision to make, although Xueyan told me that she "wouldn't be surprised if she chose to stay." The new hospital definitely provides better opportunities for professional development, better equipment, and facilities. It also has a more clearly defined hierarchy, whereby doctors are clearly marked with ranks and respected for their professional expertise in a way doctors in the hinterland provinces (*neidi*) are not; Xueyan mentioned several times how nurses deferred to and obeyed doctors in the new *danwei*. According to her, 70 percent of her patients are Hong Kong residents and the patients patronizing her hospital come from more than forty countries. As a result, she is able to use English for communication purposes for the first time in her professional career—something she takes great pride in.

The choice made by Xueyan is worth highlighting, since in spite of her uncertainty about the future, she is one of the few people who have indeed actually taken the plunge and put herself in such a state of transition. She is, considering the circumstances in which she left, capable of risk-taking and adventures. Xueyan told me that most people back in Bengbu, including her husband, would not have the confidence to leave a tenured job in the state sector, in spite of their proven professional competence. "They do not trust their own ability, nor do they want to prove it by putting themselves in a situation where there is no way back." Her observation about her colleagues back home points to a common blind-spot in the study of translocal practices and social imagination: while there is a tendency to associate translocal practices with those on the move, those who have left home or are returning home, little attention is given to the daily dilemmas confronting many not so "courageous" people who do not (yet) leave but who nevertheless entertain the idea of leaving. After all, leaving can take place not only in a geographic and physical sense, but also in a psychological sense. Unless this sense of restlessness and the attendant feeling of anxiety resulting from having to make a decision—experienced alike by both those who have left and those who have not—are both taken into account in the investigation of translocal practices, such inquiries are doomed to reveal little about the processes of the formation of subjectivity.

Xueyan was still undecided about her future when we had a second interview two months later, in April 2002. In fact she seemed more cautious and reflective about the new job. She wondered if her decision to leave Bengbu was a decade too late, and if she could ever get used to the demanding nature of the new job, and if she could live with the insecurity of working in an untenured position in a private enterprise, with little guarantee of long-term job security:

> I should have decided to leave ten years ago. I'm approaching 40. It's taking time to get used to the change in work environment. I wonder if it's worthwhile throwing away the benefits I've enjoyed at the state hospital all these years. True, the old hospital doesn't offer exciting prospects and doesn't really respect doctors' expertise, but at least there is not that much need to prove myself. I was in control there and I was under no pressure to please the

patient. Here the patient is God and can do no wrong! If there is one complaint about me from a patient, I will be finished! With this job, the workload is heavy, the pace is fast, and the pressure never lets up. There is a lot to adjust to, and it's not that easy for someone my age. It's as simple as this: if you work for *gongchandang* (the communists), you have an easy job but little money. If you work for *zibenjia* (capitalists), you will make money, but you have got to work very very hard.

She told me during the second interview that she had just come back from Bengbu, where she sat for one of the exams as part of her postgraduate studies. Her *danwei* in Bengbu was still in the dark, assuming that Xueyan was trying to finish her postgraduate qualifications during her long service leave. It transpired that getting used to the fast, busy and high-pressure job was more difficult than originally expected. Many years' experience of working in the state sector and of being immersed in its work ethos was proving to be baggage too entrenched to discard, yet too heavy to live with. Her repeated expression of regret for not having left Bengbu ten years earlier points to the difficulty for some translocals in "travelling light." Inhabiting a liminal space, unable to choose between the state and the public sector, the habitat of the past, and prospects for the future, and between here and there, she seemed to have come to a more balanced view of the choices facing her.

"Shanghai belongs to everyone, not just to Shanghainese"

Yang[24] is also a native of Anhui. His experience of leaving Anhui, though less of a secretive affair than that of Xueyan, is nevertheless more torturous, and certainly equally entangled. Upon graduating from Hefei Industrial University, a prestigious university in Anhui in the early 1980s, Yang was assigned to work as an engineering designer in the Institute for Industrial Engineering in Bengbu, a subsidiary of China's Ministry of Industry. Thanks to his professional competence and leadership skills, Yang was dispatched to Shanghai by the Institute to lead the Shanghai-based branch. During his period of four years as the middle manager of the research team, Yang was able to cultivate an extensive professional and business network. His satisfactory performance at work, however, did not translate into job satisfaction: Yang had to live separately from his wife and his son, both of whom were still based in Bengbu. Yang's Institute refused to support Yang's effort to bring his family to Shanghai. In order to preserve the sanctity of his family and secure the future education of his son, Yang decided to resign from the Institute, a move that was never accepted by his *danwei*. As part of their punitive measures, Yang's Institute to this day has refused to release his personal dossier to Yang's current employers, forbids him from selling his apartment in Bengbu which he had purchased under the *danwei*-sponsored housing scheme, and refuses to provide the official transfer document needed in order to enrol his son in a state-funded school in Shanghai. Despite all these hurdles, or perhaps precisely because of them, Yang and his family took the plunge three years ago, severed his ties with the Institute, and joined one of the burgeoning real-estate companies in Shanghai. By mobilizing his personal networks, Yang, as a real-estate agent specializing in sales, leasing, and residential development, was able to impress his boss. Yang now has bought an apartment which is worth 300,000 yuan, secured a Shanghai *hukou* for both himself and his family, and has a company car at his disposal. He has traveled to Italy and Spain on the job, and enjoys a *xiaosa*[25] lifestyle which, according to him, combines a busy working schedule with a reasonable amount of time for recreational activities.

Yang attributes his success in job change and settlement in the new city to Shanghai's flexible policy of attracting skilled migrants from outside Shanghai:

> I got my *hukou* permit within two months of joining the company. *Hukou* is no longer a big hassle. All you need to apply for a Shanghai *hukou* is a *danwei* that is happy to employ you, a residential address, and an application fee of 2000 yuan. You don't even have to lodge the application yourself; there are human resources service centres[26] that will do it on your behalf. I heard that these days, you can even lodge your application electronically on the Internet, and you may have to wait no more than three days for the permit to come through.

To Yang, the flexible and efficient policy adopted by Shanghai city's government is in sharp contrast to the impersonal, rigid and inefficient bureaucracy of his Institute back in Bengbu: "They" (the management of the Institute), Yang remarked, "are so out of touch with the logic of the market economy!"

Yang is acutely aware of the resentment against outsiders like himself:

> Sometimes, Shanghai residents have difficulty accepting the fact that outsiders like me and my family could secure a Shanghai *hukou* just like that. They find it hard to accept this. Mind you, these people tend to be of older generations, and since I don't deal with them on an everyday basis, they don't bother me. The fact is that Shanghai does not just belong to Shanghainese; it belongs to anyone who can contribute to making it a better city. Nowadays people come to Shanghai from everywhere, from China and overseas. You can no longer tell who is a Shanghainese and who is a *waidiren* (outsider).

The city as Yang experiences it is an open and accessible space, and as such, belongs to the world. Indeed, for new arrivals like himself, Shanghai is futuristic, full of promise and opportunities, but unburdened with nostalgia and memories of the past. A Shanghai *hukou* opens the door to many things, including securing business licences, free education for off-spring in the public school, medical benefits, a superannuation scheme, and passport and travel documents. This view of the city is in sharp contrast to the experience of the city of some rural women from Anhui who have come to Shanghai to work as cleaners and domestic servants.[27] Such a contrast highlights the spatial experience and imagination of the city as both gender- and class-specific. It speaks of the state-facilitated ease and convenience benefiting a burgeoning skilled workforce in the global economy. Servicing the process of flexible capital accumulation are those whose knowledge, expertise, and experience are highly desirable, transferable—from the state to the private sector—and relocatable—from northern to southern cities.

Compared with Haiyang and Xueyan's husband, Yang seemed to be more prepared to take risks. Rather than facing uncertainty and family separation, Yang seemed neither secretive about leaving the old *danwei* nor angst-ridden by a possible return. Recently, Yang has been contemplating extending his burgeoning real-estate business to Bengbu. In spite of the draconian regulations and inflexible investment infrastructure, Yang seems unfazed: "It is my hometown, and I have many resources there."

Although it is obvious that Yang's decision to sever his ties with the Institute in Bengbu was motivated by reuniting with his family in Shanghai and providing a better future for his son in Shanghai, it was equally motivated by the prospect of professional development, and opportunities for actual use of his management skills. "I simply wanted to have the chance to *do a few things*" (*zuo dian shi*), he said a number of times during the interview—to be able to "do a few things" implicitly requiring being in a space which allows things to get done. This expression of a desire to do be able to "do a few things," a rationale given to me as a throw-away remark, nevertheless seems to signify a fashionable repudiation of the state bureaucracy, with its supposedly known inefficiency, inertia, and waste. It also signifies a romanticization of the private sector, again with its generally assumed features such as innovation, creativity, and initiative. "In my old *danwei*, we did what we were assigned to do; now I am my own boss, and I look for things to do." While the general disillusionment with the bureaucratic culture of the public and state sector, and the desire to move from the public sector to the private sector for that reason, are global,[28] this phenomenon seems to have assumed a distinctively spatial dimension in contemporary China. In other words, the shift from state/public/governmental to private/commercial/civilian is conflated with the move from the north to the south, from the inland to the coastal, and from the national to the transnational.

Yang's story may read like one of triumphs of individual agency over the will of the state. True as it may be, it is important to note that while the state was portrayed as restraining and constraining in Yang's pursuit of an autonomous life, it has also provided him with valuable resources in his project of self-refashioning—a fact less appreciated and acknowledged by him. Four years of experience as an institutionalized researcher working in the state sector had prepared him adequately for the subsequent challenge in the "free market." His success in the private sector was also contingent on his ability to effectively mobilize the network which he had cultivated while working for the Institute. His capacity to exploit his connections with the state bureaucracy and his acute sense of timing seemed crucial to his success. Unlike Haiyang, whose departure from Bengbu was timely but directionless, and Xueyan, whose departure was "too late," Yang was able to engineer his exit from the state sector at a time most opportune and suitable to himself. The ease and facility with which he shed the identity of a state bureaucrat and took up global citizenship was as much a tribute to Shanghai's open policy as his capacity to appropriate state resources—both social and symbolic—for self-refashioning.

"I am a lazy person, and I want to be safe"

Ming[29] is not one of the managerial elites, being a junior public servant (*gong wu yuan*) in the Bengbu Taxation Office. Her life, however, has been in more than one way affected by the translocal practices of people surrounding her. Ming's older brother, Gao, an engineer from the Institute for Industrial Engineering (the same as Yang), had managed to negotiate a transfer to its Shenzhen branch in 1996, but he had to wait for three years before the Institute agreed to transfer his personal dossiers to Shenzhen and allowed his family to join him. Gao's wife quit her job in Bengbu and joined her husband, leaving their 5-year-old son in the care of Ming for three years before he was able to join his parents in Shenzhen. When I asked Ming what made the Institute's management finally relent, she put it down to "networking."[30] Ming's younger sister, Feng, formerly working for the People's Bank in Bengbu, has also moved south. She is now the branch manager of a bank in Fushan City, a branch of the Shenzhen Development Bank. Feng works and stays in Fushan during the week, and drives back to spend the weekend with her husband, now a surgeon in a public hospital in Shenzhen. With both her siblings in the south—her parents have also migrated south to be with their children— Ming has been to Shenzhen a few times to visit her siblings and parents, but decided that she would not like to live there. The reason she gave may sound both perplexing and simple: "I don't like to live in a place where there is no clear change of season. I like winter." However, Ming, at the time of interview, was grappling with the question as what to do with her own life. Confronted with the exodus from the Institute, her husband, Jie, an engineer in the Design Institute for Glassware (the same as Haiyang's parents) was also contemplating leaving for Shanghai. To go or not to go was indeed a difficult question. There would be much to lose by quitting. He would lose the *danwei*-given apartment, have his personal dossier transferred to the Personnel Exchange Centre,[31] and would have to pay a compensation fee of 20,000 yuan to the Institute, for his professional development.[32] However, the future, if he were to stay, was rather dim: the Institute was stagnating; his salary was meagre compared with his in-laws in the south, and the couple had to think about the future of their daughter. When I asked how close they were to make a decision, she said, "Ask me in two months' time."

I conducted a second interview with Ming two months later, to get an update on their situation. She was just as determined as two months ago that her husband should make the move, and that the destination should be Shanghai:

> There's no point in moving unless you get out of Anhui. I wouldn't even settle for Jiangsu. Beijing is no good: too much wind and sand. Shanghai is the city to be, and it's bound to get even better. It will be good for my daughter, as

she will be exposed to "a wide range of good things" (*jian shi guang*). My husband will take her to Shanghai, but I will stay in Bengbu. I am a lowly public servant and to get a proper transfer I would need to pass the public servant's test. I am a lazy person. I don't think I want to go through all that. I will stay in my job so that I will be entitled to a retirement pension when I retire [she was 40 at the time of my interview]. Shanghai is only four hours' travel from Bengbu so I should be able to see them fairly regularly. Many of my friends say that I should go with them, but I really don't know if it's a good idea. My husband shares my sentiments. I may decide to follow him, if it transpires that with my husband's salary, I would not need my public servant's pension, but for now, I think I still should play it safe.

Ming's husband, although sharing her sentiments, was not as keen to make the move, though he has agreed to go to Shanghai to "look around" and "check it out" (*kan yi kan*). He is concerned that being over 40 himself, he may seem to be "on the old side." Sensing her husband's hesitation, Ming seemed a bit more impatient with him during the second interview. Although Ming understood her husband's concern—he does not want to start from the beginning again, competing with "young people" (i.e. people in their twenties), and he is reluctant to face the initial discomfort of being physically displaced—she seemed convinced that her husband needed to become more decisive, enterprising, and liberal-thinking:

> I know I am more keen than he is about the move. But he has to go. People out there are earning 10,000 yuan a month, ten times as much as he earns here. The choice is obvious. You don't want to become irrelevant in this competitive world.

Her determination to stay put in the state sector in Bengbu, and her judgment of the suitability—or lack of it—of southern places such as Shenzhen on the basis of weather, may look to some as symptomatic of the inertia, lack of initiative, and inflexibility associated with the ethos of the state sector bureaucracy and an inland mentality. Yet to talk about her experience outside the framework of translocalism would be deeply misleading. Despite her own dislike of the south, Ming's everyday life has been dramatically affected by the translocal practices of people in her family, manifesting itself most directly in the care of her brother's son while her brother and sister-in-law first went south. She also talked about her sister (who is a bank manager) with pride, telling me of the car she drives and how easy it is for her to go to Hong Kong. In other words, what she seems to practise is a form of displaced, delegated, and delayed translocality, whereby the reward of translocality is experienced vicariously, relationally (through people close to her, including her family) and partially: the prospect of commuting between Bengbu and Shanghai to see her husband and daughter is nothing short of a translocal practice. Ming's story seems to point to the conceptual and practical need to regard translocalism as, first, consisting of both imagination and material practice; and second, involving both the individual traveler and others whose lives stand to be affected by the travel.

People move to high places like water flows down: a taxonomy of translocalism

The experiences of the individuals presented here are by no means unique to people from Anhui. Indeed, they describe the opportunities, conundrums, and dilemmas facing a particular segment of the whole population of China: those who possess knowledge and expertise that is much needed by global capitalism, but whose dreams of becoming members of the new knowledge class are sometimes inhibited, prohibited, or held in check by the high stakes of moving. Their spatial imagination is borne aloft by urban myths, folklore, and narratives of social mobility and economic success, but their social mobility is premised upon a reality of displacement. Finally, their subjectivity is mobile and deterritorialised yet their identity continues to be inscribed with a sense of where they come from, and the habits and life-world specific to that place. For these reasons, the migrant's body, mobile as it may be, increasingly becomes a site for negotiation between various tensions, contradictions, and ambiguities. Similarly, social imagination about place and space is hardly meaningful without considering the relationship between places and spaces and the body which traverses them, both vicariously and physically. As Louisa Schein points out in her chapter in this volume, "places are not only constituted by their location and physical features," but also by the "specific, often regulated, forms of bodies that inhabit them." It is precisely because "bodies," as Schein observes, "can serve as dislocated signifiers of places," that I am able to talk about the rigidity and burden of Anhui through the bodies of those who have already departed from it.

It is clear that the experience of individuals presented here has its literal dimension: the movement of people from one place to another—where, how, and why they move—their strategies of survival, and their everyday practices. It also has a symbolic dimension: the ways in which individuals "travel" through successive "regions"—from state to civic spaces; from bureaucratic to commercial spaces; from the public to the private sector; from a socialist work ethos to that of the transnational market—as well as the impact such travel has on their conception and practices of personhood. Furthermore, such experience also has a metaphorical dimension, specifically in the production of an individual affect in which geographic relocation and cultural displacement interface with a subjectivity poised between the burden of the past and the promise of the future.

The constellation of forces which are productive of power and privilege in the social lives of individuals in China has changed during the last decade or so. This results in the reconfiguration of social relations, with some people moving upward, others coming down. In the post-*hukou* era, a semiotic of social mobility is invariably imbricated with physical and geographical movement. Such social-spatial imbrication is most vividly embodied in an often heard remark, "people travel to higher places, just as water flows to lower places" (*ren wan gao chu zou, shui wang di chu liu*). Such an epigram of traditional wisdom provides a handy philosophical rationale for many individuals in China, who, swept along by the whirlwind of mobility, become palpably restless and indeed contemplate making risky decisions in life, such as the decision to leave their home (town), quit their job, or change professions. Although all draw on the wisdom of "people moving to higher places," some pay a higher price for moving, run more risks, and stand to lose more. The desire to reach the top is strong, but the road to higher places, as the stories presented here suggest, is lined with uncertainty, or even fear.

My interviewees clearly face a range of conundrums and possibilities. They have made—or are in the process of making—a range of decisions in view of their respective and constrained circumstances. The differences between these individual decisions are therefore the differences in the ways in which the self negotiates with the regime of the family, workplace, and the state in order to exploit the logic of the situation. What seems to have emerged from these individual negotiations is a diverse range of "rational" choices, or a taxonomy of translocalism. Such a taxonomy includes what I call *collateral* translocalism, involving those who have no intention of moving themselves, but whose lives are nevertheless changed or transformed by the movement of people around them. Haiyang's parents and Xueyan's husband fit into this category; it also includes *delegated* translocalism, practised by those who enjoy the rewards of moving but decide to let others do the moving on their behalf. Ming's decision to stay on in Bengbu whilst supporting her husband and daughter's move to Shanghai is an act of delegation. The taxonomy also includes what we might think of as *tactical* translocalism,[33] engineered by those wishing to move, but who need to do so either deceptively or secretly because such an action is not endorsed by, or is even against the wishes of, those in power. Xueyan's attempt to straddle both jobs while manoeuvring for more time is tactical, as is Ming's brother's bribery of the *danwei* officials to secure his dossier transfer. Finally, this taxonomy should also include those who do not want, or dare, or care, to move, but who nevertheless experience the pleasure of identifying with those who do travel. I refer to this as *vicarious* translocalism, and it is practised in everyday life by hundreds of thousands of people whose spatial imagination is fueled by contemporary tales, myths, and narratives about the successes and failures of the migrants, which are circulated widely both in the media and among members of their own community. Such a taxonomy, though patchy and not exhaustive, is nevertheless useful in alerting us to the processual nature of moving: leaving is seldom a clean departure from the past; nor is arrival a totally fresh start. Second, it points to the difficulty of "traveling light." Movement is always multiply motivated and experienced, involving cultural and psychological as well as geographical dislocations and adjustments. It is a journey not only between physical locations but also, more significantly, between different habitats and life-worlds. Lastly and most importantly, it highlights the unequal and variegated nature of translocalism—a nationwide phenomenon in contemporary China. While some parts of China are connected and become desirable due to the flow of mobile people and deterritorialized capital, other parts still have their hands tied by the state bureaucracy as well as by the inertia and memory of the past.

Such a taxonomy, which describes an array of translocal practices, is not complete until and unless we also consider it in juxtaposition with the power of translocal imagination. Translocalism can be perceived as having both a physical and psychic dimension. While the former—what is sometimes described as "translocal practice"—refers to the materiality and logistics of moving from one place to another—the latter—what I describe as "translocal imagination"—consists of mental activities such as making decisions (to leave or not to leave), imagining other places through exposure to various images (with fear or desire), and identifying (with or against) these places. In other words, translocal imagination, equally as important as subjectification, can exist with or without the actual movement of the self and others. Therefore, questions about subject-formation at any given moment are necessarily questions regarding the ways in which translocalism operates at the levels of both translocal practice and translocal imagination. While conflating these two levels risks losing conceptual clarity and precision in our study of translocality and translocalism, cutting either out of the loop would equally risk flattening out the texture and layering of experience, reducing translocalism to a less than productive concept.

Individuals described in this chapter all experience tension, contradiction, and ambivalence of some kind when practising translocalism, and resort to strategies, tactics and manoeuvres to negotiate with the regimes of power imposed by the family, the *danwei*, and the state. The transnational capital, mobility, and power of the Chinese state have conspired to (re)produce an uneven and unequal translocalism. As a result, the contour and the shape of translocal processes are indeed intricate. These processes are diverse, fluid, sometimes confusing, and always complex. They are marked with, first, an interface between the material (the flow of people) and the symbolic (the flow of images); second, a convergence between the private and the public; third, a coalition of individuals' sentiments and state desires; fourth, a fusion of looking toward the future (imagination) and looking toward the past (memory and identity); and fifth (related to the fourth), a conflation of space (here or there) and time (now or then).

Notes

1 The most recent evidence of the tenacity of such images can be found in Wang Xiao Shuai's film, *Guniang Biandan* (*So Close to Paradise*, 2002), set in Wuhan, Wubei Province. The film is about rural migrants in the city, and at one point in the film, Dongzi, an inarticulate country lad eating a bowl of noodles in a roadside noodle hut, decides to show off to his friend by requesting two shabbily dressed itinerant singers to stand by his table and sing a tune. The tune they sing is *Tianxianpei*, a Huangmei folk opera indigenous to Anhui.

2 Both these tropes are extensively discussed in Sun (2002b).

3 Of course, I am fully aware of the ways in which these tropes relate to and overlap with one another. Many rural migrants' mobility, for instance, straddles the trope of "going to the city" and "going south."

4 Nomadism has emerged as an important concept in the study of mobility in the West. In delineating the difference between diaspora, exile, and nomadism, Peters (1999) argues that the nomad is one who makes a home everywhere, has a mobile and constructed identity, and is necessarily a cosmopolitan.

5 Information about mobility and urbanization comes from *China Economic Times*, http://www.cet.com.cn/20010108/GUONEI/200102084.htm (accessed December 11, 2001).

6 There are half a dozen research and design institutes like this in Bengbu, including Design Institute for the Department of Engineering and Machinery, Design Institute for Glassware and Building Materials, and No. 40 Research Institute for Electronics.

7 An interviewee (Haiyang), the son of two senior scientists, told me that during the 1970s and 1980s his family and other staff living within the compound had swimming pools exclusively for the use of staff, a hot water system, and access to bottled gas, when these were largely unavailable to the local community.

8 They were described in colloquial terms as "eating royal grain" (*chi huang liang*).

9 I thank Louisa Schein for this point about the south being productive of transnationalism, and for several other points in this chapter.

10 The media's construction of the "successful people" and the "new rich" using the south as a backdrop is discussed at length by Wang Xiaomin (2000).

11 As a native of Anhui Province, I maintain regular contacts with friends, family and relatives there, and have an ongoing interest in economic development and social change in the province, particularly the phenomenon of the Anhui *baomu* (maid).

12 Haiyang is my interviewee's given name. He indicated in my interviews with him that he preferred to be identified using his real name, but without his surname.

13 Haiyang explained to me that all staff members of the Institute and their families live in an apartment provided by the workplace. The compound consists of a cluster of well serviced apartment buildings separated from the local community by a wall with a guarded gate. (See also note 9.)

14 Australian–Lebanese sociologist Ghassan Hage (1998) appropriates Bourdieu's notion of cultural capital, and argues that within the nation, cultural capital takes on a "national" dimension. He calls it "practical nationality," which can be understood analytically as the sum of accumulated nationally sanctioned and valued social and physical cultural styles and dispositions adopted by individuals and groups, as well as valued characteristics within a national field: looks, accent, demeanor, taste, nationally valued social and cultural preferences, and behavior, etc. To have national capital, therefore, is to be able to claim national belonging.

15 This obviously originated from Hong Kong Chinese people's description of mainland Chinese. It is interesting that Guangzhou residents adopt this label to refer to the Chinese from outside Guangzhou, thus betraying a desire to identify with the spatial imagination of the transnational Chinese, that is Hong Kong, rather than that of China.

16 The word "lao" defies precise translation. It connotes someone who is a gold-digger, a bludger, or someone who is undeserving of the wealth bestowed upon him or her.

17 "Daole Beijing cai zhidao guanxiao, daole Guangzhou cai zhidao qianshao."

18 For a good case where the notion of the subaltern is applied to the Chinese context, see Michael Dutton (1998).

19 Harvey (1989) talks about the agility and flexibility of corporations in the context of the political economic transformation of late twentieth-century capitalism from Fordism to flexible accumulation, whereby the financial system is de-linked from active production of real commodities.

20 Urry (2002) defines cosmopolitan qualities as consisting of an openness to difference, a readiness to learn about other cultures and people, and a capacity to understand the cultural symbolism of other cultures. Ulf Hannerz (1990) also talks about cosmopolitanism along these lines.

21 Like Haiyang, Xueyan prefers to use her real given name with surname withheld.

22 Xueyan explained to me that the status of associate principal doctor (*fu zhuren yishi*) is more or less equivalent to that of associate professor in a university.

23 Although she did not explicitly talk about the quality of her relationship with her husband, she did convey the impression that there was not much left to the relationship. The couple have no children.

24 Yang is his real name; for identification purposes he prefers to use only his surname.

25 Yang mentioned a few times how he wanted to live a "xiaosa" lifestyle. The nearest equivalents of *xiaosa* in English are "cool" and "insouciant." *Xiaosa*, when used to describe people, refers to those who do not try too hard to impress other people, but nevertheless effortlessly excel due to sheer talent. Yang said that in a society which is marked with restlessness and social mobility, *xiaosa* becomes the rarest quality.

26 Human resources service center: *Rencai fuwu zhongxing*. "*Rencai*" literally means people with talents and special skills. Yang mentioned a number of times that his move to Shanghai was a result of the city's desire to attract *rencai* like him.

27 I have conducted interviews with a group of cleaners and domestic servants in Shanghai. See Sun (2005).

28 See, for instance, Du Gay (1992).

29 Ming is her real name. She prefers to use her real name for purposes of identification but wants to leave out her surname. It is also her preference to identify her siblings and husband by their first name only.

30 I asked Ming if "networking" (*la guanxi*) means dining and wining and briberies with gifts and cash, she replied: "Something like that."

31 Everyone I interviewed, with the exception of one (Haiyang), expressed some anxiety about either not being able to obtain their personal dossier from their *danwei* when they transfer jobs, or having their dossier transferred to the Personnel Exchange Centre. Nobody could give a clear explanation of why dossiers continue to hold such significance; however, most still considered a transfer with dossier a better way to go.

32 This fee is called *beiyangfei*, and the rationale for charging such a compensation fee is that employees should repay the costs of training and professional development they have received from the *danwei* if they decide to leave.

33 I am following de Certeau's (1984) distinction between "strategies" and "tactics." According to de Certeau, strategies are the means of the strong and powerful, whereas tactics are the means of avoidance and deception deployed by those in weak or socially disadvantaged positions.

References

Cartier, C. (2001) *Globalizing South China*, Maldon, MA: Blackwell.

Certeau, M. de (1984) *The Practice of Everyday Life*, Berkeley, CA: University of California Press.

Chi, Z. (1996a) "Jingdai huaibei Haiyangmin wenti de jige cemian" (Some aspects of peasant migration north of the Huan River in modern times), *Ershiyi Shiji* (21st Century) 38: 37–45.

—— (1996b) *Zhongguo Jingdai Haiyangmin* (The Drifting Population in China in Modern Times), Hangzhou: Zhejian Renmin Chubanshe (Zhejiang People's Press).

China Economic Times (2001) "Anhui Gaige Huji Zhidu" (Anhui plans reforms of Hukou system), Online version: http://www.cet.com.cn/20010108/GUONEI/200102084.htm (accessed December 11, 2001).

Du Gay, P. (1992) "Organizing identity: entrepreneurial governance and public management," in S. Hall and P. du Gay (eds) *Questions of Cultural Identity*, London: Sage Publications, 151–169.

Dutton, M. (1998) *Streetlife China*. Melbourne: Cambridge University Press.

Hage, G. (1998) *White Nation: Fantasies of White Supremacy in a Multicultural Society*, Sydney: Pluto Press.

Haiyang (2002) interview, January 16, Guangzhou.

Hannerz, U. (1990) "Cosmopolitans and locals in world culture," in M. Featherstone (ed.) *Global Culture*, London: Sage.

Harvey, D. (1989) *The Condition of Postmodernity*, Oxford: Basil Blackwell.

Ming (2002) Interview, February 4 and April 13.

Nonini, D. and Ong, A. (1997) "Chinese transnationalism as an alternative modernity," in A. Ong and D. Nonini (eds) *Ungrounded Empires: The Cultural Politics of Modern Chinese Transnationalism*, London and New York: Routledge.

Peters, J. D. (1999) "Exile, nomadism, and diaspora: the stake of mobility in the western canon," in H. Nacify (ed.) *Home, Exile, Homeland*, London and New York: Routledge, 17–44.

Sun, W. (2002a) "Discourse of poverty: weakness, potential and provincial identity in Anhui," in J. Fitzgerald (ed.) *Rethinking China's Provinces*, London and New York: Routledge, 153–178.

—— (2002b) *Leaving China: Media, Migration and Transnational Imagination*, Lanham, MD: Rowman & Littlefield.

—— (2005) "Anhui Baomu in Shanghai: gender, class and a sense of place," in J. Wang (ed.) *Locating China: Space, Place and Popular Culture*, London and New York: Routledge.

Urry, J. (n.d.) "The global media and cosmopolitanism," Online version: http://tina.lancs.ac.uk/\sociology/soc056ju.html, accessed March 2002.

Wang X. (2000) "Introduction" in X. Wang (ed.) *Zai Xinde Yishixintai de Longzhao Xia* (Under the Dominance of the New Ideology), Nanjing: Jiangsu Renmin Chubanshe.

Xueyan (2002) interview, February 16 and April 11, Guangzhou.

Yang (2002) interview, March 7, Shanghai.

Index

Dicken, P. 131 n.1
Dongbei 80
Dongfanghong 198
Drum and Gong Troupes 61, 63, 68, 71
Duara, P. 52, 171–172, 179, 181
Du Juan 209 n.4
Dushuchenglin 201
Dutton, M. 6, 177

"earth-bound" ideology 5, 14, 18, 36–38, 43–44, 51, 176
Ebola 193
economy, heavy industry 58
Elle 142
empire in China and cosmological mimesis 176–177
enterprise, incentives to 94
enterprising practices 118–124
ethnicity 143–144, 168, 179, 221, 225
Europe 11–12, 17, 57, 91 n.1, 115, 170, 174, 177–179, 186
European Union (EU) 11–12

Farmer, P. 193–196
Faure, D. 4–6, 14, 19, 28, 51 n.2, 75, 93, 176
Fei, X. 18, 36–38, 51 n.1
Feld, S. 28
Feng, C. 4, 7, 13–14, 22–25, 27, 254
Fenjiu 61
Ferguson, J. 132 n.13, 223, 225
festivals: Chrysanthemum 45, 48–50; Coconut 88; *Junpo* 88; Third March 88
Feuchtwang, S. 4–5, 177, 189 n.6
Fitzgerald, J. 13–15
flexible: accumulation 26, 228, 259 n.19; citizen 26, 218
Forbes, D. 119, 133 n.22
Foster, R. J. 193
Freedman, M. 41
Free Trade Zone 109
Fujian 38, 40, 43, 80, 82, 143

Gansu 82, 196
geography 20, 130, 214; globalization 7, 26, 77, 156, 217
global, transnational 25–27
Godley, M. 178
"golden age" of 1930s 44
Golden Triangle 24, 196–197
Goodman, B. 19
Goodman, D. S. G. 4, 7, 14, 19, 23–24, 28, 132 n.6

Gordon, C. 123
Grand Canal 38
Guan Di *see* Guan Yu
Guangdangjiu 205
Guangdong 38, 43–44, 49, 51 n.3, 52 n.10, 78, 81–84, 87–88, 115, 143, 145, 148–150, 156, 167, 196
Guangxi 46, 80–2, 88, 143, 182, 196–7, 200, 244
Guan Yu 64
Guattari, F. 17, 20
Guilin 185
Guiyang 185, 224, 236 n.6
Guizhou 13, 28, 39, 80, 82, 167, 169, 182–184, 218–233, 244
Guldin, G. 15
Guniang Biandan 258 n.1
Guojia Minwei 218
Gupta, A. 132 n.13, 225
guxiang see native place
Gu Yanwu 3

Hage, G. 259 n.14
Hainan 13–14, 23, 25, 47, 166–169, 181, 239; designation of 27; economy in 75; foreign capital 77; Haikou, the capital of 81; *hukou* 86; identifying with 86; issues of translocality in 82; major destination 75; market reform and opening-up of 75–79; migrants to 23; new migrants in 79–82; new migrants' identification with 74–91; and translocalism 82–89; translocality in 74; translocal projects in 4
Haizhou 57, 64
Han *see* Minzu
Han Dynasty 88
Hangzhou city 95, 103, 105, 148; Orient Culture Park 180
Hannerz, U. 259 n.20
Harvey, D. 18, 25, 259 n.19
health 8, 29, 86, 115, 157, 202, 229, 247
Heaven and Earth Society 38, 41–42
Hebei 82, 246
Heilongjiang 78, 80, 82, 115
Heitu 183–186 *see* village
Henan 80–82, 145, 197, 209 nn.2, 3
Hendrischke, H. 7–8, 17
Hendry, J. 174–176, 181
Herod, A. 16, 216
hierarchies, scales, and social practice 96, 97, 188, 214–217; "*hukou*-hierarchy" 139
Hitchcock, M. 181, 189 n.7